The Struggle for Democracy

The Struggle for Democracy

Paradoxes of Progress and the Politics of Change

CHRISTOPHER MECKSTROTH

OXFORD
UNIVERSITY PRESS

OXFORD
UNIVERSITY PRESS

Oxford University Press is a department of the University of Oxford. It furthers
the University's objective of excellence in research, scholarship, and education
by publishing worldwide. Oxford is a registered trade mark of Oxford University
Press in the UK and certain other countries.

Published in the United States of America by Oxford University Press
198 Madison Avenue, New York, NY 10016, United States of America.

© Oxford University Press 2015

First issued as an Oxford University Press paperback, 2019

All rights reserved. No part of this publication may be reproduced, stored in
a retrieval system, or transmitted, in any form or by any means, without the
prior permission in writing of Oxford University Press, or as expressly permitted
by law, by license, or under terms agreed with the appropriate reproduction
rights organization. Inquiries concerning reproduction outside the scope of the
above should be sent to the Rights Department, Oxford University Press, at the
address above.

You must not circulate this work in any other form
and you must impose this same condition on any acquirer.

Library of Congress Cataloging-in-Publication Data
Meckstroth, Christopher.
The struggle for democracy : paradoxes of progress and
the politics of change / Christopher Meckstroth.
pages cm
ISBN 978–0–19–021392–3 (hardcover : alk. paper); 978–0–19–093551–1 (paperback : alk. paper)
1. Democracy. 2. Democratization. I. Title.
JC421.M53 2015
321.8—dc23
2014046019

To my father and the memory of my mother

CONTENTS

Acknowledgments ix
Texts and Abbreviations xi

Introduction: Democracy and the Politics of Change   1

1 A Historical and Socratic Theory of Democracy   9

PART ONE

2 The Socratic Elenchus   61

3 Kant's Critique of Morality   80

4 Kant on Politics   114

5 Hegel on History   139

PART TWO

6 The Four Conditions of Principle (II)*   177

7 Cases   208

Conclusion   242

Appendix 249
Bibliography 253
Index 265

ACKNOWLEDGMENTS

This book began as a dissertation at the University of Chicago, where I benefited from a research exchange grant to the École Doctorale of the Institut d'études politiques de Paris, and an ACLS-Mellon Dissertation Completion Fellowship. Bob Gooding-Williams, Bernard Harcourt, Nancy Luxon, and Jennifer Pitts all provided helpful comments on chapters, and Luxon also helped teach me how to teach. Michael Forster's comments on Chapter 3 pushed me to refine my reading of *Groundwork* I. Sankar Muthu read and commented on the entire dissertation, and our exchanges on Kant continue to shape my thinking. I also thank Andrew Dilts, Thomas Fossen, Loren Goldman, Mara Marin, and J. J. McFadden for countless discussions. I am particularly indebted to Fossen, Goldman, and McFadden for shared time spent wrestling with Hegel. I owe a permanent debt to Iris Young, who advised an earlier project on Habermas's democratic theory. My advisors Patchen Markell, John McCormick, and Bill Sewell provided unfailing support and criticism all along the way, and since, as well as models of scholarship. In addition to the intellectual debts I owe Markell, it was he who provided me the example of a scholar, both creative and humane, that inspired me to throw in with this line of work.

I thank my colleagues and students at Harvard's program in Social Studies, and for discussions of the work I thank Kevin Caffrey, Rodrigo Chacón, Bo-Mi Choi, Matt Landauer, Libby Newman, Thomas Ponniah, Nicolas Prevelakis, Lisa Stampnitzky, Bonnie Talbert, Ioanna Tourkochoriti, and Carla Yumatle. Landauer offered helpful suggestions on the same-sex marriage case. I am grateful to Andy Jewett for discussion and inspiration. I owe a particular debt to Richard Tuck, who commented on an early version of what became Chapters 4 and 5, and who did so much to make Social Studies both personally welcoming and intellectually engaging at the highest of levels. I will forever be indebted to his example of what it means really to think for oneself.

Among those who have discussed or commented at conferences over the years, I extend particular thanks to Angélica Bernal, Maeve Cooke, Ellisabeth Ellis, Eva

Erman, James Ingram, Pauline Kleingeld, Inder Marwah, and Paulina Ochoa. At Cambridge, I thank all my colleagues and students who commented on a version of the chapter on Kant's political theory, and for welcoming me this past year into the faculty. Special thanks also to Isaac Nakhimovsky and Mike Sonenscher, who read the paper in its long form and provided incisive comments. The book owes a great deal to my excellent editor Angela Chnapko, and to three very thoughtful anonymous reviewers for Oxford University Press. Chapter 2 contains pieces previously published in "Socratic Method and Political Science," *American Political Science Review* 106, no. 3 (2012): 644–60. A few of the claims in Chapter 1 appeared in "The Struggle for Democracy: Paradox and History in Democratic Progress," *Constellations* 16, no. 3 (2009): 410–28.

My greatest debts are first of all to my parents, who first taught me to love writing and ideas, and did so much else besides. And then to my wife Giulia, without whom neither would this book have been possible nor would I be the person I am.

TEXTS AND ABBREVIATIONS

Where feasible, I have cited by book and chapter or by section number, to facilitate comparison across editions. Plato and Aristotle are cited from the Oxford Classical Texts. All translations throughout are mine unless otherwise indicated.

Rousseau

All citations are to the *Pléiade Œuvres complètes*, 5 vols., eds. Bernard Gagnebin and Marcel Raymond (Paris: Gallimard, 1959–1995).

CS. *Du contrat social ou principes de droit politique*. 1762.
PV. *Du contrat social ou essai sur la forme de la république (première version)*.

Kant

All citations are to the Akademie edition, *Kants gesammelte Schriften, herausgegeben von der Preussichen Akademie der Wissenschaften zu Berlin* (Berlin: Walter de Gruyter, 1902–).

G. *Grundlegung der Metaphysik der Sitten* [Groundwork of the Metaphysics of Morals]. 1785.
KpV. *Kritik der praktischen Vernunft* [Critique of Practical Reason]. 1788.
KrV. *Kritik der reinen Vernunft* [Critique of Pure Reason]. 1781; 2nd ed., 1787. Cited in A/B editions.
MS. *Die Metaphysik der Sitten* [The Metaphysics of Morals]. 1797.

Hegel

Where not otherwise noted, citations are from Hegel's *Gesammelte Werke, herausgegeben von der Rheinisch-Westfälischen Akademie der Wissenschaften* (Hamburg: Meiner, 1968–).

SK.   *Werke in zwanzig Bänden.* Eds. Eva Moldenhauer and Karl Markus Michel (Frankfurt am Main: Suhrkamp, 1971).

Enz.   *Enzyklopädie der philosophischen Wissenschaften* [Encyclopedia of the Philosophical Sciences]. 3rd rev. ed., 1830. Cited by section number.

PhG.   *Phänomenologie des Geistes* [Phenomenology of Spirit]. 1807. Cited by section number.

PhR.   *Grundlinien der Philosophie des Rechts* [Outlines of the Philosophy of Right]. 1821. Cited by section number except for the preface, cited in Meiner.

VPG.   *Vorlesungen über die Philosophie der Geschichte* [Lectures on the Philosophy of History]. Cited from Vol. 12 of the *SK*.

WL.   *Wissenschaft der Logik* [The Science of Logic]. 2nd rev. ed., 1832. Cited in Meiner.

The Struggle for Democracy

Introduction

Democracy and the Politics of Change

It is difficult to read through the global news today without running across struggles for democratic change. Most spectacular are revolutions and counter-revolutions, such as the ambivalent events of the Arab Spring or recently, as I write in 2014, in Ukraine. But even where democracy has long been established, struggles over social and political reform often fill the headlines. In the United States, for instance, the first decades of the twenty-first century saw an equal rights movement mobilize for same-sex marriage and Occupy protestors challenge the legitimacy of economic inequality, at the very time a Tea Party organized to roll back Keynesian economic stimulus and Obama's health insurance reforms. In France, new challenges were raised to long dominant secular principles, both by proponents of multicultural inclusion and by resurgent traditionalists who rallied en masse against legalizing "marriage for all."[1] In Europe more broadly, responses to the economic crisis and subsequent austerity led in countries including Spain and Greece to an explosion of extra-parliamentary politics on the left, repeatedly pitting elected governments against massive street protests and general strikes. In other countries (and again in Greece), new and old antisystem parties surged on the right, claiming to speak for people unrepresented by unaccountable elites and redefining more narrowly the boundaries of the people that ought to rule. In Latin America, the rise of populist and indigenous movements since the 1990s produced profound constitutional changes in a number of states, many of which remain highly divisive and unstable. And in Egypt, mass protests toppled one former general and paved the way for the country's first ever freely elected president, before another round of protests accused the same presidency of sliding into dictatorship and helped another general come to power. What all these stories have in common is that in each of

---

[1] The website of the principal French anti–same-sex-marriage organization characterizes its fight as one of "democracy versus gender theory" (http://www.lamanifpourtous.fr/en/why/democracy-versus-gender-theory).

them, many (if not all) sides vied actively for the mantle of democracy; opposite proposals were each said to make good on democratic values or to represent the will of the democratic people, and it was, at least in large part, on these grounds that they staked their claims to the justice of their cause.

If democracy is not the only live political creed left in the twenty-first century (advocates of theocracy and undemocratic liberalisms also survive—so often pitted against each other), it nevertheless remains far and away the most powerful, and by now it must be admitted that it has proved its appeal to peoples on every continent and of every major cultural and religious tradition on earth. But if this is a genuine, if qualified, triumph, it has not meant the end of history or the end of politics. To the contrary, the lesson we ought to have taken from the last two centuries of democracy's successes and failures is that ongoing struggles over what "democracy" means are themselves an integral part of democratic politics. The "struggle for democracy" in this book's title thus refers not only to the struggle to realize "democracy" but also to the struggle for the right to decide what it will mean. On the one hand, "democratization" has not been merely a linear story of advances and setbacks en route to some inexorable final state of postpolitical repose; rather, democracy has commonly succeeded where its contours first emerged through a contextual political process whose results were not set wholly in advance, and it has too often failed precisely where one or more sides insisted on their right unilaterally to impose their own preferred version of "democratic" institutions when their preference was not shared by others. On the other hand, we have seen that part of life in a democracy, where it has taken hold, is that citizens continually engage each other in political struggles to make their democracy a better one, even though these same citizens commonly disagree, often passionately, over what a "better democracy" would mean. Recall, for instance, how in a famous speech during his first run for the U.S. presidency in 2008, Barack Obama described American history as a continuing struggle to more fully realize the promise of the "core ... ideal of equal citizenship under the law" embedded in the U.S. Constitution, and the American "experiment in democracy" as the launching of the project of "a union that could be and should be perfected over time."[2] But who is to say what would make that union "more perfect"? Certainly major turning points in American history have been defined by disagreement over this, from the Civil War to the Affordable Care Act—with those on both sides commonly defending their views in the name of the same underlying value of the people's right to govern themselves. It would be a mistake to suppose we can confidently wait for history to resolve these disagreements for us. Unless we could somehow prove that history

---

[2] "Transcript: Barack Obama's Speech on Race," New York Times, March 18, 2008, http://www.nytimes.com/2008/03/18/us/politics/18text-obama.html. The speech is titled "A More Perfect Union."

can only advance without reversals along an inevitable arc of justice, then we can never be certain that the side that has so far won out is also the side that deserves to. And hindsight anyway comes too late when it matters most—*in medias res*, when the struggles are still live and the future of our shared democratic life hangs in the balance.

The need for a theory of democratic change has thus never been more urgent. But today most mainstream democratic theories define democracy as a set of timeless principles or institutions.[3] This does not mean that such theories never have anything to say about democratic revolution or reform. But it does mean they offer only a very narrow range of ways of understanding the role of change in democratic politics. If democracy is defined in terms of timeless principles or static institutions, then democratic change can be understood in one of two principal ways: either it is whatever brings us closer to that ideal, or else it is whatever change the existing democratic system allows, if that system is taken already to satisfy the ideal reasonably well.

Neither of these options is good. The problem with the second is easy to see: it asks citizens to surrender their democratic judgment entirely to existing powers, preserving no independent check against the risk of self-justifying biases in those powers that might reproduce and entrench undemocratic decisions over time. Although it is not impossible that even flawed institutions may sometimes reform themselves for the better, one cannot safely presume this must happen or that those institutions themselves always deserve the final say. Recall, for instance, how the U.S. constitutional system before 1860 was structured to perpetuate the existence of slavery and shield it from democratic challenge, and

---

[3] Major approaches of this sort include procedural, epistemic, and deliberative theories. (This book is concerned with normative rather than empirical democratic theory.) For the first, see inter alia Robert A. Dahl, *Democracy and Its Critics* (New Haven, CT: Yale University Press, 1989); for the second, David Estlund, *Democratic Authority: A Philosophical Framework* (Princeton, NJ: Princeton University Press, 2008), and Hélène Landemore, *Democratic Reason: Politics, Collective Intelligence, and the Rule of the Many* (Princeton, NJ: Princeton University Press, 2013); for the third, Bernard Manin, "On Legitimacy and Political Deliberation," *Political Theory* 15, no. 3 (1987): 338–68, Amy Gutmann and Dennis Thompson, *Democracy and Disagreement* (Cambridge, MA: Harvard University Press, 1996), and Joshua Cohen, *Philosophy, Politics, Democracy: Selected Essays* (Cambridge, MA: Harvard University Press, 2009). Other static theories build in both procedural and substantive criteria; see Corey Brettschneider, *Democratic Rights: The Substance of Self-Government* (Princeton, NJ: Princeton University Press, 2007); Thomas Christiano, *The Constitution of Equality: Democratic Authority and Its Limits* (Oxford: Oxford University Press, 2008); and Anna Stilz, *Liberal Loyalty: Freedom, Obligation, and the State* (Princeton, NJ: Princeton University Press, 2009). Jeffrey E. Green, *The Eyes of the People: Democracy in an Age of Spectatorship* (Oxford: Oxford University Press, 2009) and Eric Beerbohm, *In Our Name: The Ethics of Democracy* (Princeton, NJ: Princeton University Press, 2012) raise issues from the point of view of democratic agents but continue to argue in terms of static principles. By contrast, democratic change has received important treatments in recent years from theorists including Bruce Ackerman, Seyla Benhabib, Jürgen Habermas, and Bonnie Honig, discussed below.

how action outside the established system (in that case, war) was required to build what nearly everyone today would call a more democratic nation. Those who place their trust entirely in the self-reforming powers of existing institutions must bite the bullet and admit that this would have ruled out, for instance, any basis for questioning the legitimacy of slavery in the United States before the Civil War. Nor is the problem easily solved by suggesting that democratic systems must meet some minimum threshold before they can be trusted.[4] This only pushes the dilemma one step further back, for who is to define that threshold and to judge in a particular case if it has been met? Here again, one must either let some actual institution decide or else appeal directly to a timeless constitutional ideal.

The other option, then, is to define as democratic any change that moves us closer to realizing a model democracy, where this model is specified by reason, quite apart from the views of the actual persons who will have to live with its results. But this, too, invites problems: for struggles over democratic change are in one sense always struggles over the interpretation of the same underlying ideal, and who is to decide which interpretation is best? Unless we want to leave this question to the existing system, it appears one must argue that reason authorizes a specific democratic model (or range of models) both sufficiently detailed to decide real-world contests over reform and so rationally inescapable that it deserves to trump the judgment of actual democratic citizens acting through the normal political process. The danger, of course, is that the theorist's judgments in the name of democratic reason come to stand in for those of actual citizens, who ought on democratic grounds to be the ones deciding how to govern themselves. A flight to ideal theory here blinds one to the political stakes involved in deciding who decides, and risks collapsing either into well-intentioned utopian schemes wholly disconnected from actual citizens' concerns, or else into rationalizations for undemocratic vangaurdist projects of sociopolitical engineering from above. In extreme cases one concludes that a dictatorship of the proletariat is a democratic republic, or that the aim of liberating Iraq from tyranny should justify its indefinite occupation by a foreign military power.

These are dangers for any wholly ideal theory of politics, but they are especially troublesome for democrats. For to show how an ideal of *democracy* could be specified directly by right reason, one would first need to show why one's preferred democratic model is objectively binding and deserves to overrule any contrary views expressed by actual citizens. But as a democrat, one must do this in some way that shows why the same arguments ought *not* also to justify similarly overruling the views of citizens in the making of normal law. That is, one must explain why it is that reason—or the philosopher king who interprets

---

[4] Stilz, *Liberal Loyalty*, 89–98.

it—simultaneously *must* be allowed to legislate the details of a democratic constitution, and yet *must not* be allowed to legislate normal laws, leaving this instead to the choice of citizens through a democratic process. This is a very hard circle to square, since most of the arguments against allowing reason to legislate directly at the level of normal law would seem to apply at the constitutional level, too.[5] I do not believe that any of the democratic theories that defines democracy in terms of timeless principles or institutions has yet provided a convincing solution to this problem, nor is it easy to see how they could.

Indeed, because they cannot escape from these dilemmas, mainstream democratic theories of this sort court both theoretical and political incoherence. The problem is not merely academic, because it means arguments for democratic change may all too easily flip over, in practice, into their opposites—rationalizations of an undemocratic status quo, on the one hand, or of reforms pushed by unaccountable elites, on the other. And just because static theories cannot reliably tell the difference, they also reinforce the suspicions of those who readily conclude that therefore talk of democracy is always and everywhere only a mask of power, and so we might as well give up on criticizing antidemocratic politicians and movements, or even join them in twisting democracy's meaning however we like to serve our own political ends.

Quite apart from this, a second problem with static theories of democracy is simply that they ignore an entire field of political phenomena central both to the establishment of democratic states and to ongoing political life within them. Politics, after all, is not only about programs and ideals, but also—and perhaps foremost—about the actions and interactions of citizens as they pursue those ends and ideals and navigate their inevitable conflicts and disagreements. Consider first that struggles for democratic change are not only a public exchange of reasoned arguments. A central concern of social and political movements, both reformist and revolutionary, has long been not only to advance a brief for their cause, but also to build representative mass organizations that might call into question the existing political system's claim adequately to represent the views of democratic citizens on the issue.[6] Even when mainstream democratic theories consider political protest or activism as part of democratic politics, however, they often see it only as raising free-floating arguments or reasons, and ignore the crucial element of organization and mobilization to which such arguments are tied and which are meant to undergird actors' competing

---

[5] Frank Michelman provides an extended argument to this effect in his "Constitutional Authorship," in *Constitutionalism: Philosophical Foundations* (Cambridge, UK: Cambridge University Press, 1998), 64–98.

[6] Although largely ignored by theorists, this topic has received extensive attention from empirical scholars of democracy; see, for instance, Theda Skocpol, *Diminished Democracy: From Membership to Management in American Civic Life* (Norman: University of Oklahoma Press, 2003).

claims to representative legitimacy.[7] This too-narrow focus overlooks an entire world of politics—sometimes democratic and sometimes not—both inside movements for change and in the dynamic relation of such movements to formal organs of the state.

Another notable fact about struggles over change is that both established states and the movements who challenge them often ground their claims to legitimacy in the history of other struggles that came before. Now it might be that this is a logical mistake or nothing but a rhetorical ploy, but this does not go without argument. If one imagines democracy entirely as a set of timeless principles or institutions, then one must either conclude that history has no bearing at all on present decisions, or else one could begin from premises whose historical contingency is acknowledged but which are nevertheless thought to bind us because we continue to recognize them as "our own."[8] I will argue to the contrary, however, that history may indeed matter for democratic judgment, not because it binds the future with the dead hand of the past, but because it can play a vital role in helping us to interpret the significance of the democratic decisions we are making in the present. On this view, the value of history for democratic thinking is not that it is old but that it trades in particularities, that it helps us to attune judgment to specific elements of situation and context that matter greatly in sussing out the sometimes radically different meanings of formally similar political decisions in disparate circumstances.

This book, then, is about the problem—and the promise—of change in democratic politics. It defends a distinctive democratic theory that builds in at its core attention to democracy's historical dimension, and it shows how a certain way of doing this offers the only chance of escaping the perplexities into which every theory of timeless democratic principles or institutions falls when confronted by struggles over founding and reform. But the logic of the argument reaches far beyond these particular struggles. For among the reasons that these struggles are both so politically consequential and so difficult to theorize is that they draw out and bring to a head latent tensions in underlying claims to democratic legitimacy that had never really been resolved. That is, the reason it is so hard to sort out who speaks for "the democratic people" in struggles for reform is that we do not really have a good answer to how we know the political system speaks

---

[7] For example, John Rawls, *A Theory of Justice* (Cambridge, MA: Belknap Press of Harvard University Press, 1971), 364–91; Jürgen Habermas, "Civil Disobedience: Litmus Test for the Democratic Constitutional State," *Berkeley Journal of Sociology* 30: 95–116, and *Between Fact and Norms: Contributions to a Discourse Theory of Law and Democracy* (Cambridge, MA: MIT Press, 1996), 382–4; Kimberley Brownlee, *Conscience and Conviction: The Case for Civil Disobedience* (Oxford: Oxford University Press, 2012).

[8] The first position is defended, for instance, by Michael Otsuka in his *Libertarianism without Inequality* (Oxford: Oxford University Press, 2005), 132–50; the second by Rawls in *Political Liberalism* (New York: Columbia University Press, 2005).

adequately for them before such struggles break out, either. And so a theory of democratic change of the sort offered here is also a general theory of democratic legitimacy, and indeed I mean to go so far as to argue that any viable theory of democratic legitimacy must be also a theory of democratic change.

Finally, this far I have written as if it were obvious that "democracy" is the central value we ought to pursue in politics. But one might well be more concerned with other values—individual freedom, perhaps, or equality or the public good—and political movements often are. There is nevertheless good reason to focus on democracy, because there is good reason to think democracy, rightly understood, is today the only value that can consistently underwrite the legitimacy of collective decisions that must be enforced also against citizens who disagree. Later chapters consider the detailed arguments, but the basic thought is that any other basis of political legitimacy would require proof of some foundational principle showing why someone *other* than all the citizens subject to a political authority ought to have a say in that authority's decisions, or why some *other* value ought to trump those citizens' right to decide how they want to govern their relations for themselves. Democracy, in other words, is the only legitimate form of government not because it has a secure theoretical foundation, but just because it is the only form that needs no further foundation whatsoever. This is not to suggest that this logical feature had predetermined those historical successes democracy has had or might still have in the future, but it does point to one possible reason that the value admits such widespread appeal, and why it has so often in recent centuries remained in a position to pick up the pieces after competing political projects had collapsed. What this means, then, is that a democratic theory is also a general theory of political legitimacy, and so we can see how focusing on the question of democratic change—a question so neglected in mainstream political theory—allows one to approach some of the most central and enduring questions of political thought from a new angle. The rest of this book is an extended argument to show that this angle is an illuminating one.

The plan of the book is as follows. Chapter 1 lays out the general theoretical argument for what I call a historical and Socratic theory of democracy, and shows how it responds to a crucial paradox entailed by the problems of democratic founding and change. This theory is further developed in Part Two of the book, where Chapter 6 further elaborates key claims and Chapter 7 puts them to use in considering some exemplary cases of democratic struggle. But first, Part One considers three of the major thinkers to whom the theory is most indebted. Chapter 2 examines Socrates's characteristic mode of indirect argument by refutation, or "elenchus." Chapters 3 and 4 argue that Kant used a similar sort of argument in his moral and political theory, arriving at broadly republican conclusions that pointed, however, to the need to consider political legitimacy in relation to historical change and the problem of historical judgment. Chapter 5 then shows how Hegel's philosophy of history approached the same problem by adapting a Socratic style of argument in a somewhat different way—one that did not, like Kant's, require trusting in the authority of an existing political system to reform itself, but instead finally showed how one might determine whether or not change was justified by comparing the legitimacy claims of competing orders to see which holds up best strictly on its own terms.

Part One of the book thus serves three ends. It aims to recover an underappreciated and often misunderstood way of arguing in the absence of any certain foundations, with roots in Socrates and later powerfully developed by both Kant and Hegel. This will turn out to be essential for escaping certain paradoxes that inevitably arise when one tries to argue over the meaning of terms like "democracy" or "freedom" in any other way. Discussions of Plato, Kant, and Hegel directly challenge familiar pictures of them all as paragons of the search to ground politics on rational foundations—the problem is that this misunderstands the deeply critical and radically antifoundational sort of Socratic "reason" all these thinkers employed to such great effect. And in the case of Kant and Hegel, this matters also for understanding their place in the history of political thought, since their use of this sort of argument broke significantly with mainstream approaches in eighteenth-century rational natural law. On the other hand, Kant and Hegel each offered a version of a distinctive sort of turn to history that conceived history as a space of political judgment—irreducible to any sort of laws of historical progress that might be expected to do our judging for us. This is what distinguished their "idealisms" from other, more straightforward sorts of historicism in the period, which largely won out later in the century and with which Kant's and particularly Hegel's views have ever since too often been conflated. The third aim of Part One is to present some of the key arguments and approaches actually worked out by Kant and Hegel that support the general claims of the contemporary democratic theory defended in Part Two.

It is possible, therefore, to read Part One by itself if one has no interest in contemporary theory, or Chapter 1 and Part Two if one has no interest in the history of political thought, although I would very strongly suggest at least also the chapter on Socrates because otherwise it will be very difficult to follow the sort of argument I make elsewhere. And one would still need to accept a general orientation in democratic theory, the arguments for which were provided by Rousseau and Kant and considered in Part One. It is also possible for those allergic to Kant or moral philosophy to skip Chapter 3 and focus on the more directly political Chapters 4 and 5, although then one must be willing to accept my claims about Kant's larger strategy. But the case is at any rate much the stronger, and the vision behind it and the sense in which to take it clearer, when one considers all the pieces together.

1

A Historical and Socratic Theory of Democracy

In order to address the problems considered in the preceding Introduction, this book defends what I call a *historical* and *Socratic* theory of democracy. I call it the theory of *democratic elenchus*, but one may also refer to it simply as a historical and Socratic theory. "Elenchus" is the original Greek term (in Romanized form) for Socrates's characteristic style of argument; it is a more precise way of describing what is commonly called "Socratic method," and the point of using the term is that it allows one to focus clearly on what one means in calling the theory "Socratic," which might otherwise suggest any number of things.[1] When I argue for a "Socratic" theory of democracy, then, what I mean is that this theory makes use of a very specific way of arguing for its conclusions, a distinctive way of working out what we ought to take "democracy" to mean and of resolving conflicts over its interpretation. (This theory has nothing to do, in particular, with either Socrates's or Plato's own political doctrines, neither of which were kind to democracy.[2]) The key point about this way of arguing is that it works even in the absence of any certain foundational principles. When Socrates argued, he did not attempt to deduce his conclusions directly from any obviously true starting point. Instead of preaching his own beliefs or claiming special knowledge for himself, he made his case entirely by questioning the coherence of others' claims to knowledge and authority. This will turn out to be a particularly useful way of

---

[1] Literal translations include "refutation," "cross-examination," "testing," and "proof" in a court of law. Henry George Liddell and Robert Scott, *A Greek-English Lexicon* (Oxford: Clarendon Press, 1996). Christina H. Tarnopolsky insightfully discusses another sense, "shaming," in *Prudes, Perverts, and Tyrants: Plato's Gorgias and the Politics of Shame* (Princeton, NJ: Princeton University Press, 2010).

[2] Although there remains some discussion of this in the literature, my concern here is not with Plato's politics but rather with the way Socrates's method might serve democratic ends by undercutting undemocratic claims to authority, along the lines suggested, for instance, by J. Peter Euben, *Corrupting Youth: Political Education, Democratic Culture, and Political Theory* (Princeton, NJ: Princeton University Press, 1997).

arguing when one needs to sort through competing interpretations of democracy. But although elenchus and related forms of argument played a crucial role in the history of the philosophical tradition, and experienced occasional revivals, they have since fallen into relative obscurity, and their potential value for democratic theory has never been fully explored. Indeed, today the term itself is hardly known outside specialist circles in ancient philosophy. One of the major aims of the first part of this book, then, will be to show how renewed attention to this tradition—to both the strengths and limitations of ways this sort of argument has been put to use in the past by some of its greatest practitioners—could shed new light on some of the more pressing and intractable difficulties in contemporary democratic theory.[3]

The rest of this chapter introduces the major principles of the theory of democratic elenchus and shows how they fit together. The detailed arguments in favor of the theory are developed in later chapters, but before one can judge them, one needs a clear overview of the position they are meant to support.

Principles (I) and (II)

The first characteristic that sets this theory apart is that it is *historical*. What I mean by this is that when we inquire into the democratic legitimacy of a given political order, we ought to ask two sorts of questions. Mainstream, static theories ask whether or not that order is properly arranged, so that one can say (in one sense or another) that in it the people govern. A historical theory of democracy asks this, too, but it goes on to ask additionally whether or not it can also be said that the people have chosen this order for themselves. Whereas the first question is formal (or synchronic), the second introduces into democracy a second, historical (or diachronic) dimension. According to a historical theory, a good democratic system must meet both conditions at the same time. To see why this might make sense, consider first a case in which two different countries live under identical constitutional laws, but in the first these laws were freely adopted by the citizens themselves, whereas in the second they remain in force only through constant military repression (either foreign or domestic). The democratic legitimacy of the two constitutions is not indistinguishable, though the institutions

---

[3] Part of this project is distinguishing the logical core of this tradition from some of the ways it was later developed in nineteenth- and twentieth-century discussions of "dialectic." Although the term "dialectic" was also originally used by Plato to describe his mode of argument in the dialogues, more recent uses have stretched it beyond all recognition. Because "dialectic" today conveys so little and carries so many misleading associations, I have preferred to emphasize the alternate, unambiguously Socratic term "elenchus," to mark the status of what I aim at reclaiming as a *way of arguing* in the absence of secure first principles, rather than any sort of metaphysical or causal theory.

they describe are exactly the same. On the other hand, consider another case in which two countries use the same free and open political process to ratify new constitutions. If, however, one of the two constitutions hands legislative power permanently to an unaccountable executive—by plebiscite, for instance, or *Ermächtigungsgesetz*—then the democratic legitimacy of the resulting orders is not the same, although we have identical grounds for supposing each of them to have been chosen through a popular process. A historical theory of democracy captures these crucial differences, obscured by static theories, because it considers democracy always simultaneously along two distinct dimensions.

Now there are many ways of spelling out what it might mean to say that a democratic order is properly arranged, or that it has been chosen by the people. The theory I defend builds on a way of thinking about the first question with roots in Rousseau and Kant, and which has been pursued by a number of contemporary theorists. There are good reasons for thinking this the right approach to take, as discussed in later chapters. Yet apart from a few exceptions considered later, this line of thought has most often focused only on democracy's formal side, while neglecting its historical dimension. (Some of the difficulties in Kant's own view of historical change are considered in Chapter 4.) So the first major claim of this book is that democratic theory needs to extend this way of thinking to democracy's historical side as well, and this is expressed in the first of the theory's two core principles:

Principle (I): A legitimate democracy must (a) respect all citizens' equal freedoms, both in the content of its decisions and in the process through which those decisions are authored, and also (b) do so through a political system those citizens have chosen for themselves.

To clarify, the reference to legitimacy does not imply a threshold dividing "legitimate" from "illegitimate" regimes. Rather, we will see that the principle is only meaningful for comparisons, that what it allows one to judge is the *relative strength* of the competing legitimacy claims of parties locked in democratic struggles. "Citizens" is meant here, and always throughout the book, to refer to all members of the political community; it does not exclude by definition resident aliens or undocumented immigrants, but leaves open the question of whether and in what ways they might be included or excluded from full membership in that community.[4] Where I write of a democracy's "decisions," it is

---

[4] This is itself a question open to democratic struggle. Because struggles concerning borders and interstate relations raise even more complex questions, however, I cannot also address them in this work. But this does not mean the theory here denies the reality of the problem; it is just that on the one hand, not every struggle is over borders, and on the other, it makes sense to work out a response to the problem of change first in the simpler case where this further issue does not arise, before going on to consider also the more complex case in which it does.

more traditional to use "laws," but it has often been alleged, in the course of democratic struggles, that not only formal laws but also other sorts of coercive social relations should be understood as decisions of the community which must therefore be brought under democratic control. "Decisions" is thus preferred to avoid building into the theory itself any particular stand on this issue, to highlight instead that what counts as a political decision is itself a political decision, and therefore ought to be judged by using the theory in particular cases, not at the outset by definition. (My own position on the current state of this question is discussed later, but one can accept the general theory even if one disagrees with those conclusions.)

The first point about Principle (I) is that it is not directly institutional. It does not define democracy as majority rule, for instance, but admits a wide range of institutional arrangements so long as those count both as chosen by the citizens themselves and as respecting those citizens' equal freedoms. The basic idea, which extends a thought from Rousseau and Kant, is that politics requires making decisions that can be enforced even against citizens who disagree, and dissenting citizens can be obligated to obey only if those decisions count as self-imposed by the citizenry as a whole. What we would call democracy (what Rousseau and Kant called a republic) is the only legitimate constitution,[5] therefore, because in it even dissenting citizens can be said to be bound only by their own free choice, and "volenti non fit iniuria" (as Kant put it, citing the familiar principle of Roman law).[6] The reason democracy deserves to rule, then, is not that it is most likely to make good decisions, or that it best promotes some external value (such as freedom, equality, or happiness, independently defined). The more fundamental political question is who has the power to decide what counts as "good" or which values politics ought to pursue, and then to enforce those judgments even on citizens with other views—if need be by violence. It is this eminently political authority that can only rightly be attributed to the citizenry as a whole.

Now if this is the point of democracy, then it is easy to see why it cannot be defined directly by any institution. Even majority rule, for instance, although it may often be a good idea, cannot define democracy in the sense required to show why it deserves to rule.[7] For as history shows, it is only too possible

---

[5] The only peremptorily just constitution, in Kant's later writings.

[6] "No injustice is done to the willing" (6:313).

[7] Some think it mistaken to define democracy in ways that tie it logically to concepts of value. But this depends entirely on the questions one means to ask, and here we are concerned with questions of legitimate political authority—just the sort that come to a head in democratic struggles and revolutions. This should not be mistaken for a claim that any outcome we find morally objectionable is ipso facto undemocratic, but it does mean that even majorities can act in undemocratic ways if they violate logical conditions of attributing their decisions to the people as a whole—for instance, by disenfranchising minorities.

for majorities sometimes to disenfranchise, to enslave, or even to massacre a minority of their compatriots, and in those cases majority rule looks less like the entire citizenry legislating for itself and more like one large faction imposing its will unilaterally on everyone else.[8] This is why Rousseau, for instance, admitted that majority rule is only surely just if one supposes "that all the characteristics of the general will remain in the majority" (*CS* IV.II, 3:441).[9] But the problem, of course, is hardly unique to majorities, since countermajoritarian institutions (up to and including those requiring consensus) may just as easily be exploited by minorities for their own factional ends. So since no institution can guarantee the legitimacy of its decisions, merely by being the sort of institution that it is, a further ground is thus required to explain why decisions taken by any of several sorts of institutions ought sometimes to count as legitimate because attributable to the citizenry as a whole.

The first clause of Principle (I) provides a different sort of solution. It holds that a public decision counts as self-imposed by the citizenry, and therefore as democratically legitimate, if it respects all citizens' equal freedoms, both in its content and in the process through which it was authored. Rousseau suggested the idea behind this double requirement when he redefined a "republic" not as a specific form of government but as any state ruled by laws, where "laws" were held to mean general decisions authored by the sovereign people as a whole (II.

---

[8] One can even write a sort of proof: if democracy is simply majority rule without qualification, then a majority decision disenfranchising a minority is democratic. And if that decision is democratic, so is a second decision whereby a majority of those remaining disenfranchises another minority who made it through the first round. By this route one arrives sooner or later at the result that a minority of all citizens retains the right to rule over all the rest. Ergo, if majority rule is justified unconditionally, then so is rule of a minority. But once one accepts any limiting condition at all, then democracy cannot simply be *defined* as majority rule. And this points to a real political danger; one could argue that a messier but similar scenario played out twice during the French Revolution, once under the Convention, culminating in the Terror, and again under the Directory, clearing the way for Bonaparte.

[9] Cf. II.III, 3:71–2; I.V, 3:359. If Rousseau were a majoritarian proceduralist, it should be impossible to account for his distinction between the general will and the will of all (II.III–IV), or for his favorable view of the Roman *comitia centuriata* in IV.IV. John P. McCormick rightly emphasizes this last point in "Rousseau's Rome and the Repudiation of Populist Republicanism," *Critical Review of International Social and Political Philosophy* 10, no. 1 (2007): 3–27, but I think it shows something other than that Rousseau took the general will for an objective common interest that might be best known by the few. Rather, because Rousseau defined the "people" as the whole rather than as one social faction among others, his interest in the *comitia centuriata* was how they alone included all (IV. IV, 3:452) and worked to bring them to agreement on an actual single will—they were not majoritarian but included moderating influences to prevent their capture by factions perceived as such by other citizens and therefore divisive. They thus worked rather like the lawgiver and civil religion to "persuade without convincing" (II.VII, 3:383). We will see this is essentially the same strategy used later by Sieyès and Hegel, and though I do think it ultimately indefensible on democratic grounds, it points to a real difficulty in working out who speaks for the democratic "people" and to the need for a theory of the sort I will defend.

VI, 3:379). But he also invited confusion by suggesting that only laws passed in person by the assembled citizenry could count as authored by the people, and from this later democrats have often dissented.[10] A more defensible interpretation has recently been offered by Jürgen Habermas and developed by Corey Brettschneider, who have argued that legitimate law must respect all citizens' equal freedoms not only as its "authors" but also as its "addressees."[11] It is easy to see why a law should be undemocratic if imposed on citizens excluded from an equal role in the lawmaking process. But it is no less important that the law's content should not violate citizens' equal freedoms after it is passed. The reason is that the subsequent *enforcement* of such a law can be legitimate only if one can *continue to see it as binding* on all citizens because self-imposed. And so a law that enslaves a part of the population, for instance, could never legitimately be enforced, because slavery abolishes the civil freedom and personhood of the very persons it claims to obligate, and this is absurd if the only source of law's authority is the free will of those who author it for themselves (as Rousseau famously observed in the parallel case of enslaving oneself by contract).

But if slavery is an extreme case, one can see how the same logic might apply, for instance, to laws disenfranchising certain classes of citizens, or as Brettschneider emphasizes, those depriving some citizens of an equal right to sue in court or of equal protection from arbitrary state detention. If instead both the process through which a law is authored and the content of that law respect the equal freedoms of every citizen, then because all citizens are treated similarly as free persons under laws of their own making, none has grounds for claiming the resulting law cannot consistently be enforced. Although some citizens have been outvoted, one may nevertheless suppose each also to agree to accede to the choice of the whole, despite his or her personal views (as one must if any decision is to be possible without universal agreement). By contrast, this supposition is absurd—like a contract selling oneself into slavery—whenever the collective choice violates the equal freedoms one must attribute to each citizen in supposing them freely to have so agreed (as one must if the collective

---

[10] Though Rousseau had reason enough for suspecting the sort of representation typified by the eighteenth-century British Parliament to amount to an abdication of popular sovereignty, developments since the American and French Revolutions have shown it is at least conceivable that elections could be used not only to decide contests among rival grandees for the right to rule over others, but also as a means of holding representatives accountable to popular views, and therefore as part of a larger process of democratic will-formation. On these changes, see Bernard Manin, *The Principles of Representative Government* (Cambridge, UK: Cambridge University Press, 1997) and Nadia Urbinati, *Representative Democracy: Principles and Genealogy* (Chicago: University of Chicago Press, 2006).

[11] Habermas, *Between Facts and Norms: Contributions to a Discourse Theory of Law and Democracy*, trans. William Rehg (Cambridge, MA: MIT Press, 1996), Chapter 3, and "Constitutional Democracy: A Paradoxical Union of Contradictory Principles?," *Political Theory* 29, no. 6 (2001): 766–81; Brettschneider, *Democratic Rights: The Substance of Self-Government* (Princeton, NJ: Princeton University Press, 2007), 28–53.

decision is to bind them as their own).¹² The first clause of Principle (I), then, explains what it means to say that sometimes the citizenry as a whole can be said to govern itself, even though individuals continue to disagree, and why in those cases public decisions are legitimate and binding.

Yet this is not enough. The democratic theory defended here breaks with static theories like Brettschneider's by adding a further requirement, expressed in Principle (I)'s second clause. This theory is *historical* because it holds that a legitimate democracy must not only meet the formal conditions just described, but must also do so through a system that the citizens have chosen for themselves. In recent years, a number of leading theorists have drawn attention to this historical dimension of democracy, but what this entails and whether it is indeed necessary remain highly controversial.¹³ Among the book's aims, then, is to strengthen the case for historical theories by showing why one can no longer rightly dismiss the demand that citizens should be able to choose for themselves which institutions they will recognize as democratic. The detailed case is made later by working through powerful arguments adduced by Rousseau and Kant in their own, not entirely successful, attempts to grapple with this issue, but the basic point can be introduced as follows.

The content of Principle (I)'s first clause will depend entirely on how one spells out what it means for public decisions to respect all citizens' "equal

---

¹² This is the core thought behind Rousseau's notion of the general will, from which all the limits on sovereign power, including its inalienability, derive. (Although, as Rousseau duly noted, this does not yet answer the further question of how to recognize the general will in practice.) A difference is that I follow other recent interpreters in insisting on *equal* freedoms, whereas Rousseau and Kant thought it enough for law to respect freedom and apply to everyone. As the rest of this chapter will make clear, my view is that differences of this sort cannot be sorted out wholly a priori, but depend in part on historical struggles of the kind that have managed to establish the principle of legal equality in many democratic polities since the time that Rousseau and Kant wrote.

¹³ See Habermas, *Between Facts and Norms*; Bruce Ackerman, *We the People*, 3 vols. (Cambridge, MA: Harvard University Press, 1991–2014); Frank I. Michelman, "Constitutional Authorship," in *Constitutionalism: Philosophical Foundations*, ed. Larry Alexander (Cambridge, UK: Cambridge University Press, 1998); Jed Rubenfeld, *Freedom and Time: A Theory of Constitutional Self-Government* (New Haven, CT: Yale University Press, 2001); Elisabeth Ellis, *Kant's Politics: Provisional Theory for an Uncertain World* (New Haven, CT: Yale University Press, 2005), and *Provisional Politics: Kantian Arguments in Policy Context* (New Haven, CT: Yale University Press, 2008); Seyla Benhabib, *Another Cosmopolitanism*, ed. Robert Post (Oxford: Oxford University Press, 2006), and *Dignity in Adversity: Human Rights in Troubled Times* (Cambridge, UK: Polity Press, 2011); Kevin Olson, *Reflexive Democracy: Political Equality and the Welfare State* (Cambridge, MA: MIT Press, 2006); Melissa Schwartzberg, *Democracy and Legal Change* (New York: Cambridge University Press, 2007); Jack Knight and James Johnson, *The Priority of Democracy: Political Consequences of Pragmatism* (Princeton, NJ: Princeton University Press, 2011); Paulina Ochoa Espejo, *The Time of Popular Sovereignty: Process and the Democratic State* (University Park: Pennsylvania State University Press, 2011); Craig T. Borowiak, *Accountability and Democracy: The Pitfalls and Promise of Popular Control* (Oxford: Oxford University Press, 2011); Axel Honneth, *Freedom's Right: The Social Foundations of Democratic Life* (Cambridge, UK: Polity Press, 2014).

freedoms." The most common way of doing this is to derive a priori a schedule of specific rights and institutions directly from the general principle. (Another is to hand authority to do so to an institution like the U.S. Supreme Court.) The obvious problem is that this involves the theorist (or Court) in drawing up a list of rights or institutions that actual citizens may not accept, but that nevertheless must trump, in cases of conflict, what would otherwise appear to be those citizens' own self-legislating will, expressed through elections or other political channels. Defenders of this approach reply that because these rights and institutions are just those conditions that make a political process democratic in the first place, any public decision that contradicts them cannot be considered the real will of the democratic people—even if it is supported, for instance, by an electoral majority or referendum.[14] Now I agree with the general principle that any democratic process and decision must respect the equal freedoms of all citizens. But this does not mean there is no danger in stipulating a priori a schedule of specific rights and institutions that would prejudge the constitutional decisions of actual citizens everywhere in the world and for all future generations. Unless we can be very certain that every other conceivable list may be ruled out on strictly a priori grounds, a final judge will always be required to decide which—among those offered up by different theorists, jurists, or political actors—deserves to be imposed with the force of law, in a given polity, even on those who disagree. And this raises again at the constitutional level the familiar question of political authority we already encountered at the level of the normal laws. Now I think there are good reasons for supposing it impossible to reason a priori from the general principle directly to particular rights and institutions (without camouflaging contestable judgments as apodictic rules of reason), but what is certain is that it would take a very ambitious argument to prove the opposite, and that in the absence of such an argument, the point cannot safely be presumed.[15] Furthermore, recall that any conceivable proof would need to avoid entailing the further conclusion that a priori reason ought also to suffice for establishing the legitimacy of normal laws, since otherwise one ends up with a rather undemocratic sort of democratic theory.

---

[14] See Habermas, *Between Facts and Norms*; Brettschneider, *Democratic Rights*; Anna Stilz, *Liberal Loyalty: Freedom, Obligation, and the State* (Princeton, NJ: Princeton University Press, 2009); and John Hart Ely, *Democracy and Distrust: A Theory of Judicial Review* (Cambridge, MA: Harvard University Press, 1980), although they differ about how to respond to potential conflict.

[15] It is not enough to reply with Stilz that there may exist a minimal list on which every reasonable person would agree (*Liberal Loyalty*, 91). The problem is that these rights and requirements matter just because they are meant to be enforced against actual third parties who disagree nonetheless, and this requires a stronger authorization than our own unilateral judgments of the range of dissent hypothetical persons might admit (just because our own judgments, in themselves, cannot rightly bind third parties who do not share them).

For all these reasons, a historical theory of democracy takes an entirely different tack. Rather than avoiding the question of who decides, it confronts that question head-on and answers that any binding decisions on the content of democratic rights or the shape of democratic institutions must be left to citizens themselves. Such questions cannot be resolved a priori at the level of a general theory, but this does not mean that anything goes or that democratic theory has nothing more to say. We have already seen that decisions at the level of normal laws count as democratic only if they respect all citizens' equal freedoms. A historical theory now applies the same point also at the constitutional level. It holds that a democratic system, too, must count as chosen by the citizenry as a whole, just because those citizens have chosen it in a manner respecting the equal freedoms of them all. This yields the second clause of Principle (I). To make the point more explicit, one may also write out this clause more completely as holding that a legitimate democracy must respect all citizens as authors and addressees, (b): "through a political system those citizens have chosen for themselves in a manner respecting the equal freedoms of them all." (Here, I write of a "manner" rather than a "process" because a legally codified procedure would already be part of the constitutional order that needs to be chosen.)

Taken as a whole, then, Principle (I) is an entirely different sort of principle than that familiar from static theories. It is not a general rule under which specific democratic rights and institutions fall as instances; instead, what it does is to specify the conditions under which it may meaningfully be said that a citizenry has chosen its democratic institutions for itself. This means that it does not ask us to substitute our own a priori judgments for those of citizens, but to interpret as best we can what judgments those citizens themselves have made, insofar as the citizenry as a whole (and not only a faction acting despotically) can be taken to have made any judgment at all. For a democratic system to count as chosen in this way by the "people," it must respect all citizens as both "authors" and "addressees," just like normal laws. The second clause of Principle (I) explains what it means for citizens to count as its "authors." And the system will count as respecting all citizens also as its "addressees" just in case it also meets the double condition already laid out in the first clause.

Because Principle (I) does not permit philosopher kings or political scientists to derive democratic rights and institutions a priori, it allows a wide range of institutional variation across time and place. And because it insists on building up the argument in every case from local political realities, it builds in a strong presumption against extending one's own preferred interpretation of democracy too readily to other contexts, without attending to the views of those actual persons to whom one would see it applied. But this respect for context does not slide into relativism, because the principle still provides a standard for explaining why some political orders are more democratic than others, and why certain reforms to a given order might be good or bad on democratic grounds. By offering a *general* framework for thinking about what counts as a *particular* and local decision, then, this approach stakes out new ground in familiar debates for and against "universal values," from which it cuts straight through a number of confusions that have made those debates so intractable. (Certainly, more is needed to show why this amounts to more than simply transposing familiar worries to a new key, but this will be a major theme of the book.)

Readers will doubtless object, because it seems at first that Principle (I) only pushes back the problem of political authority to the constitutional level, rather than resolving it. We want to say the people themselves decide what will count as respecting their equal freedoms, but how can we tell what "the people" have decided unless we already know which equal freedoms a decision of "the people" must respect? Or put another way, how could the people ever choose their own constitution, since they must already be constituted in some form or another before they could choose anything at all? Here, we seem to encounter a vicious circle or infinite regress, what Bonnie Honig has called a "chicken and egg problem."[16] This is not a mere logical quibble but a very real political danger, because it points out how difficult it is to know whether or not an existing democratic regime harbors self-perpetuating exclusions and violence—while also reminding us that every conceivable alternative faces similar risks. In recent years, a number of theorists have drawn attention to related formulations of "democratic paradox" that approach this problem from various angles.[17] I believe the underlying issue is best understood as follows. It appears that a democratic regime both requires an independent authority to ratify its legitimacy and yet at the same time cannot possibly admit any such authority. If final authority is truly independent of the democratic system, then that authority is the true sovereign and the people can be said to govern only at its pleasure. If instead the democratic system retains sole and final authority for itself, then we have no reason better than its word for supposing it to

---

[16] Honig, *Emergency Politics: Paradox, Law, Democracy* (Princeton, NJ: Princeton University Press, 2009), 14.

[17] See Claude Lefort, *Democracy and Political Theory*, trans. David Macey (Minneapolis: University of Minnesota Press, 1988); Pierre Rosanvallon, *Le peuple introuvable* (Paris: Gallimard, 1998); William E. Connolly, *The Ethos of Pluralization* (Minneapolis: University of Minnesota Press, 1995), *Identity/Difference: Democratic Negotiations of Political Paradox*, rev. ed. (Minneapolis: University of Minnesota Press, 2002), and *Pluralism* (Durham, NC: Duke University Press, 2005); Michelman, "Constitutional Authorship"; Chantal Mouffe, *The Democratic Paradox* (New York: Verso, 2000); Habermas, "Constitutional Democracy"; Alan Keenan, *Democracy in Question: Democratic Openness in a Time of Political Closure* (Stanford, CA: Stanford University Press, 2003); Benhabib, *Another Cosmopolitanism*; Sofia Näsström, "The Legitimacy of the People," *Political Theory* 35, no. 5 (2007): 624–58; Kevin Olson, "Paradoxes of Constitutional Democracy," *American Journal of Political Science* 51, no. 2 (2007): 330–43; Jason Frank, *Constituent Moments: Enacting the People in Postrevolutionary America* (Durham, NC: Duke University Press, 2010); Honig, *Emergency Politics*; Ochoa Espejo, *Time*; Angélica M. Bernal, "The Meaning and Perils of Presidential Refounding in Latin America," *Constellations* 21, no. 4 (2014): 440–56.

represent the people's democratic will. I call this dilemma the "paradox of authorization." The infinite regress previously described arises when one tries to escape it by tracing the legitimacy of the current system back to some prior foundation; but then either the authority of that foundation is independent of the people's choice, in which case it is inconsistent with democracy, or else it depends on that choice, in which case one needs a further foundation to assure us it is what they have chosen. This problem was a central concern for major figures in the social contract tradition from Hobbes to Kant, underlying the way they theorized the legitimacy of revolutions and the founding of new states. It slipped from view in the nineteenth century, but has finally begun to attract attention again with the rise of interest in normative theories of democracy since the end of the Cold War and as critics continue to point out difficulties in some of the ways ideas with roots in eighteenth-century theories of justice have been revived since the 1970s.

Although many of the historical theories of democracy proposed in recent years have wrestled with this problem, none has yet managed convincingly to resolve it. Some, like Bruce Ackerman's or Jed Rubenfeld's, ignore the paradox, whereas accounts like Jason Frank's or Pierre Rosanvallon's draw valuable attention to its historical significance but do not attempt a solution. Discussions by Claude Lefort and Chantal Mouffe can be read to suggest that the paradox is intrinsic to democracy and attempts to solve it misguided and perhaps dangerous. Bonnie Honig and Paulina Ochoa Espejo have each, in different ways, suggested that the difficulty may best be met by reimagining a constitution or a people not as a discrete and static entity but as part of an "infinite series" (Honig) or as an ongoing "process" (Ochoa Espejo). Finally, Jürgen Habermas and Seyla Benhabib have argued that a democratic constitution should be understood as a "reflexive" project of self-revision pointing into the future (Habermas), in which constitutional ideals are continually reinterpreted to challenge injustices and exclusions through an unending series of "democratic iterations" (Benhabib).

What none of these different responses provides, however, is a defensible standard for judging when constitutional changes are moving in the right or wrong direction. Even Habermas and Benhabib, who have done a great deal to advance discussions of broadly Rousseauian and Kantian principles, have left this problem unresolved. On the one hand, although their notions of a reflexive constitution and democratic iterations do show how legitimate democratic change is *possible* and how it might be conceived, neither on its own does anything to tell us which actual changes may or may not be merited in a given case—how to tell the difference, in other words, between a "democratic iteration" and an undemocratic one.[18] On the other, if at the end of the day democratic standards

---

[18] Consider Honig's objections in "Dead Rights, Live Futures: A Reply to Habermas's 'Constitutional Democracy,'" *Political Theory* 29, no. 6 (2001): 792–805, and "Another Cosmopolitanism? Law and Politics in the New Europe," in Benhabib, *Another Cosmopolitanism*, 111–12. Benhabib appears

are simply the principles of discourse ethics appropriately applied, then the question of who decides in the final instance how to interpret and apply them looms as large as ever. It is not enough to say that citizens themselves will sort this out in the public sphere or through the interaction of formal and informal publics, because the reason we need democratic government in the first place is that citizens disagree and cannot always be trusted to do the right thing, and so we need a final authority to interpret and enforce what will count as the self-legislating will of the citizenry as a whole.

Here, too, the theory of democratic elenchus takes a wholly different tack, and this is what makes it not only historical but also Socratic. Now the paradox of authorization is a serious problem that cannot safely be ignored, but it appears as an insoluble logical paradox only on certain commonplace assumptions. The right way of understanding this paradox is like a Kantian antinomy—once we see that certain assumptions render it inescapable, this ought to explode the obviousness of those assumptions and show the need for a different sort of democratic theory that can do without them. (And this, of course, is a broadly Socratic sort of argument.) In this case, the assumption that must be dropped is that the notion of the democratic people's will refers to a natural object in the world, prior to any political decisions over who counts as part of that people and how those parts are to be counted. The reason we are tempted to suppose this is that if such an impossible object could be found—what we might call the *Volk an sich selbst* [the people in itself]—then its authority would be self-evident and incontrovertible, and—most important—readily borrowed by anyone with correct insight into its nature as a means of sorting out present political controversies. Then we would not need to consider our democratic judgments as themselves political acts requiring political justifications, but could pass them off as entirely epistemic—as determined directly by the nature of the world rather than by free acts for which we might be held responsible, even though their point is to justify not propositions of truth but coercive relations among persons. This, however, is to mistake a practical question for a theoretical one (in the Kantian sense of these terms), and it invites us to apply categories like causality where they cannot really apply. Hence the ease with which we look to stories of causal origins to fill in for political justifications of present regimes, and the familiarity of this move in social contract theories that posit a unified people prior to the constitution of sovereign political authority. Rousseau and Kant, by contrast, followed Hobbes in radically rejecting this latter supposition, and this set them off sharply from

---

to acknowledge a related point in *Dignity*, 152. For a fuller discussion, see my "The Struggle for Democracy: Paradox and History in Democratic Progress," *Constellations* 16, no. 3 (2009): 410–28.

others in the period including Locke, Pufendorf, Vattel, and Achenwall, who preferred in various ways to cling to it.[19]

The alternative is to consider the idea of a democratic people not as an object but as what Kant called a practical postulate, a principle necessarily presupposed in judging what we ought to do. In other words, "the democratic people" is not something out there to be found or observed like a physical phenomenon, but a conceptual constraint we take on when we ask what sort of public decision might fairly be imposed on all citizens. Only a decision that can count as the will of the whole people may rightly be imposed, because any other would amount to the will of a faction tyrannizing over the rest, and that would violate the equal freedoms of all citizens that every binding decision must respect. But this means we do not need to know that "the people" exists in any empirical sense—in fact, it would be impossible ever to know that, since "the people" is a political idea that cannot be directly experienced. What actually exists, in a literal sense, is only a bunch of citizens making judgments in a certain way—by asking whether or not different ways of governing themselves can be defended as consistent with the principle of a democratic people freely legislating for themselves.[20] Making and defending these sorts of judgments, and working to organize political power in line with them instead of in some other way, are already a form of political action, and need to be included in any theory of democratic politics. One of the greatest dangers in democracy is to suppose, to the contrary, that one has somehow located the *Volk an sich selbst*, and thus to attribute to some set of particular persons, organized to come to decisions in some particular way, the plenary powers that only this wholly ideal entity could ever rightly possess. This is dangerous because it hides the political act involved in claiming authority to make that attribution and to enforce its consequences on others, by pretending that "the people's" true will shines forth naturally of itself, prior to any politics. It is the old populist trick through which calls to seize all power for "the people" become the surest means of mastering them.

---

[19] The decisive issue is whether sovereignty can be both alienated and yet revoked for violating a trust or contract between the people and the rulers. Hobbes, Rousseau, and Kant agree in collapsing any gap of this sort between the people and the sovereign (although they do not, of course, derive identical consequences from this).

[20] To anticipate: although the idea of "the people" does not exist, it has a practical use because anyone claiming to speak for the people must be able to defend a claim that *does not contradict* that idea, and when different parties compete for the right to speak for the people, one can compare the consistency of their respective claims with this idea all of them presuppose. So the idea is a formal constraint useful in sorting through competing interpretations of the same empirical data on grounds of consistency, but it is not itself an empirical entity we might ever simply "find." Kant's categorical imperative and ideal republican constitution and Hegel's notion of spirit as the self-actualization of freedom are also ideas of this sort, considered in the following chapters.

The right way to think about a principle of democratic theory like Principle (I), then, is not as describing a thing but as an assumption internal to an act of democratic judgment.[21] If we consider again Principle (I)'s two clauses, we can now see that the paradox of authorization arises only if one assumes the point of the second clause is to secure an independent ground of authority for the first. This could work only if we knew we had indeed located the *Volk an sich selbst*, and that kicks off the regress because it is no more possible at the constitutional level than at that of ordinary legislation. The alternative is to give up entirely on the supposition that one of the principle's two clauses might ground the other—either logically or historically—and instead to consider them simply as two equal conditions to be satisfied at the same time. This means that only those political systems able to meet both conditions without inconsistency can possibly be defended. And therefore we can rule out any system that cannot satisfy both clauses *on the same interpretation of citizens' equal freedoms, even if we do not know that this (or any) particular interpretation of those freedoms is, in fact, the true one*. Instead of searching for a direct proof of the one true view (which cannot be found), we start by ruling out all views that cannot consistently be defended, and then take whatever is left. For instance, a plebiscite that hands legislative authority to an unaccountable ruler fails to meet both conditions on the *same* interpretation of citizens' equal freedoms. And so does a "popular democracy" imposed by a vanguardist putsch (unless it is subsequently ratified through some other more consistent channel). The problem with these views is not that we know that some other one is right instead, but that if one starts to explain what it is that makes them "democratic," one ends by contradicting oneself and talking nonsense.

This move is inspired by one of the central claims in Hegel's *Philosophy of Right*, that any just constitution must count as respecting simultaneously what Hegel calls citizens' "objective" and "subjective" freedom (§146–7). In referring to "objective" freedom, he meant that the constitution must, in fact, be organized to respect the liberty of all the citizens, and by "subjective" freedom, that these same citizens must also be able to recognize for themselves that it is thus organized, so they also freely accept it as their own. Only if both conditions are satisfied at the same time can it be said that the constitution is truly free. Hegel, however, was no democrat, and so he had rather different ideas than I will defend about what is required to satisfy this double condition. (Chapter 5 discusses his views in detail.) But the general point is nevertheless a great insight; what it allowed Hegel to do was to define the institutional requirements of political freedom indirectly, merely by working out the conceptual conditions of any

---

[21] Throughout the book, I use "judgment" neither in the technical Kantian sense of the third *Critique* nor for Aristotelian *phronēsis*, but in the political sense familiar from debates in the social contract tradition over who is to be final judge in the face of political disagreement.

interpretation of political freedom that might hold up as internally consistent. He then went on to argue that the reason the modern state was superior to earlier political forms was just because this state can be shown to resolve inconsistencies in the accounts of freedom and justice through which those earlier forms had tried and failed to justify themselves.[22] This approach escapes the paradox of authorization because it does not attempt to prove the positive legitimacy of the present constitution by deriving it from any independent ground. Instead, it reasons strictly by elimination, ruling out those alternatives that cannot be defended without self-contradiction and admitting only those that can. This is the sort of reasoning Hegel called "dialectic," which he reported to have learned from Plato and Kant.[23]

The second principle of the theory of democratic elenchus reworks Hegel's Socratic insight in democratic terms:

> **Principle (II):** In a contest over democratic change, that party counts as representing the choice of the democratic people which more consistently meets its own interpretation of Principle (I) than any other party.

This is not another substantive principle to be ranked with Principle (I). Rather, it explains how Principle (I) should be used, what it means in a practical case when we face two or more competing democratic visions to say that one of them satisfies that principle better than another. The key point is that Principle (I) is strictly a negative or limit-principle (what Kant calls a *Grenzbegriff*). It cannot pick out any particular constitution to which it corresponds; all it allows us to do is to rule out as self-contradictory certain constitutional programs we actually encounter in the course of historical struggles. So we judge these competing programs not by asking which best approximates some independent standard of the one true democratic constitution, but by working through each of them on its own terms to see which among them holds up best in its claim to be the program chosen by the citizens. This is strictly a test of consistency, but Principle (I) helps add some teeth to it by drawing out and making explicit the conceptual conditions that any consistent interpretation of democracy would have to meet.

It is important to stress that Principle (II) lends itself only to comparative judgments; it does not suppose that a rote application of Principle (I) allows us to draw a bright line between "consistent" and "inconsistent" programs, full stop. Rather, all it asks us to do is to compare the actual programs involved in a

---

[22] This is the general thesis of the *VPG* and the closing sections of the *PhR*.

[23] *WL* 12:242. Cf. *PhG* §71, *Lectures on the History of Philosophy 1825–6*, 3 vols., trans. and ed. Robert F. Brown (Oxford: Oxford University Press, 2006–2009), 2:124–155, 2:175–224. Original in Hegel, *Vorlesungen*, 17 vols., ed. C Becker et al. (Hamburg: Meiner, 1983–2007).

particular controversy, to see which makes the stronger case to be consistently defensible as the one chosen by the democratic people.[24] The judgments it permits are thus always local and historically situated; whether or not they may also be more broadly generalizable is a question that requires making further judgments as occasions for them arise. Neither of the two principles is an algorithm. Together, they invite us to pose a certain sort of question of proposals for or against democratic change. This question is Socratic: it asks each side why its vision of democracy should be believed, and examines the answers for consistency on their own terms. This never allows us to prove conclusively that any one democratic program is legitimate in an absolute sense. But it does allow us to reason indirectly, by elimination, in order to say which among available programs at a given time and place has made the best case, the case that has held up better than any other. And this is just as much as we need to show, because in politics what we need to decide is which among several democratic visions to support in the midst of struggles over change. The absolute legitimacy of a given democratic system is a question that neither admits nor ever needs an answer, either in philosophy or in politics.

Principle (II)*

A historical and Socratic theory of democracy is defined by Principles (I) and (II). The second explains how to make use of the first, and together, they comprise a complete theory of democratic legitimacy and democratic change. But more must be said, because Principle (II) will strike many as too permissive to be of any real use. One may well suppose that nearly any interpretation of democracy can be formulated so as to meet the minimal requirement of consistency if considered strictly on its own terms.[25] Surely, one might think, if one is to rule out any particular view, one must challenge its terms directly to show they begin from the wrong assumptions, and this requires proving some other set of assumptions right. Now a major aim of the book is to show at least that this does not go without saying, that another sort of strictly internal argument is both logically valid and capable sometimes of producing significant results. Chapters 2–4 show how this sort of *elenctic* argument was developed and put

---

[24] Some may ask why we ought to care about consistency in the first place. In the sense in which it is invoked here, it is not an independent value based on any sort of moral claim, for instance, that a consistent life is better than some other sort. The point is simply that if we are to mean anything in calling some politics more democratic than others, then we must be able to explain what we mean by this in some way without flatly contradicting ourselves. Chapter 3 discusses this in detail.

[25] This is also, of course, a famous objection to Kant's categorical imperative, based on a misunderstanding considered in Chapter 3.

to use by Plato, Kant, and Hegel, but this requires a good deal of textual work to overcome familiar misreadings that insist on mistaking these authors' arguments for foundationalist ones—perhaps, one suspects, because it is presumed too quickly that otherwise they could not be any good.

Perhaps it is true that any interpretation of democracy can be made consistent if taken at face value. But the way the Socratic elenchus works is by questioning bald assertions in order to draw out and make explicit the assumptions on which they depend and the consequences they entail, to show that sometimes these assumptions or consequences do not sit well with what one originally meant to assert. So the way one gains critical purchase in elenchus is not by proving foundations true or false, but by working out in greater detail the relations among ideas and claims internal to the position one is considering. In principle, each of these moves is open to challenge in dialogue—as illustrated by Plato's use of the dialogue form—but one may also summarize certain moves found repeatedly successful in order to provide general guidelines, so that every discussion of a particular case need not begin by reinventing the wheel. Principle (II)* (read "two-star") is a guideline of this sort. It is not a different principle from Principle (II); it is only a further specification that works out in greater detail some of the conditions a particular democratic program will have to meet in order to hold up as consistent. It is another formulation meant to be more immediately useful in practice, and it shows one way it is at least possible to put some teeth into Principle (II)'s requirement of consistency. But even if one disagrees with some of these more specific conditions, one can still accept Principle (II) and the general framework of the theory.

Principle (II)*: In a contest over democratic change, the party which best satisfies Principle (II) is that which meets the following four conditions:

(1) It puts forward some consistent interpretation of Principle (I) that supports its program.
(2) It demonstrates popular support for its interpretation, on that interpretation's own criteria for identifying popular support.
(3) Its interpretation is consistent with the results of past contests that continue to carry the presumption of representing decisions of the democratic people, in the absence of positive evidence that those decisions have subsequently been reversed.
(4) No other party meets the preceding three conditions equally well.

I call these, respectively, the *conceptual* condition (1), the *practical* condition (2), the *historical baseline* (3), and the condition of *exclusivity* (4). Here, I will only introduce the basic ideas behind them; Chapter 6 treats them in detail.

The first, conceptual condition holds that a proposed democratic system must be defensible on some consistent interpretation of the equal freedoms of all citizens. One need not show this is the one "true" interpretation, only that it distinguishes in some consistent manner between systems that do respect these freedoms and others that do not. The idea is that if one cannot manage even this, then one has failed to provide even a possible answer to why we ought to consider one's program more "democratic" than any other. Without any consistent standard at all, every program is equally well described as "democratic" or "undemocratic" and the terms lose meaning altogether. Of course, one might argue that Principle (I) already builds in too much content, that there might exist a consistent interpretation of what democracy is (and what it is not) that does not insist on freedom or equality or the inclusion of all. This question is considered in Chapter 6, although it should be pointed out that the theory is open to revising any of these formulations if arguments to that effect should turn out to win. One has to start somewhere, but if and when specific interpretive controversies arise, the theory invites one to work them out in Socratic fashion.

The second, practical condition is that the proposed system enjoys some observable popular support, consistent with its own interpretation of how popular support can be observed. We do not need to show that this represents the one true will of "the people" [*das Volk an sich selbst*], only that it is consistent with what we should *expect* to see on the proposed system's own interpretation of how that will is to be recognized, since every democratic system must commit itself to some answer to this question. The general idea is that although any number of views of democratic freedom might sound good in the abstract, if in a given polity, one's preferred view can be maintained only by force because other citizens reject it, then insisting on it nonetheless may lead lofty emancipatory ideals to flip over, in practice, into apologies for despotism. Or to give a more prosaic example, majority rule is, in general, a perfectly consistent way of organizing a polity in accordance with Principle (I), but if in a certain country a majority votes instead for a consociational system, then it is very hard to argue that majority rule is the vision of democracy those citizens have chosen for themselves. On the other hand, protections of minority rights are not obviously ruled out simply because they lose a majority vote, nor is majority rule clearly rejected when a consociational constitution is ratified through a consociational process (as it was, for instance, in the United States). In each case we must go on to ask further questions, as considered in Chapter 7.

Condition (3) requires that the proposed system be compatible with other democratic principles established by previous struggles and which have a good claim to retain the people's present allegiance. I call these principles collectively "the historical baseline." It is always possible that a present struggle will turn out to justify overturning established principles, but this can be so only when one side puts forward (a) a consistent interpretation of citizens' equal freedoms backed by (b) popular support for overturning those principles (c) *in a consistent fashion*, meaning everywhere they appear in the existing constitutional order rather than by picking and choosing in a manner that belies the claim that overturning the underlying principles is really what the people now have willed.

This condition will likely be controversial. One might suppose history irrelevant to democracy, especially since I have argued that the legitimacy of present orders cannot be derived from historical foundations. But there is another way history can be used in democratic theory, not as a foundation but as a source of context for interpreting the present. Now democratic systems are typically complex and contain many parts bearing on the same underlying principles. For instance, if equal protection of the laws is a recognized principle in a democratic system when it comes to racial discrimination, then in considering related issues such as discrimination by gender or sexual orientation, one should do so in a way consistent with that underlying principle. This might mean extending it also to these cases, or it might mean distinguishing those cases by showing why the principle does not apply to them or does so in a different way—but either choice requires an argument, and any argument one makes must also be consistent with other baseline principles as well as the constraints of conditions (1) and (2). The reason we care about consistency here is that what we are really interpreting is the vision of democratic rights and institutions endorsed by the democratic people. Of course, it may well be that the people have not yet taken a consistent view on some particular issue. But if we do not consider even general principles of a given democratic system as consistent (when we can), we are left with no way of distinguishing more and less democratic systems or justifying the authority of constituted powers in any system to make and enforce law (since that authority always depends on attributing popular authorization to the system as a whole). If a certain people's view of even the most general principles is indeed incoherent, then its political system is in crisis—but this should be a particular finding and not a general presumption.

The reason history matters in this is that democratic systems commonly evolve through a series of political struggles that revisit underlying principles from different angles. This means that our evidence for interpreting the people's present view includes evidence of decisions they may be taken to have made in the past. These should be understood as standing decisions until positive evidence is provided that the people have changed their minds. For instance, it might be possible to interpret recent movements against same-sex marriage in the United States or France as movements to overturn the principle of equal protection or legal equality. But these principles were established in the United States and in France through very dramatic popular struggles (the Civil War and the French Revolution), and although in each case the results were repeatedly challenged over the better part of a century, I think most would agree that in the long run the principles were quite conclusively affirmed. In the absence of evidence that the American or French people have recently decided to throw out legal equality in other areas (by reconsidering the admissibility of slavery or feudal privileges, e.g.), we ought to interpret recent struggles instead as accepting the general principle and contesting only its interpretation and applicability in certain cases. And this yields a very different picture of present struggles than we would have if we considered them in a vacuum—in this case because the principle of legal equality may be considered internal to positions on each side, we have more to work with in evaluating their consistency than we would if those earlier struggles for equality had never happened.[26] The notion of the historical baseline thus allows us to draw principled connections across cases and across time, and to see how the background of prior struggles may sometimes help to define more clearly the issues at stake in present controversies. The reasons for taking it seriously parallel the rationale for Dworkin's "adjudicative principle of integrity," according to which one ought to view the law at a given point in time as a consistent and principled whole, including past decisions in the absence of evidence that these have since been reversed.[27]

It is important to stress that this notion of the historical baseline is neither Whiggish nor intrinsically conservative. Although the results of some past struggles should count as standing decisions of the democratic people, this is not true of them all. One must consider the history of particular struggles in order to determine which among them merit that presumption. Nor may one presume that future struggles ought to continue in any particular direction. Any baseline principle can be overturned at any time, and what looked like progress at one moment in history may later appear to have been the opposite, and perhaps still later something else again. All the notion of the historical baseline is meant to suggest is that at a given time one's judgments ought to be justifiable against the background of the history one actually has. But because the people

---

[26] Here, we see how I consider the history of struggles after Rousseau and Kant wrote to have shifted the going baseline interpretation of the conditions of a general will to include legal equality and a ban on privileges. The interpretation of principles like Principle (I) is always inflected by historical context in such a way that one cannot sort out strictly a priori what may be a priori and what historical within them. But this is not a problem, because in any given struggle one must argue it through in any case from the standpoint of all participants to reach a conclusion that can be justified relative to the range of positions actually brought to the table. The principles and conditions spelled out here are useful because they help to draw out contradictions in those positions, but if a position proves able to defend itself, then it may be the principle or its interpretation that needs to change, and the theory is entirely open to this. This is another sense in which it is historical.

[27] "History matters in law as integrity: very much but only in a certain way. Integrity does not require ... that judges try to understand the law they enforce as continuous in principle with the abandoned law of a previous century or even a previous generation. It commands a horizontal rather than vertical consistency of principle across the range of legal standards the community now enforces." Ronald Dworkin, *Law's Empire* (Cambridge, MA: Harvard University Press, 1986), 227.

are always free to change their minds, one can never anticipate the future—one can only continue to interpret what it is that they decide. It was for a similar reason that Hegel held the owl of Minerva only flies at dusk.

The first three conditions narrow down the range of admissible proposals in any actual democratic struggle. When more than one remains, the fourth condition decides; it holds that a legitimate system must be *uniquely* supported over all others by some argument satisfying conditions (1) through (3). Coherence alone is not enough. The thought is this: among equally consistent and arbitrary alternatives, none may, consistent with the equal freedom of all citizens, be imposed by force on those who endorse another, because there is no reason for the latter to see that view as binding. And so any legitimate solution must be uniquely favored over others by some unanswered argument (compatible with the first three conditions) that tips the balance in its favor. This does not require proving that argument ultimately "true," only that we cannot prove it false and that it is not countered by an equally admissible argument on the other side. If no one side's proposal is any more consistent or less arbitrary than the others, then this is itself often an argument in favor of a compromise solution that might be justified simultaneously from more than one point of view. Other times it may be that no compromise is possible and so the set of legitimate solutions is, as best we can tell, presently empty. That possibility may be tragic, but it cannot for that be ruled out. Theory cannot solve all the problems of democratic politics; sometimes it is political realities that first would need to change.

Taken together, the four conditions of Principle (II)* spell out the requirements that any interpretation of democracy must meet if it is to count as chosen by the citizens of an actual polity. But that interpretation must also *be* chosen in a particular case, and this cannot be deduced from the theory. Rather, one must turn first to the history and present political circumstances of a given polity to see which rival programs are actually on the table, what arguments have been mustered, what sort of popular backing organized, and which actions taken by competing sides to test the strength and consistency of each other's claims. The conditions of Principle (II)* provide an interpretive scheme that allows us to make sense of these circumstances and to judge among competing claims to represent a particular people's decision at a particular point in time. And because they do this without invoking any external authority that would compete with that people's right to decide how they will govern themselves, they allow us finally to escape the paradox of authorization.[28]

---

[28] The astute reader will ask why this does not merely reproduce the paradox at yet another level, since someone must still interpret and apply Principle (II)*. It is true that at the end of the day individuals and collective actors must interpret these conditions and can be expected to disagree. But this is inescapable in any theory that admits any sort of principles or conditions at all. What matters is what these agents ask themselves: either what *they* think is just or else what *the people as a whole* may best be taken to have decided is. If the latter sort of judgment is not demonstrably wrong, there

Applying these conditions is not a one-off exercise. It requires continued attention to the shifting balance of argument and organizing among competing democratic actors on the ground. At a given moment one can determine which (if any) available program would be most democratic under present conditions, but one should also try to identify potential developments in the near future that might require revising that conclusion. This is an important feature of the theory, because it allows us to make provisional judgments in the course of ongoing struggles, while also drawing attention to divergent future possibilities that might corroborate or challenge the judgments we have made. It also matters for citizens who participate in these struggles, since it can help them to identify which among several courses of action might do the most to bolster their democratic position, or to challenge their opponents'. It can also provide them with principled grounds for distinguishing cases where democracy demands compromise and others in which it requires sticking to one's guns. The theory of democratic elenchus can be used not only by theorists but also by any citizen, whenever and wherever one debates the legitimacy of an existing democratic system and proposals for change. Unlike Rawls's political liberalism, however, it does not suppose that justice requires the public to accept the theory itself. Its more modest claim is that if one is going to make headway on controversies concerning democratic legitimacy and change, one does better to debate them in these terms than in others.

Common Institutional Principles

The point of a historical and Socratic theory is that it allows one to work through the details of particular democratic struggles—both contemporary and historical—to judge them on a case-by-case basis. The very fact that it forces democratic theory to build up its arguments from particular political and historical contexts is an important challenge to more familiar approaches, both those that seek to legislate a priori for all the world and those that shrink from defending principled judgments altogether. Chapter 7 will work through a number of

---

is no contradiction in enforcing the results (just because these may be held to be willed by the people). But even if the former were right, there would *remain* a contradiction because one's individual judgments of justice and injustice do not immediately bind others (*unless* they also count as chosen by the people). So democratic elenchus does not imagine it will eliminate disagreement, but asks people to disagree about different things—which among competing institutions or collective actors has the best claim to speak for the people. In practice, this invites theorists and citizens to make judgments that turn on interpreting the significance of *other citizens' political acts and views* in a way mainstream theories do not; logically, it means that although disagreement will (rightly) continue, it need no longer take the form of a paradox that undermines every judgment of democratic change.

cases in this way, chosen partly for their intrinsic interest but also as examples of how the theory might be put to work in any number of other struggles.

But it will also be helpful to introduce here some of those institutional principles most commonly established in the historical baselines of democracies today—though one must be careful not to take these the wrong way. It cannot be stressed too vigorously that no democratic people is bound by the choices of another, so the fact that a constitutional principle is established in many democracies lends no justification whatsoever for applying it anywhere else where it has not been chosen by the local citizens.[29] But comparing across polities can nevertheless serve a strictly heuristic purpose to give some sense of the type and range of principles we will be looking for in particular cases. And because, in fact, variations on the same principles do turn up repeatedly across national traditions, partly due to the historical influence of certain constitutional models, some familiarity with similarities and differences across countries can also be of help in making sense of historical choices within a given tradition, since these were often taken with reference to earlier models or contemporary developments elsewhere.

The following list is culled from two types of sources—a line-by-line comparison of the contemporary and historical constitutional texts of forty-seven countries today widely considered democracies, and a broader study of the legal, intellectual, and political histories in which these constitutions were fashioned and refashioned over the past few centuries.[30] It does not purport to be complete or final, but it does identify many of those broad institutional principles most widely accepted across democracies today, and may accordingly serve as a starting point for discussion. One must not take it in a Whiggish way; the fact that these principles are widely accepted today does not mean either that earlier constitutional history was aiming at them or that they can be expected to develop further in a similar direction in the future.

The principles may be divided into two broad headings—political and social. Political principles concern the organization of the state itself, whereas social principles concern the relation of that state to the larger society of which it is a part. The seven major political principles are: (1) the state must secure for citizens the protection of law and the administration of justice; (2) the state must act in accordance with the rule of law; (3) the powers of the state should be internally distinguished and divided; (4) the state must respect a range of civil rights and civil

---

[29] This is not because "peoples" are real discrete entities, but because in the current international system only states are considered to legislate directly in their citizens' name. The UN system, in particular, is founded on respect for the sovereign authority of member states and expressly rejects any democratic requirements for states seeking international recognition. Although some recent developments aimed at protecting human rights have raised new issues, none presently comes anywhere near establishing in international law democratic requirements for state legitimacy.

[30] See the Appendix.

liberties that limit its direct political control over life beyond its borders; (5) laws must be authored either directly by the people or by a body chosen by them as their representatives, and the executive (although not necessarily the head of state) must be accountable to the people or that body; (6) laws must be universal in respecting the equal freedoms of all citizens; and (7) the constitution must be both popularly ratified and open to popular revision. All these are established in some form or another in the constitutions of nearly every contemporary democracy, although each may be interpreted more or less strongly and in various ways. For instance, principles (3) and (4) are taken quite strongly in the United States, whereas in the United Kingdom their status is rather more tenuous and always in flux. Most other democracies fall somewhere in-between.

The seven political principles had been established in most of Europe and several former British colonies by the end of the First World War, in the cresting of the so-called first wave of democratization (although in much of Europe, of course, they would not hold). The aftermath of the First and Second World Wars also leant a dramatic impetus to the development of social principles, though some had earlier roots. These social principles number five: (1) the state should emancipate citizens from private domination; (2) it should protect them through legislation against abuses in market relations; (3) it should guarantee social minimums to all citizens (although not necessarily provide them itself); (4) it should enforce citizens' right to organize independent unions; and (5) the state may intervene in the market economy in a wide variety of ways to pursue democratically chosen macroeconomic ends, but may not do so by taking direct control of the economy as a whole. This last principle, in other words, reconciles a far-reaching public planning power with respect for private property and markets. Of course, during much of the twentieth century Communist states adopted a different model, but there is little reason for supposing that choice defensibly democratic; where political freedom followed after the fall of the Berlin Wall, citizens of those states voted in every case neither for Communism nor for laissez-faire, but for versions of the same five social-democratic principles already established in other democratic states.[31]

Each of these five social principles is written into the constitutions of between 74 and 90 percent of the forty-seven contemporary democracies mentioned above (and this figure is conservative, because it excludes countries such as the United States where many of the same principles are instead codified in major legislation).[32] No third category of principles, besides the political and the social, presently enjoys anything approaching such widespread support. For instance, although environmental protections are also common, they are typically framed

---

[31] Allende's Chile might have proved an exception had it been allowed to run its course, and the Venezuela of Chávez and Maduro is a borderline case.

[32] See the Appendix. Percentages are even higher among constitutions written since 1945 and higher still since 1975. I have not bothered to chart the political principles because they are included in nearly all these constitutions.

in terms of citizens' right to a healthful environment and best understood as a subset of the social minimums a state ought to guarantee.[33] Rights to state support for cultural preservation are also social minimums, whereas other sorts of cultural rights are best understood as specifications of political principles—for instance, by expanding the list of civil liberties to protect linguistic expression alongside freedom of conscience, or by structuring federal systems to represent cultural or linguistic minorities instead of strictly geographic ones. Finally, a few constitutions include principles governing relations to other states.[34] This is the only area in which one finds some evidence of what could be a third sort of democratic principle on a par with the political and the social. But these international principles appear only in a few constitutions, and so cannot at present be said to enjoy anything like the widespread acceptance of the other two.

As I have stressed, this list of principles is strictly heuristic. It does not distill the essence of history or dictate to specific polities. But it does offer an initial sense of the type and range of principles likely to turn up also in the baselines of particular states. It also points to two interesting facts—first, the very wide scope of agreement across contemporary democracies on broad institutional principles, and second, the sophistication and general coherence of the view of democratic institutional principles that emerges from this sort of reconstructive study. Actual constitutional traditions have integrated a range of principles with diverse historical roots and justifications. However, many political theories—both contemporary and historical—consider only some of these concerns while neglecting others. For instance, many contemporary theories of social justice focus wholly on the distribution of resources, whereas this touches on only one of five distinct social principles very widely recognized across actual democratic constitutions today. This illustrates one of the ways a historical and Socratic theory might help to broaden conceptual horizons and raise new and interesting questions for democratic theory, by asking theorists to consider not only other theories but also evidence of the positions actual democratic citizens have arrived at over time through the course of political struggles.

Conclusion

A historical and Socratic theory asks us to judge democratic struggles not by some external yardstick, but by interpreting what citizens themselves have decided is required to govern themselves in a democratic way. The four

---

[33] Section 45(a) of the Spanish Constitution is typical: "Everyone has the right to enjoy an environment suitable for the development of the person, as well as the duty to preserve it."

[34] For instance, Austria's Federal Constitutional Law incorporates provisions governing participation in the European Union (Art. 23).

conditions of Principle (II)* show how this can be done, beginning always from the particular political and historical context in which a given struggle unfolds. Arguing this way allows us to judge who (if anyone) deserves to win out in present struggles, to point out some ways future events might alter these judgments, and to make sense of and evaluate the history of those struggles that got us to this point.

This approach has several advantages over familiar alternatives in democratic theory. It finally escapes the paradox of authorization that bedevils every other theory, because it provides a standard for democratic judgment without appealing to any foundational authority that would compete with the people's right to decide how to govern themselves. The reason it can manage this is that it uses Socrates's characteristic style of argument, elenchus, to judge among democratic programs strictly by ruling out those that cannot be defended even on their own terms. In doing so, it also resolves a longstanding confusion over what makes a democratic "people" a "people." A people is not a sociological entity, but a practical principle presupposed in asking a certain sort of question: What (if any) collective decisions may justly be imposed even on citizens who disagree? We then posit a people as corresponding to the scope of the jurisdiction of the public power we are asking about—individuals are part of a "people" only for practical purposes. The important thing is not any characteristic fact of culture, race, history, or social position that might make a "people" one; to the contrary, a "people" means simply all those persons subject to a certain political power, considered as free and equal. Of course, this does not yet solve the "boundary problem" of how to resolve controversies over who should be in and out of a particular jurisdiction. But it already does a great deal, by showing both what is wrong in the dangerous claims of antipolitical nationalisms and populisms, but also why the democratic notion of popular sovereignty, rightly conceived, is not open to familiar criticisms that cannot tell the difference.[35] Finally, because a historical and Socratic theory provides a *general* framework for interpreting the decisions of *particular* communities as to how they will govern themselves, it offers a more productive alternative to familiar arguments for and against "universal values."

These advantages of democratic elenchus are clearest if one compares it to other influential theories. Before closing, I will briefly consider three: Rawls's political liberalism, Ackerman's dualist democracy, and Habermas's discourse theory of law and the democratic state.

---

[35] For example, Joseph A. Schumpeter, *Capitalism, Socialism and Democracy* (New York: Allen & Unwin, 1976), 250–68; Isaiah Berlin, "Two Concepts of Liberty," in *Liberty* (Oxford: Oxford University Press, 2002), 166–217; William Riker, *Liberalism against Populism: A Confrontation between the Theory of Democracy and the Theory of Social Choice* (Prospect Heights, IL: Waveland Press, 1982).

Rawls offers a particularly sophisticated example of a familiar way of taking broadly Kantian principles, which might be called a proselytizing liberalism. In this view, everything ultimately depends on trying to convince one's fellow citizens that they share liberal beliefs about justice—at least deep down, on reflection, and despite their disagreements over moral and religious doctrines. Society will be just if its basic structure reflects this "public conception of justice" on which all citizens agree.[36] This view allures because it promises to purge politics of coercion. Political theory need not focus on showing how those who dissent from one's own (particular version of liberal) politics may nevertheless sometimes justly be coerced, because it aims instead to open everyone's eyes to the fact that they all already agree—not on everything, to be sure, but at those decisive levels required to justify the system and its outcomes. This is a variant on a very familiar approach in the history of political thought,[37] but one that aligns Rawls not with Kant—who famously insisted to the contrary that erecting a just constitution was possible "even for a race of devils" (8:366)—but with other thinkers including Protestant reformers and Hegel.[38]

The key to understanding *Political Liberalism* is to see that the whole argument continues to depend ultimately on reflective equilibrium.[39] "At the first stage," Rawls explains, "justice as fairness ... proceeds from shared political

---

[36] "[L]et us say that a society is well-ordered when it is not only designed to advance the good of its members but when it is also effectively regulated by a public conception of justice. That is, it is a society in which (1) everyone accepts and knows that others accept the same principles of justice, and (2) the basic social institutions generally satisfy and are generally known to satisfy these principles" (John Rawls, *A Theory of Justice* [Cambridge, MA: Harvard University Press, 1971], 4–5). Cf. Rawls, *Justice as Fairness: A Restatement* (Cambridge, MA: Harvard University Press, 2001), 8.

[37] The variation is that consensus no longer applies to religion but only to "political conceptions of justice." But the latter are meant to play just that role the former no longer can: "[G]iven the fact of reasonable pluralism, a well-ordered society in which all its members accept the same comprehensive doctrine is impossible. But democratic citizens holding different comprehensive doctrines may agree on political conceptions of justice. Political liberalism holds that this provides a sufficient as well as the most reasonable basis of social unity available to us as citizens of a democratic society" (Rawls, *Fairness*, 9).

[38] Rawls cites Hegel's influence on this point in his *Lectures on the History of Moral Philosophy* (Cambridge, MA: Harvard University Press, 2000), 366–7. The mere fact that Rawls entertained plans to become a Protestant minister before opting for philosophy after serving in the Second World War did not dictate that his later theory would see philosophy as filling in for religion in the public role of securing a societywide community of (at least second-order) belief taken for the necessary basis of social order and justice. But that is indeed how the later texts describe philosophy's role. Cf. Rawls, *A Brief Inquiry into the Meaning of Sin and Faith* (Cambridge, MA: Harvard University Press, 2009), and *Lectures*, 3–13.

[39] In *A Theory of Justice*, Rawls compared reflective equilibrium to Socratic method, suggesting that "[m]oral philosophy is Socratic" because "we may want to change our present considered judgments once their regulative principles are brought to light" (*Theory*, 49); this paragraph is cut in the second edition (Cambridge, MA: Harvard University Press, 1999), 42–3, but see 507. The differences between our understandings of Socratic method thus bear directly on contemporary theory.

conceptions of society and person that are required in applying the ideals and principles of practical reason."[40] These particular conceptions are "implicit in the public political culture of a democratic society,"[41] and we, as democrats, can see this by systematizing our own settled judgments about justice in reflective equilibrium.[42] The reason we care about "overlapping consensus" and "reasonable disagreement," then, is not that they provide any independent ground or content for principles of justice,[43] but only because *once we already presume* the liberal conceptions of society and person Rawls thinks we all will reach by reflecting on our considered judgments, it would be inconsistent of us *as liberals* to interpret our liberal ideas in ways that cannot also be accepted by those committed to other reasonable doctrines: "[I]f justice as fairness were not expressly designed to gain the reasoned support of citizens who affirm reasonable although conflicting comprehensive doctrines—the existence of such conflicting doctrines being a feature of the kind of public culture that liberal conception itself encourages—it would not be liberal" (143). Rawls's view, then, depends entirely on working out "from within" the fundamental ideas of "a certain political tradition" (14). All his other concepts, including "public reason" and respect for "reasonable disagreement," derive from this foundation that constrains them.

But consider what such a thoroughgoing conventionalism entails. First, it leaves nothing to say to anyone who does not already share liberal assumptions or who, on reflection, finds herself more committed to an illiberal judgment than to liberal principles. Indeed, it follows that slavery (and worse) is wholly justified in any public political culture that consistently embraces it. Second, it presumes a unitary (liberal) political culture to get the argument off the ground, even though the subsequent case for taking seriously "the fact of reasonable pluralism" due to the "burdens of judgment" would appear to challenge that presumption. Third, it wrongly supposes that one person's private reflection on her own moral views is sufficient to justify principles that will also bind others, or—on the most charitable reading—that a dialogue among some persons over which views they happen to share can then justify imposing those views also on third parties. The underlying problem is that Rawls's reflective method ignores the signal fact that in politics (unlike in pure philosophy) normative ideas will be used to justify coercion even against persons who do not share them. But one cannot fairly presume a consensus on one's preferred (liberal) principles in order

---

[40] Ibid., 141–2. Although *some* ideas of this sort are required by "practical reason," *which* ideas are determined by our historically contingent political culture, in which Rawls emphasizes the fallout from sixteenth- and seventeenth-century wars of religion (xxiv).

[41] Ibid., 43, cf. 18, 20. He later calls these "fundamental ideas that we seem to share through the public political culture" (150). Cf. Rawls, *Fairness*, 5–6, 19–20.

[42] Rawls, *Political Liberalism*, expanded ed. (New York: Columbia University Press, 2005), 8, cf. 26; *Fairness*, 31.

[43] Rawls, *Political Liberalism*, 39–40.

to justify imposing them on actual dissenters. One would need to show either that they were rationally inescapable (which *Political Liberalism* denies), or else that one's fellow citizens can be taken actually to have chosen them through a democratic process—not only that one has convinced oneself they "would" choose them if they thought about it the right way.[44]

A historical and Socratic theory differs on all counts. First, it presumes no starting cultural consensus. Instead, it provides an argument for the most basic democratic principles drawn directly from the need to justify coercion *because* citizens do not necessarily agree, rather than grounding them in any shared political culture.[45] Second, it justifies its principles not by inviting one to reflect on one's own value commitments but by showing that these principles count as chosen by those citizens on whom they will be imposed. Finally, it does not argue directly from any arbitrary set of conventional assumptions, but always by elimination *across* the competing positions defended by one's interlocutors. That is, rather than presuming the justice of our own most deeply held convictions and working out what follows from them, a genuinely Socratic argument begins from *the viewpoints of others*, to see which among them holds up best on its own terms—not on ours. In each case, where political liberalism asks us to reflect (first and decisively) on what *we believe*, democratic elenchus asks us to interpret what *other citizens have decided*. Of course, Rawls sees his theory as a contribution to public debates that will be resolved by citizens through democratic institutions. But political liberalism and democratic elenchus ask citizens to engage these debates and struggles on very different terms.

Unlike Rawls, Bruce Ackerman's *We the People* takes an approach that puts popular sovereignty front and center. He argues that "the People" author their constitutional laws in two different ways: in normal times they act through a formal amendment process, but in periods of "higher lawmaking" (including the American founding, Civil War, New Deal, and civil rights era), the same people can make their voice heard another way, when institutional powers compete for the right to act in "the People's" name by taking their case directly to the voters. Genuine higher lawmaking can be distinguished from an unconstitutional power grab because it unfolds through five characteristic stages: (1) "signaling," when a reform movement wins a victory in some branch of government; (2) "proposal," when all branches are ready to pass reforms; (3) a "triggering election," in which a first reform effort is either rewarded or punished by voters;

---

[44] Cf. Rawls, *Theory*, "[A] society satisfying the principles of justice as fairness comes as close as a society can to being a voluntary scheme, for it meets the principles which free and equal persons would assent to under circumstances that are fair. In this sense its members are autonomous and the obligations they recognize self-imposed" (1st ed., 13). But in this sense alone! The original position continues to function this way later on; cf. Rawls, *Fairness*, 17–8.

[45] This does not make it "metaphysical" rather than "political," because the argument derives not from philosophical premises but from the political need to decide what to do when citizens disagree.

(4) "mobilized elaboration," when the reform party controls all branches and is able to push through a broad agenda; and (5) a "ratifying election," in which former opponents switch and embrace the new order in a phase of consolidation.[46] This is a powerful theory that brings much-needed attention to the problem of democratic change. A historical and Socratic theory shares Ackerman's focus on the need to sort through competing claims to represent "the people" and on ways the actions of contending parties and the unfolding of events can help to strengthen or undercut the case for one side or another. But it also differs in a crucial way.

In Ackerman's five-stage process, controversies over who speaks for "the people" are finally decided by repeated victories in elections. But why should we trust any existing electoral system to represent "the people's" one true voice? And how can we presume this, especially in constitutional crises when parts of the existing system are called radically into question? Ackerman's faith in elections overlooks three important possibilities. First, the existing electoral system itself may harbor biases and exclusions that should be held undemocratic. Second, even if the electoral process is procedurally fair, the outcome may still violate some citizens' equal freedoms, and therefore should not count as authored by "the people" as a whole (e.g., American slavery). Third, in struggles over "higher lawmaking," citizens often organize themselves outside formal electoral channels in ways that challenge those channels' exclusive right to speak for "the people." Although such movements do appear in the background of Ackerman's story, what counts as a "democratic" outcome is always decided by courts and officials elected through existing channels. But in many of his cases, citizens also organized mass demonstrations, strikes, civil disobedience, and other forms of collective action that directly challenged the democratic legitimacy of parts of the existing political system long before they won victories in national elections. Obviously, one cannot presume extra-electoral movements to represent the *Volk an sich selbst* better than elections, for just the same reasons. But they may at least open real questions as to whether the existing system deserves the final and unilateral say, even if they do not also win according to that system's own rules.

This is perhaps clearest in historical cases, such as the 1848 Revolution in France, when a protest campaign organized through a national circuit of public banquets showed up the narrowness of the representative claim of a government supported by elections on a strict property qualification. In that case the reformers had a very strong democratic claim even though they were never able to win in an electoral system stacked against them, and that was why extra-parliamentary action—in that case, up to and including revolution—was

---

[46] *We the People*, Vol. III, 3:43–6. Although Ackerman refers specifically to the United States, the broader argument can be generalized mutatis mutandis.

ultimately justified and not simply a power grab. Although such radical outcomes are unlikely to be justified in countries today widely considered democratic, they play a central role in both historical and contemporary democratic revolutions, and even in established democracies interpreting the democratic valence of election results may require attention to the wider context of political organizing and mobilization in which they transpire. This was certainly the case, I would suggest, for the civil rights movement and for more recent controversies over same-sex marriage, even before reformers won major victories in courts and legislatures.

Ackerman's theory, then, would be too positivist, too state-centric, and ultimately too friendly to existing constitutional orders to serve as a general theory of democratic legitimacy or democratic change. This is not necessarily a fault, however, because it is meant instead as a theory of the sources of positive constitutional law. And if our question is what the law already is, then it is indeed appropriate to limit ourselves to legally recognized sources of legitimacy like elections. But what the foregoing shows is why one also needs a broader theory of democratic legitimacy to alert us to when the existing constitutional framework may not be its own best judge. Consider, for instance, the American Civil War, one of Ackerman's main examples. On his theory, before 1860 slavery was a straightforward and unambiguous part of the constitutional order fully backed by the democratic voice of the American people. I would argue that although this is correct as a point of constitutional law, one must be careful to distinguish this from the suggestion that the same order also represented the unambiguous democratic will of "We the American People," full stop. The point is not to let that people off the hook but to point out that the legitimacy of slavery, disenfranchisement, and the electoral overrepresentation of those who benefited most directly from them were not unassailable on democratic grounds even before Lincoln made it to the White House. I have stressed that this raises a great conceptual difficulty, because as soon as one moves from interpreting constitutional law to assessing its claim to democratic authority, one runs directly into the paradox of authorization. What should be clear, however, is that one cannot escape the problem simply by calling elections, first because someone must always already have set the terms on which those elections will be called, and second because even a fair process may yield results (like slavery) incompatible with the principles on which the authority of that process depends—hence the need for a historical and Socratic theory to judge when election results or Court decisions count as speaking for "We the People."

If Rawls focuses too narrowly on principles, and Ackerman on process, Jürgen Habermas rightly focuses on how to relate the two. We already saw that democratic elenchus builds on the principle Habermas draws from Rousseau and Kant, that democratic laws must respect all citizens as both authors and addressees. Habermas also sees how applying this principle courts the paradox of authorization. A historical and Socratic theory, however, responds to this paradox very differently than he.

According to Habermas, what makes a democratic system legitimate is not that we ever know it has gotten the interpretation of citizens' equal freedoms right. Instead, what matters is that every act of democratic founding "creates the possibility of a process of self-correcting attempts to tap the system of rights ever more fully," since "each citizen of a democratic polity can at any time" take up the founding principle of equal freedoms for all *in a critical fashion* to challenge existing biases and exclusions.[47] In other words, a democratic system counts as chosen by the people not because we know they actually signed off on its present interpretation of rights, or that such an interpretation is true, but because the people always remain free to change the current interpretation should they no longer accept it. Now this is fair enough, but it does not tell us what to do whenever citizens disagree. For Rousseau and Kant, the point of republican government was that someone needs to interpret and enforce the citizens' general will. Rousseau concluded that all assembled citizens must vote regularly on whether or not to keep their present form of government, Kant to the contrary that only the existing sovereign can decide, whoever that may be—individual citizens may publicly dissent but must ultimately obey. Habermas takes a different tack. According to his "two-track model," citizens formulate their common will both in the "formal publics" of elected legislatures and in the informal communicative flows of the "anarchic" public sphere.[48] When things work well, public opinion generated in the public sphere steers the deliberations of state officials and holds them accountable through elections, while electoral and parliamentary procedures filter public opinion in line with the equal rights and freedoms required by deliberative principles before translating it into law. Crucially, although Habermas admits that institutionalized power may perpetuate biases and exclusions, he insists these can always be challenged in the public sphere where citizens relate through persuasion rather than power: "Because publics cannot harden into organizations or systems, there is no exclusion rule without a proviso for its abolishment" (374, cf. 363–4).

Now this does show why a good democratic system should respect those civil liberties required for a vibrant public sphere, since otherwise it would be much easier for a particular way of organizing state power to perpetuate itself over time by monopolizing the political space in which citizens might begin to articulate and organize alternatives. But it cannot show more than this. Because there can be no reason for supposing any actual public sphere to correspond to the idea of a realm of pure moral suasion unsullied by strategic thinking and relations of power, we can never know that empirical public opinion

---

[47] Habermas, "Constitutional Democracy," 775–6, emphasis in original.
[48] Habermas, *Between Facts and Norms*, Chapters 7 and 8.

represents the general will of the *Volk an sich selbst*, or does so better than formal institutions of the state (where spokespersons may after all at least have been elected and may sometimes be dismissed). Nor can we presume actual opinion will naturally coalesce of its own accord into a clear and general consensus, which means we still require an authority to determine which among citizens' opinions will count as "public."[49] And even if the notion of a wholly communicative community were indeed realizable on earth, it should remain exceedingly difficult to see how that community might bring the state's coercive machinery to heel without the intermediary of some power that would compromise its moral authority (for instance, by campaigning to influence elections, in which strategy, resources, and organized relations of power are inescapable).

Ultimately, Habermas leaves us with the familiar dilemma: either we suppose the ideal of "the public sphere" and a "self-correcting" constitution to correspond to *actual* public spheres and constitutions (at least often enough), and so resign ourselves to trusting the existing system to reform its own abuses. (As in Kant, we can help by raising arguments but the system is the sovereign judge.) Or else we take those concepts as critical principles *we* can apply to judge the democratic system, but then we place our own individual judgment above any (like the system's) with even a prima facie case to count as belonging to the people as a whole. I think this part of Habermas's project is accordingly best understood as, like Kant's philosophy of history, more hortative than analytic—as an effort to defend both democracy itself and a role for principled argument in democratic politics against the suspicion that democracy is best

---

[49] How deeply Habermas's position depends on the contrary assumption is perhaps clearest in his 1960 review of Reinhart Koselleck's *Critique and Crisis: Enlightenment and the Pathogenesis of Modern Society* (Cambridge, MA: MIT Press, 1988), written as he was composing *The Structural Transformation of The Public Sphere* (Cambridge, MA: MIT Press, 1989), published in 1962. According to Habermas, Koselleck's worry that the eighteenth-century *Aufklärer* invited perpetual civil war by ignoring the need for a sovereign judge in cases of political disagreement turned on misidentifying "private sentiment with public opinion" ("Verrufener Fortschritt—Verkanntes Jahrhundert: Zur Kritik an der Geschichtsphilosophie," *Merkur* 14 (1960), 471). Because "filtering" "private *opinions*" in the plural through public debate transforms them into "public *opinion*" in the singular (Habermas's emphases), making this enlightened opinion (identified with Rousseau's general will) decisive in politics allows one to invert the Hobbesian principle *auctoritas non veritas facit legem* (472). What Koselleck—following Schmitt—saw as the danger in French Revolutionaries' moralizing refusal to admit the need for a final judge, Habermas took as their failure to follow through on the demand for sovereign publicity with sufficient thoroughness in the direction later pointed by Marx, thus effectively misidentifying the true interests of the nation as a whole with the class interests of the bourgeoisie. One need not accept Koselleck's polemical conclusions to see that, despite all of Habermas's later shifts, it is this disagreement over what to do with political disagreement that remains what is really at stake in Habermas's notion of the public sphere, and later also those of discursive democracy and communicative power, all the way down to *Between Facts and Norms*.

understood as only another form of domination.[50] In this it continues a long tradition, not least in Germany, that sees modern politics as a struggle between two ways of organizing society—one through mechanisms of power guided by reason of state, the other as a moral community united by consensus on ethical beliefs (or the ongoing good-faith pursuit of such consensus). Influential postwar interpretations of the twin catastrophes represented by Hitler and Stalin turned on whether they were best understood as the former triumphing over the latter, or instead of the latter triumphing and undermining itself.[51] But if one is already prepared to take democratic principles seriously, then it is not clear how much further one gets by thinking along these lines. One might well rather follow Kant when he denied, in his political theory, that justice requires any anchor in moral community—even in the final instance—since it is concerned not with belief or motivation but only with removing hindrances to hindrances of freedom, and so with structuring power in ways that admit a principled defense.

Although a historical and Socratic theory accepts many of Habermas's claims concerning principles and institutions (drawn from Rousseau and Kant), it thinks differently about political action and historical change. Habermas's discourse theory, like other forms of deliberative democracy, too quickly reduces democratic politics to persuasive speech, and conceives its goal as subordinating political power as thoroughly as possible to something approximating pure communication (and hence ultimately to reason). But power is inescapable in politics, and so one does better actively to organize power in ways that counteract inequality and domination. A historical and Socratic theory sees nothing wrong with organized pressure and political struggle, fighting coercion with coercion, competition to hold powerholders accountable, and negotiations

---

[50] On this aspect of Kant's theory, see Sankar Muthu, *Enlightenment Against Empire* (Princeton, NJ: Princeton University Press, 2003), 162–9; Loren Goldman, "In Defense of Blinders: On Kant, Political Hope, and the Need for Practical Belief," *Political Theory* 40, no. 4 (2012): 497–523.

[51] For the former, see inter alia Friedrich Meinecke, "Mass Machiavellism," in *The German Catastrophe: Reflections and Recollections* (Cambridge, MA: Harvard University Press, 1950), 51–5, in light of his earlier *Machiavellism: The Doctrine of Raison d'Etat and Its Place in Modern History* (New Haven, CT: Yale University Press, 1957); for the latter, both Max Horkheimer and Theodor Adorno, *Dialectic of Enlightenment: Philosophical Fragments*, trans. Edmund Jephcott (Palo Alto, CA: Stanford University Press, 2002), originally published 1944; and Koselleck, *Critique and Crisis*, originally published 1959. In *The Theory of Communicative Action* (Boston: Beacon Press, 1984–1987), Habermas countered Weber's emphasis on the instrumental rationality of the modern state and economy by adapting the notion of a normatively integrated community, inherited by way of Parsons from Durkheim, who had modeled it explicitly as a functional analogue for religion. That Habermas's approach to politics through the lens of a fundamental contest between moralism and immoralism—a view he shares with Schmitt and Koselleck, while differing over which is the dangerous term—has remained constant from *The Structural Transformation* to *Between Facts and Norms* may be gleaned from his early review of Koselleck and the title of the more recent work [*Faktizität und Geltung*].

among interested parties (even in the final instance). What matters is whether or not all this supports the claim that political power is exercised in a way chosen by all citizens under conditions of equal freedom. Identifying democracy with pure deliberation is politically perilous, even as an ideal, because it deflects attention from questions of who is actually making political decisions, how those persons are or are not accountable to their fellow citizens, and what relations of power are involved when some citizens go on to enforce those decisions on others. (Of course, Habermas's "two-track" theory is particularly sophisticated just because it incorporates a role for the institutions of the democratic state, thus tempering the more anarchistic implications of *The Theory of Communicative Action*, but the point of the whole system continues to turn on maintaining the appropriate hierarchy of communicative rationality over institutional power.) Democratic elenchus, by contrast, invites citizens not to eschew power but to engage it and to struggle to organize it in ways more defensible as representing decisions freely chosen by them all. It neither purges politics of principle nor reduces it to the exchange of arguments, but considers arguments always against the background of the organized power that tests their claims to popular backing and makes possible enforcing their results.

Finally, a historical and Socratic theory thinks differently about democratic change. It does not suppose that particular changes are best justified by describing them as democratic iterations that reflexively extend the existing system's founding principles. Since every application requires another authoritative judgment, this sort of story (if taken as a justification) would reproduce the paradox of authorization whenever citizens disagree. As we have seen, democratic elenchus always argues instead *across* the range of competing interpretations political actors bring to the table to see which holds up best on its own terms, and this avoids stacking the deck in favor of any particular principle or system.

This also allows it to suggest a unique interpretation of the much-contested notion of "progress." It sees stories about progress not as describing objective historical truths, but as moves in ongoing political struggles over the future course a society ought to take. But this does not mean they are only mystifying fictions, so long as one is careful to see them for what they are—a sort of political argument. The reason "progress" stories are both so attractive and so dangerous is that any struggle over reform tacitly poses a question about whether it would improve the status quo. And if we care about the outcome of reform struggles in the present, we ought to care for the same reasons about the ways past struggles bear on the principles they involve. So if we want to know, for instance, whether establishing a right to same-sex marriage is democratically justified today, we ought to consider whether or not it can be justified in a way that takes into account past struggles—say, over religious freedom, and against racial and gender discrimination—the results of which we continue to think have made our constitution a more democratic one. This is why it is not simply a mistake to think that arguments over the interpretation of history might sometimes play a limited role in present political judgments.

The danger is when these stories are presented, not as contestable interpretations as part of a larger debate to be judged on democratic grounds, but as true descriptions of historical necessities or independent sources of political authority. Then it seems as though getting history right, or penetrating to its hidden laws, would mean history could make our political decisions for us, and lift our responsibility for justifying those decisions in a democratic way. It is also the mistake that leads one to suppose that historical developments must be linear or that they allow one to predict what ought to happen into the future (because it confuses evaluative interpretations with causal laws). There is no reason to suppose that whatever looks like "progress" today will not appear very differently tomorrow; every democratic judgment is local and must remain always open to review. But if one keeps all this clearly in mind, then there is nothing wrong with asking whether or not a certain reform proposal seems, at the moment, an improvement over the status quo, in light of a critical appraisal of what has come before.

In this way, "progress" can be understood not as something that might or might not be true of history, but as one sort of question one might ask of competing sides in struggles over reform, in the course of coming to a democratic judgment. This is a radically deflationary account of "progress," but it is one that refuses to throw out entirely the possibility of judging and sometimes justifying democratic change. The great nineteenth-century theories of progress were not simply mistakes, because they responded to the prominence of reform struggles after the French Revolution and the need for a language in which to make sense of them. There are good reasons why those particular theories have since collapsed, but that does not mean we ought also to give up thinking in a principled way about the questions of reform and revolution that inspired them. These questions are today as live as ever, and demand a democratic response.

A historical and Socratic theory of democracy, then, builds on the general democratic turn in much political theory since the 1990s. Although it shares concern for equal freedoms with other sorts of theories, including Rawls's, it insists that these are defensible only if reinterpreted in a resolutely democratic way. Among democratic theories, it draws inspiration from the attention to historical struggle in Ackerman's, but it rejects a wholly positive account of popular sovereignty. Instead, it agrees with Habermas that a democratic order must count both as chosen by the citizens and as protecting those equal freedoms citizens must retain to remain in a position to choose. But although Habermas also recognizes that this entails a paradox, the two theories respond in different ways. Where Habermas broadly follows Kant in asking us to trust in the self-reforming tendencies of democratic founding principles and the public sphere, democratic elenchus begins from the site of actual struggles to work out which among competing views of democracy holds up best, on its own terms, as chosen by the people. In this it follows not Kant but Hegel. The rest of the book explains more fully what this entails, and how it helps make sense of the problem of democratic change.

PART ONE

Chapter 1 introduced the basic ideas behind a historical and Socratic theory of democracy. Part Two of the book will examine in more detail the conditions of Principle (II)* and consider some examples of how these might be used to work through particular cases of democratic struggle. But first, Part One considers the three figures in the history of political thought to whom democratic elenchus is most indebted—Plato, Kant, and Hegel.[1] The first reason is that most of the best arguments for the theory I mean to defend were already made by them—although none put all of them together in quite the way I suggested in Chapter 1—and so a good way of approaching these arguments is to examine the particularly sophisticated cases these figures made for them.

The second reason for engaging closely with Plato, Kant, and Hegel matters for the history of political thought. All three are commonly taken for paragons of foundationalist metaphysics, but I will argue this is almost entirely wrong—that all three are to the contrary profoundly antifoundational thinkers, and that the sophistication and power of their theories depended precisely on the ways they always argued, at the deepest level, not from any self-evident first principles (apart from the presuppositions involved in taking up certain sorts of questions), but strictly by challenging the consistency of competing positions on those positions' own terms. This was why Kant called his philosophy a "critique" and Hegel his "dialectic," and it is no less true for the high idealist Plato of middle dialogues such as *Republic* than for the Socrates of the early aporetic dialogues.

Not only does this challenge familiar readings of these figures, it also sheds new light on the development of German idealism from the 1780s to the 1830s by showing how it drew on a tradition of antifoundational

---

[1] Although Rousseau is also important, I consider him more briefly in the chapter on Kant's political theory since I view Kant to have taken on the most relevant arguments from Rousseau.

thought with roots reaching back to Socrates. This tradition had been buried over intervening millennia as the critical side of Plato was eventually eclipsed by dogmatic interpretations of Neoplatonists and Christian syncretists, and it required a new encounter with skepticism—famously, in Kant's case, by way of Hume—to revive interest in it in Germany at the end of the eighteenth century. But many of Kant's and Hegel's interpreters (then as now) have not seen that this radically antifoundationalist response is the sort they meant to give, and this has led to all sorts of dogmatic misinterpretations. Already in the early nineteenth century, opponents of German idealism sought to bolster their positions by relegating it to a bygone age of "metaphysics." This view has since been widely taken up, and when one considers also more recent criticisms of rational foundations in general, the prevailing consensus on how to position Kant and Hegel is very broad indeed (if not universal)—not only among their critics but also their defenders. But the effect of Kant's and Hegel's critical engagements with metaphysics and practical reason was to explode older notions of politics as governed directly by natural law and to replace them with a project of working out from inside the conditions of a political order compatible with a radically foundationless conception of freedom. In this Kant built on Rousseau, on ground opened up by Hobbes, whereas Hegel drew on Kant by way of Fichte and Schelling but reacted against Kant's republicanism with arguments drawn largely from Montesquieu, in light of the widely perceived failures of the Jacobin Revolution.

What is most distinctively shared by the political thought of Kant and Hegel, beyond their radical antifoundationalism, is the way they placed the act of political judgment before arguments for one or another political regime.[2] This is not always obvious to readers of the political texts, because it concerns the way their political doctrines relate to their larger

---

[2] Other Kantians and idealists commonly failed fully to appreciate this point. Fichte was generally the best reader of Kant in the period, but though he wrote a good deal about political action and change, even he never integrated those concerns into a theory that defined justice by way of a theory of political judgment, the way Kant and Hegel did. His early 1793 works on the French Revolution and his 1794 *Lectures on the Vocation of the Scholar* leaned towards anarchism, whereas his *Foundations of Natural Right* (1796–1797) and *The Closed Commercial State* (1800) emphasized a strong role for a rationally-constituted state. This tension remained unresolved in his later lectures on the *Fundamental Characteristics of the Present Age* (1806), his 1807 tract "On Machiavelli as an Author," and his *Addresses to the German Nation* (1808), but came to take on new political salience after Jena and Austerlitz. On the evolution of Fichte's political thought see Isaac Nakhimovsky, *The Closed Commercial State: Perpetual Peace and Commercial Society from Rousseau to Fichte* (Princeton, NJ: Princeton University Press, 2011).

philosophical projects. Neither Kant nor Hegel derived political institutions directly from any positive law or end. Rather, in somewhat different ways each began by arguing that justice is defined by the freedom it presupposes, and then went on to consider the conditions under which a political order might be judged compatible with that freedom. Both were quite clear that this does not mean, as in the older social contract tradition, that one must imagine actual citizens at some point in history literally to have signed up for their present constitution—theirs is not a positivist or voluntarist notion of freedom of the sort we saw in Ackerman. What is involved is rather a theory of the conditions presupposed in *judging* any constitution to count as free, and the shape of a rightful constitution is to follow from those conditions. Although Rousseau opened the door to this sort of argument with his idea of the general will, he did not step through it, because he approached the problem of applying that idea as one of motivation rather than judgment. For Rousseau, citizens may be trusted to vote on their form of government, assuming they are motivated by the general will, and it is up to the lawgiver to secure the requisite motivation by providing them with good laws. But this is just to describe the conditions under which the problem of judgment does not arise because the lawgiver has somehow cajoled all citizens to agree.[3] (And that is a bad solution because if everyone agreed there would be no political problem left to solve with a concept like the general will.) Although Hegel took an analogous approach in *The Philosophy of Right* (by different means), his philosophy of history and Kant's political theory instead placed the act of judgment front and center.

For both, history came to play a distinctive role bound up with the act of judging constitutions in terms of freedom, so that in their works the notion of right itself came to incorporate a reference to historical change. This was not a role history played in Rousseau, nor in the same way even in the most sophisticated of contemporary historicisms such as Herder's or Fichte's, which described the development of freedom not as a problem of recursive judgment, but in different ways as a progression of predetermined stages into the future. When, later in the century, the idealism of Kant and Hegel was largely displaced in social and political thought by other sorts of historicism and by evolutionary positivisms, what was put down was not "metaphysics" but this radically antifoundational way of

---

[3] See Bonnie Honig, *Emergency Politics: Paradox, Law, Democracy* (Princeton, NJ: Princeton University Press, 2009), 14–23, although one need not also accept that showing the problems in this argument was Rousseau's aim.

arguing about politics and this nuanced way of thinking about the priority of political judgment and its relation to change.[4] What triumphed in social and political thought by the later nineteenth century was not a clear-eyed science of politics and history liberated from metaphysical illusion, but in most cases other, more literal and less reflective theories of progress. Even later nineteenth- and early-twentieth-century efforts to revive Kant or Hegel often lost sight of the problems of political disagreement and judgment, by assimilating them with competing traditions that had risen to predominance in the meantime.[5]

The problem is that the victory of various historicisms and positivisms by the mid-twentieth century was so resounding that it has proven difficult to shake the hold of the terms in which they painted themselves as the natural outgrowth of everything in the late eighteenth and early nineteenth centuries. So even when many forms of historicism fell into disrepute after two world wars, one influential line of interpretation sought a pluralist middle ground between "Enlightenment" faith in unilinear progress and "Counter-Enlightenment" irrationalism.[6] Another extended to

---

[4] This is not to deny that Hegel, in particular, had a wholly untenable philosophy of nature embedded in largely untenable claims about the relation of logic, nature, and spirit. But neither Kant's nor Hegel's political theories depended directly on positive "metaphysics" in the way of the natural law theories they challenged (as I argue at length in Chapters 3–5), and so the decline of idealism as a leading school of political thought cannot fairly be described as a demystifying shift from metaphysics to positive history or social science. If anything, it was the developmentalist assumptions shared by historicism and the evolutionary positivisms of the nineteenth century that continued, to the contrary, to ground claims of justice in empirically unfalsifiable ontologies. Kant had already criticized this sort of assumption in Herder's *Ideen* in 1784 as "still metaphysics, indeed even very dogmatic [metaphysics], however much our author rejects it because that is what the fashion demands" (8:54).

[5] British idealism largely conflated Hegel with religion; leading strands of German neo-Kantianism and Dilthey took Kant and Hegel in the direction of positive cultural sciences; and American pragmatism interpreted change in a way that downplayed the need for critical standards by privileging consensual social integration and progressive learning over political conflict and the arbitrating role of the state—which is to say by accepting the broadly developmentalist and antipolitical assumptions common to period positivisms and historicisms. Although Gentile in Italy focused on politics, his "actual idealism" played up the role of organicism and reason of state in Hegel in line with competing historicist and nationalist traditions, but in radical contravention of Hegel's own insistence on rational justification and critique. And Heidegger would eventually collapse the rational content of idealism into a phenomenology with roots tracing back to Schleiermacher's theological hermeneutics. Partial exceptions included Croce in Italy and some neo-Kantians such as Windelband and Rickert, who became major influences on Simmel and Weber.

[6] Isaiah Berlin, notably *Freedom and Its Betrayal: Six Enemies of Human Liberty* (Princeton, NJ: Princeton University Press, 2002 [1952]), *The Roots of Romanticism* (Princeton, NJ: Princeton University Press, 2013 [1965]), *Against the Current: Essays in the History of Ideas* (Princeton, NJ: Princeton University Press, 2013 [1979]).

historicism itself the critique of "metaphysics" positivism and historicism had elaborated in parallel in the Napoleonic period to criticize the Jacobin Revolution.[7] And a third continued to accept Marxism's view of itself as the inexorable culmination of enlightenment, but went on to ask how then one might come to terms with the self-undermining consequences that had followed.[8] All these accounts continued to carve up history on historicists' terms, even if they went on to make an additional move that inverted their valuations. But the distinctive historical place of German idealism from Kant to Hegel is obscured by insisting on periodizations invented by their opponents. In fact, idealism was one among several alternatives competing to replace traditional metaphysics in the aftermath of the French Revolution, Kant's first two *Critiques* having been written just beforehand. These included Romanticism, positivism, and historicisms including the nationalist-leaning variety of the German historical school of law and the socialism first developed in France. Because the line of thought associated with Kant and Hegel was the major opponent of the historical school in Germany, later assimilations of Hegel's philosophy of history to their nationalist and developmentalist historicisms are particularly misleading.[9] But neither were Kant and Hegel the last great metaphysical theorists of politics.

Reinterpretations of Kant and Hegel have also played a major role in the revitalization of Anglophone political philosophy since the 1970s led by figures such as Rawls and Taylor. But these debates revolved around a postwar North Atlantic liberalism that owed little to Kant, and also a reaction to the rise to dominance of positivist approaches in the human sciences in the decades after the war, in which context Kant and Hegel were read as sources for reintroducing properly moral and ethical concerns into

---

[7] Karl Popper, *The Poverty of Historicism* (London: Routledge, 2002) [first published as a series of articles in *Economica* in 1944–5], *The Open Society and Its Enemies* (Princeton, NJ: Princeton University Press, 2013). One must remember that nineteenth-century positivisms, such as Comte's and Spencer's, were stories of evolutionary progress that shared developmentalist assumptions with other sorts of historicism.

[8] Max Horkheimer and Theodor Adorno, *Dialectic of Enlightenment* (Palo Alto, CA: Stanford University Press, 2002 [1944]).

[9] Consider, for instance, the *Kodifikationsstreit* of 1814 that pitted Kant's former student Anton Friedrich Justus Thibaut against Friedrich Carl von Savigny; Hegel was a personal friend of Thibaut's and took a strong stand for codification in the *PhR* (§211). See Thibaut, *Ueber die Nothwendigkeit eines allgemeinen bürgerlichen Rechts für Deutschland* (Heidelberg: Mohr & Zimmer, 1814), and Savigny, *Vom Beruf unserer Zeit für Gesetzgebung und Rechtswissenschaft* (Heidelberg: Mohr & Zimmer, 1814). Beiser provides a good discussion in *The German Historicist Tradition* (Oxford: Oxford University Press: 2011), 233–45. For more on conflicts between Hegel and the historical school in Berlin, see Beiser, 258–61, and Terry Pinkard, *Hegel: A Biography* (Cambridge, UK: Cambridge University Press, 2000), 531–41.

the study of politics.[10] But here, too, the gravitational pull of later narratives has skewed interpretation, commonly privileging Kant's moral theory over the continuities with Hobbes in his political thought and the implications of his larger critical project, and the ethical side of Hegel's political theory, with its emphasis on recognition and reconciliation, over his critical reflections on the problem of historical change. What drops out from these accounts are the radical antifoundationalism, the priority of political judgment, and the particular way of conceiving change that distinguished Kant's and Hegel's projects from their contemporaries', and also those that followed. This is particularly unfortunate because forcing Kant and Hegel into these later stories has the effect of reinforcing contemporary divisions between "analytic" and "Continental" approaches that, when presumed sharply competing and exhaustive, conspire to obscure the possibility of other ways of thinking about political change.

The Argument Chapter by Chapter

Chapter 3 introduces elenchus by working through its original source in Plato's Socratic dialogues. It aims to establish three crucial points. First, elenchus shows how positive conclusions may sometimes be defended strictly by elimination, in the absence of any certain first principles. Second, conclusions reached this way count as justified just because elenchus also shows the impossibility of any more direct route to knowledge. Plato, in other words, invented or discovered the *method-dependence of knowledge*, according to which what distinguishes knowledge from mere belief is nothing more or less than whether it can withstand withering and systematic criticism from every available point of view. It is not the content of a belief that makes it true or false, but whether or not it can be "tied down with reasons" in dialogue (*Meno* 98a). This is the key to understanding both Plato's idealism and the later idealisms of Kant and Hegel. Third, "ideas" in Plato are not, as widely supposed, freestanding truths to which we might ever have direct access. To the contrary, they are presuppositions to which we commit ourselves in asking certain sorts of questions.[11] So if

---

[10] The situation was somewhat more complex in Germany, where Heideggerian and Marxian interpretations loomed large also against a background of rising positivism, but where serious studies of Kant's and Hegel's positions in their own right had also revived after the war.

[11] This is not to say that for Plato ideas are *only* presuppositions that are not also "real." It is profoundly anachronistic to attribute to Plato a position either way on this distinction he never drew. What matters and what is clear is that Plato denied any other *route* to knowledge outside dialectic (*Republic* 533a), and this is the decisive point—concerning the relation of *ideas* to the *action*

I ask, for instance, "What is just?," I commit myself to supposing that some things can be shown to be just and others cannot. This is not because I also presume the independent authority of any logical rules, but just because if I do not accept this, then I cannot answer the question without contradicting myself and speaking nonsense. So as long as I am interested in asking this sort of question, I must accept as binding the assumptions it entails. Plato's ideas are assumptions of this sort and do not represent a turn away from the radically destabilizing approach of Socratic elenchus. To the contrary, they follow from a further working out and making explicit of just the logic already at work in Socratic questioning, which made elenchus work by leading Socrates's interlocutors into self-contradiction and *aporia*.

This chapter focuses closely on how elenchus works in Plato's dialogues, rather than on Plato's substantive political views or the historical setting in which he wrote, not because those are unimportant but because they have been covered extensively by others. For understanding what it might mean to say that Kant's and Hegel's arguments, too, are radically antifoundational, what is most important is to see how elenchus works and what follows from it, and for this there is no better source than the texts of Plato's dialogues.

Chapter 3 then considers Kant's moral theory, arguing that it should be understood as turning on a fundamentally similar sort of antifoundational argument. The categorical imperative, in particular, is a regulative assumption built into the act of moral judgment, or in other words, an idea presupposed in asking the question "What ought I to do?" This understanding of Kant's moral theory resolves a number of longstanding confusions, including over why a test of "contradiction" should be the standard of morality, and why we are bound by the moral law in the first place—the reason is just that we must consider ourselves so bound whenever we ask whether anything is right or wrong. Although Kant did also presume a widespread consensus on common-sense moral beliefs, the key point is that he did not also presume those particular beliefs true or reserve to common sense unaided by philosophy the authority of final judge. Rather, Kant suggested that common sense functions for him as for Socrates (G 4:404); it furnishes beliefs to be interrogated but critical argument is required to distinguish which (if any) among those beliefs actually turn out to be justifiable.

---

or method of Socratic dialogue, not to any *object* that might or might not exist outside of dialogue. Some of the finer distinctions with Kant are considered in Chapter 4.

Three important points follow. First, because Kant's moral theory is antifoundational and Socratic, it is a mistake to suppose it depends on any tendentious positive "metaphysics" or theoretical views of human nature, human agency, or final ends. The whole argument is built by working out assumptions internal to the act of raising questions concerning right and wrong, and this is just why it is so powerful. Second, the positive conclusion of Kant's moral theory is that every claim of obligation presupposes universal respect for freedom—what he calls "autonomy." Although the moral theory considers only the case of an individual deciding what she ought to do, the same point will apply when Kant goes on to consider the case of *political* obligation in which we ask when we may rightly compel others. So Kant manages to provide a wholly antifoundational and extremely powerful argument for why we ought to place universal freedom above any other consideration in morality and politics. Third, because Kant's case for autonomy is negative and indirect, it does not mean that politics ought to aim directly at promoting freedom or morality. Autonomy is only a practical idea internal to an act of judgment, and no state or political power can produce autonomous citizens by force. All politics can do is to protect people from the actions of others that would prevent them from exercising their own free judgment, and this means politics must not aim at realizing the kingdom of ends on earth, but only at removing "hindrances to hindrances" of external freedom (6:231). This is an argument not for a minimal state (as for Wilhelm von Humboldt[12]), but for a state of laws with a republican constitution (in the best case), because these are the conditions, as Rousseau had argued, under which the public power required for securing freedom is itself compatible with the freedom it is meant to secure. In effect, Kant's moral theory argues that to think politics is about applying morality is to misunderstand not only politics but also morality itself and the sort of freedom it presupposes. And this means contemporary theories that apply Kantian moral principles directly to politics misrepresent Kant's position and ignore the powerful arguments he actually provided against just such a mistake. Once again, the confusion is that people focus too narrowly on the ideas assumed in certain acts of judgment, while forgetting that since these are only regulative principles, one must always consider also who is judging. Kant is not a political moralist, but continues a resolutely political line of thinking running from Hobbes to Rousseau,

---

[12] Humboldt, *The Limits of State Action* (Cambridge, UK: Cambridge University Press, 1969), originally published as a series of articles in 1792.

and indeed is more radical than Rousseau in distinguishing categorically between questions of political judgment and issues of moral motivation, which led him to drop Rousseau's traditional republican fixation on guarding against faction by inculcating civic virtue.

Chapter 4 then considers Kant's political theory. It challenges views of Kant as narrowly liberal and unconcerned with the republican or democratic question of whether the people can be said actually to make the laws. Kant's views became more republican over time, and by the time he wrote his most substantial political works, he came to follow Rousseau's defense of a republican constitution under laws as the necessary condition of civil freedom (in principle). Because Kant tied this to the elenctic case for freedom first developed in his moral theory, however, where Rousseau had taken the priority of freedom for granted, what Kant provided was a wholly antifoundational argument that only a republican constitution under laws can be definitively just. This argument refuted religious and other competing claims of justice from the inside, by working out the consequences of the very idea of obligation they presupposed in arguing against the people's right to choose how to rule themselves. The underlying case for democracy in a historical and Socratic theory follows this broadly Kantian argument (although I go further in prohibiting legal inequality, on grounds considered in the prior chapter). On this theory, democracy is the only legitimate form of government, not because we can ever prove it ultimately just, but because every other basis of political legitimacy can be shown to be self-defeating, and democracy is therefore the only sort of regime we do not have good reason to rule out. To paraphrase Winston Churchill, what we can fairly say of democracy is that it is the least legitimate form of government except all those other forms that have been tried from time to time. And this will be just as much as we need to say to show why we are justified in demanding democratic government over any other sort and in judging struggles over change in democratic terms. The power of democracy is not that it rests on the right foundations, but that it is the only sort of government that requires no foundation whatsoever.

Kant is often thought to defend an undemocratic liberalism, because he argues that citizens must obey even a monarch who rules by laws the people "could" have authored, and because he denies any right of popular revolution. But the chapter shows that Kant's argument actually turns on the problem of judgment: by his later political works, he argues that the *idea* of a just constitution can only be a republic under laws, but just because this is only a regulative idea, one must also consider the political question of who is in a position to apply it. He concludes, following Hobbes, that only the existing sovereign may consistently be held to represent the decision of the entire people. Although this answer is not entirely satisfying, it is not undemocratic in principle and it is not easily proved wrong. Kant rejects revolution not because he rejects republicanism, but because he argues that reform through the existing system is the only route to change consistent with the republican ideal at which it aims. And to show why this does not amount to demanding the impossible, he appeals to a philosophy of historical progress he insists is valid only for practical purposes. In doing this, he makes the legitimacy of the present constitution depend on a theory of how citizens might be understood to judge it, rather than on any external measure of justice or historical foundation. And he builds into that theory of judgment an intrinsic reference to change. This is a very radical reinterpretation of older social contract and republican traditions, following directions opened by Hobbes and Rousseau, which reworked elements of late medieval and early modern theories of resistance and institutions inside a framework that prioritized the act of popular judgment and possibilities for ongoing change. It built into older political theories of principles and ends also a theory of conflicts over the right to interpret and apply them.

This move to a theory of the conditions of popular judgment opens the possibility of a response to paradoxes of authorization that had arisen in the course of the English and French Revolutions (and would arise in the United States with the Civil War). But did Kant also get these conditions right? Although Kant was right that traditional resistance theories begged the question in conflicts over who represents the sovereign people, he was wrong to conclude (with Hobbes) that this meant sitting "sovereigns" must always be their own judge. He ignored a third possibility—that one might be able to work out a theory of the conditions under which a people could be taken to have endorsed one representative over another, just because the contrary supposition cannot consistently be defended. Although Hegel does not approach the problem in the same terms, Chapter 5 argues that his philosophy of history amounts to just this sort of theory.

The chapter makes three main points. First, Hegel's political theory in the *Philosophy of Right* was undemocratic because it too narrowly followed Montesquieu against Rousseau, identifying freedom not with popular decision but strictly with a mixed constitution and a complementary public spirit that reconciles the people to the laws. Although political theorists have focused overwhelmingly on Hegel's resulting concept of *Sittlichkeit* [ethical life], this is perhaps the least defensible notion in his political thought, and it offered no good answers to criticisms of demands for ethical consensus that we saw had already been made by others, including Kant.[13] Second, although Hegel's philosophy of history is widely supposed to the contrary indefensible because it is grounded in an untenable teleological metaphysics, this misunderstands the logic of his arguments. A major conclusion of Hegel's logic and philosophy of nature was to establish that "spirit"—the human world of politics, culture, and history—is irreducible to the other two and must be interpreted in its own native terms of freedom. Hegel's philosophy of history does have a real problem, however, because it wrongly presumed that the most defensible interpretation of freedom must ultimately win out. But this did not depend on insight into some panlogical cosmology or providential design—to the contrary, the problem lay in the thoroughly empirical view of history Hegel took (once again) particularly from Montesquieu, which presumed that social order can only survive when grounded in ethical consensus. And again, we have seen that Kant and others had already given good reasons to doubt this.

What this means for contemporary theory is that one must entertain in a way Hegel did not the possibility that indefensible and unfree orders will nevertheless win out (the possibility that later so preoccupied Max Weber), and this changes in some important ways how one ought to take his remaining arguments and what they mean for politics. But it does not mean one must throw out entirely Hegel's approach to thinking about what it could mean to interpret history in terms of freedom—as long as one is careful to recognize that such an interpretation can only hold for practical purposes and never also as a causal explanation or predictive law. Although Hegel invited confusion by employing developmentalist language common in the period, what distinguished his theory radically from the Romantic and historicist views he excoriated in later works was that he took the familiar trope of a self-perfecting freedom as an interpretive presupposition useful in sorting through competing judgments of actual history. He did not simply presume that whatever had happened was also caused that way—as Kant had rightly criticized

---

[13] This is not to suggest that the notion of a mixed constitution of the sort invoked by Montesquieu can have no role in modern democratic theory, but that to do so, it must be rethought in a way that reconciles it with popular sovereignty (as, for instance, in Madison and then Tocqueville). As mentioned in the first chapter, some division of powers is widely accepted among contemporary democracies. My view is that the appropriate degree must depend on negotiations among citizens over the sort and severity of contingent historical divisions in their particular polity.

Herder for doing in his *Ideen*. Instead, Hegel suggested that if the present social order is to be legitimate, then this could only be because it can be seen as a more consistent and defensible interpretation of citizens' freedom than the orders it replaced. And then he went on to examine actual history to see whether it indeed made sense to see it this way, or whether to the contrary some other order's claim to be free turned out to hold up better than the modern state's. Hegel's philosophy of history was radically unlike others in the period, then, because it depended not directly on the force of analogies to organic development (although he used them), but always instead on the dialectical or elenctic arguments he provided to show why a particular social order did or did not hold up on its own interpretation of justice and freedom. Critics of Hegel's philosophy of history are usually criticizing Herder instead, or any of the many other literal organicists of the period who, unlike Hegel, did not provide detailed immanent refutations of competing interpretations of history to show *why* we ought to conclude that freedom had, in fact, progressed, but simply asserted that we must.

Once one sees that this is what Hegel's philosophy of history is for, then one can appreciate some of his insights into certain conditions under which a given social order's claim to be free will or will not hold up. Strictly speaking, the details of every case must be worked through on their own terms, as Hegel himself did—but one may also draw out some general guidelines concerning sorts of contradictions likely to repeat themselves. The chapter closes by considering some important examples from across Hegel's works. Hegel's criticism of the Jacobin Terror illustrates the general point that any interpretation of citizens' freedom must be institutionally specific enough to distinguish between freedom and tyranny, or else one risks aiming at the former and ending with the latter. Hegel's discussion of Socrates's trial, which he describes as tragic rather than simply an injustice committed by the Athenians, makes the point that even a view of justice like Socrates's that is defensible in the abstract may not also be defensible in a particular historical situation if it is rejected by one's fellow citizens. And Hegel's interpretation of the *Antigone* and *Orestia* shows, among other things, why it is not enough to provide a consistent defense of one view of justice unless one can also show that competing views cannot similarly be defended on their own terms, and thus why sometimes only a mutually acceptable third alternative can be justified. These conclusions will be familiar from the preceding chapter as among the conditions of Principle (II)*, which are meant to help us in thinking through what it could mean to say that a particular interpretation of citizens' equal freedoms holds up better than others as that chosen by the citizens themselves. Although the case for those conditions does not depend directly on the interpretation of Hegel, Hegel's texts provide a rich resource for thinking about how one might begin to pose these sorts of Socratic questions of history.

The discussions of Plato's Socrates, Kant, and Hegel in the following chapters are meant to challenge familiar, foundationalist interpretations of these thinkers and their place in the history of political thought. They are also meant to familiarize the notion of elenchus, and give a sense of some of the sorts of things it can do. At the same time, they work through the core arguments for the general framework of what I have called a historical and Socratic theory of democracy. Some of these come from Kant and some from Hegel, while the sense in which they are to be taken comes across best in Plato's inimitable dialogues. I should stress that the view one is left with is not meant to be directly attributable to Hegel or to Kant or anyone else, although I think it is best reached by thinking through and across positions defended here as genuine interpretations of these authors' works. These chapters are heavily textual, not because this is always the most fruitful way to approach historical works, but because in this case it is just the difficulty in appreciating the distinctive logic of the arguments at play that has most interfered with rightly situating them in relation to other, better-understood views in the period.

2

The Socratic Elenchus

The Greek term "elenchus" [*elenchos*] can be translated as "cross-examination," "testing," or "refutation." What is most distinctive about Socrates's refutations are that they proceed strictly by posing questions: when Socrates examines his interlocutors' claims to knowledge of virtue, he does not present some counter-argument of his own that begins from a competing first principle. Instead, he asks a series of questions that push his interlocutor to clarify and draw out the implications of his own views; as he puts it at *Meno* 75c–d: "The more dialectical [way] is perhaps to answer [charges] not simply with what is true, but also through things that the person questioned concedes he knows."[1] Ultimately, it becomes clear that some of these consequences contradict others, and this shows the interlocutor's position to be incoherent. It is thus refuted not on Socrates's terms, nor according to any abstract and timeless rules of inference established ex ante, but always in a strictly immanent manner. Unlike direct deduction or induction, then, this method of argument allows us to arrive at determinate conclusions without presuming the truth of any positive foundational premises whatsoever.

The key difficulty is understanding how, if at all, such a strictly negative method could ever justify more than negative conclusions. The answer is not obvious, and continues to be hotly debated in the literature, while many deny it is possible at all.[2] I think Plato clearly believed there to be an answer, but that

---

[1] I use the male pronoun throughout because, with the exception of Diotima's reported speech in *Symposium*, the interlocutors in the dialogues are male.

[2] Gregory Vlastos famously called it "*the* problem of the Socratic elenchus," *Socratic Studies* (Cambridge, UK: Cambridge University Press, 1994), 3–4. Those who have denied that elenchus can lead to positive knowledge include George Grote, *Plato and the Other Companions of Socrates*, 2nd ed. (London: John Murray, 1888); the early Vlastos in "The Paradox of Socrates," in *The Philosophy of Socrates: A Collection of Critical Essays*, ed. Gregory Vlastos (New York: Anchor Books, 1971); Hugh Benson, *Socratic Wisdom: The Model of Knowledge in Plato's Early Dialogues* (Oxford: Oxford University Press, 2000); and Dana Villa, *Socratic Citizenship* (Princeton, NJ: Princeton University Press, 2001). Competing versions of the contrary, "constructivist" view are found in the later Vlastos, *Socratic Studies*; Richard Kraut, "Comments on Gregory Vlastos, 'The Socratic Elenchus,'" *Oxford Studies in Ancient Philosophy* 1 (1983): 59–70; Ronald Polansky, "Professor Vlastos' Analysis of Socratic

this answer too is necessarily indirect. It is best understood as an argument in three steps. In the first step, Socrates refutes a particular interlocutor as just described. These refutations lead not directly to new positive knowledge, but to *aporia*, the radically negative realization that we in fact know nothing at all of what we thought we knew. In the second step, however, we are asked to reconsider this result from a different point of view: rather than focusing narrowly on the doctrinal content of particular beliefs or propositions, we come to see that Socrates's systematic elenctic critique of everything existing poses a fundamental challenge to an entire traditional conception of knowledge. Socrates is not asking us, or his interlocutors, simply to trade one set of naive moral doctrines for another; more profoundly, he is inviting us to recognize that the truth of a belief is inseparable from the method by which it can be tested, criticized, and defended. It is in this sense that Socratic method is not merely one method among others, but rather the very *invention of method as such*—or, equivalently, of the *discovery of method as a problem*. Socrates is the first to demonstrate the general point that the validity of a belief cannot be judged simply by comparing it to some authoritative list of the "right" beliefs, but only through the process of subjecting it and its rivals to systematic critique.[3] And it is in Plato's reflections on Socratic elenchus in the transitional and middle dialogues that the term and the concept of "method" first appear in the Western corpus, at least among surviving texts.[4] This innovation is truly a watershed in the history of thought and occupies a pivotal role in the development of both the philosophical and scientific traditions.[5] At the same time, Plato's epistemic claim in the dialogues is also a hortatory or protreptic one, because the conception of knowledge he

---

Elenchus," *Oxford Studies in Ancient Philosophy* 3 (1985): 247–60; Thomas C. Brickhouse and Nicholas D. Smith, *Plato's Socrates* (Oxford: Oxford University Press, 1994); and Terrence Irwin, *Plato's Ethics* (Oxford: Oxford University Press, 1995). The view I will defend is unlike any of these because it purports to draw positive conclusions only indirectly, as a second-order result of just the sort of total critique insisted upon by the anticonstructivists.

[3] See W. C. Kneale and Martha Kneale, *The Development of Logic* (Oxford: Oxford University Press, 1962) for potential forerunners such as Parmenides and Zeno, and Plato's *Parmenides*.

[4] Henry George Liddell and Robert Scott, *A Greek-English Lexicon* (Oxford: Clarendon Press, 1996); hereafter referred to as Liddell-Scott. Vlastos emphasizes Plato's neologism (*Socratic Studies*, 1). A search in the *Thesaurus Linguae Grecae* confirms exactly zero appearances of forms of *methodos* in surviving Greek texts before Plato, who proceeds to employ it twenty-six times, always in those works generally considered middle or later. On standard chronology, it appears first in the key passages *Phaedo* 79e, 97b; *Phaedrus* 269d–270e; and *Republic* 435d, 510b, 531d, 533b–c, 596a, and is also found in *Theaetetus, Sophist, Politicus, Laws,* and the *Second Letter*.

[5] Indeed, Plato also coins the standard meaning of "philosophy" in the same pages (Liddell-Scott). Plato's use refers to a critical search to distinguish truth from mere opinion, whereas Isocrates, the only place the term appears in surviving texts of comparable age, uses it to refer more generally to a love of learning or to the systematic study of a field, such as oratory. For some of the ways Plato's invention of method bears also on questions of explanation in the empirical social sciences, see my "Socratic Method and Political Science," *American Political Science Review* 106, no. 3 (2012): 644–60.

advances poses an invitation to both interlocutor and reader to join in an ongoing dialogical project of self-examination though which one learns to think for oneself and becomes better.[6]

Socrates's unending elenctic practice thus overturns an entire world of traditional knowledge, but in doing so simultaneously establishes the possibility of a radically new conception of knowledge as that which best survives the ongoing challenge of systematic criticism. And yet one further step is required, for many of the early Socratic dialogues seem to suggest that *no* beliefs could ever survive such a demanding test, that every claim to positive knowledge must ultimately founder for being unable to justify its own foundations. Plato thus responds with a crucial third move, beginning with the introduction of the so-called method of hypothesis in the *Meno*. His insight is that only certain *kinds* of beliefs could ever survive in elenchus, and therefore *if* any belief is to be justifiable, *then* it would have to meet certain conditions. In particular, it would have to be justifiable on some universal, unchanging, and consistent principle (on some defensible interpretation of these terms), if it were to defend against elenctic objections from every competing point of view its claim to be more true than the alternatives. Otherwise, it could only be one opinion among others, but never genuine knowledge that a doubter would have some non-question-begging reason to accept. This, I contend, is the best way of understanding the Platonic theory of ideas—as regulative assumptions already implicitly built into the method of Socratic critique, which Plato draws out and further develops in middle dialogues like *Republic*. The key point is that this establishes a standard for distinguishing defensible from indefensible beliefs, which is wholly antifoundational and immanent to the critical method itself. This inverts a standard notion of method as a means to the ever-closer approximation of a preexisting objective truth.[7] Instead, objectivity here is a regulative construct that follows from the logic of method as a systematic interrogation of every claim to know; what it means for a belief to be "objective," then, is nothing more or less than that it may be *consistently defended as objective in elenchus against all competing views*.

In addition to providing an original explanation of Socratic elenchus that establishes its logical validity as a critical means of justifying positive conclusions, this interpretation shows that Plato's ideas themselves—commonly taken for the very paradigm of transcendent metaphysical foundations—are

---

[6] For more on the protrepic side, see Charles Kahn, *Plato and the Socratic Dialogue: The Philosophical Use of a Literary Form* (Cambridge, UK: Cambridge University Press, 1996); Francisco J. Gonzalez, *Dialectic and Dialogue: Plato's Practice of Philosophical Inquiry* (Evanston, IL: Northwestern University Press, 1998); and Christina H. Tarnopolsky, *Prudes, Perverts, and Tyrants: Plato's Gorgias and the Politics of Shame* (Princeton, NJ: Princeton University Press, 2010).

[7] Compare Hegel's famous discussion of the method of philosophy in the Introduction to the *Phenomenology*, §73–76.

best understood quite to the contrary as further developments within the overarching antifoundational logic of elenchus. I do not take a position on how to distinguish the historical Socrates from the historical Plato or on the standard chronology, since my argument does not depend on them. Nor do I focus on the protreptic side of elenchus or on Plato's later "method of division," or *diairesis*, which I take to build on elenchus but to have less relevance to contemporary democratic theory.[8] Finally, I should emphasize that I use "elenchus" expansively to include the later developments of hypothesis and ideas, whereas it is more common to describe elenchus as one piece of the larger "dialectic" by the middle dialogues. But "dialectic" is a diffuse concept in Plato as elsewhere, and referring to "elenchus" helps keep the focus on what I take to be essential, the notion of argument through the immanent refutation of alternatives, in the absence of any certain and authoritative foundations. Since my claim is that hypothesis and ideas draw out and make explicit logical suppositions already implicit in elenchus (even if they do so in terms borrowed from geometry), retaining the term reminds the reader that the more specific arguments around ideas are embedded in a larger dialogical investigation that remains elentic as a whole.

Refutation

The logic of Socratic refutation can usefully be compared to that of argument by *reductio ad impossibile*, also known as *reductio ad absurdum*.[9] In a standard *reductio*, one deduces from a given proposition a consequence that contradicts that proposition itself. This shows that the initial proposition cannot be true, or if one prefers, that it cannot mean anything to say that it is true, since in doing so, one commits oneself logically no less to the claim that it is false.[10] But a *reductio* sometimes allows more than this negative conclusion; for if one can show that one proposition leads necessarily to self-contradiction, while the contradictory proposition does not, and if the contradictory is properly framed so as to exclude the possibility of any third alternative, then one may fairly conclude not only that the initial proposition is false but also that the contradictory is true. Here,

---

[8] For three very different discussions, see Kenneth M. Sayre, *Plato's Analytic Method* (Chicago: University of Chicago Press, 1969); Hans-Georg Gadamer, *Plato's Dialectical Ethics: Phenomenological Interpretations Relating to the Philebus* (New Haven, CT: Yale University Press, 1991); and Melissa Lane, *Method and Politics in Plato's Statesman* (Cambridge, UK: Cambridge University Press, 1998).

[9] The terms are essentially equivalent, both deriving ultimately from the Greek *hē eis to adunaton apagōgē* (Aristotle, *Prior Analytics* 41a21). For the history of argument by *reductio*, see Kneale and Kneale, *Logic*.

[10] See for instance Gilbert Ryle, "Philosophical Arguments," in Ryle, *Collected Papers*, Vol. 2 (London: Routledge, 2009), 203–21.

then, is a clear and well-understood example of how it is sometimes possible to arrive at positive conclusions by strictly negative means. Like the *reductio*, and unlike either induction or direct deduction, Socratic elenchus allows one to justify positive claims without presuming the truth of any foundational premise whatsoever. Neither induction nor direct deduction can get off the ground unless we already possess at least one solid truth from which to begin; elenchus, by contrast, places no claim beyond criticism and depends on no epistemic authority external to the method itself. Because it is radically antifoundational in this way, it is particularly well suited for addressing fundamental disagreements in which no shared first principles, or interpretations of first principles, may be taken as already firmly established.

But if Socratic method is like a *reductio* in this first respect, it is radically different in others. For one might imagine that elenchus, even if it can do without presupposing substantive premises, must at least presuppose the procedural rules of logic, the way that induction and direct deduction do. And yet as Vlastos rightly emphasized, Socrates never simply deduces the contradictions in his interlocutors' beliefs for them; instead, he only asks them questions, and allows them to fall into self-contradiction through their own responses.[11] Every time Socrates proposes to draw a logical conclusion in the dialogues he *requires the explicit assent of his interlocutor at every step along the way*. This is an obvious textual fact about the dialogues that has irritated many an undergraduate and puzzled many an interpreter. I take it to be making a very serious theoretical point, namely, that Socrates's method does not presuppose any rules of logic whatsoever, if we understand by "rules" algorithmic procedures whose validity is secured ex ante and that need only be correctly applied to a given case.

To the contrary, rather than invoking the authority of a rule, Socrates at every step merely poses a question; if his move is accepted by the interlocutor, this shows that the interlocutor himself, on reflection, takes it to represent a valid logical consequence of his own views. But the interlocutors are always free to say no, and when they do sometimes want to change their answers or to argue off in a new direction, Socrates invariably allows this, so long as it does not render the underlying matter of dispute a moving target (*Gorgias* 499b–c; *Republic* 340b–c, 345b; *Protagoras* 349c–d). The authority by which the interlocutor finds himself convicted of incoherence, then, is always in the final instance his own, never Socrates's or that of some impersonal set of logical rules that might confront him as an alien law. This does not mean that logic has no place in the method. Rather, the sort of rules we have come to associate with "logic" can be understood as a compendium of certain moves shown to be generally and reliably successful in elenchus. Indeed, there is some reason to think that this may be their

---

[11] Gregory Vlastos, *Socrates, Ironist and Moral Philosopher* (Cambridge, UK: Cambridge University Press, 1991), 94–5.

actual historical origin, insofar as Aristotle's *Organon* can be read, in part, as an extended systematizing reflection on argumentative practices learned in Plato's Academy. But Socratic questioning remains logically prior to any of these particular rules; if they are to count as necessary truths, this is only because we have not (yet) found any coherent way of denying them, which is equivalent to saying they must continually prove themselves in elenchus.[12] Even the most basic principle of noncontradiction is first justified by Aristotle, in the *Metaphysics*, not on grounds of self-evidence but because one who denies it can be refuted on his own terms.[13] Such an "elenctic demonstration" [*to elenktikōs apodeiksai*], he suggests, is the only sort it makes any sense to demand for such a basic principle.[14] General logical truths, then, can be helpful *within* Socratic method by allowing us to build on the arguments of others, insofar as these are not in dispute; but because *the question is always prior to the rule*, even these general truths must always remain open to criticism whenever their status or applicability to the case at hand becomes controversial.

This serves to highlight an essential characteristic of Socratic arguments that contrasts sharply with induction, direct deduction, and *reductio*: it need not be *impossible to doubt* their logical soundness for them to be good arguments. All that is necessary is for Socrates to show that *on his interlocutor's own assumptions*, there is good reason to find such arguments compelling. To refute a particular interlocutor's claim to knowledge, it is sufficient to show that he cannot make coherent sense out of his own position when pressed to do so.[15] The relevant question, in the first instance, is thus not whether all

---

[12] Robinson contrasts Plato's view on this point with Descartes's, who held to the contrary that "by method... I understand certain and easy rules such that whoever has followed them exactly will never suppose anything false for true, and without uselessly wasting any mental effort, but always gradually increasing knowledge [*scientiam*], will arrive at the true understanding [*cognitionem*] of everything of which one will be capable" (*Regulae ad directionem ingenii* [Atlanta: Rodopi, 1998], 85). Robinson rightly remarks that this "is far from the spirit of Plato." *Plato's Earlier Dialectic*, 2nd ed. (Oxford: Oxford University Press, 1953), 73.

[13] The principle was first formulated by Plato at *Republic* 436b.

[14] *Metaphysics* 1006a: "But we have now posited that it is impossible for anything at the same time to be and not to be.... Some indeed demand that even this shall be demonstrated, but ... it is impossible that there should be demonstration of absolutely everything; there would be an infinite regress, so that there would still be no demonstration.... We can, however, demonstrate negatively [*esti d'apodeiksai elenktikōs*] even that this view is impossible, if our opponent will only say something; and if he says nothing, it is absurd to attempt to reason with one who will not reason about anything.... Now negative demonstration [*elenktikōs apodeiksai*] I distinguish from demonstration proper, because in a demonstration one might be thought to be begging the question, but if another person is responsible for the assumption we shall have negative proof [*elenchos*], not demonstration." This is Ross's translation, in the Barnes edition.

[15] This is how one can respond to Quine's critique of analyticity in "Two Dogmas of Empiricism"—particularly because Quine's argument uses just this sort of characteristically Socratic strategy itself. In Quine, *From a Logical Point of View*, 2nd ed. (Cambridge, MA: Harvard University Press, 1980), 20–46.

of Socrates's conclusions follow necessarily or whether his own premises are incontrovertible, but rather whether or not it is reasonable to think that the particular interlocutor he is facing would accept them. This is what is signaled by the question-and-answer format of the dialogues, and by Socrates's repeated criticisms of the more customary use of long, direct speeches as a means of pursuing knowledge (e.g., *Gorgias* 461e–462a, 466c, 471e–472c; *Protagoras* 334d–338e; *Republic* 348a–b). From this it follows, finally, that in Socratic refutation a "good argument" always means one good *relative to a given position one is trying to refute*, never (at this stage) one we need some reason to think must be good absolutely, or true in any ultimate sense. These points are commonly overlooked by analytically minded interpreters, because appreciating them requires attention to the way the dialogue form inflects the logical status of particular arguments in context.[16]

This is made even clearer by a second way in which elenchus differs from *reductio*. A single valid *reductio* is enough to establish a proposition universally: if I show once that the proposition "some unmarried man is not a bachelor" entails its own negation, because every unmarried man is, *ex definitio*, a bachelor, then we may consider this proposition definitively refuted, and its contradictory established (unless I am later shown to have erred). The proof becomes no more or less certain if I copy it out ten thousand times. This sort of universality is typical of formal logic and mathematics, which trade in general and necessary a priori propositions. But Socrates's refutations cannot be like this, I submit, because of their essentially immanent and dialogical character. Because they always begin from the contingent constellation of views an interlocutor happens to hold, the conclusion of any single refutation must always remain *relative* to that particular position. That is, while Socrates's logic is sufficiently compelling to make it dramatically plausible for a given interlocutor to be reduced to silence (at least, I hope the reader will grant, much of the time), it is typically less than airtight, and one could often imagine another interlocutor arguing back in a different way. Indeed, sometimes Plato goes so far as to dramatize this explicitly, notably in *Gorgias*, *Protagoras*, and *Republic*, where Socrates refutes more than one interlocutor in the course of a single dialogue.

The point to take is that in Socratic elenchus, unlike an analytic *reductio*, the logical status of a single refutation is inferior to that of the ongoing and systematic refutation of all competing views. For even if every individual elenchus

---

[16] Here, I agree with treatments stressing the importance of form to the interpretation of content from Hans-Georg Gadamer, *Dialogue and Dialectic: Eight Hermeneutical Studies on Plato* (New Haven, CT: Yale University Press, 1980) and Leo Strauss, *The City and Man* (Chicago: University of Chicago Press, 1964) to Kahn, *Plato*; Gonzalez, *Dialectic*; and Catherine H. Zuckert, *Plato's Philosophers: The Coherence of the Dialogues* (Chicago: University of Chicago Press, 2009).

permits only relative conclusions, one could still establish general claims, provisionally, if one were systematically to eliminate every contending claim to knowledge but one. Consider by analogy a trial in which the defense manages, through cross-examination, to lead each and every witness for the prosecution to contradict his own testimony, while at least one witness for the defense is able to maintain his story against every attempt by the prosecution to poke holes in it.[17] True, such a method could never lead to absolute certainty, since it is always possible that another argument (or another witness) might turn up that we had failed to consider. But if one accepts that we possess no self-evident starting point outside the method from which to begin (as is also the case in a trial), and if one therefore limits oneself strictly to the logic of asking questions, and to taking nothing for granted that cannot be justified in argument, then this is a conclusion that one must also accept. One would be forced to conclude that human wisdom is by nature less certain than the divine (*Apology* 20d–e, 23a–b). And if one nevertheless were not to give up on seeking knowledge, one would have to commit oneself to seeking out systematically and testing every available claim already to possess it, especially those of the most eminent experts (21e). One would also have to admit that such a search must be never-ending (23b, 37e–38a). And this, of course, is exactly how Socrates characterizes his elenctic mission.

Socratic method, then, is doubly indirect. Like a *reductio*, every refutation proceeds from the proposition to be falsified, not from a certain first principle [*archē*]. But unlike *reductio*, in elenchus it is not a single refutation that establishes a general proposition; rather, this requires an ongoing process of elimination that demonstrates internal inconsistencies in every position but one. From this it follows that the force of a given refutation is only relative to its place within this larger process of elimination. And every conclusion will be only as strong as the systematicity with which one has so far eliminated its rivals. Because in practice one can never eliminate every possible alternative view (or at least, one could never know for certain that one had already accomplished this), there can be no end to the critical search for new alternatives to challenge. Propositions that have been "demonstrated" in the past should never be considered to have been proven absolutely, only to have been shown *more defensible* than all other available positions that have actually been refuted. With these qualifications clearly in mind, however, we can now see how it may be possible to defend positive conclusions by strictly negative means.

---

[17] One might think here of Socrates's cross-examination of Meletus in *Apology* 24c–27e, or his challenge to Polus in *Gorgias* 471e–472c. There, Socrates claims to know "how to produce one witness for what I say, the very man I am debating, but the many I dismiss" (474a, cf. 475e–476a, 482b).

Aporia and Method

Several leading interpreters defend competing versions of such a "constructive" view of elenchus, based solely on the Socratic dialogues. All such views, however, face two major hurdles—one logical and one textual. First, it is not enough to demonstrate the logical possibility of such an indirect mode of justification to show why we ought to give it priority in the search for knowledge. A defender of a more traditional, pre-methodological view can easily deny that the relative and provisional results of elenchus really meet the standard of "knowledge" at all. Second, while a few Socratic dialogues do seem to result in clear positive claims to knowledge—notably *Crito* and *Gorgias*—the overwhelming majority end not in enlightenment, but in *aporia*, and usually an *aporia* in which Socrates himself avowedly shares. This is difficult to explain on the constructive view. Indeed, Socrates's disavowals of "knowledge" have been a central issue of controversy in Plato interpretation for centuries, and considerations like the foregoing have led other leading interpreters, like Benson, to deny what I have argued, namely, that elenchus is capable of demonstrating anything more than negative conclusions.[18]

Against both parties, my claim is that the tension in the text is real and marks a crucial feature of Plato's argument. Perhaps nowhere is this tension more neatly condensed than in this striking passage from the conclusion of *Gorgias*, the paradigmatic dialogue of constructive elenchus:

> All this, which was shown to be as I say some way back in our previous discussion, *is held down and fastened . . . by arguments of iron and adamant*—or so it would seem, at any rate. . . . For my account is always the same—that *I do not know how such things are*, and yet of all whom I have met, now or before, there is no one who said it in a different way without being ridiculous. (508e–509a)[19]

---

[18] Indeed, the issue is sufficiently vexed that it gave rise in the ancient world to competing schools of Platonic interpretation—whereas Neoplatonists, among others, defended dogmatic versions of Platonic idealism from the classical period to the twentieth century, Plato's own Academy became the leading seat of ancient skepticism under the leadership of Arcesilaus and Carneades, who saw themselves as carrying forward the true spirit of Platonic philosophy. See Julia Annas, "Plato the Skeptic," in *Oxford Studies in Ancient Philosophy*, supp. vol., *Methods of Interpreting Plato and His Dialogues*, eds. James C. Klagge and Nicholas D. Smith (1992), 43–72; Paul Woodruff, "The Skeptical Side of Plato's Method," *Revue Internationale de Philosophie* 40 (1986): 22–37. On the contemporary controversy, see inter alia Vlastos, "Socrates' Disavowal of Knowledge," in *Socratic Studies*, 39–66; J. H. Lesher, "Socrates' Disavowal of Knowledge," *Journal of the History of Philosophy* 25 (1987): 275–88; Paul Woodruff, "Plato's Early Theory of Knowledge," in *Ancient Greek Epistemology*, ed. S. Everson (Cambridge, UK: Cambridge University Press, 1990), 60–84; Brickhouse and Smith, *Plato's Socrates*; and Irwin, *Plato's Ethics*.

[19] Emphasis mine. Both "arguments" in "arguments of iron and adamant" and "account" in "my account" are *logos*.

Vlastos has argued for distinguishing two senses of "knowledge" or "wisdom" in passages like this: he claims that Socrates asserts only a sort of fallibilist "elenctic" knowledge, while disavowing a stronger kind of knowledge that would entail "certainty."[20] I do not disagree, but I think Vlastos misses the deeper point by suggesting the issue is essentially one of more precisely distinguishing one's terms. Rather, the ambiguity reflects the fact that Socrates's innovation appears differently when viewed from within the standpoint of the traditional knowledge it destroys, on the one hand, or from that of the new elenctic knowledge it first makes possible, on the other. This duality is important, because Plato is not merely asking us to trade one set of beliefs for another, within the horizon of the traditional view that supposes some beliefs intrinsically wrong and others intrinsically right. The crucial first step of the argument, to the contrary, is to justify a shift to a radically new perspective on knowledge by helping us to see that *every* claim to knowledge of this traditional kind—the sort whose validity is supposed to be either self-evident or else borrowed from some conventional authority like religion or the poets—will fall into self-contradiction when forced to justify itself over alternatives in the crucible of systematic elenctic critique.[21] Since we begin inside the horizon of the traditional view that assumes this is the only sort of knowledge there can be, the result appears to destroy knowledge as a whole—to teach only that one knows nothing at all.

But this negative experience of *aporia* itself also opens the way for access to a different, more genuine sort of knowledge, when the same result is reconsidered from a second point of view. For if it is true that every traditional claim can be defeated in elenchus because none can provide a coherent reason for thinking it more true than the alternatives, then by the same token it follows that *any view that could provide such a reason would be able to survive in elenchus and therefore count as true*, just because the experience of *aporia* has demolished the possibility of any ground outside elenchus that could possibly contradict it. Coming to see Plato's point, however, entails a radical paradigm shift in the meaning of "knowledge." The difference between knowledge and nonknowledge will no longer be understood as that between one list of intrinsically correct beliefs and another list of wrong ones, but rather as the difference between a belief backed with reasons and a mere opinion, *even if the content of those two beliefs is identical*. Thus, as Socrates famously explains to Meno:

> True opinions are a fine possession and perform every kind of good so long as they stay in place; they do not like to stay long [however], but run away from a man's mind, and so are of no great value until they are tied

---

[20] Vlastos, "Disavowal," 55–6.

[21] The criticism of religion and poetry in *Euthyphro* and *Ion* turns on the need for principled interpretation to overcome ostensible conflicts and contradictions among the poets and the gods.

down with reasons [*aitias logismōi*]. . . . When they are tied down, first they become knowledge [*epistēmai*], and second, they stay in place. (97e–98a)

What Plato's Socrates has done, then, is to introduce the radical claim that all genuine knowledge is method-dependent, that its truth depends not directly on its content but rather on the possibility of providing it a consistent justification. If this interpretation is correct, then the practice of Socratic method opens up a great conceptual fissure in the traditional understanding of terms like "knowledge" and "wisdom." And we should thus *expect* a radical ambiguity in Socrates's claims to knowledge, not because his terminology is imprecise but because those claims must always be open to consideration simultaneously from two competing points of view. The language of the traditional view cannot simply be discarded, because the argument is just that elenctic knowledge turns out to be more genuinely "knowledge" than traditional "knowledge" itself; that is, it better lives up to traditional knowledge's own self-image as justly authoritative belief, but it does so just insofar as it differs from that knowledge by justifying its authority wholly through the method of systematic critique. This will scan as paradox or oxymoron, however, if one does not appreciate the way the argument deliberately straddles two incommensurable epistemological points of view.

Thus, in the famous passage from *Apology*, Socrates tells the story of how he learned that the oracle at Delphi had said that no man was wiser than he, and so set out to disprove the god by finding someone wiser. When his elenctic examinations of traditional experts fail to locate such a man, Socrates concludes neither that he is, nor is not, indeed the wisest:

> For it seems every time to those who are present that I am wise in those matters in which I refute [*exelenchō*] someone else; but the fact is, gentlemen, it is likely that [it is] the god [who] is really wise and by his oracle means this: "Human wisdom is of little worth or none." And it appears that he does not really say this of Socrates, but merely uses my name and makes me an example, as if he were to say: "This one of you, human beings, is wisest, who, like Socrates, acknowledges that he is in truth worth nothing in regard to wisdom." (23a–b)

This passage can be read two ways, and the ambiguity is significant. On one reading, Socrates knows only that he does not know; but this is to use the word "know" in the traditional sense, here given voice by Socrates's interpretation of the divine oracle, from whose point of view human wisdom is of little worth or none. But the passage is just as fairly read to the contrary as an affirmation, on elenctic grounds, that Socrates is indeed the wisest and most pious of Athenians, precisely insofar as he devotes himself to the unflagging pursuit of knowledge through elenchus. And Socrates's risky and unorthodox defense, in which the story is an episode, turns on the claim that his incessant questioning is in fact the truest form of piety. Before the jury Socrates shows no faltering in his assurance of the rightness of his conduct. Indeed, he prefers to sacrifice his life before his convictions, and even to choose death, of which he claims to know not whether it is truly evil, over a lesser punishment he "knows" is evil, one that would put him at variance with himself by placing love of life over fealty to his "divine" elenctic mission.[22] This is not the behavior we should expect from a man who had learned only the negative lesson that he can be certain of nothing. The ambiguity in Socrates's professions of ignorance, then, is not an obstacle to interpretation that must be smoothed away, but a positive marker of the profound shift in perspective on the meaning of moral knowledge that Socrates invites us to make.[23]

Recognizing this allows us to appreciate the logic of Plato's argument for why one ought to prefer Socratic knowledge to the traditional view. It is crucial that he is providing an argument, not merely imposing his own view without justification (which would be inconsistent). And yet an argument for method—a justification for the need for justification—can only be roundabout. It cannot take the form of a direct deduction of the "rightness" of the view of knowledge as method-dependent, because that view itself rules out presupposing any self-authorizing positive foundation from which such a derivation might begin. Nor can it directly refute the "epistemology" of the naive, traditional view, just because the defining characteristic of that view is that it has no epistemology at all. If Socrates's argument is not to beg the question, then, it must start from within the horizon of the traditional view, and show it to be self-defeating in a language it can understand: it can only proceed, in other words, by elenchus.[24] And because that view speaks the language of example, not yet that of general principles and justifications, this means that to indict the view itself, Socrates will have to refute a series of exemplary interlocutors representing all its major recognized authorities—for instance, generals (*Laches*), lawyers (*Euthyphro*), politicians, poets and craftsmen (*Apology*), interpreters of the poets and the gods (*Greater* and *Lesser Hippias, Ion, Protagoras, Euthyphro*), as well as the leading sophists of the day

---

[22] 29a–d, and again at 37b–38c. Although the passage may be ambiguous, I read it not to depend upon immediate positive knowledge of the truth of the isolated proposition that it is wrong "to disobey one's betters, be they god or man," but rather to turn on the supposition that neither Socrates nor his interlocutors in the jury could defend another course of action consistently in elenchus, given their convictions. This reading is, I think, supported by the indirect argument of the *Crito*, which would otherwise be unnecessary there.

[23] Vlastos is thus right to consider this passage an instance of "complex irony," in which Socrates both means and does not mean what he says, but this is not, as Vlastos implies, merely a rhetorical device: it rather reflects a deep philosophical point about competing epistemologies. See *Ironist*, 31, and "Disavowal," 64–6.

[24] Charles L. Griswold Jr. is one of the few commentators in English to emphasize this point; see his "Plato's Metaphilosophy: Why Plato Wrote Dialogues," in *Platonic Writings/Platonic Readings*, ed. Griswold (Boston: Routledge & Kegan Paul, 1988), 143–67.

(*Gorgias, Protagoras*).²⁵ It follows from the logic of elenchus that this search must be both systematic and unending, as Socrates duly emphasizes at *Apology* 21a–22e.

This reading resolves key difficulties in the texts. On the one hand, we should no longer be surprised if the Socratic dialogues end in *aporia*. For we should not expect representatives of the traditional view readily to understand and embrace Socrates's radical alternative; rather, the dramatic force of the refutation will come across most powerfully if the reader is offered the spectacle of the old worldview crashing in on itself in the face of Socrates's persistent questioning. On the other hand, we can also see why it is that this need not lead Socrates to conclude that the search for knowledge is futile, but to the contrary that we must only redouble our efforts.²⁶ This is because we also come to see how it is that method-dependent, elenctic knowledge may come to count as "knowledge." Finally, however, understanding the second point *requires* an appreciation of the first: there would be no reason to accept the claim that elenctic knowledge ought to count as real "knowledge" *except that* one has come to see that every pretense to unmediated, pre-methodological knowledge is ultimately self-defeating, and thus that an elenctic justification is a sufficient one, just because there can be no other sort of knowledge that could ever contravene it. This is why Plato will continue to insist even in the later dialogues that the numbing perplexity of *aporia* is a necessary step in the pursuit of knowledge, why it must always be experienced in the first instance as both negative and total, and why Socrates cannot but share in it himself.²⁷ There is one sense in which this *aporia* is subsequently overcome, in that it no longer presents an insuperable obstacle to positive judgment. But there is another, equally real sense in which *aporia* is permanent and intrinsic to the method, because the sort of qualified claim to method-dependent knowledge that elenchus can provide always continues to depend on the unceasing refutation of every new claim to direct, final, or unmediated knowledge of the type that would require no justification.

Hypothesis and Ideas

The foregoing account of Socratic method, however, remains incomplete. If it went no further, it would be open to two fatal objections. First, it seems that survival in elenchus demonstrates only consistency of belief, not genuine knowledge,

---

²⁵ The sophists are a special case. In these epynomous dialogs, the title characters are in fact presented as continuous with traditional authorities, but other figures, like Callicles, Thrasymachus, and Euthydemus and Diyonysodorus, represent a radical challenge to traditional authority that parallel Socrates's own in crucial ways. These too must be refuted if Socrates's position is ultimately to stand (since its truth depends on the systematic refutation of all significant alternatives), but the logic of this refutation will hinge on the further step in the argument discussed in the following section.

²⁶ *Laches* 201a–b, *Apology* 23c, *Protagoras* 361c–d.

²⁷ *Meno* 80a–d, 84a–d; *Theaetetus*, repeatedly at 149a–151e, 154d–e, 155c–d, 157c–d, 161a–b, 162c–e, 167d–168c, 177b, 190e–191a, and 210b–d; *Sophist* 230b–231b and passim.

since any number of incompatible views may be internally coherent, and without access to any sort of ultimate, method-independent reality against which to check its results, the method seems incapable of discriminating among them. Second, the way Socrates actually goes about refuting his interlocutors' beliefs typically turns on securing their agreement, sooner or later, to the proposition that genuine knowledge requires the possession of a general and explanatory criterion that holds across all instances, and that might, in principle, be made explicit. This is what is commonly referred to as the "priority of definitional knowledge," and I have already emphasized that it is not an arbitrary standard that Socrates imposes, but rather a consequence of consistently thinking through the claim to authority implicit in traditional moral beliefs.[28] But whatever else Socrates may occasionally claim to know, in the early dialogues he invariably denies possessing any definitions of this sort himself. Nor is it clear how elenctic questioning alone could ever furnish them. And this seems to entail that if Socrates's own positive beliefs, for instance, in *Crito* or *Gorgias*, were subject to the same standard that he demands of his interlocutors, then they too would fail. These considerations pose a serious challenge to my substantive thesis that Socratic method manages to justify positive conclusions by strictly negative means.

It is crucial to see that Plato himself was wrestling with these problems in the dialogues, and understanding his response will help us to appreciate the way that the notions of hypothesis and ideas build on and complete the underlying logic of elenchus. For it is the introduction of the so-called method of hypothesis in *Meno* and *Phaedo* that marks the crucial breakthrough that will pave the way for the full Platonic theory of ideas in the middle dialogues.[29] And this is what finally allows him, in Book IV of the *Republic*, to arrive for the first time at a positive definition of justice.

---

[28] As William J. Prior notes in his "Socrates Metaphysician," *Oxford Studies in Ancient Philosophy* 27 (2004): 11–12, Socrates is always careful to draw out his interlocutors' assent to this standard by questioning them about their own beliefs. However, this remains another extremely contentious point in the literature; cf. Peter Geach, "Plato's Euthyphro: An Analysis and Commentary," *Monist* 50, no. 3 (1966): 369–82; John Beversluis, "Does Socrates Commit the Socratic Fallacy?," *American Philosophical Quarterly* 24, no. 3 (1987): 211–23; Irwin, *Plato's Ethics*; Richard Kraut, *Socrates and the State* (Princeton, NJ: Princeton University Press, 1984), 245–309; Paul Woodruff, "Expert Knowledge in the *Apology* and *Laches*: What a General Needs to Know," in *Proceedings of the Boston Area Colloquium in Ancient Philosophy*, Vol. 3., ed. J. J. Cleary (Lanham, MD: University Press of America, 1987), 79–115; Brickhouse and Smith, *Plato's Socrates*; Vlastos, "Elenchus"; and Benson, *Socratic Wisdom*, Chapter 6.

[29] Benson similarly portrays the *Meno* as a response to a paradox implicit in the elenctic method of the early dialogues in "The Method of Hypothesis in the *Meno*," *Proceedings of the 2002 Boston Area Colloquium in Ancient Philosophy*, Vol. 18, eds. John J. Cleary and Gary M. Gurtler (Boston: Brill, 2003), 95–126. But I do not share Benson's dissatisfaction with the "provisional" nature of this method's conclusions (126), which I rather take to be a positive result of Plato's redefining truth as inherently method-dependent.

My thesis is that the "method" of hypothesis and the ideas represent, not a repudiation of elenchus, but a further working-out of its own immanent logic, the logic of asking questions about when, if ever, we have reason to prefer any one belief to another.[30] The ideas are thus radically misunderstood if they are taken for a return to the sort of freestanding and self-evident claim to knowledge that Socrates had everywhere demolished. Only once we have fully accepted the point—learned through the experience of *aporia*—that knowledge can be attained only through a critical method, can we go on to draw the revolutionary conclusion that therefore *any assumption without which such a method cannot proceed must hold "objectively" for every possible claim to knowledge*. Such regulative assumptions of the method thus comprise what I have called the *conditions of possibility* of any consistent answer. They constrain the range of beliefs that might ever consistently be defended, simply because one cannot hope to justify any belief whose own content contravenes the necessary assumptions of the only method by which it could ever possibly be justified. And as I will show, these assumptions turn out to be equivalent to Plato's doctrine of ideas. The truth of the ideas, then, and their epistemic priority over the diversity of particular appearances, are best understood as regulative assumptions in the sense that will prove so important also for Kant, as logical presuppositions built into the very possibility of questioning the truth of our beliefs.[31]

When Plato asks us to reason to and from ideas, in other words, he is really asking us to think through the logical relations implicit in any claim we make to know something either is or is not true. He comes to recognize that every such claim tacitly commits us to two further propositions. First, we must be able to provide some sort of *explanatory account* that justifies our belief over others; in the language of *Meno* 98a, we must be able to tie that belief down with reasons [*dēsei aitias logismōi*]. Second, in doing so, we must be able to show that the entire web of logical implications in that account is *internally consistent*. If this were not the case, then our reasons could not really count as reasons for our belief in the way we need them to, since they would equally be reasons for other beliefs that, in turn, give us reasons to reject it. Plato describes such a coherence test at *Phaedo* 101d, where he explains that "if anyone attacked your hypothesis, you would be happy to let him alone and you would not answer until you had examined the results of that hypothesis, to see if, to you, they mutually harmonize or are discordant."[32]

The two conditions, however, must go together; what is required is not merely coherence but a *coherent explanation* that provides a reason for favoring

---

[30] *Pace* Vlastos, "Elenchus and Mathematics," in *Ironist*, 107–31.

[31] Chapter 3 discusses how Kant distinguishes in ways Plato had not among different types of regulative assumptions, but Kant does continue to call some of these "regulative ideas" (A642/B670–A645/B673) and traces his use of the term "ideas" explicitly Plato's (A313/B369–A320/B377).

[32] See Jyl Gentzler, "'συμφωνεῖν' in Plato's *Phaedo*," *Phronesis* 36, no. 3 (1991): 265–76. My translation here and of *Phaedo* 100a–b draws on hers.

one hypothesis over another. Thus in *Republic VI*, Plato argues that in examining a given hypothesis, we ought first to trace the logical assumptions of our beliefs back, step by step, to some general principle that would need no further justification [*to ep archēn anhupotheton*], and then to reason back "down" from this assumption to check the coherence of its consequences (510b, 511b, cf. *Phaedo* 101d–e). Only if this reasoning up and down through ideas is successful can we demonstrate that our belief is justified by reasons which are themselves coherent. And it is only this sort of belief that could ever be defended in elenchus.

This interpretation builds on important work by Gail Fine and Jyl Gentzler, both of whom argue for a "coherentist" rather than a "foundationalist" understanding of Plato's ideas.[33] But it differs in one crucial respect: I think Plato cannot simply be what contemporary analytic philosophers call a "coherentist" because he recognizes that coherence alone is no warrant for truth, whereas the coherence *of a justification uniquely favoring a given hypothesis* is. In other words, Plato is concerned with not only the coherence of our beliefs, but also the coherence of all these beliefs *and* the further proposition that this belief set, and not any other, is ultimately the true one. To test this, we need *not* have some way to prove that it is "in fact" the true one; we need only show that it can be defended in elenchus as compatible with the regulative assumption that there exists some such standard of truth and that it favors this particular view, whereas the alternatives cannot. Although both Gentzler and Fine recognize that Plato is concerned with the coherence *of explanations*, Gentzler thinks this is because explanatory claims are instrumental to "maximizing the coherence of one's belief set" (485, 487), and Fine takes coherence to be sufficient if it is "sufficiently rich" in that it integrates all branches of knowledge and (purports to) explain a satisfying number of "results" (114–15). What these readings leave out is the claim to "objective" status *as a regulative assumption* to which I mean to draw attention; doing so effectively reduces Socratic method to systematizing our preexisting beliefs (much like Rawls's "reflective equilibrium"), whereas Plato is quite ready to countenance the possibility that our initial beliefs might turn out to be of a sort that is entirely indefensible, like the shadows on the wall in the allegory of the cave.

The notion of the "nonhypothetical" principle requiring no further justification of its own provides the final piece of the story. Without such a principle, one could only trace the chain of reasons back ever further, and every justification would remain incomplete and question-begging. But the notion of an *archē anhupothetos* invites confusion, since it may seem natural to presume that Plato is saying we need to trace our beliefs back to some certain foundation outside the method. There are several reasons for thinking this cannot be Plato's

---

[33] Gail Fine, *Plato on Knowledge and Forms* (Oxford: Oxford University Press, 2003); Jyl Gentzler, "How to Know the Good: The Moral Epistemology of Plato's *Republic*," *Philosophical Review* 114, no. 4 (2005): 469–96.

thought.[34] Perhaps most telling is that Plato insists here and elsewhere on the need to reason not only *from* but also *to* such a principle. If the *archē anhupothetos* were self-certifyingly true, then it would make sense to deduce consequences *from* it, but it would not add anything to show that it was also logically presupposed by our initial belief, since we have no reason to think that that belief itself is true. If instead one thinks the point is to ascend to ever-greater truth by tracing back the logical conditions of our beliefs as far as they will go (assuming for some reason that these initial beliefs themselves can be trusted), then it is unclear why one would also need to reason back *down*. The movement in both directions makes perfect sense, however, if it is understood instead as a strictly immanent test of the coherence of the explanatory assumptions to which our initial belief tacitly commits us. Then we would indeed need to reason back to even the deepest assumptions our belief requires us to accept, and to show that other consequences that follow from these assumptions do not, in fact, contradict our initial belief. This interpretation is supported by Plato's language elsewhere, where he consistently describes the reality of the ideas not as self-evident but to the contrary, as something that must be *posited*:

> This is how I proceeded: every time *hypothesizing* the account which I judge strongest, and then whatever seems to me to accord [*sumphōnein*] with it—with regard to causes or to anything else—*I posit* [*tithēmi*] *to be true*, and whatever does not as not true. . . . I propose to go back to those familiar notions of ours and to begin from these, *hypothesizing the existence* of beauty in itself and goodness and magnitude and all the rest of them. *If you grant this and agree* that they exist, I hope with their help to explain causation to you, and to find a proof that soul is immortal. (*Phaedo* 100a–b, emphases mine)

Similarly at *Republic* 507b–509a, Socrates says that we "posit" [*etithēmi*] intelligible ideas like that of "the beautiful" and "the good" as conceptual unities in order to make sense of our everyday beliefs that particular things are beautiful or good, and that it is because it plays this role that the idea of the good "must certainly [be understood] as being the cause of knowledge and truth." Why are we justified in this positing? Not because we have direct insight into the truth of

---

[34] I agree with Fine that *anamnēsis* is a metaphor and elenctic critique the only genuine route to knowledge (*Plato on Knowledge and Forms*, 44–65). There is a good deal of textual evidence for this claim, including the fact that the examples of recollection provided in *Meno* are actually of elenctic questioning; in addition, Plato insists throughout *Republic* that "the power of dialectic alone" can reveal truth, access to which is "in no other way possible" (533a). I also agree with Jonathan Lear, "Myth and Allegory in Plato's Republic," in *The Blackwell Guide to Plato's Republic*, ed. Gerasimos Santas (Malden, MA: Blackwell, 2006), 25–43, that key allegories including the divided line and the cave are best understood as immanent critiques of the supposition that visual perception and received opinion are reliable measures of truth, presented in the very form of figurative myth itself. As such, they are at

ideas, but because "if anyone does not allow that ideas of things exist, or does not distinguish an idea for each one of these, he will have nowhere toward which to turn his thought but, denying that the idea of each thing is always the same, in this way he will completely destroy the capacity for all dialogue" (*Parmenides* 135b–c).

The *archē anhupothetos*, then, turns out to be equivalent to the doctrine of ideas itself, namely, the assumption that it must be possible to justify our particular beliefs as consequences of some general definitions that do not change with opinion, personal interest, or the vantage point of the observer but "always remain the same in all respects" (*Republic* 479e).[35] These conceptual standards must be "perfect" and "essential" in the sense that they provide *final and unique criteria*; a claim to knowledge incompatible with such criteria can only be incoherent, since it must sooner or later beg the question and thus collapses into mere belief (which is the point Fine and Gentzler seem to overlook).[36] Within the system of ideas, finally, the idea of the good plays a special role in representing the ultimate logical coherence of all other ideas under its umbrella *and* the uniqueness of this entire system's claim to truth.[37] In this way, then, we can see how tracing out the internal logic of Socrates's demand for general definitions allows us to arrive at and justify "positing" the doctrine of ideas. The methodological discussion in *Republic* lays bare the underlying logical structure to which we already commit ourselves in questioning the truth of our beliefs, the same structure that elenchus reveals in practice, and which makes elenchus work. That this continuity is real appears furthermore to be signaled by the otherwise surprising fact that Plato's terms of art for the ideas in the middle and late dialogues—*eidos* and *idea*—are the very terms Socrates had already used as early as the aporetic dialogue *Euthyphro* to describe the general definitions he was seeking (5d, 6d–e).

If there remains any doubt that the ideas are best understood as continuous with elenchus, rather than as a freestanding alternative to it, Plato explains in *Republic VII* that dialectical method must be "placed at the top of [all] the studies like a coping stone" because:

> Unless one can distinguish the idea of the good and separate it out from everything else in argument, and *make it through all elenctic refutations*

---

least compatible with my argument and likely provide it further support, although the detailed textual work required to make this case is more than can be included here.

[35] Note the elenctic argument for this conclusion, from 479a.

[36] I take it that this is the point of Plato's insistence that "an imperfect measure cannot be the measure of anything" (504c) and also of the claim that knowledge can only be of what perfectly (or entirely) *is*, while mere opinion is of what both *is and is not*, that is, that which is only on some contingent view, but unlike an idea does not "always remain the same in all respects" when considered across all contending points of view (476e–479e).

[37] Paul Natorp, *Plato's Theory of Ideas: An Introduction to Idealism* (Sankt Augustin, Germany: Akademia, 2004), describes this as "the law that objects are to be grounded in law," *viz.*

[*pantōn elenchōn dieksiōn*] as if in battle, being eager to *argue in elenchus* [*elenchein*] *not in terms of opinion but of being*,[38] and comes through all this with the argument still standing; you will say that he does not know either the good itself, or any other good? (534b–d, emphases mine)[39]

"Yes," we are assured, "by Zeus."

Rightly understood, then, Plato's ideas are not freestanding metaphysical certainties to which we could ever have direct access. Quite to the contrary, and much more radically, Plato's claim is that the only knowledge that can ever be certain or objective is knowledge of those constraining conditions of possibility logically presupposed in the elenctic criticism of every self-evident claim to "know." The only way to knowledge is through critical debate, dialectic, and the immanent refutation of alternatives (533a). But specific criteria for discriminating among positive judgments can still be provided, by working out the conceptual conditions of possibility that any generally and consistently defensible judgment would have to meet in order to survive such criticism. That is what the doctrine of ideas does. To miss the essential mediation of the ideas by critical method—as Neoplatonists and others have done for thousands of years—is to miss the entire point and force of the argument. As the following chapters show, Kant and Hegel both recognized the promise of this critical sort of alternative to dogmatism on the one hand and to relativism on the other, despite their objections to some of Plato's more specific views. Appreciating what distinguishes this approach from the other two will be the key to understanding what Kant and Hegel are really arguing, and why it is a mistake to take them in a dogmatic or "metaphysical" fashion. And as Part Two of the book will show, it will also be the key to understanding the kind of critical engagement with the views of parties in democratic struggle a historical and Socratic theory invites one to take up.

---

the logical demand for coherence and uniqueness at the most general level, encompassing all more particular truths (189–201).

[38] That is, on the regulative assumption of some "objective" criterion uniquely favoring one view over others.

[39] The passage goes on to contrast this methodological view directly with one grounded in the self-evidence of the ideas: "but if he somehow lays hold of some phantom-image [*eidōlou*] of [the idea of the good in some other way], he lays hold of it by opinion [*doxēi*] and not by knowledge [*epistēmēi*], and dreaming and dozing through his present life, before awakening here he will arrive in Hades and fall completely asleep?" (534c–d). I do not consider "distinguishing the idea of the good... in argument" in this quotation to be a step separate from elenchus, because elenchus always proceeds, even in the early Socratic dialogues, by demanding an explanatory definition that holds up under questioning.

3

Kant's Critique of Morality

Now that we have seen how antifoundational argument is possible, we may consider how it can be put to use in moral and political theory. Kant's ethics are usually understood as an endeavor par excellence to ground morality on solid rational foundations.[1] But this, I will argue, misconstrues both Kant's place in the history of political thought and how one ought to understand his central concepts including autonomy and the categorical imperative. It wrongly assimilates Kant to the sort of Wolffian rational natural law he went out of his way to contest (*G* 4:390–1, 4:443, *MS* 5:40–1), and ignores the radical break with traditional metaphysics Kant emphasized by calling his philosophy a "critique." This continues to matter also for contemporary theory, because both Kantians and

---

[1] This holds for both supporters and critics. In *A Theory of Justice*, Rawls described Kant as relying on human nature (1971, 151–7), but his later "constructivist" Kant appeals to a foundation in convention; "Kantian Constructivism in Moral Theory," *The Journal of Philosophy* 77, no. 9 (1980): 515–72; and "Themes in Kant's Moral Philosophy," in *Kant's Transcendental Deductions*, ed. Eckart Förster (Stanford, CA: Stanford University Press, 1989), 81–113. Habermas describes his own "post-foundational" discourse ethics as an alternative to Kant's two-world "metaphysics"; *Moral Consciousness and Communicative Action* (Cambridge, MA: MIT Press, 1990), 203–4. Henry Allison's *Kant's Theory of Freedom* (Cambridge, UK: Cambridge University Press, 1990) and *Kant's Groundwork for the Metaphysics of Morals: A Commentary* (Oxford: Oxford University Press, 2011), Karl Ameriks's *Kant's Theory of Mind*, 2nd ed. (Oxford: Clarendon Press, 2000), and Paul Guyer's *Kant's Groundwork for the Metaphysics of Morals* (New York: Continuum, 2007), all take Kant to seek foundations but suggest he failed to find them. Barbara Herman's *The Practice of Moral Judgment* (Cambridge, UK: Cambridge University Press, 1996) grounds Kant's ethics in a teleology of the unconditioned good. Christine Korsgaard's *Creating the Kingdom of Ends* (Cambridge, UK: Cambridge University Press, 1996) and *The Sources of Normativity* (Cambridge, UK: Cambridge University Press, 1996) attribute a "value-conferring" role to "humanity" and "practical identity." Her more recent work focuses instead on "integrity" as a condition of agency; *The Constitution of Agency: Essays on Practical Reason and Moral Psychology* (Oxford: Oxford University Press, 2008) and *Self-Constitution: Agency, Identity, and Integrity* (Oxford: Oxford University Press, 2009). She rightly sees that Kant was looking for necessary presuppositions rather than *freestanding* foundations, but continues to seek an extra-moral ground in a theoretical account of agency to show why we have to be moral; I discuss our differences later. Allen Wood follows Korsgaard, in part, in his *Kant's Ethical Thought* (Cambridge, UK: Cambridge University Press, 1999) and *Kantian Ethics* (Cambridge, UK: Cambridge University Press, 2008), but in the latter more clearly characterizes his view as a "foundational model"

their critics commonly take Kant to hold that morality means obeying reason or expressing our rational nature. For some reason or other, we are obliged to be "rational" or to develop our rational nature and Kant's arguments are meant to work out what being "rational" requires. But this was Wolff's simpler view that Kant came to reject. What Kant thought instead was that when we ask if an act is moral, what we are really asking is whether one could fairly say we had done "wrong" either by doing it or failing to—that we had violated some sort of obligation of a moral kind. Now the key to Kant's view is that just because there can be no natural, rational, or theological foundation for any moral obligations whatsoever, the only sort of act that may rightly be reproached as immoral is one that contradicts the very concept of a moral obligation as such. To call *that* sort of action "moral" would be absurd; it would be to contradict oneself. And that is all the categorical imperative means—it simply lays out the logical conditions an act must not contravene if calling it "moral" is to be anything but nonsense. It is a strictly Socratic sort of argument.

It is important to see what Kant had done in this way to morality. He had not simply placed freedom or our rational capacity to set ends at its center, or even the notion that we must develop our rational capacities in a consistent way.[2] This was all Wolff and commonplace (if not universally accepted) in late-eighteenth-century Germany, but Kant suffered a crisis of faith in the Leibnizian metaphysics underpinning this sort of rational natural law, under the influence of a skepticism he associated with both the ancient Pyrrhonists and Hume, and which famously awoke him from his "dogmatic slumber."[3] It was in working out a response to this sort of skepticism from inside that he

---

(54–5) which takes "humanity" as the "fundamental value" that "grounds the supreme principle of morality" (85). Kant's critics regularly attack him for his foundationalism. Ian Hunter charges that "[d]espite Kant's claim that his philosophy is not based on a conception of human nature... it is indeed based on a moral anthropology... of man as a self-determining intelligence... and it [derives]... norms through... reflection on what is required for the governance of man as a being with a certain kind of nature"; "Kant's Political Thought in the Prussian Enlightenment," in *Kant's Political Theory: Interpretations and Applications*, ed. Elisabeth Ellis (University Park: Pennsylvania State University Press, 2012), 181. Bernard Williams complained that Kant's ethics burden one with the "extravagant metaphysical luggage of the noumenal self"; *Ethics and The Limits of Philosophy* (Cambridge, MA: Harvard University Press, 1985), 65. See also Alasdair MacIntyre, *After Virtue*, 2nd ed. (Notre Dame, IN: Notre Dame University Press, 1984); Michael Sandel, *Liberalism and the Limits of Justice* (Cambridge, UK: Cambridge University Press, 1982); William Connolly, *Why I Am Not a Secularist* (Minneapolis: University of Minnesota Press, 1999), 163–77; Bonnie Honig, *Political Theory and the Displacement of Politics* (Ithaca, NY: Cornell University Press, 1993), 18–41; and Raymond Geuss, *Philosophy and Real Politics* (Princeton, NJ: Princeton University Press, 2008)—although Connolly and Honig are careful to qualify their objections.

[2] Cf. Korsgaard, *Self-Constitution*.

[3] 4:260. Kant had in the meantime turned toward the moral sense theory of Shaftesbury and Hutcheson, although he continued to lecture from Baumgarten's Wolffian *Initia philosophiae practicae primae acroamatice*, 3rd ed. (Halle: Carl Hermann Hemmerde, 1760). He would break, too, with the former by his critical period.

eventually developed the distinctive "critical" position that made Kant Kant: In the first *Critique*, Kant described his progress as that from reason's "dogmatic" "childhood," through the necessary step of "skepticism," and finally to reason's "maturity" in "critique" (A761/B789). The first major consequence is that this exploded the entire universe of traditional metaphysics based on tracing moral and theoretical truths back to self-evident first principles after the model of Aristotelian demonstration—which is why Kant's friend and correspondent Moses Mendelssohn called him "the all-demolishing Kant" in the preface to his 1785 *Morgenstunden*.[4] Of course, not everyone accepted Kant's view and even those who did often misinterpreted him on this point, but it was clearly one of the reasons his philosophy had the degree of impact that it did, and was widely recognized by contemporaries as a major break. I will not consider the details of Kant's theoretical philosophy here, although it matters that the broadly parallel argument of the first *Critique* strongly supports my reading of Kant's strategy in the moral theory and is likely incompatible with more familiar, uncritical interpretations.[5]

It is important to see that Kant not only provided an alternate, antifoundational interpretation and defense of morality, but also claimed to have proven the impossibility of every foundation of the traditional sort. The search for such independent final authority—even, importantly, in a "reason" understood as positive and dogmatic rather than as an active, critical faculty—was itself incoherent, because since the notion of moral obligation necessarily implies the freedom to choose whether or not to do the right thing, one cannot consistently hold oneself bound by an obligation that contradicts one's own freedom. In other words, one cannot act morally by obeying commands one has not freely authored for oneself, and that is why Kant thought it "no wonder" that "every previous effort ever undertaken to track down the principle of morality all had to come to nothing," since although "they saw the human being bound by his duty to [moral] laws, it never occurred to them that he was *only* subject to *his own* and yet *general lawgiving*" (G 4:432, emphases in original). This is a very powerful argument against traditional attempts to ground morality in human nature, theology, or directly in rational natural law, just because it is an immanent critique that turns on the notions of obligation and freedom on which those approaches themselves depended. But just for that reason one must

---

[4] *Zermalmenden* shares a root with *mahlen* ("to grind" or "to mill") and conveys the image of crushing into dust. *Moses Mendelssohns gesammelte Schriften*, Vol. 2, ed. Georg Benjamin Mendelssohn (Leipzig: F.A. Brockhaus, 1843), 235.

[5] My view of the first *Critique* broadly agrees with Allison's; see *Kant's Transcendental Idealism*, 2nd ed. (New Haven, CT: Yale University Press, 2004). I also agree with his observation in *Kant's Groundwork* of the parallel between the role of the antinomies and the refutation of heteronomy—justifying Kant's position in each case by ruling out alternatives shown necessarily to contradict themselves (261).

be very careful not to suppose that Kant was agreeing with those views simply because he continued to share some of their language, since his point in key instances was just to turn their own language against them.

To be sure, Kant was not an enemy of every conventional or religious belief. Rather, he claimed like Socrates to have shown common sense and religion their own true principles, rather than to have taught them anything new.[6] But the point of the critique was that Kant denied dogmatic approaches like traditional religion the authority of final judge, because unlike critical philosophy, they were incapable of tying down beliefs with reasons or distinguishing which among them did or did not deserve to be called knowledge. This was perhaps most explicit in the *Religion within the Limits of Mere Reason*, but Kant made the point already in the *Groundwork* (4:408), and spelled out its political implications in texts from "What Is Enlightenment?" to the *Conflict of the Faculties*. Because religion was in no position to judge, Kant insisted on the independence of the philosophical faculty and of public deliberation from religious authority. But he also argued directly against the sort of state paternalism Frederick II had used to justify his own "enlightened" rule, and which was supported particularly by the Wolffian strain of contract theory.[7] As we will see in the next chapter, although the king did retain the right to judge enforceable political obligations, this was not due to any intrinsic authority but only because Kant thought the sovereign's decision must be taken—here, too, on certain conceptual conditions required by reason alone—to represent the will of a self-legislating people.

This points to the second major consequence of Kant's moral critique: his view radically reworked moral philosophy to place the act of judgment front and center. And this changed entirely the meaning of a "moral law." Now Kant did presume that his readers shared a common-sense notion of moral duty, but unlike his predecessors in the German natural law tradition (and most natural lawyers elsewhere), he explicitly entertained the possibility that morality might nevertheless turn out to be "chimerical" (*KrV* A201/B247; *G* 4:402, 4:407, 4:445), and denied that direct perception of the moral law sufficed to justify any determinate content. That is just why all the arguments of the *Groundwork* and the *Critique of Practical Reason* were needed, and why they never began by laying out the content of the moral law—as commonly done in period treatises on natural law, following the broadly scholastic convention of first systematically laying down definitions by distinguishing terms, and then drawing conclusions held to follow.[8] Kant, however, always reasoned *to* the moral law, not in the sense

---

[6] He compares himself on this point to Socrates by name in the *Groundwork* (4:404). Cf. *KpV* 5:8 n.

[7] See Frederick II's anonymously published *Anti-Machiavel, ou Essai de Critique sur le Prince de Machiavel, publié par M. de Voltaire* (The Hague, 1740), Chapter 1.

[8] Cf. Christian Wolff, *Jus naturae methodo scientifica pertractatum*, 8 vols. (Halle, 1740–1748), and *Institutiones juris naturae et gentium, in quibus ex ipsa hominis natura continuo nexu omnes obligationes et jura omnia Deducuntur* (Halle: Renger, 1750); Baumgarten, *Initia*, and *Ius naturae* (Halle: Carl

of proving it from something else but in running up against it as the point past which no further proof was either possible or required (G 4:463, KpV 5:46–50). Rather than beginning from the law Kant began from reflection on the act of moral judgment and on those conditions that *would have to be true if* making and defending a certain sort of judgment were to be possible. The content of the law turns out to be just those conditions and nothing else besides.

This means that the categorical imperative, autonomy, and freedom are all only negative limit-conditions that serve to point out how certain moral judgments may be ruled out because when one thinks through their implications, they turn out to contradict themselves. But these are only conditions we must not contravene in the act of judging. They are not freestanding natural laws whose authority we must obey in lieu of judging for ourselves. Nor is freedom, in particular, a "thing" in the world that might ever be "produced" by a third party.[9] Because all these concepts are principles that make sense and bind us only in and through the act of judging, a valid moral or political judgment must consider not only the principles in isolation but also the act of judgment and who is judging for whom. This attention to the problem of reason's interpretation and the essential mediation of its formal categories by the spontaneous act required to apply them had roots in Kant's engagement with skepticism in the first *Critique*, but it also followed Rousseau's notion of the general will as a way of deriving the content of justice from an analysis of the formal conditions of possibility of any defensibly authoritative judge. And Rousseau had reached that view by taking over some (although, of course, not all) of Hobbes's arguments concerning the need for a sovereign arbiter in response to his own skeptical and political worries over the interpretation of natural law.[10]

An important consequence is that Kant's case for autonomy neither presupposes any question-begging account of human nature or the human good nor seeks to impose any such general view in ways that might do violence to other ways of life. That is indeed what views like Wolff's did, but the point of Kant's critique was just to rule this out as incompatible with the thoroughgoing respect

---

Hermann Hemmerde, 1763); and Gottfried Achenwall, *Juris naturalis pars posterior*, 5th rev. ed. (Göttingen, 1763). Kant also lectured from Achenwall.

[9] The end of "rational nature," that is, freedom, "must be thought of not as an end to be produced [*zu bewirkenden*], but as an independent end, and so *only negatively*, that is, as *never to be acted against* and so never merely as a means, but always *judged in every volition* simultaneously as an end" (G 4:437, emphases added). It is "independent" in the sense of independent of whatever we may want.

[10] Kant drew the parallel quite explicitly in the first *Critique*: "[T]o compel the endless quarrels of a merely dogmatic reason finally to seek peace in some critique of this reason itself and in a lawgiving that grounds itself in this; as Hobbes claimed: the state of nature is a state of injustice and violence, and man must necessarily leave it, to subject oneself to lawful compulsion which limits our freedom only in [requiring] that it could coexist with the freedom of every other and even thereby with the common good" (A752/B780).

for freedom entailed by any consistent notion of morality. Although Kant did retain some of the Wolffian perfectionist framework in his analyses of virtue and imperfect duties, the notable shift in his moral philosophy from the critical period is that he came to limit this analysis strictly within the constraints imposed by the notion of autonomous self-legislation, drawn from the competing and eminently political line of thought running from Hobbes to Rousseau. Those constraints and this political vision, based on an antifoundational, even avowedly "skeptical" method, had to take priority—especially in politics, as Kant would emphasize in the *Metaphysics of Morals* by decoupling justice from virtue, in direct contravention of the Wolffian tradition. Far from presuming a rational consensus on the substance of justice, then, the point of prioritizing the act of judging was just to explore the possibility of moral judgment in the absence of any such positive foundations. When Kant exhorted his readers in "What Is Enlightenment?" to "have the courage to use your *own* understanding" in "all things" and invited them to cast off "established rules and formulas" (8:35–6), when in the *Critique of Judgment* he contrasted the demand to "think for yourself" with the "heteronomy" of "prejudice" and "superstition" (5:294), he was not searching for positive foundations but asking us, like Socrates, to free ourselves from the unwarranted supposition that we can find our way in thought only with the aid of first principles that must not themselves be questioned.[11]

But Kant did continue to think we must be able to justify our moral and political judgments. The reason is that such judgments imply an obligation—in the moral case we want either to say someone else has or has not done wrong or to defend ourselves against potential reproach (even if only from our own conscience), and in the political case we actually mean to say certain obligations should be coercively enforced, just because the freedom of any one requires hindering in this way hindrances to it arising from the acts of others.[12] The aim is not to enforce consistency or obedience to rules for their own sake, but—as the previously cited reference to Hobbes in the first *Critique* suggests—to resolve conflicts we find ourselves facing among competing claims in the name of reason, morality, or justice. And so Kant retained Wolffian terms such as "rational nature" and "humanity"—both referring to the freedom to set one's own ends, which distinguishes persons from things—but refigured them merely as negative limit-concepts that defensible judgments must not contradict. Kant's notion of autonomy, which combines the Greek terms for "self" and "law," identified two such constraints; it held that every binding norm must be both (1) universal and

---

[11] Cf. Hannah Arendt, *Lectures on Kant's Political Philosophy*, ed. Ronald Beiner (Chicago: University of Chicago Press, 1992), 32–40; Tracy Strong, *Politics Without Vision: Thinking Without a Banister in the Twentieth Century* (Chicago: University of Chicago Press, 2012), Chapter 1.

[12] This is why they are unlike claims of taste, *pace* Arendt. Bad taste may be hard to bear, but it is not a crime.

(2) self-imposed. These closely followed the constraints on sovereign lawgiving Rousseau had expressed with the notion of the general will. (*Allgemein* is the German for both "general" and "universal.") A moral judgment that contravenes the requirement of generality by applying to others rules one refuses to apply also to oneself can only be self-serving hypocrisy dressed up as virtue (4:419, 4:424). And a judgment that contradicts one's own freedom or the freedom of others as ends in themselves cannot describe a moral obligation one has any consistent reason to obey, since as Rousseau had pointed out, only free persons may be held morally accountable for their acts.[13] All the formulations of the categorical imperative and the moral law are different ways of expressing these two conditions.

This made possible a new approach to working out what morality requires and in what sense we are bound to be moral. Both are radically antifoundational. What it means for an act to be moral is *just that it may consistently be defended as moral*, and the reason morality binds is that we take its assumptions on ourselves in asking certain sorts of questions about right and wrong—"What ought I to do?," as Kant put it in the first *Critique* (A805/B833). That is, as long as we care about whether or not any of us have any obligations, or wish to judge the actions of others or make any claims in terms of right and wrong, we thereby take up these assumptions the way Socrates's interlocutors had taken on assumptions concerning general definitions and reasons in staking claims to knowledge. The final section of the chapter considers in some detail why we should think this is Kant's view and what sort of challenge is posed by a skeptic who rejects moral justification altogether. But the point here is that this is a distinctive way of thinking about morality that begins from the act of judgment and an interest in defending one's judgments, and does not depend on any sort of external authority to impel us to be moral or teach us what morality means. This will be important particularly for politics because it points to a distinctive way of working though controversies over claims to legitimate authority and obligation that is, in principle, fully compatible with the freedom of a democratic people to determine how they will govern themselves. But because it reframes notions such as humanity, freedom—and as we will see in the next chapter, the ideas of a republican constitution and perpetual peace—not as freestanding realities but as conceptual constraints internal to an act of judgment, if forces one to consider always the active side of judgment irreducible to the concepts it employs and, crucially, who in any given case is actually doing the judging for whom. This last, consummately political question, which was also Hobbes's and Rousseau's, is what contemporary Kantians most often overlook when directly applying

---

[13] That obligation entailed freedom was widely recognized, but that this might serve in this way as a criterion for distinguishing genuine and specious obligations was not. Contrast Baumgarten (*Initia*, 4–5) to Rousseau's case for the absurdity of a contract selling oneself into slavery, targeting Grotius (*CS* I.IV).

principles from Kant's moral or political theories in the manner of the dogmatic natural law that was among the targets of his critique.

Both Kantians and their critics overwhelmingly agree that Kant's is a search for ultimate moral foundations. But a few interpreters have challenged this consensus. Hannah Arendt rightly pointed to parallels between Kant's critical method and Socrates's, but remained so captivated by the standard view of Kant's moral theory that she turned to the discussion of aesthetic judgment in the third *Critique* in an attempt to uncover Kant's "real" theory of politics—a position difficult to defend since Kant had written a political theory of his own.[14] Tracy Strong has recently advanced a thoroughly critical view that, however, also leaves the details of the moral theory to one side, whereas Shalini Satkunanandan has argued that the categorical imperative implies a freedom irreducible to the application of moral rules.[15] Onora O'Neill has done the most in English to argue for an antifoundational understanding of Kant's project.[16] But this remains a decidedly minority view. I build here on this underappreciated line of interpretation by taking on Kant's moral theory directly, showing exactly how its argument works by comparing it to the logic of Socratic elenchus, and drawing out important consequences that will matter for political theory.

Kant and Plato

There is no direct evidence that Kant ever read Plato's dialogues firsthand, but ample evidence exists that he was deeply influenced by secondhand accounts of both an ancient skepticism he associated with Socrates and Plato's doctrine of ideas.[17] Kant's famously ambivalent reception of Plato reflected the limitations

---

[14] Arendt, *Lectures*, 31–9. I think Kant's moral and political theory less opposed to the critical elements Arendt rightly notes elsewhere than she did.

[15] Strong, *Politics*, Chapter 1; Satkunanandan, "The Extraordinary Categorical Imperative," *Political Theory* 39, no. 2 (2011), 234–60.

[16] "The Kantian grounding of reason, as of morality, cannot be foundationalist. Anything that could count as foundations would be transcendent, and so alien. Once we make the Copernican turn we cannot expect any foundations to be available." Onora O'Neill, *Constructions of Reason: Explorations of Kant's Practical Philosophy* (Cambridge, UK: Cambridge University Press, 1989), 64.

[17] On Kant's debts to ancient skeptics, see notably Giorgio Tonelli, "Kant and the Ancient Skeptics," in *Skepticism and Enlightenment*, eds. Richard H. Popkin, Ezequiel de Olaso, and Giorgio Tonelli; trans. John Christian Laursen (Boston: Kluwer Academic Publishers, 1997), 69–98; Michael N. Forster, *Kant and Skepticism* (Princeton, NJ: Princeton University Press, 2008); Antonie Samsom, *Kants Kennis der grieksche Philosophie* (Alphen aan den Rijn, Netherlands: N. Samsom, 1927); and John Christian Laursen, *The Politics of Skepticism in the Ancients, Montaigne, Hume, and Kant* (New York: E.J. Brill, 1992), Chapter 8. On the influence of Plato's idealism, see especially Heinz Heimsoeth, "Plato in Kants Werdegang," in *Studien zu Kants philosophischer Entwicklung*, eds. Heinz Heimsoeth, Dieter Henrich, and Giorgio Tonelli (Hildesheim, Germany: Georg Olms, 1967), 124–43; and Max Wundt, "Die Wiederentdeckung Platos im 18. Jahrhundert," *Blätter für deutsche Philosophie* 15 (1941/1942): 149–58.

of the Neoplatonist-influenced secondhand accounts available to him, notably Brucker, but many of Kant's criticisms targeted what I have argued were actually misreadings of the logic of Plato's position. Kant stood out among his contemporaries in grasping how ideas can be understood not dogmatically but critically, as a response from inside the perspective of the skepticism he associated with Socrates and ancient Pyrrhonists rather than a flight from it.

Kant's general critical argument may be understood in three main steps: the first two effectively recapitulate the stages of *aporia* and *ideas* in Plato, while the third builds on Plato's argument by extending the Socratic demand for justification to the use of the ideas themselves. Like Socrates, Kant begins first by way of doubt, demonstrating that both moral common sense (*Groundwork* I) and theoretical reason (the "Transcendental Dialectic" of the first *Critique*) lose themselves in contradiction unless the suppositions they take for granted are reexamined and provided a critical justification. And like Plato, Kant goes on to suggest that these contradictions can be overcome only if one accepts certain regulative principles that place limits on the range of admissible conclusions, just because they represent the conditions of possibility of any coherent justification whatsoever. Rather than countering the foundationalist arguments of "dogmatists" by arguing from different foundations, Kant proposes instead to submit reason to its own critique, in order to derive evaluative criteria solely from the regulative assumptions of the critical method itself.

Kant's third step goes beyond anything in Plato, but does so by extending the critical logic of Socratic method one step further. For while Plato convicted dogmatic belief of incoherence and proposed a remedy in reason, the argument of Kant's first *Critique* is that reason, too, may fall into self-contradiction unless its presuppositions are provided a critical justification of their own. Kant drew from this three signal consequences. This first led him to distinguish in a way Plato had not between the diverse logics of practical and theoretical reason (or moral justification and empirical explanation), because as the third antinomy showed, the latter entails the regulative assumption of causal determinism, while the former requires to the contrary that of freedom. Second, from this it follows that a coherent defense of moral principles cannot contradict this assumption of freedom, and this served to impose an additional constraint on the practice of moral justification beyond those of consistency, universality, and uniqueness already identified by Plato. Of course, Kant drew this notion of freedom from a natural law tradition closely bound up with Christian theology and not from reflection on Plato, but the point here is how his critical system refigured it not as a principle of theology or even of positive metaphysics, but in Platonic fashion as a necessary hypothesis implied in asking certain sorts of questions or making certain claims. Finally, in both moral and empirical inquiry, although in different ways, Kant's argument opened up a crucial gap between the logic of analytic reasoning from definitions and judgments of objective reality. And this raised the possibility, of central concern to Kant, that the musings of reason might turn out to be nothing more than "chimerical" figures of the brain. One of Kant's central tasks, then, in both the moral theory and the theoretical, was to discriminate among the uses of various types of a priori concepts, in a way Plato had not, in order to show why some of them support valid conclusions, while others lead only to absurdity.

Kant identified his critical project explicitly with Socrates on several occasions. In the preface to the second, 1787 edition of the *Critique of Pure Reason*, he wrote that the work's value for posterity was clear "above all if one takes into consideration the invaluable advantage of putting an end for all future time to all objections against morality and religion in a *Socratic* way, namely by the clearest demonstration of the ignorance of the opponent" (Bxxxi, emphasis in original). He identified himself with Socrates's method in the *Groundwork* (4:404) and the *Metaphysics of Morals* (6:376), and with his pedagogy there (6:411) and in the *Pädagogik* (9:477).

In most cases, however, as in the logic of the antinomies, Kant's more specific debt was to ancient Pyrrhonist skeptics. He repeatedly identified his own "method of doubt" with that of skeptical or "zetetic" inquiry in his precritical period,[18] and several times identified "critique" with skeptical or zetetic method later on.[19] In the *Critique of Pure Reason* itself, he wrote that the argument of the transcendental dialectic supports "the skeptical method," of which it offers "an

---

[18] In his marginal notes to *Observations on the Feeling of the Beautiful and the Sublime*, he identified his "method of doubt" with that of the skeptics, which proceeds by "strengthening the reasons on both sides" of a given argument (20:175). Kant praised skeptical method in *Logik Blomberg* (24:204–18), and endorsed "zetetic" instruction in his "Announcement of the Programme of His Lectures for the Winter Semester 1765–1766" (2:307). As Tonelli observes, the Greek term *zetetic* is a dispositive indication that Kant had in mind not only modern, but also ancient, skeptics (70).

[19] Kant associated "critique" with Socrates in Reflection No. 4457 (c. 1772), where he described the critical method of transcendental philosophy in these terms: "Critique of science and *Organon* of wisdom (which comes more from doing without than acquiring. Socrates)" (17:558). In a marginal note to the paragraph of Meier's *Auszug* on the "methodus Socratica" and "methodus Platonica" (c. 1769–1775), Kant wrote, "dogmatic or critical (in the end skeptical)" (Reflection No. 3373, 16:803). In a Reflection of 1769 Kant suggested that "critique" should be "zetetic, skeptical, problematic" (No. 3967, 17:366), and in another of 1772, he asked, "The idea of metaphysics: is it a critique or a doctrine: is its procedure zetetic or dogmatic?" before answering that "transcendental philosophy is critique of pure reason [*Critick der reinen Vernunft*]" (No. 4455, 17:558). In another c. 1772, he outlined the project of the first *Critique*, describing its second part as "zetetic" (No. 4460, 17:560). Kant considered this skeptical or zetetic tradition to have been "originated" by "a man so famous and so very highly to be respected as Socrates," who showed how "Dogmatists" led themselves into self-contradiction by professing certainty they could not demonstrate (24:207; again at 212). In his lectures on the *Encyclopedia* (c. 1777–1782), Kant explained that when a certain part of knowledge "has a great appearance of truth and thus becomes taken as dogmatic," "only the ancients had already seen that here a skeptical method is the goal: critique" (29:28).This skeptical method of "laying out contradictions" is thus "very necessary" for speculative philosophy (ibid.). The *Jäsche Logic* (1800) described "the skeptical method" as "very useful to the critical procedure" (9:84).

example of its great utility, when one allows the arguments of reason to step out to meet each other in the greatest freedom" (A507/B535). Here, Kant appears to draw on the Pyrrhonist practice of counterposing opposite claims to reach equipollence and freedom from dogmatic illusion.[20] But Kant tended to lump together the Pyrrhonists with the Academic skeptics, including sometimes Plato himself,[21] and more than once named Socrates as the "origin" of the "method of skeptical doubt" further developed by Pyrrho (24:207–8; 24:212; cf. 24:3–4).

Kant's debt to this skeptical tradition was central in sparking the intellectual crisis that awoke him from his "dogmatic slumber" and pointed him to the problem the critical philosophy would later claim to have solved. As Forster points out, Kant twice attributed this awakening to his discovery of the antinomies, which exhibit the equipollence characteristic of Pyrrhonism (12:257–8, 20:319–20). He also more famously cited Hume's influence (4:260). But Hume described his own skeptical arguments as indebted to the ancient Pyrrhonists,[22] and Kant, like many of this contemporaries, associated the two.[23] Kant appears to have considered all these figures part of a common skeptical tradition stretching across the centuries, and he never abjured identification with this tradition, although he did argue that "critique"—which he continued to call "the skeptical method"—need not lead also

---

[20] Cf. Kant's account of the "skeptical method," as contrasted with the "dogmatic," in his lectures on the *Philosophical Encyclopedia*: it is "a method of inquiry... where man first inquires, if something is apodictically certain. The skeptical method is the method of contradiction, through which we seek to find the truth. When someone for instance argues one thing, then one argues the opposite and inquires if it is not perhaps true" (29:27–8). Cf. Sextus Empiricus, *Outlines of Pyrrhonism*, book 1, section xi: "The major principle of the skeptical system is that of opposing to every argument an equal argument; for we believe that from this we end by ceasing to dogmatize" (Cambridge, MA: Harvard University Press, 1976). Forster points to this passage and offers a helpful discussion in *Kant and Skepticism*, Chapter 4. Of course, Kant is not content to rest with *ataraxia* but insists like Socrates in pushing on.

[21] In the *Jäsche Logic*, Kant described the later Academics as "subtle, dialectical philosophers" and skeptics who "follow the first great doubter Pyrrho"; "their teacher Plato himself was the cause of this, in that he presented many of his teachings dialogically, so that reasons *pro* and *contra* were brought forward, without himself ever deciding among them, although he was otherwise very dogmatic" (9:30). Kant did sometimes draw distinctions between Pyrrhonist and Academic skeptics, but not consistently.

[22] David Hume, *Enquiry Concerning Human Understanding* (Oxford: Clarendon Press, 2000), 119–21; cf. *Treatise*, I.IV. On Hume, Pyrrhonian skepticism, and their eighteenth-century reception, see notably the work of Richard H. Popkin, *The Third Force in Seventeenth-Century Thought* (Leiden, The Netherlands: E.J. Brill), 237–41; *The High Road to Pyrrhonism* (Indianapolis: Hackett), 55–78; "David Hume: His Pyrrhonism and His Critique of Pyrrhonism," *The Philosophical Quarterly* 1, no. 5 (1951): 385–407; and Manfred Kuehn, "The Reception of Hume in Germany," in *The Reception of David Hume in Europe*, ed. Peter Jones (New York: Thoemmes Continuum, 2005), 115–30.

[23] Kant's discussion of skepticism running from Socrates through Pyrrho in the *Logik Blomberg* concludes that "in the most recent times, David Hume is especially known as a skeptic," and attributes to him the characteristically Pyrrhonist practice of expounding first the argument on one side of a question, then on the other, in order to demonstrate "the uncertainly of all our cognition

to doctrinal "skepticism" as a final conclusion (9:83–4, 24:205, 208–10, 214–5, 29:28, *KrV* B535).

If the problem that spurred Kant to develop his critical philosophy owed much to ancient skepticism, his solution owed a significant debt to Plato's doctrine of ideas. Not only did he open his discussion of "ideas" in the *Critique of Pure Reason* by invoking Plato's innovation (A313/B370), later described as the original of what he would call an "ideal" (A568/B596), but he had first invoked Plato's ideas in his pivotal 1770 *Inaugural Dissertation on the Form and Principles of the Sensible and Intelligible World*, where he first committed himself to the central noumena/phenomena distinction (2:392) as a way of extricating oneself from otherwise inescapable paradoxes that foreshadow the antinomies and paralogisms of the first *Critique* (2:410–419).[24] This partial breakthrough, he concluded, showed the necessity of embarking on a "search for a method" (2:419), and it was this search that would occupy him through his "silent decade," culminating in 1781 with the publication of the first *Critique*. The *Dissertation* explicitly associated this first appearance of the notion of noumenal perfection with "Plato's ideas" (2:396, 413). During this period, Kant was in close contact with a number of the leading figures of a Plato revival in Germany, including Moses Mendelssohn, whose 1767 adaptation of *Phaedo* Kant takes the trouble to cite and refute by name in the second edition of the *Critique of Pure Reason* (B413–22), and Hamann, who from 1761 owned a copy, in Königsberg, of Ficino's 1590 bilingual edition of Plato's *Opera Omnia*.[25]

Kant also referred to Plato in a famous 1772 letter to Marcus Herz where he first laid out the proposal for *Critique of Pure Reason* (10:131). Although

---

whatsoever" (29:217–8). Significantly, Kant's early exposure to Hume was almost certainly mediated by the self-styled Königsberg Socratic and Humean skeptic, J. G. Hamann. When Kant wrote the *Critique of Pure Reason*, he had access to the aforementioned section I.IV of Hume's *Treatise*, on skeptical doubt, only from Hamann's partial 1771 translation, published anonymously in the *Königsberger Zeitung*. See Keuhn, "Kant's Reception of 'Hume's Problem'," *Journal of the History of Philosophy* 21, no. 2 (1983): 175–93. In 1759, Hamann had published a book of *Socratic Memorabilia* dedicated to Kant and a mutual friend, in response to a private exchange in which Hamann had invoked a skeptical Hume (dubbed "the Attic philosopher") to criticize dogmatic rationalism and make room for a return to Christian faith (Hamann to Kant, 27 July, 1759, printed in Kant's *Schriften*, 10:15). The *Denkwürdigkeiten* closely associated Socrates and Hume (*Sämmtliche Werke, historisch-kitische Ausgabe*, 6 vols., ed. Josef Nadler. Vienna: Herder & Co, 1949–57, 2:73). On Kant and Hamann, see Frederick C. Beiser, *The Fate of Reason: German Philosophy from Kant to Fichte* (Cambridge, MA: Harvard University Press, 1987), 16–43.

[24] In the same section in which Plato first appears, Kant distinguished between the "*elenctic*" or negative and "dogmatic" ends the *intellectualia* may serve, although at that point he considered both valid (2:395).

[25] For Hamann's Ficino, see his 1761 letter to another of Kant's friends, J. G. Lindner, in Hamann, *Briefwechsel*, 7 vols., ed. Authur Henkel et. al. (Frankfurt am Main: Insel, 1956–1979), 2:118. On the larger revival see Heinrich von Stein, *Sieben Bücher zur Geschichte des Platonismus* (Göttingen: Vandenhoeck und Ruprecht, 1862); Wundt, *Wiederentdeckung*; and Elena Polledri, "Friedrich Höderlin e la Fortuna di Platone Nel Settecento Tedesco," *Avevum* 74, no. 3 (2000): 789–812.

Kant criticized Plato's recourse to a "prior spiritual intuition of the divine" to ground the objectivity of the ideas, the reference shows that Kant was at the time looking for a better solution than (what he took to be) Plato's own to the problem he thought Plato had also been trying to solve. Looking back on this period in two essays written in the 1790s, Kant went so far as to claim that Plato "without a doubt" had first posed what he elsewhere famously called the central question of his own critical system: "How are synthetic a priori propositions possible?" (8:391; cf. 20:323–4, 4:276, *KrV*, B19).

Kant's well-known criticisms of Plato's doctrine of ideas support, rather than contradict, the thesis of its importance for him. Kant's primary target was always an image of Plato as a mystic who grounds the objectivity of ideas in recollection of an "intellectual intuition" of the divine, whereas Kant insisted on the need for a reasoned justification of the sort he provided for transcendental idealism by showing it to be the only solution to the antinomy of pure reason. But this view of Plato, dominant for centuries under the influence of Neoplatonist and syncretist Christian interpreters, misunderstood Plato's position, mistaking his elaborate metaphorical illustrations of certain doctrines for the arguments meant to justify them. In fact, as I argued in the last chapter, Plato provided just the sort of indirect and elenctic justification Kant demanded (in so many words at *Parmenides* 135b–c). Here, it may matter that Kant's familiarity with Plato was likely based largely on secondary sources like Brucker, who dismissed Platonism as a whole for its fanciful mysticism and incoherence (and against whose criticism Kant famously defended Plato's *respublica noumenon* in the first *Critique*, A316–7/B372–4).[26] So there is more than a bit of irony in the fact that Kant distinguished his notion of ideas from Plato's in the *Critique* with the qualification that "it is not at all unusual . . . that in comparing the thoughts an author expresses about his subject, he is even better to be understood than he has understood himself, in that having defined his concept with insufficient precision, he therefore from time to time spoke or even thought contrary to his own intention" (A314/B370). Kant had certainly understood Plato, if not better than himself, at least better than Kant's sources.

But as I explained above, even where Kant really differed from Plato, his argument extended rather than repudiated Plato's central methodological insight. Kant hardly rejected the general strategy of analyzing the a priori conditions of any possible justification; what he did is to distinguish where Plato did not among

---

[26] Iacob Brucker, *Historia critica philosophiae*, 2nd ed. (Leipzig: Heirs of Wiedemann & Reich), 1766–1767. On evidence pertaining to the likelihood of Kant's exposure to originals, see Samsom, *Kants Kennis*. Kant never cites detailed arguments from Plato's texts. The *Critique* did not use the term "respublica noumenon," but in *The Contest of the Faculties*, he identified his own theory of the state as "a Platonic *ideal* (*respublica noumenon*)" (7:91) and he had referred to the notion also in the 1770 *Dissertation* (2:396).

different types of a priori concepts (categories from ideas, ideas from ideals) appropriate to different sorts of justifications (empirical versus moral, elsewhere also aesthetic).[27] He lauded Plato for rightly perceiving the central role of ideas in morality, and even credited him for drawing attention to the rational form implicit in the experience of nature (A315–9/B371–5). Where he broke with Plato's idealism is in distinguishing the two types of justification, and limiting one to the objects of experience and the other to the supersensible, whereas "before metaphysics had yet reached the point of making this distinction, it had intermingled ideas, which can only have the supersensible as their object, with *a priori* concepts, to which objects of experience are appropriate, in that it simply never occurred to it that the origin of these ideas could be different from that of other pure *a priori* concepts" (20:319). On the one hand, then, Kant argued against mystical Neoplatonist misinterpretations of Plato's argument. At times he suggested that this saved Plato's core message from his own excesses, since "the lofty language that served him in [the empirical] field is surely quite susceptible of a milder interpretation, and one that accords better with the nature of things" (*KrV*, A314/371), while at others he blamed Neoplatonists themselves for offering up a mystical "*pseudo-Plato*" that "makes Plato's idea into an idol" (8:399).[28] On the other hand, Kant extended the logic of Plato's general antifoundational strategy still further in light of a distinction among the a priori concepts that Plato called ideas, and claimed in this way to rescue the possibility of justification from its own antinomies.

The key point is that for Kant, as for Plato, the turn to "ideas" or "the synthetic a priori" extends the skeptical method by reflecting on those assumptions that lead dogmatic views into hopeless self-contradiction, and therefore the conceptual conditions any possible view would have to meet in order to avoid a similar fate. It is not a search for new dogmatic foundations. The following sections consider the arguments of the *Groundwork* and the *Critique of Practical Reason* to show that they in fact proceed this way.

The *Groundwork*

The *Groundwork*'s central argument has three main parts, corresponding to the work's three chapters. *Groundwork* I shows the need for a philosophical account of morality, one that demonstrates logical necessity by considering a

---

[27] This is nicely spelled out in the posthumous *Prize Essay* at 20:318–20, where he also shows why this duality within reason demonstrates the need for a critical justification of the objectivity of rational concepts themselves.

[28] It is thus that Plato famously became, for Kant, the "father of all mysticism in philosophy"—but this "however, not through any fault of his own (since he applied his intellectual intuition only backwards, to clarify the possibility of a synthetic *a priori* knowledge, not forwards, in order to extend the range of ideas that might be interpreted by divine reason," unlike later self-styled "Platonists" (8:398).

priori relations among ideas, rather than relying uncritically on the authority of conventional or religious examples. *Groundwork* II then poses the hypothetical question: What principle could possibly qualify as a principle of morality, *if* morality were to have any coherent meaning at all? Kant first argues that any moral principle must be compatible with the general notion of a necessary obligation, which is what morality must presuppose if it is to bind us as it claims to. Then he argues by elimination to the five different formulations of the categorical imperative, on the grounds that any other principle would contradict that general notion. Kant is very explicit that these first two chapters are "merely analytic" and do not provide any positive foundation that proves morality true (4:445). They only show what we would have to suppose *if* we were to avoid contradicting ourselves in making moral claims.

Finally, *Groundwork* III purports to show why morality indeed binds us and is more than a "chimerical idea" (ibid.). Kant's argument is essentially practical: we necessarily presuppose freedom and the moral law when we ask ourselves, from the standpoint of a moral agent, "What ought I to do?" Although Kant is often wrongly taken as attempting to provide some further positive foundation, the rest of the chapter is actually aimed to the contrary at showing how a moral bond can be understood, rebutting the charge that the freedom it supposes violates other requirements of reason, and showing up the demand for any further foundation as itself incoherent and therefore reasonably rejected. The argument is entirely antifoundational and Socratic all the way down, and this matters greatly for how its conclusions ought to be understood. Although many interpreters agree with some parts of this reading, however, nearly all of them reject other parts and fail to see how all of them fit together into a powerful elenctic whole—typically, because they insist on trying to uncover a positive foundation sooner or later somewhere along the way. They do this despite the fact that this requires both reading actively against the grain of the overall structure of the argument, which proceeds indirectly and by elimination, and also discounting Kant's repeated explicit claims to have provided no such final ground. The work's final lines conclude that although "we indeed do not understand the practical unconditioned necessity of the moral imperative, we do comprehend however its *incomprehensibility*, which is all that can fairly be required of a philosophy which strives in its principles up to the very boundary of human reason" (463, cf. *KpV* 5:46, emphasis in original). One may be tempted to discount all this if one does not see how a strictly negative argument by elimination could possibly justify positive conclusions of the sort Kant claims to have defended. But if one is familiar with the logic of Socratic elenchus (as further developed by Plato through the middle idealist dialogues), then all of Kant's claims here make sense. As we saw in the last section, Kant understood this sort of argument exceptionally well (and had built the whole *Critique of Pure*

Reason on it), and he made a point of comparing his argument to Socrates's explicitly in the *Groundwork* (as well as in the first *Critique*). I will consider the *Groundwork*'s three chapters in turn.

Groundwork I is meant, as its title suggests, to justify the "transition from ordinary rational knowledge of morality to philosophical." This explicitly Socratic argument is meant to show why moral philosophy is necessary, in order to solve a problem moral common sense cannot reliably solve on its own: if *"the common reason of humankind"* is to "escape perplexity due to claims on both sides, and not to run the risk, through the ambiguity into which it easily falls, of losing all genuine moral principles," it finds itself "impelled to go forth from its sphere and take a step into the field of *practical philosophy*" (4:405, emphases in original).[29] Seeing the point of this argument can be tricky, because Kant insists on the one hand on denying moral common sense final authority to judge, on the other that he is only teaching it what it already knows. But this, as we have seen, is exactly what Socrates did in texts like *Meno*, where he denies "teaching" anything to the slave boy while eliciting from him geometrical truths (82d, 84c–d). Kant's point is that although moral common sense—and the Christian religion intimately bound up with it for his primary audience—has some correct beliefs, it is incapable of tying these down with reasons or reliably distinguishing between correct and incorrect ones. (Compare the parallel thesis of *Religion*.) Only philosophy can do this because it demands general definitions and trades on the necessary logical relations among concepts, whereas common sense thinks only in examples whose authority it can take on faith. But this need for definitions and justifications is already implicit in common sense and religion because they rely on the concept of "duty" to make moral claims about what people should and should not do. Kant's argument very nearly parallels the way Socrates had showed naive interlocutors' claims to knowledge already tacitly to imply a need for defensible general criteria for distinguishing knowledge from nonknowledge.

The way Kant puts this is to claim on the one hand that "common human reason" already has the categorical imperative as a principle that it "has actually always before its eyes and uses as the standard in its judgments," and that "it would be easy to show how ... with this compass in hand, it knows very well how to distinguish in every case that comes up what is good, what bad, what

---

[29] "Perplexity" here translates *Verlegenheit*, a term Kant uses repeatedly at key points to describe the sort of conflict of reason with itself that had been emphasized by ancient skeptics. Cf. the very opening lines of the Preface to the first edition of the *Critique of Pure Reason*: "Human reason has the peculiar fate that in one species of its knowledge, it should be burdened with questions it cannot turn away—since they are posed to it by the nature of reason itself—but which it also cannot answer, since they exceed all the capacity of human reason. Reason falls into this perplexity [*Verlegenheit*] through no fault of its own.... [yet nevertheless, by its own efforts] it plunges itself into obscurity and contradiction...." (A vii/4:7). The German *Verlegenheit* is commonly used to translate the Greek *aporia*.

in accord with duty and what contrary to it, if one only made it attend to its own principle, as Socrates did, without teaching it in the least anything new" (4:403–4). But he nevertheless thinks it necessary to write the moral philosophy contained in the *Groundwork* and the *Critique of Practical Reason* because on the other hand, innocence, though lovely, is easily misled [*verführt*], and so even wisdom "needs science, not to learn from it, but to secure access and durability for its precepts" (4:404–5).[30] So common human reason is compelled for "practical reasons" to go "*out* of its own sphere" and into that of "*practical philosophy*," in order to escape the perplexity of the "*natural dialectic*" that arises because common sense cannot tie down its beliefs, "to receive there information and precise instruction concerning the source of its principle and its correct definition [*Bestimmung*]" (4:405, first emphasis mine, others in original).

It is easy to see how this can be mistaken for a foundationalist argument. But the key is to see that all it actually does is to furnish the concept of "duty" (see 4:406), which, because it implies the notion of categorical necessity, points to the need for a philosophical argument in terms of a priori concepts, which is the only sort that could possibly account for the requisite necessity. This is why the argument begins entirely afresh in *Groundwork* II from an analysis of the concept of a categorical imperative, rather than continuing to proceed directly from any of the substantive premises introduced in *Groundwork* I, which might otherwise have been taken for positive foundations (such as the claims that a good will is the only thing imaginable that is good without qualification, or that nothing is superfluous in nature). It also explains why Kant himself should argue from examples at the beginning of *Groundwork* I (4:393–4), before insisting at the start of *Groundwork* II that "one cannot worse advise morality than when one wishes to derive it from examples" (4:408). All this makes perfect sense once one sees that Kant's aim in the first chapter is to engage common sense on its own terms, to show that it already depends on a concept (duty) that will require general criterial definitions and justifications of a sort for which it does not yet see the need. The chapter first establishes the need for a general, unqualified standard (the "idea of the absolute worth of a mere will" 4:394—note the Platonic term), then argues by analysis to the concept of duty (4:397) and from that to the notion of acting purely from respect for the law (4:400), and finally by elimination to the first formulation of the categorical imperative (4:402). This is a Socratic argument, as Kant explicitly points out at the chapter's end. But just for that reason, because it relies at several points on beliefs Kant expects his readers to share but that have not been justified, he thinks it necessary to

---

[30] Cf. *Meno* (97e–98a): "True opinions are a fine possession and perform every kind of good so long as they stay in place; they do not like to stay long [however], but run away from a man's mind, and so are of no great value until they are tied down with reasons.... When they are tied down, first they become knowledge, and second, they stay in place."

go on in *Groundwork* II to provide a freestanding argument from the notion of a categorical imperative to its particular formulations, based entirely on necessary a priori connections among ideas, and in *Groundwork* III finally to show why morality is justified and binding in the first place, and not merely a "phantom of the brain" (4:445).[31]

Consider next *Groundwork* II. As mentioned above, the argument has three main parts. The first recapitulates the substance of the preceding case that morality cannot be defined through examples or empirical generalizations, but only by a general explanatory definition (or "idea") justified on a priori grounds, since only such arguments can provide the *"absolute necessity"* requisite "if one does not want to deny the concept of morality of all truth and relation to any possible object" (4:408). The next part then elaborates the notion of logical necessity implied by an "imperative" and distinguishes a "categorical" imperative, which would hold independent of our pursuit of any particular end, from a merely "hypothetical" one based on the notion that one who wills the ends also wills the means. The third part then goes on to derive the five formulations of the categorical imperative by elimination, by showing that they express the only possible principles consistent with the general notion of a categorical imperative, just because they abstract from any possible facultative ends that might otherwise be thought to ground an obligation. (Although there has been much debate about it, I take Kant at his word when he says he means all these ways of representing the moral principle as logically equivalent and mutually entailing, 4:436.) In the course of this, Kant repeatedly considers four examples but is very clear that these are not meant to be arguments but only illustrations of the general principles already defended on a priori conceptual grounds. The chapter then concludes by contrasting Kant's notion of "autonomy of the will as the supreme principle of morality" with those "heteronomous" views that comprise, he writes, every previous theory ever devised (4:440).

There are four main points to see. First, the argument is entirely and avowedly antifoundational. Kant emphasizes no fewer than half a dozen times that the chapter is meant only to show what morality *would have to mean, if it were to mean anything consistent*, so arguing exactly in the way I have suggested that Plato used the notion of "hypothesis" in the middle dialogues to work out the conceptual

---

[31] The literature on *Groundwork* I is radically divided and hardly knows what to make of its relation to the rest of the text, whereas a Socratic reading makes perfect sense of it. See, for instance, the range of competing views in Nelson Potter, "The Argument of Kant's *Groundwork*, Chapter 1," in *Kant's Groundwork of the Metaphysics of Morals: Critical Essays*, ed. Paul Guyer (Lanham, MD: Rowman & Littlefield, 1998), 29–50; Paul Guyer, *Kant on Freedom, Law, and Happiness* (Cambridge, UK: Cambridge University Press, 2000); Wood, *Kant's Ethical Thought*, 48–9; and Allison, *Kant's Groundwork* (8, 149).

conditions of any possible claim of truth (4:420, 4:421, 4:425, 4:431, 4:440, 4:444–5). If there is to be any case that Kant nevertheless means to provide a positive foundation in the end, it will have to depend entirely on the arguments of Chapter 3, considered later. Second, this means that Kant is very rigorous (and indeed successful) in providing a definition of morality that depends on taking for granted no positive conception of human nature, natural human ends, conventional authorities, religious doctrines, or substantive propositions of "metaphysics" or rational natural law.[32] This is no small thing because it had been widely supposed—and often still is—that without some sort of positive authority of this sort, morality could have no meaning and would fail to pick out any determinate obligations at all. Kant was doing something quite radical, then, in arguing that it is possible to work out entirely by immanent reflection on the conceptual assumptions entailed in moral judgment a determinate criterion for distinguishing which judgments are and are not defensible. Here, too, the move very nearly paralleled Plato. And indeed, of the constraints Kant came up with—universality and self-imposition—the first was the same one Plato too had found when asking a similar question concerning the nature of the virtues.

Third, this means that the way to understand the categorical imperative is as holding that *what makes an action moral is just whether or not it can be defended consistently as moral*, and nothing else besides. This clears up familiar confusions about the role of "contradiction" in Kant's theory. Kant is not saying we have some independent obligation not to contradict ourselves—either as a condition of the "integrity" of an agent or as a general rule of reason or because then the consequences will be bad or any of the other ways of providing an external theoretical warrant for this demand. The point is just that if we cannot *call what we are doing "moral" without contradicting ourselves*, then a definition of morality that calls it moral anyway will make morality into nonsense.[33] This is the worry Kant articulates over and over again when he identifies certain conceptual presuppositions of

---

[32] Kant uses "metaphysics" to mean a priori or conceptual, but that does not make his position "metaphysical" in the sense his critics charge.

[33] Hence, the key to the "contradiction in the will" is that "*if we considered everything from one and the same viewpoint, namely that of reason*, then we would meet with a contradiction in our own will, namely that a certain principle should be objectively necessary as a general law and subjectively not apply generally, but to allow exceptions" (4:424, emphasis added). The reason we need to consider things *from that perspective* is that we are already asking a moral question about what can and cannot be justified, and so the point is not that it is impossible to will this but that the fact that we fall into self-contradiction in trying to justify it on assumptions we ourselves have made shows that we are speaking nonsense. What it really shows is that we are not making a moral claim at all but only trying to make an exception for ourselves that allows us to pass off self-interest in moral language—as the preceding sentence makes clear. There is nothing mysterious about this standard Socratic argument. Cf. the lying promise at 4:422 (at 4:403 this remains implicit), and Kant's examples of absurd moral claims in *KpV* 5:25–6.

moral obligation as such and argues that if one were to contravene them, it will be impossible to find a principle of morality anywhere (4:408, 4:428, 4:433).

Fourth, it is crucial to Kant that his notion of autonomy requires moral maxims to count as actually self-imposed. This is the key difference between his view and the Wolffian notion of a moral requirement to develop one's essential human powers as a free and rational being, and Kant thinks it important enough to lump the latter view in the camp of "heteronomous" theories (4:443). Kant's language in the *Groundwork* is clear and strong: human beings have a certain "dignity," not insofar as one is merely *subject* to the moral law, but only "insofar as one is at the same time with respect to it *lawgiving* and only therefore subject to it" (4:440, emphasis in original). "Dignity," that is, depends logically on the act of giving oneself law; it is not an independent foundation in lieu of that lawgiving (cf. 4:436). This is a difficult but important point. It is true that one's judgments must not contradict the limiting condition of respect for "humanity" or "rational nature" both in oneself and in others, just as they also must not contradict the condition of generality. If they are not general, we cannot say that they are morally necessary, since if a moral obligation applies to you, it must also apply to me (insofar as we are similarly situated in relevant respects). Otherwise, we are making exceptions for ourselves and passing off our own inclinations as "morality." And if our judgments violate respect for freedom, they cannot be seen as self-imposed and therefore binding. The reason we need to respect the freedom of *others* and not only our own, however, is because of the generality condition—since we are asking what sort of *general moral obligation* is consistently defensible as such, it follows that if we must respect freedom at all, we must respect everyone's freedom. To respect only our own would be either hypocritical or absurd *as a moral claim*.

But the subtler point is that since these constraints hold only inside an act of judgment, what needs to be consistently defensible is not the principles alone but the entire act. In the moral case, when I judge in the first instance for myself, my maxims will be actually self-legislated just in case they meet the formal conditions, since I have ipso facto also chosen them. I can also judge others by putting myself in their shoes, but this does not warrant coercing them in line with what they should have judged. At most I could voice my view, but Kant is concerned above all in the moral case with the first-personal question "What ought I to do?" The gap between idea and application will become very important, however, in politics, where judgments of justice require justifying the coercion of others and it will matter whether it is enough not to violate formal conditions or whether one must also consider who is in a position to judge for whom. As we will see in the next chapter, the view that obligations must count as actually, not only hypothetically, self-imposed will strengthen the case for emphasizing the democratic-leaning elements in Kant's political theory and help to explain why Kant defends there certain otherwise puzzling conclusions.

But it is important to see that he defends this position already in the moral theory. Although it is here easier to miss because it may not change outcomes, it does affect the spirit in which we ought to take Kant's practical philosophy and key notions such as the "moral law." This spirit, I contend, is a broadly Socratic one that places spontaneity of judgment before the authority of any particular rule. The reason we care about principles when we do is only that we care about making and defending certain judgments. This is why autonomy is unlike earlier eighteenth-century rational natural law.

Consider how Kant argues strictly by elimination for all the formulas of the categorical imperative. In most cases this is obvious. After arguing that a categorical imperative cannot depend on any further end (since then morally would only be instrumental to something else we might or might not care about pursuing), Kant arrives at the formula of universal law on the grounds that since a moral law must "contain no condition by which it is limited, *there remains nothing left over* but the universality of a law as such, to which the maxim of the action ought to conform, and which conformity alone the imperative properly represents as necessary" (421, emphasis mine). He immediately emphasizes that this leaves it entirely undecided whether "what one calls duty may be an empty concept" but shows only what "that concept wants to say" (ibid.). The formula of a law of nature only rephrases this formula of universal law. The formula of the kingdom of ends is said to follow from the first, third, and fourth formulas (4:433), and the formula of autonomy to follow from the first and third (4:431), so neither relies on an independent foundation. A second argument for autonomy proceeds again explicitly by elimination. Since we cannot be bound to obey a categorical imperative only by some further "interest," the only possibility left is a law we author for ourselves and to which we bind ourselves of our own free will: in Kant's words, "*if there is a categorical imperative* . . . then it can only command that everything be done from the maxim of one's will as such a [will] that could at the same time have as object itself as legislating universal law; since only then is the practical principle, and the imperative [the will] obeys, unconditional, since it can have no interest as its ground" (4:432, emphasis mine). Any other bond would "turn out every time [in the end to be] conditional and could not at all be appropriate for a moral command" (4:433). That is, we would be unable to find any consistent moral principle anywhere.

The formula of humanity sounds the most like an appeal to a positive foundation, but we know this cannot be Kant's view both because he insists repeatedly later on that he still has not proven morality true and because the different formulas could not have the same logical status, as Kant insists they do, if all the others were only admissible hypotheses and this alone rested directly on a certain first principle. Kant argues that every action logically implies orientation to an end, but no sort of end we are simply free either to take up or not to could ever justify a *categorical* obligation. So again by elimination: "But having posited that there were [*wäre*] something the *existence of which in itself* has an absolute worth, something which as *an end in itself* could be a ground of determinate laws; then in it, and in it alone, would lie the ground of a possible categorical imperative" (4:428). The only possible answer is to take as our end *our very capacity freely to set ends for ourselves*, what Kant variously describes as "humanity" [*Menschheit*], "rational nature" [*vernünftige Natur*], or simply "freedom": "Now I say: the human being and in general every rational being *exists* as an end in itself, *not merely as a means* to be used by this or that will at its discretion; instead he must in all his actions, whether directed to himself or to other rational beings, always be regarded *at the same time as an end*" (4:428). This might read like a positive foundation, but one must note its place in the argument. It is doubly qualified, first by the preceding sentence, "having posited" [*Gesetz aber* ...] that some end exists, and second by the introductory locution "Now I say..." [*Nun sage ich:*], which seems meant to underscore the hypothetical status of what follows.[34] And even this would only count (in the subjunctive) as the ground of a "possible" categorical imperative—Kant does not say it would prove that imperative true. The end of the paragraph drives the point home, because the reason Kant gives for accepting humanity as an end in itself is not that we have any positive reason to think it true, but to the contrary only because "without it nothing of *absolute worth* would be found anywhere" and "if all worth were conditional and therefore contingent, then no supreme practical principle for reason could anywhere be found" (4:428). So the argument here is hypothetical and by elimination, just as for all the other formulas.[35]

Korsgaard's influential interpretation in *Creating the Kingdom of Ends* takes Kant instead to argue that since none of our specific ends can themselves be sources of ultimate value, we must attribute ultimate value to our own ability to set ends and "confer" value derivatively on the ends we choose.[36] But Kant's worry is not that otherwise what we thought had value will turn out not to have

---

[34] O'Neill notes this in *Constructions*, 136; cf. Kant's similar usage at 448.

[35] The recapitulation of the argument at 4:437 makes some of this elenctic logic clearer: "In the idea [*Idee*] of a will good unconditionally and without [the] limiting condition (of reaching this or that end) one must abstract thoroughly from every end to be effected; so the end must here be thought not as one to be effected, but *rather* as an *independent* end, and therefore only negatively, that is, never to be acted against, and thus it must in every volition be judged never merely as a means, but always at the same time as an end. Now this [end in itself] can be nothing other than the subject of all possible ends itself, because this is at the same time the subject of a possible unconditionally good will; *since this [will] can be subordinated to no other object without contradiction [ohne Widerspruch]*" (final emphasis mine, others in original). The claim is that a general "idea" or criterial ("unconditional") definition of the good cannot depend on any other end without contradicting itself, and so one's own freedom to set ends is the only admissible candidate.

[36] 119–24. Cf. Wood, *Kant's Ethical Thought*, 127–32. Wood later distances himself from the "value-conferral" part of the claim (*Kantian Ethics*, 92), but continues to hold that rational nature

any (and why should that not be so?), but that we will not be able to find a moral principle anywhere. In other words, the issue is not tracing back a causal chain to show how certain objects ended up endowed with value, but a wholly conceptual point about the conditions of possibility of a consistent account of moral obligation. Apart from textual considerations, the substantive advantage of this argument is that it does not invalidly conclude from the facts that I value my own freedom and that every other rational agent values hers, that each of us must also therefore value the freedom of the other.[37] At this stage we are simply assuming morality to exist in order to work out what it would have to mean if it did. The rest is supposed to wait for *Groundwork* III. Allison, by contrast, rightly emphasizes that the argument for the formula of humanity proceeds strictly by elimination, and denies finding in the text any "regressive argument" of the sort proposed by Korsgaard and Wood.[38] Although our views here are broadly confluent, however, I do not entirely see how Allison claims to make up for the lack of a universalizing warrant at this point for which he faults Korsgaard and Wood, whereas on my account this is clear because everything follows from the

---

is a fundamental value necessarily presupposed in agency as such, which then provides an independent ground for the principle of morality. I do not think Kant is trying to argue us into morality by showing us we are already committed to it in setting ends as such, nor do I see how one can make up the generalization gap without already starting from inside the moral point of view. The difficulty with reading Kant on analogy to J. S. Mill, I fear, is that for Kant everything turns on providing not only a reasonable interpretation of what we do but also a claim about the a priori necessity of doing so, because otherwise, the concept of obligation we employ would turn out to be chimerical. It is because Mill had no such worries that it would never have occurred to him to write *Groundwork* III.

[37] For criticisms on this key point, see Thomas Nagel in *The Sources of Normativity*, 207; Guyer, *Kant on Freedom*, 151; Allison, *Kant's Groundwork*, 228. When Kant writes at 429 that the existence of rational nature counts as an "*objective* principle" because—as he will show in *Groundwork* III—every rational being must represent its own existence as an end in itself "on the same rational ground that holds for me," his point is only that this positing is a priori necessary for every subject. As he argued before (427), this is a *necessary condition* of any end that might ground a moral imperative, because without such necessity, it should be impossible to account for the claim of any such imperative to bind us categorically. It is not, however, also the reason we must respect humanity not only in our own person, "but also in the person of every other"—*that* follows instead from the distinct consideration that a practical imperative must also have the form of a universal law. The fact that every rational being must respect her own humanity merely *qualifies* the principle of humanity as an "*objective* principle," as Kant writes, "from which, as a highest practical ground, *it must be possible to derive all laws* of the will" (429, final emphasis mine). But that we are concerned to derive *universal laws* follows from the fact that we are assuming for the sake of argument that some moral law exists. Some confusion is invited because 429 points ahead to *Groundwork* III, where it will turn out that the moral law is justified as a practical supposition necessary in the act of judging, but this is precisely not because there is any independent freestanding foundational authority to human nature we are teleologically obligated to obey (as for Wolff), but just because our self-legislating judgments will be inconsistent if they contradict the very freedom to judge we must employ in making them, and inconsistent as *moral* judgments if they apply different standards to others than we apply to ourselves.

[38] Allison, *Kant's Groundwork*, 225.

fact that we are examining the conceptual assumptions of a possible categorical imperative and this contains within it—along with respect for the freedom to judge—also the demand for generality.[39]

Let us turn finally to *Groundwork* III, which is at last supposed to show that morality is more than a phantom of the brain. As I have suggested, this argument has several parts that add up to a valid elenctic justification. Kant first argues that we necessarily assume freedom and the moral law in the act of practical judgment. He then goes on to show how and why it is possible to understand oneself as morally "bound" from the standpoint of an actor making such a judgment. Then he rebuts the objection that the freedom supposed is impossible because it contradicts the determinism of nature. And finally he rejects the demand for any further ground of morality by arguing that demand itself is incoherent. Before looking at the details, consider for a moment what this means.

Kant's claim is that when we take up the standpoint of a moral actor by asking ourselves, "What ought I to do?," we take on certain assumptions just by posing that sort of question. First of all, we must consider ourselves free to act on the answer we come up with—that is, if we think of ourselves simply as impelled by whichever instinct is strongest at a given moment, we cannot give any meaningful answer to the question of what we "ought" to do, nor is there any point it asking it. And so it can never turn out that I "ought," for instance, to treat myself or be treated as a slave; this is ruled out as incompatible with the freedom necessarily presumed in asking the "ought" question in the first place. Less obvious, perhaps, is why my actions also cannot contradict the supposition of a universal law. The reason is that in asking the "ought" question, we are asking something other than "What do I most feel like doing?" or "What is to my personal advantage?" Just because "ought" supposes radical freedom, we must consider ourselves free to choose whether or not to act on any given inclination or interest—otherwise, we are really taking ourselves to be determined by certain desires or ends we have not taken responsibility for choosing (4:446–7), but we cannot do this while claiming to give an answer to what we "ought" to do. Notice that it is not that we are *in fact incapable* of deciding some other way, or even of taking ourselves to have decided some other way, because of some theoretical point about human nature or human agency—of course, we could follow our instincts without thinking about it, or flip a coin, or do whatever someone else tells us to do.[40] But when we ask the "ought" question, pointing out that this is what we had done would not tell us whether we also "ought" to have done it.

---

[39] Allison suggests that "simply put, the claim is that if this is how rational nature, whether in oneself or others, rightly regards itself [as an end in itself], then this is how it ought to be treated," but on its face this seems to recapitulate rather than to solve the problem of the missing normative warrant he rightly points to just before (228).

[40] Contrast Korsgaard, *Self-Constitution*; Wood, *Kantian Ethics*.

This is what it means to say that within this practical standpoint we must consider ourselves as legislating universal law. This does not mean we cannot act on inclinations or must derive all our specific obligations from the abstract notion of law in general. This is only a limit concept, like freedom—all we need to do is to make sure the principle behind our action does not *contradict* the notion of a general law, because if we took a principle like that—"Do whatever makes you happy no matter how it affects other people"—then it would no longer make sense to say we were acting in accordance with any sort of notion of "ought" at all.

Now all this holds only *inside* what I will call "the moral point of view" and what Kant called "practical reason." One will object that it appears one has only presupposed morality in order to show why we should ask about "oughts," and then used this question to justify presupposing a certain view of freedom, and that freedom again to prove morality. And this is exactly the objection Kant himself raises in the famous "circle" passage at 4:449, which suggests that this is indeed how he was thinking. As he points out, "We cannot see in this way that we should consider ourselves as free in acting and so yet also hold ourselves subject to certain laws ... and how this is possible, and therefore *from where the moral law binds*" (4:450). Now interpretation becomes controversial. Most readers suppose Kant means to answer by providing some sort of theoretical ground that shows us why we need to take up this moral point of view in the first place. But although there are passages that may suggest this in isolation, it is exceedingly hard to square with the text as a whole. *After* all the intervening arguments usually taken to provide some sort of theoretical foundation, Kant concludes that "the subjective impossibility of *explaining* freedom is the same as the impossibility of tracking down and making comprehensible an *interest* which the human being could take in moral laws" (4:459-60, emphasis in the original, "*Interesse*" being also the term at 450). He then sums up the chapter:

> Thus the question of whether a categorical imperative is possible can indeed so far be answered, as one can indicate the single presupposition on which it is alone possible, namely the idea of freedom, and also that one can see the necessity of this presupposition, which is sufficient for the *practical use* of reason, that is for conviction in the *validity of this imperative*, and therefore also of the moral law—but how this presupposition itself is possible never permits itself to be seen by any human reason. (4:461, emphasis original)

And although the theoretical use of reason necessarily pushes always for further explanatory grounds, this demand is not always warranted (a core claim of the first *Critique*), and so "it is thus no rebuke to our deduction of the supreme principle of morality, but rather a reproach which one must bring against human reason as such, that it cannot make comprehensible the absolute necessity of an unconditioned practical law (as that of the categorical imperative must be)" (463).[41] Why not? Well, that deduction "cannot be held in suspicion because it does not wish to do so through a condition, namely by means of some interest laid down as ground, because then this could not be a moral law, that is the supreme law of freedom" (ibid.). And we saw that Kant ends the entire work by emphasizing how this means we must accept the "incomprehensibility" of the "practical unconditioned necessity of the moral imperative" (ibid.).

Now all this is rather extraordinarily explicit textual evidence that Kant takes himself to have pursued a wholly antifoundational or elecntic strategy that depends entirely on demonstrating necessary assumptions *from inside* the practical standpoint one enters by posing questions about what one ought to do, and then fighting off challenges by showing how they end by falling into self-contradiction. The intervening arguments are difficult, but since this is how Kant himself reports what he takes them to have shown, this ought to weigh in their interpretation. And there is every reason to expect this sort of strategy from Kant, given his explicit reflections on it elsewhere, considered in the preceding section, and the spectacular use he had made of it in the Transcendental Dialectic of the first *Critique*.

Consider then how Kant's argument goes. At the beginning of the chapter, he showed that the practical standpoint requires presuming freedom and generality. Now it is highly characteristic for Kant to argue that certain assumptions that cannot be proven true nevertheless hold from a practical point of view—that is, when we ask practical questions about "what ought I to do?" rather than theoretical ones about "what can I know?" Indeed, freedom is among the classic examples. Kant is always very clear that to warrant this use of a concept only "for practical purposes," all theoretical reason needs to do is—not to provide any reason whatsoever for thinking it independently supported—but only to show it does not contradict anything else that *can* be proven true and that would rule it out. Kant makes this move over and over again after introducing it in the first *Critique*, and he uses the same language in the *Groundwork*. The final sections of *Groundwork* III give just his sort of immanent refutation of the charge that the freedom the practical standpoint must suppose is inadmissible because it contradicts the determinism of nature. Although "the freedom attributed to [the will] seems to stand in contradiction with the necessity of nature . . .

---

[41] One should not be misled by the term "deduction," since Kant consistently uses it not to refer narrowly to demonstrations from first principles but in the broader sense of a necessary justification. See Dieter Henrich, "Kant's Notion of a Deduction and the Methodological Background of the First *Critique*," in *Kant's Transcendental Deductions: The Three Critiques and the Opus Postumum*, ed. Eckart Förster (Stanford, CA: Stanford University Press, 1989); Rüdiger Bubner, "Kant, Transcendental Argument and the Problem of Deduction," *Review of Metaphysics* 28, no. 3 (1975): 453–67; and Lewis White Beck, *A Commentary on Kant's Critique of Practical Reason* (Chicago: University of Chicago Press, 1960), 176.

the illusion about the contradiction rests on this, that we think of the human being in a different sense and relationship when we call him free than when we consider him as a part of nature, and subject to [nature's] laws" (455–6). This is the condensed argument of the first *Critique*, and it is important to see that (whatever one thinks of it there) here Kant is explicit that his appeal to the distinction between worlds of sense and understanding worlds is no ontological claim, but to the contrary, "The concept of a world of understanding is only a *standpoint* that reason sees itself compelled to take, outside appearances, *in order to think itself as practical*" (458, emphases are Kant's).[42] So Kant's argument here is eminently Socratic, aimed at refuting a charge of contradiction not by furnishing freedom a positive warrant of any kind but merely by showing up as unfounded others' overweening claims to know: for "where determination by laws of nature ends, there all *explanation* ends as well, and nothing is left over but *defense*—that is, to repel the objections of those who pretend to have seen more deeply into the essence of things and therefore boldly explain freedom to be impossible" (459, emphasis in original).

The most difficult point remains the "circle." One ought to take Kant's response as follows. Kant's initial worry is that it "seems as though" [*scheint also, als*] we have only presupposed morality in order then to justify it, because we are inclined to *presume* that what it means for morality to bind must be that some theoretical reason impels us to take up the moral point of view. This is how every heteronomous theory thinks of "binding." But one of the key claims of morality as autonomy is that this way of thinking is wrong and incoherent, and he is very explicit again at the end of the chapter that we cannot possibly be shown to be bound *this way*, by proving some "interest" in the moral law—a law we were bound to *that* way could not be moral. So how does the introduction of the two standpoints at 4:450 respond to this problem? By showing another sense in which we can take ourselves to be "bound"—*already inside the moral point of view*—in a way nevertheless compatible with our freedom. He concludes the section with just such an explanation: "If we think of ourselves as obligated, we view ourselves as belonging to the sensible world and yet simultaneously to the intelligible world" (4:453), and describes the result in a way that reads less as a claim to have secured a foundation than to have shown why it was wrong to suspect the practical argument of having relied upon a question-begging foundation in the first place. The next

---

[42] Cf. similar locutions at 450, 452. I take it that Allison and others have decisively won the argument for the "two-standpoint" view over the "two-worlds view" in the first *Critique*. See his "Transcendental Idealism: The "Two Aspect" View," in *New Essays on Kant*, eds. Bernard den Ouden and Marcia Moen (New York: Peter Lang, 1987), and *Kant's Transcendental Idealism*, 2nd ed. (New Haven, CT: Yale University Press, 2004). But even if one does not accept this, Kant is emphatic in the *Groundwork*. I fail to see how quotes like these could possibly be accounted for on the contrary reading, whereas it is obvious that every prima facie reference to two worlds can be taken as a metaphor.

section, which recapitulates and develops the argument, referred to as a "deduction," is titled "How is a categorical imperative possible?" (4:454–5), and this is what it claims to show. Now in reasoning or in contemplating examples of virtue, one becomes aware of a capacity for spontaneous judgment, over and above anything determined by nature's laws (4:452, 4:454). And when we accordingly think of ourselves as free (as either theoretical or moral judgments require us to do, insofar as the theoretical also requires an ability to adjust our beliefs based on whatever we turn out to show is true), we "transfer ourselves" [*sich versetzen*] into the world of understanding (4:453, 4:455). Because this world comprises the *"ground of the world of sense and therefore of its laws,"* we can consider ourselves bound as members of the latter by our own will as members of the former (4:453). All this really means is that we can think and argue, and that whatever we accept as turning out to be right or true in argument will have to count as right or true vis-à-vis any unjustified beliefs or impulses we might have. This is all very nearly the classic idealist position of the priority of argument (*logos*) to knowledge, although Kant here emphasizes also a distinctively moral side where Plato ran theory and morality together. So this is a rather metaphorical way of pointing out that when we argue about truth or rightness, we have to consider the answers authoritative over unjustified impulse or belief.

But is this a foundational proof of freedom from which morality follows? Kant insists over and over that it is not, including on the following page where he emphasizes again that "freedom is only an *idea* of reason, the objective reality of which is itself open to doubt" (4:455), and that the world of understanding is only a standpoint reason sees itself compelled to take up *"in order to think itself as practical"* (4:458, emphases in original).[43] Most of Kant's locutions appear to be describing how we must think if we are to think consistently once we are already in the space of reasons—his example of the scoundrel, for instance, at 4:454–5 is something of a non sequitur if taken for an argument to convince the scoundrel to be moral, but Kant's point seems to be rather that even a scoundrel can reflect on right and wrong and thus make sense of the notion of an "ought." Kant invites confusion at two points by suggesting that autonomy follows immediately from freedom, whereas it has been rightly objected that independence from causal determination qua spontaneity is not the same as a lawful will.[44] But Kant's move still makes sense if his aim is not to argue us into lawfulness. If we are already reasoning about what is true or right, then lawfulness does

---

[43] A footnote at 4:448 could hardly be more explicit: "I opt for this way—assuming freedom, sufficiently for our purpose, as laid down merely in idea by rational beings *in their conduct* as its ground—so that I may *not find myself bound also to prove [beweisen] freedom for theoretical purposes.* Since even if this last is left unaccomplished, still the same laws are valid for a being that cannot act except under the idea of its own freedom, as would bind a being that were truly free. *We can thus here free ourselves from the burden that weighs upon theory"* (emphases mine).

[44] See Allison, *Freedom*, 227–8; Ameriks, *Mind*, 206–8.

indeed follow as a presupposition, in just the way Socrates first showed. And Kant always (in the *Groundwork*, almost always elsewhere) takes for granted that his interlocutors take themselves to act through free wills (in the lawful sense) because they are already concerned with judgments of right and wrong.[45]

The mistake is to suppose Kant was arguing against a moral skeptic who needs a theoretical reason to take up moral reasoning in the first place. But it is quite clear that Kant's worries were different. Part of his argument, we saw, was to confute fatalists who deny the possibility of freedom on which morality depends—not because they do not care about morality but because they propound an incoherent, fatalistic moral theory.[46] But his major opponents in *Groundwork* II and III were defenders of traditional heteronomous moral theories of all kinds that sought moral authority in natural goods, human nature, rational perfection, or natural law understood as independent and prior to the act of autonomous self-legislation. His knock-down argument against such theories was that they contradicted themselves because they could not show how morality can bind without positing some sort of "interest" that amounted to a compulsion incompatible with the freedom moral obligation must presume. But although Kant's own theory of autonomy does not face the same contradiction, *it would still run afoul of Kant's own criticism* unless it managed to provide *some other way* of explaining what moral obligation means, or how the moral law can "bind." What the appeal to the two standpoints does is to provide the missing account, in lieu of any "interest" or explanation by tracing to a further ground. It has to do this if morality is to make any sense *from the inside*, but it does not also need to argue us into morality. The real point is, quite to the contrary, clearly to distinguish moral reason from both the theoretical and from mere sensibility. As Kant emphasized in a review of Schulz's *Attempt at an Introduction to a Doctrine of Morals for all Human Beings Regardless of Different Religions* in 1783, "The practical concept of freedom has nothing to do with the speculative," since when I ask a practical question, "as to how I came originally to be in the state in which I am now to act, I can be completely indifferent; I ask only what I now have to do, and then freedom is a necessary practical presupposition and an idea under which alone I can regard commands of reason as valid" (8:13). He concluded that "[e]ven the most stubborn skeptic [*Skeptiker*] grants that, when it comes to acting, all sophistical worries about a universally deceptive illusion must fall away" (ibid.)—but *only when it comes to acting*, because it is our own free participation in the project of asking after the rightness or wrongness of actions, not any theoretical truth about metaphysics

---

[45] Hence, immediately following: "All human beings think of their will as free. From this comes every judgment of actions as such that they *should have happened even though they did not happen*" (4:455, emphasis in original).

[46] See, for instance, Kant's 1788 critical review of Ulrich's *Eleutheriology* (8:455).

or our essential natures, that commits us in Socratic fashion to the regulative presuppositions on which morality depends.

The "Fact of Reason" and the Moral Skeptic

It will be objected that Kant introduced in the second *Critique* the famous dictum that the moral law should be considered "like a fact of pure reason, as it were" [*gleichsam als ein Factum der reinen Vernunft*], the objective reality of which can in no way be grounded through any further deduction, and yet which we must nevertheless accept as a priori certain (5:47). This reads on its face like a foundation, but interpretation of the claim and its relation to the *Groundwork* is deeply controversial.[47] I think it best understood not as a positive foundation at all, but to the contrary as a marker of the impossibility of any extra-moral ground for morality, and so not a "reversal" of Kant's position in the *Groundwork* but, if anything, a more emphatic statement of it. I will briefly consider the text before turning to the question of how one might respond to the sort of radical moral skeptic Kant never took on in a full and systematic way.

Kant first calls the moral law a "fact of reason" at 5:31,[48] where he writes that:

> One may call the consciousness of this fundamental law a fact of reason [*ein Factum der Vernunft*] because one cannot reason it out from antecedent data of reason . . . [and] because it instead presses itself upon us of itself as a synthetic a priori proposition that is not grounded on any intuition, either pure or empirical. . . . However, one must note well, in order to consider this law without misinterpretation as *given*, that it is not an empirical [fact], but rather the sole fact of pure reason which, through it, makes itself known as originally lawgiving (*sic* volo, *sic* jubeo).[49] (5:31, emphasis in original)

---

[47] Allison and Ameriks number among proponents of a "great reversal" according to which Kant had grounded morality on freedom in the *Groundwork* but reversed himself in the second *Critique*, although both also think the arguments fail. See Allison, *Freedom*, Chapter 12, and *Kant's Groundwork*, Chapter 12; Ameriks, *Mind*, Chapter 6. But Kant never mentions a reversal and suggests continuity with the *Groundwork* in the *KpV* (5:8), and any reversal is denied by equally eminent scholars including Lewis White Beck, "The Fact of Reason: An Essay on Justification in Ethics," in *Studies in the Philosophy of Kant* (Westport, CT: Greenwood Press, 1965), 200–14, and Dieter Henrich, "Die Deduktion des Sittengesetzes: Über die Gründe der Dunkelheit des letzten Abschnittes von Kants *Grundlegung der Metaphysik der Sitten*," in *Denken im Schatten des Nihilismus: Festschrift für Wilhelm Weischedel*, ed. Alexander Schwann (Darmstadt: Wissenschaftliche Buchgesellschaft, 1975).

[48] Although "Factum" appears in the Preface at 5:6.

[49] The Latin follows Luther's widely distributed "Sendbrief vom Dolmetzschen," in *D. Martin Luthers Werke* (Weimar: Böhlau, 1883), 30:635, slightly misquoting Juvenal, *Satires* VI.223: "*Hoc volo, sic jubeo, sit pro ratione voluntas*": "What I will, I command, let will stand for reason." This points to the practical interpretation I defend.

On the one hand, this law is a "fact" just *because it cannot be reasoned out from any antecedent positive premise*, either empirical or rational. On the other, it is not merely a "datum" that happens to appear intuitively true but whose truth cannot be justified. That would amount to merely a contingent psychological law, and such a law could never bind us morally (5:96–7). To the contrary, the moral law "forces itself upon us of itself as a synthetic a priori proposition," which means there must be some reason for supposing not only that we do think it, but that we do so *necessarily*. ("Of itself" means only "without any further ground on which it depends.") Kant emphasizes repeatedly that "the objective reality of the moral law cannot be proved through any deduction, by every effort of reason theoretically, speculatively, or empirically supported" and yet "it nevertheless stands fast by itself" (5:47). So what other sort of justification can it have?

The main reason Kant's exposition invites confusion is that he is always already assuming the moral point of view that cares about asking ,"What ought I to do?"—that is why the book is a "Critique of Practical Reason," which means an immanent critique (5:16). So we can make Kant's claims clearer by making this point of departure explicit: hence, *if we inquire into the rightness or wrongness of our actions, then* the moral law "forces itself upon us of itself as a synthetic a priori proposition"; and *if we inquire into the rightness or wrongness of our actions, then* although no theoretical deduction can be provided for that law, "it stands nevertheless firmly established by itself." While the crucial first (practical) premise is usually left implicit, Kant does allude to it often enough to assure us that this must be his thought. Two pages before the first mention of the "fact of reason," he explains that "we become immediately aware" of the moral law "as soon as we draw up maxims of the will for ourselves," which is to say when we take on the standpoint of practical reason by considering our actions in terms of principles that may or may not turn out to be justified (5:29). And just after introducing the "fact of reason," Kant claims that it is "undeniable" since "one may simply analyze the judgment that people pass on the lawfulness of their actions" in order to see its necessity in operation (5:32). One can then see that the force of the argument, by ruling out explicitly any attempt to provide a positive deduction or to derive morality from freedom, serves to block any confusion about the independence of the moral point of view. The moral law is clearly not presupposed in the manner of traditional natural law theory, which presumed the content of the law could be worked out from self-evident first principles in the manner of Aristotelian demonstration. It is instead presupposed in making judgments of right and wrong, in the sense that Socrates showed his interlocutors' claims to knowledge to presuppose standards of truth they could not, in fact, meet, and this is why the intervening arguments must proceed always indirectly and by elimination, by reflecting on the conceptual conditions of any interpretation that could count consistently as "moral."⁵⁰ If Kant meant something else, his arguments would be much simpler.

So where does this leave Kant's view? One can draw out some of its strengths and limits by considering the radical moral skeptic Kant never seriously engaged. Kant had opened a radical gap between moral and theoretical argument, by showing that each had its own logic on incompatible assumptions. He thus established the autonomy of moral thinking, clearly demarcating justification from causal explanation or inquiry into nature.⁵¹ But this means we have no extra-moral ground for taking up the moral point of view in the first place. To the contrary, in it we must consider ourselves bound just because we freely author its commands for ourselves. So what sort of challenge is posed by someone who simply has no interest in that standpoint? First, the fact that someone may not care about moral questions does not invalidate the self-imposed obligations of those who do. Indeed, a consistent moral skeptic cannot even deny that she is under moral obligation, since to do so is already to take up the moral point of view by posing the question of justification. To paraphrase, if there is no morality, then it is not that all is permitted but that terms like "permitted" have no meaning—all could be permitted only if one accepts, in principle, that some things might not be and then provides an argument to show instead that they are. So all a consistent moral skeptic can say is that she does not care about morality, and that is not an argument a defender of morality need refute. This is not, of course, to say every question is a moral one, or that taking up another standpoint like, say, Nietzsche's or Foucault's is not also possible and perhaps illuminating and important. But Kant's point is that there is not really a conflict here just because these are different sorts of questions to ask.

---

⁵⁰ To take up the moral point of view by asking moral questions or making moral judgments is to open oneself to demands to justify one's conclusions. It means accepting what Rainer Forst has called others' "right to justification." *The Right to Justification: Elements of a Constructivist Theory of Justice* (New York: Columbia University Press, 2007). I share Forst's criticisms of Henrich, Korsgaard, and Apel (though not necessarily of Kant). If we differ here, the point is a fine one over the sense in which respect for others might be said to "ground" morality; Forst means to emphasize with this "second-order insight" that justification is prior to direct insight into a moral law in the manner of traditional natural law, and on this we agree, since this is just the way elenchus or dialectic is prior to those regulative assumptions it employs. But the "ground" holds only within the moral point of view as a reconstruction of what it means to take it up, and we are not so much "finite beings who use reasons" (61) as beings who may sometimes choose to do so (and who, in doing so, must regard ourselves and others this way), as Plato took pains to dramatize. This matters because we must also choose the moral point of view and consider that others may not, and although Forst does not deny this, focusing heavily on justification places less emphasis than Kant on self-legislation and coercion—particularly in politics.

⁵¹ This is very close to what Charles Larmore calls "the autonomy of morality"—except that he presents this as the opposite of Kant's view. *The Autonomy of Morality* (Cambridge, UK: Cambridge University Press, 2008). Cf. Forst, *Justification*, 43–60.

The real moral challenge posed by skeptics who reject the moral point of view is how those who do accept it ought to treat them. For if obligations must be self-imposed, then forcing an obligation on others entails a risk not on the skeptic's principles but on Kant's own. This is a risk Kant himself took seriously, by denying any right to enforce virtue and at several other places in his political theory. Notice, however, that this risk cannot even appear for the skeptic herself: if one accepts her view, then no coercion can be "wrong." So if this problem is real, skepticism is not an answer. Consider next that the Kantian does not contradict herself in an ideal case in which it is known with certainty that the skeptic really rejects moral justification entirely and the Kantian has rightly interpreted autonomy. That is just because what "autonomy" requires is for the Kantian to respect even a skeptic's own right to judge morally for herself, while restraining her actions only insofar as they present external hindrances to the equal freedom of others. So although the skeptic may not want to engage in justifying her actions, this does not mean that she has a positive right to act in ways that violate others' freedom (including other skeptics'). Nor does it mean that she surrenders her own right to equal respect. If she truly refuses to engage in justification, those who do take up the moral point of view must still respect her autonomy as best they can, although they must do so *ex hypothesi* in the absence of her own willingness to participate in defining what that could mean. And so they would have to make necessary collective judgments as conscientiously as they can while refusing to compel her to be "better" or "more free." In some cases concerning children or the legally incompetent, for instance, others have no choice but to act *bona fide* in a fiduciary capacity, while always holding open in principle the possibility that the other may one day come to enter the moral point of view and take up for herself the interpretation and judgment of her actions, her rights, and the reciprocal rights of others.

The real risk is that one can never really know that what one takes for a contest between morality and amoralism is not actually a conflict over the meaning of moral justification itself. It may always turn out in encountering the other that we are the ones who ought to realize that our own prior conception of autonomy was too narrow, and that we are the ones thus obligated to revise our views. But this can be determined only through dialogue with actual others, in which we hold ourselves and the other to the same critical standard—that we be able to justify our particular conceptions of freedom, morality, or justice and to defend their claim to obligate against objections from every competing point of view. A permanent openness to such engagement is thus the hallmark of an appropriately moral stance toward a person we take to deny the authority of morality. I think Arendt is right to emphasize the political significance of these sentiments in Kant, and I think they are also well illustrated by Socrates's example in Plato's dialogues. They indicate the spirit in which a historical and Socratic theory means to approach political struggles over the meaning of democracy.

Here, the skeptical objections run out. If we understand what it means to take up the moral point of view in this way, there is no sense in which it requires any further, extra-moral ground. We are not moral because we cannot help it. It is instead a way we can choose to be, and which, once we take up that point of view, we can also say we *should* choose to be.[52] But what it means is to commit oneself to making and defending responsible judgments, across a range of interlocutors that can never be delimited in advance. And this is why it is so important not to hypostasize any particular formulae or to mistake principles that we need to acknowledge in judging for ourselves for freestanding authorities which, once demonstrated, we need only singlemindedly to follow. I have suggested that, despite some common caricatures, this is actually an important part of how Kant thought about morality, too. In the next chapter, we will see that the argument for autonomy as a necessary presupposition of any obligation will apply to political obligations as well. But we will also see that there the further question of who is in a position to decide for others comes to take center stage. What Kant's moral theory had shown was a distinctive, critical way of understanding freedom and its role in defending judgments, and also why supposing that politics should serve morality directly—even Kantian morality—is to misinterpret what morality itself requires.

---

[52] Thomas Fossen defends a related view of political obligation in "The Grammar of Political Obligation," *Politics, Philosophy & Economics* 13, no. 3 (2014): 215–36.

4

Kant on Politics

The last chapter argued that Kant's moral theory provided a powerful and thoroughly antifoundational argument that every obligation must be autonomous—that if it is to bind, it must count as both universal and self-imposed. But what follows for politics? First of all, if the argument is good, it refutes from inside every moral and political claim based directly on traditional metaphysics, natural law, theories of human nature, or religion.[1] Properly understood, Kant argued, any of these frameworks can only demonstrate its own insufficiency and the need to work out principles of justice instead strictly in terms of universal freedom. This backed freedoms of religion and expression already characteristic of Frederick II's Prussia, and it broadly supported the sovereign claims of Frederick's centralizing state over traditional corporate authorities and aristocrats. But it also challenged Frederick's claim to rule for the good of the people rather than in accord with their freedom, the view supported across the range of mainstream academic social contract theories running from Pufendorf through Wolff and Achenwall.[2] That view saw the prince as bound by fundamental laws set through an actual compact between prince and people, which granted the prince more or less complete powers to promote the *salus populi*. Kant instead followed Rousseau in arguing that the point of the contract idea was to show that only a government that respects citizens' freedom could ever count as one those citizens had bound themselves to obey. Only a constitution in which the general will rules could be sovereign, and sovereignty was not like a piece of property the people could alienate at will—or in effect, be taken always already to have alienated. In one sense or another, then, a legitimate sovereign must

---

[1] Cf. Christian Wolff, "Since *natural law* has its sufficient reason in the very nature [*rerum*] of men and things, it therefore *contains a natural obligation*, which is immutable and necessary" (*Intsitutiones juris naturae et gentium* [Halle: Renger, 1750], §40, emphases in original).

[2] See, for example, Frederick II, *Anti-machiavel* (The Hague, 1740); Samuel Pufendorf, *De jure naturae et gentium libri octo*, 2 vols. (Oxford: Oxford University Press, 1934), first published 1672; Wolff, *Jus naturae methodo scientifica pertractatum*, 8 vols. (Frankfurt, Leipzig, and Halle: Renger, 1740–1748); Gottfried Achenwall, *Ius naturae in usum auditorum*, 5th rev. ed., 2 vols. (Göttingen: Victorinus Bossiegelius 1763).

count not as merely someone the people have accepted to rule in their best interest, but as the people ruling themselves.

This is a controversial reading of Kant, and this chapter makes three major claims about why one ought to accept it and why it matters. First, it is essential to see that Kant was not a moralist in politics: indeed, he took his view of morality to require drawing a very sharp line between morality and justice. Because this is well established among interpreters of Kant's political theory, I will not argue for it here;[3] but it is important to keep in mind because it has often been overlooked by Kantians who focus too narrowly on the moral theory—in Kant's day as in ours. The basic point is that if autonomy is the only moral law, then morality requires acting for the right reasons, and since this cannot be coerced by external powers like the state, the pursuit of virtue and moral perfection must be left to individuals. The state's role is to secure citizens' external freedom by enforcing a rule of law in such a manner that those laws count as imposed by the omnilateral will of the citizens themselves. This creates space for individuals to act both justly and morally as they interact with each other and with objects, by hindering hindrances to their external freedom—but it does not aim at making moral citizens. This matters because since justice must be enforced, a theory of justice requires a theory of the conditions under which any particular persons have the right to judge and enforce their judgments on others, and this is why one needs a theory of the state. Kant's moral theory thus carves out space for politics from the inside.[4]

Here again, we see Kant insisting that since freedom and the moral law are principles of judgment, they cannot rightly be understood without reference to the act of judgment in which they are employed. In this, Kant broke not only from natural lawyers like Wolff, but also from the emphasis on civic virtue Rousseau had carried over from the republican tradition. Whereas Rousseau sought to solve the problem of how the general will should be known by bringing all citizens to share a good-faith orientation to its pursuit, Kant recognized that one cannot engineer virtuous citizens or moral consensus, and that since disagreement was to the contrary inescapable in politics, only a theory of political judgment could hope to respond to it in a principled way. Otherwise, one will be tempted to mistake every political controversy for a conspiracy of sinister interests, and either to conclude with the Jacobins that dissensus is best resolved

---

[3] Particularly good discussions may be found in Authur Ripstein, *Force and Freedom: Kant's Legal and Political Philosophy* (Cambridge, MA: Harvard University Press, 2009), and Anna Stilz, *Liberal Loyalty: Freedom, Obligation, and the State* (Princeton, NJ: Princeton University Press, 2009).

[4] In much the way the first *Critique* had carved out a space for morality from inside "metaphysics." As Kant put it in *Religion within the Boundaries of Mere Reason*: "But woe to the lawgiver who would wish to bring about through coercion a constitution directed to ethical ends! For he would not only thereby effect the opposite of the ethical [end], but also undermine his political ends and make them insecure" (6:96).

by purging the dissenters, or else to find oneself politically paralyzed and soon sidelined by less scrupulous actors whenever one's own moral doctrines fail to inspire universal acclamation, as the *quarant-huitards* discovered once the dust settled on their revolution and they actually had to try to govern France.

But if Kant distinguished politics from morality, what sort of politics did he call for? The chapter's second claim is that Kant's political theory was not, as is often thought, narrowly liberal, but was by his later writings thoroughly committed to the republican or democratic claim that a rightful government is one in which the people make the laws. In particular, Kant did not propound a theory of either "hypothetical" or "modal" consent—of the sort defended, for instance, by Rawls—but instead required attributing actual consent to the people *as represented* by a sovereign held to act through their general will.[5] But interpreters who agree with me in emphasizing Kant's republicanism sometimes overstate the case, because it is also true, as is well known, that Kant always continued to insist that even absolutist monarchs have a legitimate claim to be obeyed, and that he ruled out any right to popular revolution. This apparent tension has given rise to a string of controversy stretching from the 1790s to the present day.[6] I defend the following view. Although by his later

---

[5] Contrast inter alia Allen Rosen, *Kant's Theory of Justice* (Ithaca, NY: Cornell University Press, 1993); Elisabeth Ellis, *Kant's Politics: Provisional Theory for an Uncertain World* (New Haven, CT: Yale University Press, 2005); Frederick C. Beiser, *Hegel* (New York: Routledge, 2005), 238; and Onora O'Neill, "Kant and the Social Contract Tradition," in *Kant's Political Theory: Interpretations and Approaches*, ed. Elisabeth Ellis (University Park: Pennsylvania State University Press, 2012), 25–41.

[6] A number of early Kantians criticized Kant for "betraying" his principles in rejecting a right to revolution. See Ludwig Heinrich Jakob, *Antimachivel: Oder über die Grenzen des bürgerlichen Gehorsams* (Halle, 1794); Johann Benjamin Erhard, *Ueber das Recht des Volks zu einer Revolution* (Jena and Leipzig, 1795); and Paul Johann Anselm von Feuerbach, *Anti-Hobbes: Oder über die Grenzen der höchsten Gewalt und das Zwangsrecht der Bürger gegen den Oberherrn* (Erfurt, 1798). More recently, see Werner Hänsel, *Kants Lehre vom Widerstandsrecht, Kant-Studien Egränzungsheft* 60 (1926); Frederick C. Beiser, *Enlightenment, Revolution, and Romanticism: The Genesis of Modern German Political Thought, 1790–1800* (Cambridge, MA: Harvard University Press, 1992), 48–55; Sarah Williams Holtman, "Revolution, Contradiction, and Kantian Citizenship," in *Kant's Metaphysics of Morals: Interpretive Essays*, ed. Mark Timmons (Oxford: Oxford University Press, 2002), 209–31; and Thomas E. Hill Jr., "Questions about Kant's Opposition to Revolution," *The Journal of Value Inquiry* 36 (2002): 283–98. Others have tried to save Kant from this charge, either by emphasizing the threat of censorship (Domenico Losurdo, *Autocensura e compromesso nel pensiero politico di Kant* [Napoli: Bibliopolis, 1983]), or by suggesting that he meant to permit revolutions when so-called states failed to meet minimal criteria of legitimacy. See (Kenneth R. Westphal, "Kant on the State, Law, and Obedience to Authority in the Alleged 'Anti-Revolutionary' Writings," *Journal of Philosophical Research* 17 (1992): 383–426; Dieter Henrich, "On the Meaning of Rational Action in the State," in *Kant & Political Philosophy*, eds. Ronald Beiner and William James Booth (New Haven, CT: Yale University Press, 1993); Arthur Ripstein, *Force and Freedom: Kant's Legal and Political Philosophy* (Cambridge, MA: Harvard University Press, 2009), 325–44; B. Sharon Byrd and Joachim Hruschka, *Kant's Doctrine of Right: A Commentary* (Cambridge, UK: Cambridge University Press, 2010); Reidar Maliks, *Kant's Politics in Context* (Oxford: Oxford University Press, 2014), 112–43. Christine Korsgaard tries to defend a similar conclusion by suggesting that ethics may sometimes permit what justice disallows,

works Kant was genuinely committed to republican institutions in principle, he also insisted that consistently applying this principle required a theory of who was in a position to judge. So he rejected revolution not because he rejected republican principles, but because he argued that reform through existing sovereign institutions was the only sort that could be defended as compatible with the notion of a people ruling themselves through general laws, rather than as some number of individuals arbitrarily imposing their own interpretation of justice on everyone else.

One might say, then, that Kant's theory was not antirepublican but metarepublican, because it was not merely a theory of institutions but first and foremost a theory of the political judgment through which one might assess any institution's pretense to legitimacy.[7] This was a significant revision of the social contract tradition, which shifted the role of history from securing a putative foundation in the past to opening up a horizon of ongoing popular judgment always receding into the future—history became a field of action. This built a reference to historical change into the very notion of right itself, but it did so in a very different way than historicisms like Herder's that Kant criticized. In most of his writings, Kant presented the idea of historical progress as a practical assumption valid only as part of an ongoing act of political judgment, which always demanded justification in terms of right. He never took it for a providential fact of history of the sort that might save us the work of making and defending judgments for ourselves. Kant's was a way of historic*izing* justice that was not a historic*ism*, in the sense that term would come to take in nineteenth-century Germany, and it set him off equally from timeless or backward-looking theories of natural law and from the developmentalist historicisms that would come to dominate the nineteenth century.

---

in "Taking The Law into Our Own Hands: Kant on the Right of Revolution," in *The Constitution of Agency: Essays on Practical Reason and Moral Psychology* (Oxford: Oxford University Press, 2008), 233–62. Others think Kant did rule out all revolutions and this reveals his tacit authoritarianism. See Isaiah Berlin, "Two Concepts of Liberty," in *Liberty: Incorporating Four Essays on Liberty* (Oxford: Oxford University Press, 2002); Jean-Bethke Elshtain, "Kant, Politics, & Persons: The Implications of His Moral Philosophy," *Polity* 14 (1981): 205–21. Still others agree Kant ruled out all revolutions but argue this is defensible and compatible with democracy because of the possibility of reform. See Gunnar Beck, "Autonomy, History, and Freedom in Kant's Political Philosophy," *History of European Ideas* 25 (1999): 217–41; Ellis, *Kant's Politics*; Katrin Flikschuh, "Sidestepping Morality: Korsgaard on Kant's No-Right to Revolution," *Jahrbuch für Recht und Ethik* (2008): 127–45. Lewis White Beck suggested a similar view while ignoring Kant's own arguments for reform, in "Kant and the Right of Revolution," *Journal of the History of Ideas* 32 (1971): 411–22.

[7] This is not to suggest that Kant's view of revolution and reform followed originally from republican principles; in fact it predates his conversion to republicanism in the 1790s. The problem it addresses is common to any government that derives its legitimacy from representing the people, be it republican or monarchical, and so when Kant eventually took up republican principles he reworked his existing theory to arrive at a consistently republican result.

The chapter's third claim concerns what we ought to make of this view today. I think Kant was broadly correct in following Hobbes to argue that the various strands of traditional resistance theory were unable to provide a consistent and non-question-begging answer to the problem of judging change (although I do not argue the point in detail here). But if reconceiving the problem as one of historical judgment opened the possibility of a solution, that does not mean Kant's particular answer was also right. Kant insisted we must presume the legitimacy of every existing sovereign because otherwise in judging the sovereign, we contradict the very notion of an established final arbiter that is required if justice is ever to be attainable. But he failed to consider a conceivable (and historically common enough) case in which two or more pretenders vie for sovereign authority over the same citizens. Then one cannot avoid somehow judging—but this would mean arguing not over the people's right to "resist" but over the very different question of who has the most defensible claim to represent "the people." And—to anticipate—one might answer without contradiction if one could show that some pretenders' claims were themselves inconsistent and so untenable, while others' were not. In the next chapter, I argue that Hegel came to defend a version of such a theory, although in rather different terms. But the point here is to see, first, that Kant's general turn to historical judgment need not rule out every case of revolution—although it does give reason for suspecting those conflicts may not be best described as "resistance" struggles pitting a tyrant against "the people." And second, Kant's own, genuinely antirevolutionary solution was not a simple mistake or a betrayal of his principles—indeed, it is more consistent than many of the grounds on which he has been criticized for it. Unlike political moralists or liberal rationalists whose views are not ultimately democratic, Kant felt compelled to face up to what I have called the paradox of authorization. And although I will argue that Kant's solution was not ultimately satisfying, the fact that he provided such good reasons for taking seriously the problem suggests that more recent efforts to revive Kantian principles and other eighteenth-century ideas may need to consider it as well.

From Hobbes to Kant

Part of my thesis is that Kant's political theory should be understood in significant part as an intervention in an eighteenth-century debate over how to respond to Hobbes.[8] The dominant framework for political thought in

---

[8] Here, I build on a recent direction in scholarship emphasizing Kant's "Hobbesianism." See Richard Tuck, *The Rights of War and Peace: Political Thought and the International Order from Grotius to Kant* (Oxford: Oxford University Press, 1999); Katrin Flikschuh, "Elusive Unity: The General Will in Hobbes and Kant," *Hobbes Studies* 25 (2012): 21–42; and a related view in Jeremy Waldron, "Kant's Legal Positivism," *Harvard Law Review* 109 (1996):1535–66, and "Kant's Theory of the

eighteenth-century Germany was a version of social contract theory taken to run from Grotius through Pufendorf, Thomasius, Wolff, Vattel, and Achenwall, among others. Within this broad tradition, major divisions pitted a strand descended from Leibniz and developed by Wolff, relying heavily on rational metaphysics, against the less metaphysical strand of Pufendorf and Thomasius.[9] But despite their differences in how to go about it, all agreed on the need to counter Hobbes by preserving a role for natural law irreducible to the decision of the political sovereign.[10] One of the most striking things about Kant's political theory at the time was how his arguments aligned him with the widely reviled views of Hobbes. Although Kant is often mistaken for a wholesale critic of Hobbes, his criticisms followed Rousseau's and were internal to the general framework that distinguished both Hobbes and Rousseau from Grotius, Pufendorf, and Vattel as Kant understood them, whom he famously dismissed *en bloc* as "only sorry comforters" (8:355).

Deeper than divisions between Pufendorf and Wolff was a fundamental disagreement concerning the basis of social order and its justification that ranged all the German natural lawyers against Hobbes and Rousseau. The avowedly anti-Hobbesian view dominant in Germany built on an older interpretation of the social contract that—to generalize—understood society as built up through a series of expanding corporate associations, including the family, and crowned at the top by political society, as one further association with its own particular end of securing internal and external peace (and sometimes of also the means of self-sufficient life). Hobbes had famously rejected this

---

State," in *Perpetual Peace and Other Writings on Politics, Peace, and History*, ed. Pauline Kleingeld (New Haven, CT: Yale University Press, 2006), 179–200. But this direction remains highly controversial. Cf. Patrick Riley, "Kant Against Hobbes in *Theory and Practice*," *Journal of Moral Philosophy* 4, no. 2 (2007): 194–206. Reidar Maliks dissents in part, in his "The State of Freedom: Kant and His Conservative Critics," in *Freedom and the Construction of Europe*, Vol. 2, eds. Quentin Skinner and Martin van Gelderen (Cambridge, UK: Cambridge University Press, 2013), 205. Howard Williams allows for some continuities but emphasizes contrasts in *Kant's Critique of Hobbes* (Cardiff, UK: University of Wales Press, 2003) and "Natural Right in Hobbes and Kant," *Hobbes Studies* 25 (2012): 66–90.

[9] These contrasts, however, were clearer at some times than at others; Achenwall and even Wolff drew explicitly from both traditions. See J. B. Schneewind, *The Invention of Autonomy: A History of Modern Moral Philosophy* (Cambridge, UK: Cambridge University Press, 1998); Ian Hunter, *Rival Enlightenments: Civil and Metaphysical Philosophy in Early Modern Germany* (Cambridge, UK: Cambridge University Press, 2001); T. J. Hochstrasser, *Natural Law Theories in the Early Enlightenment* (Cambridge, UK: Cambridge University Press, 2004). Although one might rather emphasize continuities among Grotius, Hobbes, and to a lesser degree Pufendorf, Kant accepted the eighteenth-century tradition's anti-Hobessian self-description and took Grotius and Pufendorf for opponents.

[10] One should note, however, that this did not necessarily make them any more favorable to popular resistance—Pufendorf and Wolff agreed in rejecting any such right, whereas Achenwall defended it.

by insisting that social order was political through and through. This changed the role of the contract idea—instead of a series of associative agreements, one was left with a single contract authorizing coercion and constituting a united sovereign people. This was obviously a way of putting down challenges to state authority from traditional corporate bodies and appeals to heaven. But its force lay in the way it, in effect, demanded a political justification of the authority of any associative alternative to the state. And one should recall that the sort of pre-political duties defended by Grotius and Pufendorf included duties of slaves to obey their masters (an issue central to Rousseau's critique of Grotius).

Pufendorf responded with a doctrine of two social compacts, the first creating society and the second a political sovereign who promises to care for the *salus populi* in return for obedience.[11] This kept alive the older view of a consensually integrated society independent of political authority, on which the latter ultimately depended and by which it was constrained. In this, the notion of natural sociability came to play an important polemical role as no longer merely a story of how polities came to be that pointed to their purpose, but as an argument for the possibility of a pre- and extra-political society as an alternative to the amoral Hobbesian state (not least, of course, in international relations where in Hobbes the absence of a state left only anarchy). At issue was a deep divide over whether political conflicts required a political solution—one that conceived the problem as one of justifying sovereign judgment and coercion—or whether principles of right might instead be worked out to apply even in a "society" conceived as a free and consensual association, as an alternative to power politics in the state. Although the former certainly had its perils, the danger with the latter was, as Kant would point out, that if organized power actually decides anyway, then principles that refuse to acknowledge this will end up serving more often as rationalizations than effective checks: "Although the legal code of Hugo Grotius, Pufendorf, Vattel, and the like (only sorry comforters), philosophically or diplomatically formulated, has not the slightest *legal* force, nor could it have (since states as such do not stand under a common external power), [it] always leads to an ingenuous *justification* of aggressive war, without there being a single example in which a state was ever moved by arguments armed with the testimony of so important men to give up its [warlike] projects" (8:355). This polarity would have a long and influential history in the nineteenth and twentieth centuries, not least in Germany, and one might well see aspects of the more recent

---

[11] Pufendorf, *De jure naturae*, VII.II.VIII; *De officio hominis et civis juxta legem naturalem libri duo*, 2 vols. (Oxford: Oxford University Press), first published 1673, II.VI. Achenwall concurs in *Ius naturae, pars posterior*, §91-§98. It is an interesting question how the society united by the first compact is to take a united decision for a particular constitution *before* agreeing to a common sovereign who will henceforth represent their common will as a single moral person.

Kantianisms of Rawls and Habermas as rather closer on this point to Pufendorf than to Kant (although Rawls was closer to Kant in his international theory).

Rousseau and Kant wholly rejected this anti-Hobbesian turn. Despite their criticisms of Hobbes, each accepted the fundamental point that political conflicts require political solutions involving justified coercion, and ruled out appeals to any extra-political authority.[12] But against Grotius, Pufendorf, and the Hobbes of *De Cive* together, Rousseau also argued that sovereignty cannot be alienated or transferred, and (even if he did not have Hobbes's *Leviathan* directly in mind) that neither can it be vested in a representative by an authorizing act. The arguments of the first sections of *The Social Contract* suggested that any such transfer or authorization would be tantamount to selling oneself into slavery and could not meaningfully be considered binding (I.II–V). Moreover, on the same grounds that a contract can hold only for persons considered free, Rousseau also insisted on the need for limits to the sovereign power in the generality of the laws and respect for the equal rights of its addressees (although he did not think this ruled out established privileges and classes). The brilliance of this move was that, rather than attempting to constrain from outside the logic of Hobbes's act of constitutive sovereignty—by which a multitude is first endowed with a single will—Rousseau claimed to work out limits on that power entirely from within the political logic itself. If sovereignty cannot be alienated, then the initial moment of direct citizen legislation Hobbes required only for choosing a sovereign must instead be permanent (cf. *De Cive* VII.V; *Leviathan* II.XVIII, despite their differences), and the legislative power can belong only to the general will expressed through the actual decisions of the assembled people. The government, now distinguished from the sovereign, may be delegated. If one way of describing the force of Hobbes's position, then, is as leveraging the paradox of authorization against resistance theories, one can say that Rousseau turned that paradox back against Hobbes to point out that his solutions continued to rely on a moment of authorization ultimately incompatible with his own critique.[13]

---

[12] Rousseau emphasized his continuity with Hobbes on this point in the *Social Contract* when writing "of all the Christian authors, the philosopher Hobbes is the only one who has rightly seen the evil and the remedy, who proposed to unite the two heads of the eagle [church and state], and bring everything under a political unity, without which neither state nor government will ever be well constituted.... It is not what is horrible and false in his politics, it is what is just and true, that has made him hated" (IV.VIII, 3:463). But the larger positioning is perhaps clearest in the earlier manuscript draft *PV* I.V, "False Notions of the Social Bond," which opens with the assertion that "[t]here are a thousand ways of assembling men, but only one of uniting them" (3:297), and closes with a critique of Grotius's defense of slavery (3:305).

[13] Here, I build on arguments Tuck has made in *Laws of War and Peace* and in public lectures on the notion of "the sleeping sovereign," but my concern is with how this passes on an unresolved paradox in a new formulation. I agree with Tuck's critique of (at least a certain sort of) constitutionalism, but mean to emphasize how a reciprocal critique also applies to alternatives such as majoritarian plebiscites.

But this left a difficulty, since Hobbes's sovereign had been required to solve the problem of how to create a unified will attributable to the state as a whole, meaning the people considered as a unity. In ruling out a representative solution, Rousseau was left with the need to establish *actual unity of will* among the individual citizens, and this is why the figure of the legislator and civic education played such a decisive role for him.[14] Kant was unwilling to follow Rousseau's solution, however, since as we saw, he provided powerful arguments in the *Metaphysics of Morals* that right is a matter only of external coercion, and ought not to depend on the virtue of the citizens, which is a matter for individual conscience. Kant's solution was instead to retain the notion of constitutive representation from Hobbes, while adapting it to Rousseau's demand that the sovereign can rightly rule only through the general will.[15] Kant suggested that the existing sovereign must be taken as the representative of the people's general will not in the sense that sovereignty had been alienated by the people, but rather in that this unity of representation is a logical condition of attributing a will to the united people in the first place: there must be some particular constituted actor who will decide for the people, and also one to enforce those decisions, and this would be no less true if one attributed that power to some actual assembly than to a monarch. Whereas Rousseau achieved unity by civic soulcraft, Kant saw it as instead a logical precondition that must be presumed if any rightful state is to be possible. That is, Kant considered both the original contract and the general will only practical principles that must be assumed in judging a given constitution, not empirical facts that might be directly experienced or engineered into existence. This placed Kant rather closer to Hobbes even than was Rousseau, and even farther from Grotius, Pufendorf, and Vattel. But it also continued in Rousseau's expressly republican direction, while adding

---

[14] That "the legislator" is Rousseau's response to the problem of judgment, as the sovereign is Hobbes's, is clear from *CS* II.VI, 3:380, and even more so in the manuscript *PV* I.VII, 3:309–II.II, 3:318.

[15] There is good reason to think Kant took this view directly from Hobbes. In Feyerabend's notes from Kant's 1784 lectures on natural law, Hobbes's is the only proper name to appear in the section on *jus publicum*, where Kant cites Hobbes's argument for the necessity of a state to solve conflicts of individual judgment and enforce common judgments against bad wills: "Hobbes is therefore wholly right when he says: *exeudum est e statu naturali*" (27:1382). On that page and the next, Kant goes on to rebut a right to revolution on the grounds of constitutive union/representation: "Once a mass of persons comprises a people," it cannot question the supreme power since "the *summus imperans* is either the people or the representative of the people" (27:1383). Cf. 27:589 on the same point: "This is what, among all scholars of natural law only Hobbes assumes as the highest principle of the *status civilis: exeundum esse ex statu naturali*"; or again in *Religion* at 6:97. Where Kant cites Hobbes, he always cites *De Cive*, where Hobbes wrote only of "union," whereas "representation" in this sense was introduced later in *Leviathan*. But as the *Naturrecht Feyerabend* passage shows, Kant uses both terms, and he was at least familiar enough with *Leviathan* also to refer explicitly to the notion of "Leviathan" in Hobbes as the "supreme power and ground of public right" or again as "a symbol of Hobbes's for a state, whose soul is a prince," in his unpublished notes (19:99, 15:710), and again to Hobbes's use of the Leviathan as a symbol once in his lectures (25:771).

a historical dimension to the problem of political judgment that had already been foregrounded by Hobbes.[16]

Only when one appreciates that Kant was deeply concerned with the sort of question of representation raised by Hobbes can one see clearly that when Kant wrote, "*What a people cannot decide [to impose] upon itself, a legislator also cannot decide [to impose] upon a people*" (8:304, emphasis in original)—this was not meant, as has often been supposed, as a "hypothetical" or "modal" condition sufficient to establish the justice of the laws directly. Kant was not saying that any conceivable law is valid simply because it is general, and therefore those subject to that law *would* or *could* agree to it—as in Rawls's original position. Rather, Kant's point was that even a lawful representative of the people's general will *will not be acting consistently in its role as representative* if it passes a law to which the people as a whole could not possibly have agreed, because that law itself contradicts the very notion of the free and self-determining general will of a united people. (For instance, Kant's example is a law that bestows a hereditary privilege of ruling rank, 8:297.) The constraint comes directly from the logical analysis of what it means to represent the people's general will;[17] and so what makes a law just and binding when it is so is that when a lawful representative makes a law that does meet these conditions, it can fairly be said—not that we *could* or *would* agree to it—but that in fact, acting through our representative, *we have already so agreed*. The theory of justice, in other words, turns out to depend on a theory of political representation that takes as its point of departure fundamental disagreement over the rational requirements of justice that gives rise to the political need for a sovereign judge.

What allowed Kant to reconcile a Hobbesian insistence on constitutive representation with Rousseau's general will was the way he came to insist on the "merely ideal" status of both the original contract and the notion of the general will that followed from it (8:297).[18] Whereas for Hobbes and Rousseau an

---

[16] My argument does not depend on whether one takes Hobbes's own arguments to be proto- or antidemocratic. Kant followed Rousseau in using the concept of the general will to point Hobbes's brief for sovereignty in an avowedly republican direction. Room for controversy would have to turn on Rousseau's argument against representation, but the difficulty with that is to see why a majority in a popular assembly should nevertheless, in effect, be taken to represent the whole. For the debates on Hobbes, see particularly the pieces by Richard Tuck, Kinch Hoekstra, and Quentin Skinner in *Rethinking the Foundations of Modern Political Thought*, eds. Annabel Brett and James Tully (Cambridge, UK: Cambridge University Press, 2006); and David Runciman, "Hobbes' Theory of Representation: Anti-Democratic or Proto-Democratic?," in *Political Representation*, eds. Ian Shapiro, Susan C. Stokes, Elisabeth Jean Wood, and Alexander S. Kirshner (Cambridge, UK: Cambridge University Press, 2009), 15–34.

[17] Kant is quite explicit about this: just before reaching the conclusion cited above, he points out that the supreme commander's "will gives orders to the subjects as citizens only through representing the people's general will" (8:304).

[18] Sieyès offers an instructive counterpoint, since he was wrestling with the same sort of problem. (Although there is no evidence of Kant ever considering ideas specific to Sieyès, Kant did once write him a flattering letter at the behest of an associate; see Alain Ruiz, "Neues über Kant und

existing constitution either was or was not, in fact, legitimate, Kant shifted the focus to the ongoing act of judgment through which any constitution might be justified. For Kant, one must act on the *presumption* that every existing regime is legitimate, *for practical purposes*, since rebellion is always immoral, but one may—and indeed must—nevertheless publicly criticize the failings of that state to live up to the idea of a true republic. As Kant put it at the end of an addition to the second edition of the *Doctrine of Right*, the requirement ruling out revolution "lies already a priori in the idea of a civil constitution as such—that is in a concept of practical reason—and although no example in experience is *adequate* to be put under this concept, still none must contradict it as a norm" (6:372, emphasis in original).[19] For

---

Sieyès: Ein unbekannter Brief des Philosophen an Anton Ludwig Théremin (März 1796)," *Kant-Studien* 68, no. 4 (1977): 446–53.) Sieyès famously distinguished the nation's *pouvoir constituant* from its *pouvoirs constitué* and *commettant*, in order to justify the Etats Généraux reconstituting themselves as an Assemblée Nationale and seizing sovereignty from the king in 1789. This repeated the classic resistance theory move turning on the notion of a pre-political "society" already possessed with a common will before transferring some powers to a state, but defined that society in a novel way through economic division of labor rather than contract, and by insisting on its unity in the Third Estate against traditional corporate powers (Roberto Zapperi, ed., *Qu'est-ce que le Tiers état?* [Geneva: Droz, 1970], V.178). Sieyès saw the paradox of authorization: "Even if the nation had regular [sessions of the] Estates-General, it would not be up to this constituted body to pronounce upon a difference of opinion touching its constitution. There would be in that a *petitio principii*, a vicious circle" (V.184). But how to secure unity of national will without a similar *petitio* for the National Assembly? Sieyès's complex representative schemes over the following decade sought to engineer actual unity of will through integrative political institutions through what he called "*adunation*," as an expressly monarchical alternative to democratic "polycracy"—thus privileging popular unity over actual popular control. But this is inconsistent with the claim of the pre-institutional will of the *pouvoir constituant*—or to put a finer point on it, if you need a plebiscite to ratify Bonaparte's coup d'état, then for the same reason the nation should not be able to alienate its legislative power to a system in which a Grand Elector effectively determines laws from the top down. When Sieyès appealed to the necessity of representation to fend off challenges from the Jacobins in the early 1790s, he had already defined the sovereign nation, in Istvan Hont's words, so that "its 'constituent power' could be exercised only through the unitary representative system of the National Assembly as a constituted power" (*Jealousy of Trade: International Competition and the Nation-State in Historical Perspective* [Cambridge, MA: Harvard University Press, 2005], 489). This is convenient if one's power base is in the Assemblies, as opposed to the sections or Jacobin clubs, but it is also logically incoherent. And this is just the difficulty of showing how defending one's own revolution does not also legitimize every subsequent revolution against the new regime one hopes to set up, which we will see is the crux of Kant's competing, more consistently Hobbesian position. On these issues in Sieyès, see Hont, *Jealousy of Trade*; Murray Forsyth, *Reason and Revolution: The Political Thought of the Abbé Sieyès* (Leicester, UK: Leicester University Press, 1987); François Furet and Ran Halevi, "Introduction," in *Orateurs de la Révolution Française, I, Les Constituants* (Paris: Gallimard, 1989); Pasquale Pasquino, *Sieyes et l'invention de la constitution en France* (Paris: Jacob, 1998); Michael Sonenscher, "Introduction," in Sieyès, *Political Writings* (Indianapolis: Hackett, 2003); and Isaac Nakhimovsky, *The Closed Commercial State: Perpetual Peace and Commercial Society from Rousseau to Fichte* (Princeton, NJ: Princeton University Press, 2011), 22–35.

[19] He emphasized this unbridgeable gap between ideal and reality a page earlier: "Every fact (actuality) is an object in *appearance* (to the senses). Opposed to this, the thing in itself is what can

Kant, there always remains an unbridgeable gap between the mere *idea* of a united people governing itself through its own general will and the actual fact that some empirical persons must be empowered to act in that people's name if the people are to be said to have a single will at all. As he had famously written in the *Idea for a Universal History with Cosmopolitan Intent* in 1784:

> One may begin however one likes, but it cannot be seen how one could obtain a supreme authority of public justice that would itself be just, whether one seeks it in an individual person or in a society of many persons selected for [that end], since each of these will always misuse his freedom when he has no one above him that exercises power over him in accordance with the laws. The supreme authority should however be just *in itself* and yet also a *human being*. This task is therefore the hardest of all; indeed its complete solution is impossible: out of such crooked timber, as that from which men are made, nothing entirely straight can be hewn. Only approximating to this idea is required of us by nature. (8:23, emphases in original)

This is the problem Kant addressed in his version of social-contract theory by introducing an explicitly historical and future-oriented dimension opened up by the gap between reality and ideal, according to which all right will remain only "provisional" until the establishment of a perfect and universal federation of republics that succeeds in guaranteeing perpetual peace and justice for the entire world. This is the gap that must be filled by the act of judgment. In these works, Kant was explicit that we did *not*, in fact, know history will reach this happy end. Rather, he argued that since the mechanism of unsocial sociability

---

be represented only by pure reason and must be counted among the *ideas*, to which no object given in experience can be adequate—and of this sort is a perfectly *rightful constitution* among human beings" (6:371, emphases in original). Cf. *Contest of the Faculties:* "The idea of a constitution in accord with the natural rights of human beings—namely that those who obey the laws should at the same time, united, make them—lies as the ground of all forms of state, and the common essence which, thought through pure concepts of reason, is called a platonic *ideal* (*respublica noumenon*), is not an empty phantom of the brain but an eternal norm for every civil constitution whatsoever, and of avoiding all wars. A civil society organized in accord with this is the representation of such according to laws of freedom through an example in experience (*respublica phenomenon*), and can only be attained through many laborious struggles and wars. But this constitution, once achieved in the main, is qualified as the best of all... and to end war; thus it is a duty to reach it, and provisionally (because this does not so soon come to pass) it is the duty of monarchs, although they rule *autocratically*, nevertheless to govern in a *republican* (not democratic) way" (7:91). Note the explicit reference to Plato's ideas and the clearly practical conclusion grounding a duty; also that here merely governing in a republican manner is explicitly a temporary stopgap measure en route to actual constitutional change. "Democratic" here, of course, means the classical sense Kant rejected, without rule of law or a separation of legislative and executive powers.

makes it at least possible to imagine how a condition of perpetual peace under rightful constitutions could come about—even for a race of devils—this means there is no solid empirical or theoretical ground that could *rule out* the pursuit of that goal, without which justice is impossible, as incoherent or chimerical.[20] Kant's universal federation is also an "idea," not to be achieved directly by revolution, but one that if pursued by "gradual reform in accord with solid principles" can lead "in *continual approximation* to the highest political good, perpetual peace" (6:355, my emphasis). As he explained:

> [T]he question is no longer whether perpetual peace is a [real] thing or an absurdity. ... Rather, we must act as if the thing is [real], though perhaps it is not; we must work toward founding it and the kind of constitution that seems to us most suitable to it (perhaps the republicanism of all states, severally and together) in order to bring it about.... And even if reaching the completion of this goal remains always a pious wish, still we are certainly not deceiving ourselves in taking on the maxim of working incessantly toward it, for this is our duty. ... (6:354–5)

Kant's is an argument about the active orientation of citizens who must judge their constitutions, and also the orientations of sovereigns who ought to open themselves to reform. It is not merely an edifying sermon promising future

---

[20] This is quite explicit in *Theory and Practice* (8:309–10), *Perpetual Peace* (8:362, 8:368), and the *Metaphysics of Morals* (6:354–5), Kant's most systematic political works, where he comments on how one ought to take the political significance of the third *Critique*'s argument concerning teleology in history (5:430–4). Consider also his parallel argument for the possibility of moral progress in *Religion*. On the other hand, he clearly took the opposite position once in the late *Conflict of the Faculties* (7:88–9), based on the new argument from participation in sympathy with the French Revolution. This last, however, is brief and popular and does not obviate the more systematic arguments of the earlier texts, which cannot therefore be said to depend on it. Indeed, even in other earlier, popular texts, where Kant wrote mostly in an assertoric mode, he also signaled his practical aim: In the "Idea for a Universal History," he ended by suggesting that writing a history presuming a plan of nature "must be regarded as possible" and that the chance to justify providence this way "is no unimportant motive for choosing a particular standpoint for considering the world" (8:29–30). In the 1786 "Conjectural Beginning of Human History," he emphasized that "conjectures may not push their aspirations for assent too highly, but must rather present themselves always as only a movement of fancy [*Einbildungskraft*], granted in the accompaniment of reason for the recreation and health of the spirit, not however as a serious business" (8:109). But such a presentation of history is nevertheless "useful" for "instruction and edification" because it shows people not to blame providence for their suffering (8:123). Henry Allison offers a broadly sympathetic account in "Teleology and History in Kant: The Critical Foundations of Kant's Philosophy of History," in *Kant's Idea for a Universal History with a Cosmopolitan Aim: A Critical Guide*, eds. Amélie Oskenberg Rorty and James Schmidt (Cambridge, UK: Cambridge University Press, 2009). For a largely contrasting account, see Pauline Kleingeld, *Fortschritt und Vernunft: Zur Geschichtsphilosophie Kants* (Leiden, The Netherlands: Königshausen & Neumann, 1995).

salvation, because it emphasizes that change requires both active work and ongoing judgment in accordance with critical principles. It is best understood as a way of radically reworking the republican demand for self-governance to build in a theory of how ongoing constitutional conflict might be resolved in a way consistent with republican principles—what I have called a meta-republicanism, if the neologism can be excused.

Rejecting Revolution

Of course, one might instead read Kant's idealizing move simply as another way of shutting down actual republican revolutions—a way he has often been read. I think the interesting question is whether Kant's political theory ought to be understood deep down as democratic or undemocratic in principle, and this is a well-known interpretive puzzle as old as Kant's theory itself. On the one hand, Kant defines the ideal of a "true republic," which every government ought to strive gradually to approximate in effect, as a *"representative system* of the people ... by all citizens united and mediated by their delegates (deputies)" (6:41).[21] And he defines citizens as "colegislators [*Mitgesetzgebers*]" (8:294), each of whom possesses the rightful attribute "inseparable from his essence (as a citizen) ... of obeying no other law than that to which he has given his consent" (6:314).[22] He also famously maintained throughout his life enthusiasm for the French Revolution even when he criticized its methods.[23] On the other hand, in the same writings Kant rejects "democracy" as despotic (8:352–3), advocates the disenfranchisement of "passive citizens" (6:314–5), and most famously insists that the people have no right to resist their rulers, even tyrannical ones (6:318–23).

Consider first two related cases where Kant appears to reject the requirement that the people can be said to govern itself—his disparaging of "democracy" in *Perpetual Peace* and his insistence on excluding "passive citizens" from the vote in both *Theory and Practice* and *The Metaphysics of Morals*. In each case, a closer look shows that Kant's objection is not based on rejecting popular sovereignty, but instead on a claim about the conditions under which the people can fairly be said to rule.

When Kant equates "democracy" with "despotism" in *Perpetual Peace*, and suggests that monarchy or aristocracy may be preferable, he is, of course,

---

[21] He also used "republic" earlier in the more limited senses of any state under common laws, and again as a state that separates executive from legislative powers (8:352).

[22] Note that although Kant sometimes writes of laws to which the citizens "could have" given their assent, here he uses the indicative.

[23] For example, *Contest of the Faculties* (7:85–7).

referring to the classical conception of democracy in which the assembled people wielded not only legislative but also judicial and executive authority (6:352–3). It is to this universal participation in the executive, not the legislative, that Kant objects, "because [democracy] establishes an executive power where all decide on and in any case also against one (who does not agree), so that all, who are nevertheless not all, decide, which is a contradiction of the general will with itself and with freedom" (8:352). Far from rejecting the notion of popular rule, then, Kant rejects a direct democracy of this sort on the grounds that in it "the people" are not really ruling, since the same persons must single out individuals in such a way that if they are taken also as passing laws, this partiality will render their will that of a faction rather than of the whole. Kant frames the argument here expressly in Rousseauian terms as a self-contradiction of the "general will"; this is clearly an argument about the conditions of popular rule rather than an alternative to it.[24]

Consider next Kant's famous endorsement of the distinction between active and passive citizens, on the grounds that the latter lack the independence required to participate actively as co-legislators; his examples include apprentices, domestics, women, and anyone dependent on another (except the state!) for his livelihood (6:315, cf. 8:295–6). This distinction is required only because Kant earlier identified the "essence" of a citizen with the right to vote and the "attribute of obeying no other law than that to which he has given his consent" (6:314, cf. 8:294). But even the argument against allowing "passive" citizens to vote depends on a democratic principle: he objects that such persons' "dependence upon the will of others" is incompatible with freely legislating for oneself (6:315). He does not worry that they lack the intellectual *capacity* to judge the laws rightly; instead, he worries that their lack of independence means that they would only reflect, with their votes, the will of those on whom their livelihood depends, and that this would therefore distort the representation of the people's general will. If what mattered to Kant was only the rationality or generality of the laws, then his objection would be couched in terms of *knowledge or intelligence* rather than *dependence* and *will*—terms also emphasized by Rousseau. And if Kant were really concerned only with hypothetical or modal consent (imputed from formal universality), then his distinction between "active" and "passive" citizens would be meaningless, since every citizen would be "passive" in just the sense that he describes (or mere "co-protectees" [*Schutzgenossen*] as opposed to "citizens," in the language of "Theory and Practice," 8:294). Note finally that the reason *state* dependence is uniquely *not* a problem for Kant is that the state represents the general will of the entire people and so dependence on it does not preclude one from legislating autonomously for that people, as dependence on someone else's

---

[24] Cf. Rousseau's very similar criticism of Athens at *CS* II.IV, 3:374, and his related objections to "democracy" at III.IV.

merely private will does.[25] My point here, of course, is neither to praise nor to blame Kant's particular *judgments* about who should count as too dependent to will for themselves, nor his general suggestion that such inequalities should be accommodated by the political system rather than reformed as incompatible with its principles—contrast Rousseau's famous claim that "no citizen should be so rich that he could buy another, and none so poor to be constrained to sell himself" (*CS* II.XI, 3:391–2). My point is simply that these are disagreements *within* a shared framework that requires actual popular consent, not an opposition between one thinker who cares about actual self-governance and another who does not.

Let us turn finally, then, to Kant's repeated claim that monarchical and aristocratic governments may be legitimate, and that "the people" have no right to resist them or to replace them by force of arms. Now it is clear that Kant came to hold first that only a "patriotic" government (in *Theory and Practice*), and then a "true republic" (by *Perpetual Peace* and the *Metaphysics of Morals*) is finally, rather than only "provisionally," legitimate.[26] And Kant holds that in every state the established authority "is obligated ... to change the kind of governance gradually and continually so that it agrees *in its effect* with the only constitution that accords with right, namely that of a pure republic, so that all the old empirical (statutory) forms, which served merely the *subjection* of the people, give way to the original (rational) form, which alone makes *freedom* the principle and indeed the condition of all *coercion*, as is required by a rightful constitution of a state in its proper sense" (6:340–1, emphases in original). This "is the final end of all public right," Kant writes, since without such a constitution all right remains in the final analysis *"provisional"* as in the state of nature (6:341). Or as he puts it in *Perpetual Peace*, "The republican constitution is ... as far as right is concerned, in itself that which every kind of civil constitution has originally as its basis" (8:350). So although Kant will not declare other sorts of government illegitimate, he clearly presents them as second-bests to the idea of such a "true republic" (defined as a representative system of the people acting through its deputies), and insists that other governments also ought to govern in accordance with its spirit (8:351).

So why does he countenance such second-bests at all? His core argument is perhaps clearest in an important footnote to the *Contest of the Faculties*, where he writes that a free being can and should "demand no other government for the people to which he belongs than one in which the people are co-legislative," but that nevertheless "this right is however always only an

---

[25] Cf. Rousseau, *CS* II.XII, 3:394.

[26] For the evolution of Kant's views, see particularly Werner Busch, *Die Entstehung der kritischen Rechtsphilosophie Kants, 1762–1780* (Berlin: De Gruyter, 1979); Beiser, *Enlightenment*; Pauline Kleingeld, *Kant and Cosmopolitanism: The Philosophical Ideal of World Citizenship* (Cambridge, UK: Cambridge University Press, 2012); and Reidar Maliks, *Kant's Politics in Context*.

idea of which the realization is limited by the condition of the accordance of its *means* with morality, which the people may not overstep, and this may not occur through revolution, which is always unjust" (7:87). Because Kant's Europe was dominated by undemocratic constitutions, therefore, and because it was impermissible to overthrow these by force, Kant concludes that "to have autocratic rule [by a single legislator] and yet to govern in a republican way, that is, in the spirit of republicanism and on an analogy with it" is the way "to make a people satisfied with its constitution" (7:87). In other words, Kant's refusal to disallow autocratic governments does not reflect unconcern for popular rule in principle, but depends entirely on the further argument that revolution is always impermissible, since to deny the legitimacy of non-republican governments would be tantamount to calling for the revolutionary overthrow of virtually every state in Europe. As ever for Kant, what one needs to justify is not a mere ideal, but an actual course of political action in reference to that ideal.

Now one can easily imagine undemocratic arguments against revolution; one might, for instance, argue with Guizot or Rawls that a just constitution does not require the authorization of the people so long as it is rationally justified. But Kant's objection is strikingly different: he argues that the existing constitution must be respected *just because* it is the only one that may consistently be defended as expressing the people's general will. If direct rational justification of constitutional principles were the only standard, then revolution would be justified almost *everywhere* in accordance with Kant's own radical "idea" of a truly self-governing republic. What existing constitutions have over revolutionary aspirations is emphatically *not* that they are more "rational" in this sense; pace Rawls, it is not that they better represent what the people "would" will under ideal conditions, but to the contrary that they have a more consistent claim than the revolutionaries to be authoritative interpreters of what the people as a whole *already actually will*.

Kant's reasoning is this: if every individual and every band of insurgents have a right to determine for themselves whether or not the existing constitution represents the people's general will, then we remain, in effect, in a state of nature, defined by the lack of a definitive arbiter of justice backed up by a public enforcing power. But then any constitution successful revolutionaries might set up will be vulnerable to similar objections from others, and in the end it will be impossible ever to establish a rightful condition. That condition, however, is the only one in which the people—both severally and collectively—can be understood as genuinely self-governing (so far as their external actions are concerned). So if the revolutionaries' claims are accepted, both justice and popular rule are impossible; and since those claims are themselves advanced in the name of rightful popular self-governance, the revolutionaries' position turns out to be self-contradictory (8:301, 6:320,

6:372).²⁷ By contrast, an established constitution that reforms itself in a republican direction involves no such contradiction, and so only the latter is morally admissible. Kant's objection draws on the Hobbesian notion that a people without a sovereign is only a multitude, and therefore cannot possess a single will (8:303, 6:322 n.).²⁸ Unlike Hobbes, however, Kant insists that the sovereign must continue to govern in accordance with the people's general will. Here too, then, Kant's is not an argument from undemocratic principles, but one about the conditions of possibility of interpreting and enforcing the ideal of popular self-government in a consistent way.

Consider, by contrast, Onora O'Neill's view that Kant's argument requires only "modal" consent, neither hypothetical nor actual but merely the logical possibility that a certain constitution could be agreed to by an entire people.²⁹ Now Kant certainly does require such a possibility as one condition, but taken by itself, the "modal" condition fails to explain why we are *bound* by a constitution to which it is only logically possible that we might consent even though we have not done so. Or consider it this way: if actual consent does not matter, then why should it matter whether or not such consent is even logically possible? Is it not clear that the reason possible consent matters is *just because it is real consent*

---

[27] In *Perpetual Peace*, Kant adds a further charge of self-contradiction: rebellion is unjust because it cannot be publicly advocated without frustrating its own purpose (8:383). The point of what Kant there calls "the transcendental formula of public right"—namely, "all actions bearing on the right of others are unjust if their maxims are incompatible with publicity"—is to rule out as self-contradictory certain claims of public right, much the way the formula of universal law in the *Groundwork*, for instance, is meant to rule out as self-contradictory certain claims of morality. The thought is that since only an act defensible on a principle that might be seen as freely self-imposed by the entire public can consistently count as just, therefore any act that depends on secrecy for its success because "it would inevitably arouse the resistance of all against my project" cannot really count as one willed by the people as a whole. Instead, such a project is given away as an attempt to pass off a private interest as a claim of justice generally defensible (just the way failing the universalization test reveals one's tacit aim to foist a "moral" duty on others while effectively retaining an exception for oneself). Cf. Reflection 7204 (19:284).

[28] This point was established early in Kant's thought. See, for instance, Reflection 7810, from the period 1773–1775: "The highest obligation is to the body politic [corpus civile]. If the Monarch in his actions no longer represents this, the people thus [would have] right against him, *if it comprised a body politic without him*. But in a sovereign government this is not so, and thus the multitude [multitudo] has no right at all and every individual does the people injustice, to contest the basis of the civil union [unionis civilis]. Thus although the sovereign as an individual person has no right to make himself a tyrant, the subjects however also have no right of coercion against him..." (19:523, emphasis added). This is one of Kant's marginal notes to the copy of Achenwall's *Ius naturae*, from which he lectured on natural law between 1767 and 1788, and where Kant refers to Hobbes repeatedly by name. Kant's debt to Hobbes on this point is perhaps clearer in the manuscript notes to "Theory and Practice" (23:133–4) than in the final version; by framing his view "against Hobbes" Kant does not mean to reject Hobbes' view entirely but, while following Hobbes against Achenwall, to draw a further crucial distinction he thinks Hobbes failed to draw (8:303–4).

[29] O'Neill, "Social Contract Tradition."

that ultimately binds us, and yet if a certain act cannot possibly be consented to for logical reasons, then this shows us that it cannot *a fortiori* be an act to which we have, in fact, consented? (Rousseau's analogy to selling oneself into slavery remains a useful example here.) See how both the logic of Kant's argument and his use of modal language make perfect sense if one takes the condition of logical possibility only as a "touchstone" (*Probirstein*)—as Kant calls it—that reveals whether or not one can consistently *attribute* to "the people" actual consent through its lawful representative (8:39, 8:297).[30] But this only applies to laws passed by that lawful representative, since to count as self-legislated, a law must be both logically compatible with the people's general will and actually passed in the name of that will by the authority that represents it. This explains why, already in *What Is Enlightenment*, Kant suggested that the modal criterion matters just because "what a people may never decide for itself, so much less may a monarch decide for the people; *for his legislative authority rests just on this, that he unites in his will the will of the entire people*" (8:39–40, emphasis mine).[31]

There is a good deal of further textual support for the claim that this must be Kant's view. For instance, if representing the people's actual will does not matter, how is one to make sense of Kant's explanation of Louis XVI's alleged unintentional abdication, through which "the sovereignty of the monarch wholly disappeared ... and went over to the people" since "in it (the people) is found

---

[30] It is true that Kant writes "if it is *only possible* that a people could agree to it, it is a duty to consider [a] law just, even supposing that the people were presently in such a situation or manner of thinking that, were it to be consulted about the law, it would probably refuse its consent" (8:297). But this duty holds for a subject whom Kant is asking not to second-guess the sovereign, who must in general be reserved final judgment "not to make the people happy against its will, but only to make it so that the people exists as a collective entity" (8:298–9), and Kant's phrasing at 297 strongly suggests a case in which the people's present condition should not necessarily be taken to express their true and considered will. Keep in mind that the mark gold leaves on a "touchstone" is not what makes it gold.

[31] Kant also suggested in *What Is Enlightenment?* that a government with freedom of expression may be better than one with civil freedom because the former can allow citizens to cultivate their capacity to think freely. But this was 1784, before Kant's clear conversion to republicanism, and even here the point was to allow a people gradually to become "capable of *freedom* in acting," which would then require a corresponding reform in "the principles of government" (8:41–2). Similarly, in the *Natürrecht Feyerabend* notes also from 1784, Kant said, "A despotic law can be just, when it is made so that it could have been made by the entire people" (27:1382). But what reason is given? Just this: "The legislator is *summus imperans*, sovereign. The sovereign is therefore the people" (ibid.). As previously mentioned, this comes in the middle of an argument citing Hobbes, which concludes against a right to revolution on the grounds that the *summus imperans* always either is or represents the people. So although Kant was not yet committed to the republicanism of his later writings, he already insisted that the point of the "hypothetical" condition was an argument about who can be taken to represent the people's will. What changed was that he came to see these conditions also to include reference to the idea of a republican constitution, most likely while reading Rousseau's *Social Contract* sometime between these writings and the publication of the *Groundwork* the following year, in which the notion of autonomy first appears.

originally the supreme authority from which all rights of individuals ... as officials of the state ... must be derived," or why whoever has "the right of supreme legislation ... can only control the people through the united will of the people, but not that united will itself" (6:341–2)?[32] Whatever one thinks of Kant's arguments here, they clearly depend on who represents the people's will and not wholly an abstract logical test of universalizability.[33]

One important qualification remains. Even in the late *Metaphysics of Morals* and *Contest of the Faculties*, where Kant's republican sympathies are most pronounced, he continues to suggest that one should not literally change monarchies to democracies:

> Now this change cannot consist in this, that the state constitute itself from one of the three forms into one of the other two, for example that the aristocrats agree to subject themselves to an autocracy, or want to dissolve into a democracy, or vice-versa, just as if it rested on the free choice and pleasure of the sovereign, to which constitution it wished to subject the people. Since even if it decided to change itself into a democracy, it could still do the people an injustice, because they might themselves detest this constitution and find one of the other two more advantageous. (6:340)

And we saw that he suggests that a constitution must come to harmonize with that of a pure republic only "in its effect." Notice, however, that it is impossible to read this passage as a rejection of the sort of meta-republicanism I have attributed to Kant, since the grounds on which it suggests a sovereign could do wrong by creating a democracy are that the people might disagree.[34] The point Kant is making is the good Rousseauian point that the sovereign cannot alienate sovereignty at will; it has no right to abolish itself or to hand a

---

[32] Cf. Kant's language to the very similar passage in Rousseau *CS* III.XIV, 3:427–8. See also Reflection No. 8055, 19:595.

[33] It is true that some passages appear prima facie to point in the other direction, for instance, in the first of Kant's two open letters to Nicolai "On Turning Out Books" (8:434). But one cannot rely on those in isolation and must at least show why they should not also be taken in the sense more clearly expressed elsewhere. In this case, Kant's point was to refute the assertion by Justus Möser, in a polemic against Kant's "Theory and Practice" published posthumously in 1796, that it is likely that an empirical people might, in fact, opt to alienate its sovereignty to a particular class; Kant's counterclaim is that to do so violates the conceptual conditions of genuine sovereignty. See Möser, *Vermischte Schriften*, Vol. 2 (Berlin: Nicolai, 1798), 86–105. So the fact that these conditions are a priori does not mean popular consent is not required for laws; they rather comprise conditions under which a decision by certain empirical persons should count as a legitimate and binding decision of the people as a whole. Consider that Rousseau, too, did not think that the people can alienate their sovereign will even if they vote to, but that hardly means he did not care about popular sovereignty.

[34] And in the *Contest of the Faculties*, he explains that one of the two "moral causes" of the legitimate sympathy felt by onlookers of the French Revolution is "the *right* that a people must not be hindered by other powers from giving itself a civil constitution that seems to it to be good" (7:85, emphasis in original).

right to obedience over to someone else because the legitimacy of any such act depends not merely on the empirical sovereign's pleasure, but like any other law on whether it is attributable to the general will of the people—and an abdication or transfer of sovereignty, Kant suggests, is never so attributable. Now many of us might agree this makes sense if one thinks of a Reichstag voting to hand all power to Hitler, or one prince giving away his kingdom to another, but Kant thinks the argument goes both ways. The logical point appears to be that if the old sovereign abolishes itself in this way, its grant of powers would immediately cease to bind—why should anyone continue to obey the new power simply because someone who is no longer sovereign once told them to? This would amount to the dissolution of any constitution at all in the intervening moment, and accepting this view would have the consequence of forcing one to trace the legitimacy of present titles back to records of past grants in a way very familiar in eighteenth-century Europe but which competes in principle with the right of the people to determine their constitution for themselves in the present. So to avoid all this, Kant thinks one must maintain continuous sovereignty while reforming "every old empirical (statutory) form" in line with the idea of "a pure republic." Although Kant does not address the issue in detail, it seems to me clear that this should allow the sort of radical transformation in effect one would see in the nineteenth and early twentieth centuries in Britain, much of northern Europe, and Canada, Australia, and New Zealand. And Kant is very clear that should republics emerge—either because kings do, in fact, abdicate although they have no right to (like Louis XVI) or because they are defeated in war—then there can never be any reason for demanding them to hand back power. In the next section, I will make an argument for questioning Kant's absolute prohibition on even more radical change, but it is clear that his position is neither antirepublican nor antidemocratic (in the modern sense, admitting representation), but to the contrary turns on an argument about what it could mean to assert that a constitution counts as actually chosen by the people.

A Dilemma Unresolved

The best prima facie response to Kant's total prohibition on revolution is that it would appear to hold only if we are already in a civil state, and so if the current government does not meet the necessary minimum conditions of such a state, we need not consider ourselves bound to obey.[35] But this is not really

---

[35] Recently, see Ripstein, *Force and Freedom*; Stilz, *Liberal Loyalty*; Maliks, *Kant's Politics in Context*. Another tack, also considered by Maliks, builds on Kant's suggestion that the state cannot obligate one to violate "inner morality" (*MM* 6:371, *Religion* 6:99). But Kant was a staunch defender of the state's supremacy in its ongoing negotiations with religious authorities who challenged it on moral grounds, and of the Prussian policy of religious toleration whose origin as a solution to a history of

good enough—it might work if we *were certain* that we were not already in a civil state but in a mere state of nature, but the reason we need a state in the first place is just that individual judgments of this sort typically disagree, and so we cannot claim a direct right as individuals to impose our own judgment in such matters also on others who judge differently. But whenever we find ourselves under a putative sovereign who *claims* already to rule by law, then our individual refusal to accept that claim can only be partial and arbitrary (since at least that sovereign does indeed dissent, and typically many others besides). To claim a general right to impose our own judgment in such a case, then, would entail the reciprocal right of others later to reject the authority of any new legal order we might hope to establish. The only case in which this vicious circle would not arise is one in which *no one* already claimed to exercise lawful sovereign authority, just because then everyone would, in fact, agree (*ex hypothesi*) that we were in a state of nature. In that case alone could a seizure of power be justified without thereby also justifying every subsequent revolt. Hence, as Kant concludes:

> Unconditional subjection of the will of the people (which is in itself not united and thus lawless) to a *sovereign* will (uniting all through *one* law) is a *deed* that can commence only by seizing supreme power, and so first establishing public right. To allow any resistance to this absolute

---

interconfessional wars was well remembered—as emphasized, for instance, in Schiller's widely read 1791-1792 *History of the Thirty-Years War*. Indeed, this was much of the upshot of Kant's move in the *Metaphysics of Morals* to sever the dependence of justice on virtue, against Leibniz and Wolff, and in *Religion within the Boundaries of Mere Reason* to distinguish sharply between juridical and ethical communities. Kant's qualifications on obedience were meant to underscore this separation rather than to roll it back: because the state is sovereign only over questions of external right, one is not bound to obey also on matters of "internal morality," in which it is the adoption of a certain motive or belief that the state aims to compel. So when Kant concluded a long passage denying, against Achenwall, any natural law basis for resistance to "external" laws by reiterating that the people must never resist "except in those cases that can never occur in a civil union [*unionem civilem*], e.g. religious compulsion. Compulsion to unnatural sins: assassination, etc., etc." (Reflection 8051, 19:594-5), he meant not that morality trumps the state but that the idea of an original contract authorizes *imperium civile* only in matters of right, concerning hindrances to hindrances of external freedom. Achenwall uses "unio civilis" invariably in the construction "pactum unionis civilis," and Kant is much more explicit at 19:479, 19:489-90, 19:519-20, 19:565, 19:579-80, and especially at 19:569. The note at *Religion* 6:99 is to a passage distinguishing ethical law from juridical just because the former applies directly to "inner morality" unenforceable by external coercion; hence the permission to disobey a statutory command "evil in itself" because it "immediately contradicts the ethical law" must there, too, refer to laws attempting to compel inner motive or belief. Kant neither subordinates justice to morality nor qualifies the state's authority as final judge of the former. Rather, as he insists in several of these same passages, it must be the public sovereign to rule on what justice requires, although he did clearly allow for disobedience in the case of an avowedly antiethical law put forward with no pretense to a ground in external right.

power ... is to contradict oneself; since then this [power] (which may be resisted) would not be the lawful supreme power, which first determines what is to be publicly right or not. (6:372, emphasis in original)

Note that the seizure of power is criterial and establishes public right *regardless* of its content, since that power "first determines what is to be publicly right." (In Kant's terms: this fact provides the object of experience to which the concept of a rightful constitution may be applied, although it is not adequate to that concept.) The entire force of Kant's argument is to rule out any temptation for individuals to second-guess whether such power might be wielded "wrongly" in a way to void its possessor's authority; and this is particularly clear when one considers in context Kant's criticisms of Achenwall on the point, which placed him clearly on one side of this running debate.[36]

The point, then, is not that we already in fact know that we are in a civil state. Rather, we *must assume that we are*—except in the single case in which there exists not even a pretender to such authority with sufficient power to exercise it (as in the international arena)—because the alternative assumption is tantamount to abandoning all hope of ever consistently establishing a rightful condition. This is a necessary assumption of practical judgment. Consider how Kant explains the analogous role of the notion of perpetual peace:

If someone cannot prove that a thing is, he can try to prove that it is not. If he succeeds in neither (a case that often occurs), he can still ask whether it *interests* him to *assume* one or the other (as a hypothesis), either from a theoretical or from a practical point of view. ... [In the moral case, which requires adopting a certain end as a duty] ... What duty obliges is . . . to act from the idea of this end, even if there is not the slightest theoretical probability that it can be attained, so long as its impossibility is equally indemonstrable. (6:354, emphases in original)

And as Kant earlier explained, one must assume the possibility of perpetual peace in this way just because the moral law "pronounces its irresistible veto: *there is*

---

[36] Cf. 19:592 and a note that Schubert reports Kant wrote in the mid-1790s, "For a *pactum sociale* to found a republic (in the *Rousseauian* sense of a state without consideration to the form of the constitution), there must already be a republic there: it follows that this can be founded no other way than by violence, not through insight" (Schubert, *Immanuel Kants Biographie: Zum grossen Theil nach handschiftlichen Nachrichten* [Leipzig: Leopold Voss, 1842], 145). Ripstein emphasizes to the contrary Kant's analytic distinctions in the *Anthropology* lectures among anarchy, despotism, barbarism, and a true republican constitution (7:330). But the distinctions themselves do not speak to the question at issue, which is who is entitled to apply these categories with force, and elsewhere Kant appears clearly to commit himself to the view that a sovereign who at least claims to rule by law must be obeyed in external matters, regardless of the content of his or her decisions.

to be no war," and so therefore to do our duty, we must "act as if the thing [perpetual peace] is [real], which it may not be," since to do otherwise would be to "admit that the moral law within us is itself deceptive" and "would put forward the wish, which arouses our abhorrence, of sooner casting off all reason and regarding ourselves thrown by our principles along with the other classes of animals into the same mechanism of nature"—that is, to give up entirely on justice and morality as shams and to surrender politics wholly to the play of power (6:354–5).

So Kant's argument requires us to assume we are in a civil state whenever we find ourselves subject to a lawgiver who has "seized supreme power"; and although we are obligated to criticize the failings of the constitution, we are not empowered to overturn it. This is an argument of practical judgment—a question of the principles and assumptions on which we ought to act, even though we cannot ever prove, on theoretical or empirical grounds, that a given state is in fact legitimate.

This is a powerful argument that is not easily answered, and particularly not by resistance theories that fail to provide any comparably rigorous account of how one could ever judge who is to exercise the people's right to judge. But it is not airtight. Even if Kant's reasoning is correct, it depends on assuming we face only two alternatives—either the existing constitution or a state of nature (in which revolutionaries are free to pursue whichever constitution their private judgment tells them is best). But what if we face instead a situation in which two rival governments each claim authority over the same citizens (for instance, one in Tripoli and one in Benghazi, or one in Versailles and one in Paris in the Hôtel de Ville)? In this case, Kant's argument no longer tells us what to do—he can tell us we *ought not* to view the situation that way, since it entails a conflict with no sovereign judge, but this does not tell us *which* of the two pretender governments to recognize as rightful. Friedrich Bouterwek's 1797 review of Kant's *Rechtslehre* had raised just this objection: "Is it to be one and the same," he asked, "that [one should] recognize *sovereignty* and *supreme authority* [in the abstract], and that one should hold a priori as his lord *this or that* person, whose existence is not even given a priori?" (6:371, emphases in original). Kant replied in the second edition by reiterating the logical necessity of a final arbiter, but ignored the problem of how to decide between "this or that" potential sovereign. Even if we know that a final authority is required, however, so long as we do not also know who that final authority is, we cannot be said to have left a state of nature, and Kant cannot solve the problem by suggesting, for instance, that we must always prefer the "sovereign" who was "there first," since he explicitly argues that a successful revolution (even if itself immoral) thereby creates a new constitution that must henceforth be respected, and that one may not rightly try to overthrow it on the grounds of its illegitimate origins (6:323).

Although Kant never directly addresses this problem in the domestic context, he does acknowledge an analogous situation in international affairs in *Toward Perpetual Peace*, where he allows that although (according to the fifth preliminary article) no state may forcibly interfere in the constitution and government of another, "this would be entirely different [for] a state, through internal discord split into two parts, each putting itself forward as a particular state and laying claim to the whole ... (for this is anarchy)" (8:346). Here too, Kant could cogently conclude that such a condition is a state of nature and that therefore whoever ultimately succeeds in seizing supreme power must henceforth be recognized as the lawful sovereign. So the problem is not that Kant's view is inconsistent. The problem is rather that it offers no guidance for political judgment or political action whenever sovereignty becomes seriously contested in this way. And these sorts of challenges to existing constitutional orders in the name of freedom's progress would only become more central in the centuries after 1789. Ultimately, then, Kant's argument succeeds against revolutionaries who ignore the problem of authorization, interpretation, and enforcement by claiming to act directly in the name of "justice" or "the people." But it gains no traction against those who instead claim to speak already for a shadow government that precisely mirrors the representative pretensions of its rival, and real cases of revolution are often at least as plausibly described in the second manner as in the first. This is the problem of democratic change. Kant's political theory showed up the inability of traditional theories of justice and freedom to come to terms with this problem, and opened the door to a new way of approaching it through a theory of popular political judgment. But his version of that theory left a crucial dilemma unresolved. The following chapter shows how Hegel came to offer a different way of approaching it that, at least on this one point, did better.

5

Hegel on History

This chapter argues that Hegel's philosophy of history provides an original and ingenious response to the problem we saw Kant ultimately unable to resolve: When does a constitution count as freely affirmed by a people as a way of organizing their own freedom? Kant argued that one can only trust the existing sovereign to judge itself in the people's name. But Hegel suggests another possibility. If some constitutional orders are best understood as already divided, then we have no choice but to sort through competing claims to final authority to see which holds up best. Now, because Hegel agrees with Kant that authority depends on the freedom of the citizens, it follows that any claim that cannot be defended on the basis of that freedom without contradicting itself may fairly be ruled out. And so this Socratic sort of argument allows Hegel to show how one might justify a constitutional order strictly by showing up alternatives as self-contradictory. To see whether our present order should count as free and therefore rightful, then, rather than asking the sitting sovereign, we should look at the history of the orders it replaced. If it can be shown that each of them depended on interpretations of freedom that led necessarily to contradictions which the present order escapes, then the new order will count as more truly free and therefore justified. We will not be guilty of unfairly presuming history to progress toward ever more perfect freedom, or that whatever comes later is therefore better. Rather, we will have "assumed" the *idea* of self-actualizing freedom only as a principle of interpretation and judgment, to *ask* whether or not the present order can be defended as compatible with that assumption—just because if it cannot, then it cannot consistently be defended at all. Whether the answer turns out to be yes or no will depend entirely on the details of the actual history by which that order came to be, and the quality of the immanent refutations of earlier orders we may or may not be able to provide. Unlike Kant's, then, this sort of argument does not ask us to presuppose the authority of any given order ex ante. (In this sense Hegel is less willing than Kant to let might make right.) Nor does it—as is often supposed—require belief in any tendentious metaphysics, cosmology, or empirical teleology. But just for that reason neither does it allow us to predict the future; it is only a way of judging the present in relation to the past. This is the sort of argument, I contend, that Hegel gave to justify the modern state.

The reader will have noticed that this flies in the face of more familiar ways of understanding Hegel's philosophy of history and its relation to politics, and so it requires some defense. Contemporary political theorists interested in Hegel have focused overwhelmingly on the *Philosophy of Right* and the concepts of *Sittlichkeit* [ethical life] and recognition, while largely neglecting Hegel's philosophy of history.[1] But this is unfortunate, because contrary to what is widely supposed, the latter is more productive and defensible, particularly for democratic theorists. This chapter first briefly suggests that Hegel's constitutional theory, although not without interest, is fundamentally flawed because of its dependence on the notion of *Sittlichkeit* or ethical life. This notion builds on a way of understanding free institutions that Hegel drew particularly from Montesquieu, as inflected by authors of the Scottish Enlightenment, notably Smith (and although it also retained important religious undertones for Hegel). Hegel used this constitutionalist way of understanding political freedom to counter the dangers he saw in the voluntarist republicanism he associated with the failed Jacobin Revolution and with Rousseau, but at least in this form it competes fundamentally with the democratic idea that the people must author their own laws, and it cannot stand up to criticisms of the sort that had been made by Kant.

The chapter then moves to Hegel's philosophy of history, arguing for the interpretation just introduced. This requires showing that Hegel's position does not, as often supposed, depend in any positive sense on faith in a providential, developmentalist cosmology. Long-running debates over whether or not Hegel's position is "metaphysical" risk missing the point, since everything depends on what one means by "metaphysics" and what one supposes to follow from it.[2] Three substantive points are at issue. First, Hegel's larger system is, like Kant's,

---

[1] See Charles Taylor, *Hegel and Modern Society* (Cambridge, UK: Cambridge University Press, 1979), 125–69; Michael J. Sandel, *Liberalism and the Limits of Justice* (Cambridge, UK: Cambridge University Press, 1982); Allen W. Wood, *Hegel's Ethical Thought* (Cambridge, UK: Cambridge University Press, 1990); Allen Patten, *Hegel's Idea of Freedom* (Oxford: Oxford University Press, 1999); Frederick Neuhouser, *Foundations of Hegel's Social Theory: Actualizing Freedom* (Cambridge, MA: Harvard University Press, 2000), 82–174. See also Axel Honneth, *The Struggle for Recognition* (Cambridge, MA: MIT Press, 1996); *The Pathologies of Individual Freedom* (Princeton, NJ: Princeton University Press, 2012), and *Freedom's Right: The Social Foundations of Democratic Life* (Cambridge, UK: Polity Press, 2014). Honneth also turns to history, but his "normatively guided reconstruction of social development" (61) takes over pragmatist-positivist assumptions of normative integration and societal evolution from Durkheim and Parsons (elsewhere also from Dewey). The difference between our readings is that I take Hegel, in the *Phenomenology* and philosophy of history, to insist that the problem of political and interpretive disagreement over norms demands a dialectical or elenctic response proceeding strictly through the refutation of alternatives, and thus to reject direct appeals to progressive learning of the sort widely available in period treatments of *Bildung*.

[2] Major antimetaphysical or post-Kantian views include Klaus Hartmann, "Hegel: A Non-Metaphysical View," in *Hegel: A Collection of Critical Essays*, ed. Alasdair MacIntyre (Notre

thoroughly antifoundational and Socratic, and so not "metaphysical" in any dogmatic sense.[3] Second, the core claims of Hegel's logic and philosophy of nature are meant to show precisely that one cannot derive conclusions concerning history and politics directly from these other spheres, but must instead work them out always in terms of freedom, the characteristic presumption of any claim concerning human action (*Enz* §381).[4] Third, despite this independence of politics and history from nature, Hegel nevertheless supposes that arguments and explanations in all these different spheres must be homologous and converge in their results, because he rejects the distinction between logics of theoretical and practical reason defended by Kant.[5] This last point is indefensible and responsible for much of the confusion in Hegel. But what it really means is not that Hegel wrongly derives political conclusions from metaphysics, but to the contrary, that he wrongly supposes one can justify empirical claims in the same way one argues to justify conceptual and normative principles. So what needs

---

Dame, IN: Notre Dame University Press, 1972); Robert Pippin, *Hegel's Idealism: The Satisfactions of Self-Consciousness* (Cambridge, UK: Cambridge University Press, 1989), and *Hegel's Practical Philosophy: Rational Agency as Ethical Life* (Cambridge, UK: Cambridge University Press, 2008); Terry Pinkard, *Hegel's Phenomenology: The Sociality of Reason* (Cambridge, UK: Cambridge University Press, 1994); John McDowell, *Having the World in View: Essays on Kant, Hegel, and Sellars* (Cambridge, MA: Harvard University Press, 2009); Paul Redding, *Hegel's Hermeneutics* (Ithaca, NY: Cornell University Press, 1996); Béatrice Longuenesse, *Hegel's Critique of Metaphysics* (Cambridge, UK: Cambridge University Press, 2007). Leading metaphysical accounts include Charles Taylor, *Hegel* (Cambridge, UK: Cambridge University Press, 1975); Michael Rosen, *Hegel's Dialectic and Its Criticism* (Cambridge, UK: Cambridge University Press, 1982); Frederick Beiser, *Hegel* (New York: Routledge, 2005), 53–79; and Rolf-Peter Horstmann, "The *Phenomenology of Spirit* as a 'Transcendentalistic' Argument for a Monistic Ontology," in *Hegel's Phenomenology of Spirit: A Critical Guide*, eds. Dean Moyar and Michael Quante (Cambridge, UK: Cambridge University Press, 2008). For a good overview of the ongoing debate, see James Kreines, "Hegel's Metaphysics: Changing the Debate," *Philosophy Compass* 1, no. 5 (2006): 466–80.

[3] Defending this requires an interpretation of the *Logic* with which I will not burden readers here, but the clearest signal is the discussion of the problematic character of a "beginning" with which that work begins (21:53–66).

[4] Beiser's argument for a metaphysical Hegel on the grounds that Hegel believed "everything must be shown to be a part of the organism of nature" and maintained "the organicist thesis that the mental and the physical, the ideal and real, are only different stages of development of degrees of organization of a single living force," seems to underplay this central thesis (*Hegel*, 80–1). For Hegel it is not spirit that is part of nature but nature that is part of spirit. The view Beiser describes is fairly attributed to Herder, but not even to Schelling, much less to Hegel. Cf. Schelling, *System of Transcendental Idealism*: "Thus is freedom always already presupposed in nature (*nature does not bring it forth*).... [A]lthough *up to this point* nature is entirely the same as intelligence, and passes through the same powers, freedom [if it is at all] must be above nature (*natura prior*)" (3:633, emphasis added).

[5] This is the conceptual point really at stake in all the criticisms of Kant's merely "subjective" idealism and his account of pure reason as self-limiting. One can see this from the way Hegel's criticisms all stem from the same objection to Kant's antinomies, most particularly the third; see notably *WL* 12:157–9. Political implications are considered below.

to go is Hegel's philosophy of nature, adapted from Goethe and Schelling; what one should make of Hegel's philosophy of history depends not on this, but on whether or not it turns out to be a useful way of thinking through what it could mean for one view of political freedom to hold up better than another.

Because Hegel was unwilling simply to rely on providence or cosmology to explain the course of history, he turned instead to leading empirical theories of the period in the works of Montesquieu, the Scottish Enlightenment authors, and Gibbon. Although it is well known that Hegel was deeply influenced by these authors, scholarly attention has focused almost entirely on their impact on Hegel's theories of the state and civil society, rather than on their equally profound influence on his philosophy of history.[6] This clearly set Hegel's theory of history apart from the Romantic and historicist alternatives with which it is often conflated and whose language it sometimes shared, but which took no similar interest in the Scottish tradition and often defined themselves in explicit opposition to it, as did Herder and Adam Müller. But it is also crucial to understanding Hegel's key concept of the "cunning of reason" and why he wrongly supposed that political orders based on indefensible conceptions of freedom must sooner or later break down and be replaced by more defensible ones. In this Hegel extended a central thesis of the line of historical thought running from Montesquieu to Gibbon, according to which the stability of a legal order depended on maintaining the appropriate spirit among the people required to support it. Hegel certainly had philosophical reasons for wanting to see in history the progress of human freedom, but he thought he also needed to show on strictly empirical grounds why this should turn out to be the case, which is

---

[6] Exceptions include Georg Lukács's *The Young Hegel* (Cambridge, MA: MIT Press, 1977), whose *Marxisant* interpretation I will argue takes the import of Hegel's debt in just the wrong way, and Norbert Waszsek's excellent "Hume, Hegel, and History," *Clio* 14, no. 4 (1985): 379–92, which is however extremely brief and does not discuss in detail implications for understanding later works. Jean Hyppolite's *Introduction to Hegel's Philosophy of History* (Gainesville: University Press of Florida, 1996) notes the early influence but stops before the *Phenomenology*; Raymond Plant's *Hegel: An Introduction*, 2nd ed. (Oxford: Basil Blackwell: 1983) contains a brief discussion relying on Paul Chamley's *Economie politique et philosophie chez Steuart et Hegel* (Paris: Dalloz, 1963) and limited entirely to Steuart; and Ernst Bloch devotes two lines to the issue in *Subjekt-Objekt: Erlaüterungen zu Hegel* (Berlin: Aufbau Verlag, 1951), 220. Important treatments of the Scottish influence with little to say about its role in the philosophy of history include Shlomo Avineri, *Hegel's Theory of the Modern State* (Cambridge, UK: Cambridge University Press, 1972); H. S. Harris, *Hegel's Development*, 2 vols. (Oxford: Clarendon Press, 1972–1983); Manfred Riedel, *Between Tradition and Revolution: The Hegelian Transformation of Political Philosophy* (Cambridge, UK: Cambridge University Press, 1984); Laurence Dickey, *Religion, Economics, and the Politics of Spirit, 1770–1807* (Cambridge, UK: Cambridge University Press, 1987); Norbert Waszek, *The Scottish Enlightenment and Hegel's Account of "Civil Society"* (Boston: Kluwer, 1988); and Paul Franco, *Hegel's Philosophy of Freedom* (New Haven, CT: Yale University Press, 1999), 249–77. Discussions of the historical sections of the *Phenomenology* and the later lectures on the philosophy of history commonly associate Hegel either more one-sidedly with the lineage of post-Kantianism, or alternately with the Romantics.

why he had such interest in Montesquieu and the Scots. Where Hegel attributed causal necessity to a certain direction of historical development, then, this did not single him out as a German metaphysician but placed him firmly in the mainstream of the most empirically-minded French and British historical thinking. And it sharply distanced him—at least by the time he wrote the *Phenomenology*—from the Romantics and historicists with whose theories of history his is too often conflated, but whom he had made a point in his lifetime of opposing.[7]

But there is also a conceptual point. Once one sees how the logic of Hegel's argument concerning freedom in history works, entirely through the immanent refutation of alternatives rather than by grounding the "best" order directly on any positive metaphysical foundation, one can see how different a sort of answer this is than either Kant or anyone else had ever given before to the question of how to work out what count as "free" political institutions. I suggest then that one look in Hegel's philosophy of history not for a doctrine, and certainly not an institutional doctrine, but for a series of brilliant and thought-provoking examples of what it might look like to approach questions of freedom and historical change in this Socratic sort of way. The final section considers three episodes from across his writings that illustrate recurring ways in which particular interpretations of freedom might turn out to undermine themselves. Part Two of this book will draw on some of these examples in working out the conditions of what I have called Principle (II)* of a historical and Socratic democratic theory.

Against Ethical Life

One key to understanding Hegel's constitutional theory is to see why he so opposed the democratic idea that a just constitution is one in which the citizens make the laws. The answer is not that Hegel was unconcerned with citizens' freedom (as once widely supposed); rather, it is that his view of a free constitution followed in its essentials Montesquieu's. Hegel's debt to Montesquieu is explicit,

---

[7] The *PhR*, for instance, makes a point of criticizing both Romantics and historicists for misunderstanding the relation of critical reason to judgment and to history. See notably criticism of Schlegel for misconstruing Socratic irony at §140, and of Hugo (14:29–30) and Haller §258 for conflating historical fact with justification. Hegel's response to Hugo's critical review is included in the Meiner *Werke*, Vol. 14, 2. As John Edward Toews noted in his *Hegelianism: The Path Toward Dialectical Humanism, 1805–1841* (Cambridge, UK: Cambridge University Press, 1980), 60, Ranke described the University of Berlin in the 1820s as one in which "two parties stood opposed to one another, the philosophical [represented by Hegel] and the historical [represented particularly by Savigny, Eichhorn, Neibuhr and Schleiermacher]" (Sämmtliche Werke, 54 vols., Leipzig: Duncker & Humblot, 1867–90, 51/52:588). On Hegel's critique of the Romantics, see Otto Pöggler, *Kegels Kritik der Romantik* (Munich: Fink, 1999).

emphatic, and widely recognized.[8] The constitutional view Hegel took from him has two parts: it argues for a certain arrangement of institutions and it argues that institutions must be appropriate to the spirit of a people.[9] Consider first the arrangement: Montesquieu held that citizens' liberty is best secured by a complex constitutional monarchy ruled by means of "fundamental Laws" that route political authority through "subordinate and dependent intermediate powers," since "if there is nothing in the State but the momentary and capricious will of one alone, nothing can be fixed and consequently [there can be] no fundamental Law."[10] In other words, the key is to arrange a mixed constitution such that power is divided and every power dependent on the others, so that none may act alone to impose its arbitrary will on the rest. Such a moderate government must include a legislature in which the people are represented, since otherwise, they would be subject entirely to the rule of another, but that legislature should also include the body of the nobles and a monarchical veto (XI.VI). So the aim is not to make laws subject to the popular will, but that no part of society should be entirely left out and subject to the arbitrary domination of another, while every part is reciprocally checked to prevent it from dominating the whole. The laws are prior to the will of any part and even to the will of the whole. Montesquieu emphasized how this competes with voluntarism and democracy:

> It is true that in Democracies the people appear to do what they want, but political Liberty does not at all consist in doing what one wants. . . . Liberty is the right to do everything the Laws permit; and if a citizen could do what they forbid, he would no longer have Liberty, because the others would have this power just the same (XI.III, 2:4).[11]

These are all views Hegel would share.[12] One can see the appeal of this sort of constitutionalism to anyone seeking a liberty-based answer to Rousseau and alternative to Jacobinism—Tocqueville, for instance, would later use it for

---

[8] Michael A. Mosher provides an overview in "The Particulars of a Universal Politics: Hegel's Adaptation of Montesquieu's Typology," *American Political Science Review* 78, no. 1 (1984):179–88.

[9] Hegel's early notions of spirit and ethical life in the 1790s also drew on religious and Greek models, but when he turned his attention to political and constitutional questions, the way he interpreted the relevance of those models for the modern world was inflected by the framework he took from Montesquieu, as he repeatedly emphasized. Montesquieu's view was a reworking of the familiar republican defense of the mixed constitution as bulwark against domination, in favor of a constitutional monarchy along broadly English lines.

[10] Montesquieu, *De l'esprit des Loix*, rev. 2nd ed. (Amsterdam: Chatelain, 1749), II.IV, 1:31.

[11] Although Rousseau and Kant would agree with much of this, they would insist on adding that the laws must be authored by the people's general will, which rather changes the point.

[12] As is well known, Hegel also insisted strongly on the sovereign unity of the state, on the one hand, and on permitting relative freedom for subordinate powers within that unity, on the other, as particularly emphasized in the early essay "The German Constitution" (*SK* 451–610; English

similar ends. And indeed, the general argument is not necessarily incompatible with democracy, if one reinterprets it with Madison and Tocqueville not as an alternative to popular sovereignty but as a modality in which the latter might be exercised.[13] But Montesquieu and Hegel took it instead as a freestanding competitor, and this is why Hegel's political theory would be vulnerable to democratic criticisms by the 1840s, particularly once the success of the 1830 Revolution in France caused many (but not Hegel, in the final year of his life) to rethink their harsher judgments of the initial Revolution.[14]

Hegel innovated on Montesquieu in several ways, particularly in incorporating modern civil society into the system of mutually dependent constitutional powers and in the role he assigned to the "universal class" of civil servants. He also took over from Fichte a distinctive view of freedom as mutual recognition.[15] But the key is to see how none of the particular institutional consequences Hegel drew follow directly from that view—indeed, Fichte had used it to support very different institutions, and when Hegel used arguments from Schelling to criticize Fichte's conclusions, the discussion amounted to further philosophical ballast for the constitutionalist alternative to voluntarism Hegel found already in Montesquieu.[16] What Hegel took to follow depended on his opting for Montesquieu's constitutionalist framework against Rousseau's and Kant's in light of his criticism of the Jacobin Terror. There is a certain irony here, because much of what was long seen as most Prussian, autocratic, and even

---

trans. in *Political Writings*, ed. Laurence Dickey [Cambridge, UK: Cambridge University Press, 1999], 6–101)—but the question here is how that sovereignty is to be organized.

[13] Recently, see Philip Pettit, *On the People's Terms: A Republican Theory and Model of Democracy* (Cambridge, UK: Cambridge University Press, 2012).

[14] See particularly "On the English Reform Bill," published in 1831 (*SK* 11:83–128, cf. 11:553–5; *Political Writings* 234–70). Cf. Marx's criticisms of the "mysticism" and "formalism" of Hegel's conception of representation in the Estates and Marx's contrary insistence on the centrality of universal suffrage in his *Critique of Hegel's Philosophy of the State*. As Marx put it: "Hegel proceeds from the state and makes the people [*den Menschen*] into the state internalized [*versubjektivierten*]; democracy proceeds from the people and makes the state into the people [*den Menschen*] objectified" (*Marx-Engels Gesamtausgabe* [Berlin: Dietz, 1982], 2:31).

[15] See Fichte's *Foundations of Natural Right from the Principles of the Wissenschaftslehre* (1796–1797) and *System of Ethics* (1798). For discussions, see George Armstrong Kelly, *Idealism, Politics, and History: Sources of Hegelian Thought* (Cambridge, UK: Cambridge University Press, 1969), and Robert R. Williams, *Recognition: Fichte and Hegel on the Other* (Albany: State University of New York Press, 1992).

[16] See particularly Hegel's 1802–1803 essay "Natural Law," which begins with these speculative discussions and ends by siding with Montesquieu on politics and history (*SK* 2:524, *Political Writings* 102–80). Hegel's criticisms of "social contract" theory always read as somewhat misplaced, since the real disagreement was over intermediary powers but Hegel insisted on framing the objection as part of a philosophical critique of subjectivism that neither was particularly fair to Rousseau or Kant nor clearly justified his institutional conclusions unless one accepts the crucial intervening interpretation of the French Revolution as "absolute freedom and terror" presented most fully in the *PhG*, §582–95.

nationalist in Hegel's politics did not depend on an organicism of a distinctively German or speculative kind. Although Hegel did use that language, the institutional analysis he took it to support came from Montesquieu's reworking of the traditional republican defense of the mixed constitution on the model of the English monarchy. As he emphasized in the *Philosophy of Right*, "[I]t was above all Montesquieu, in his famous work *The Spirit of the Laws* [*Der Geist der Gesetze*], who fixed before our eyes, and also tried to work out in detail, the thoughts that even private law depends on the particular character of the state and the philosophical view that the part is to be considered only in its relation to the whole" (§261).

The second part of the view Hegel took from Montesquieu was that a good constitutional order must be not only good in itself, but also suited to the spirit of the particular people it is to govern. It was "*Montesquieu* [who] indicated the true historical view, the genuine philosophical viewpoint," Hegel wrote, which "consider[s] legislation in general and in its particulars not in isolation and in the abstract, but instead as dependent moments of *one* totality, in connection with all the other determinations made up by the character of a nation and an age" (*PhR* §3, emphases in original). Hegel also took Montesquieu's emphasis on the vital pedagogical role of legislation; a good constitution must make all laws and institutions accord with its principle so as to reinforce and sustain in citizens the spirit proper to their constitution, on which its enduring force ultimately depends. Now this view drew on a long classical tradition and was shared also by Rousseau, as later by Tocqueville. Hegel made two great modifications. First, he reinterpreted the notion of a people's spirit in terms of rational freedom. The principle of Hegel's modern state was not virtue, honor, or fear but freedom, understood along the lines in which Fichte had developed Kant. For Hegel, a good constitution must be loved because the citizens recognize it as securing the conditions of their liberty. Hegel's "spirit" was modeled not on passions but on a rational freedom that questions every claim to authority and accepts only those that can be justified to it with reasons. Hegel thought only a shared way of life built around reflectively justifiable claims of this sort could hold up under modern criticism, as the Reformation and Enlightenment had shown. So for Hegel the laws must teach citizens not only or primarily to be honorable or virtuous, but above all to be free, and to see for themselves how their freedom depends on preserving their constitution.[17]

Hegel's second innovation was to argue that institutions' role in cultivating this spirit of rational freedom should be in large part indirect. Rather than the state itself training citizens in what to think and how to behave, it should instead secure a space for the family and for civil society, where individuals learn

---

[17] *PhR* §150, §273, where Hegel explicitly distinguishes himself on this point from Montesquieu.

to act on their own account for their particular ends. It is through citizens' own experience of the limits of these purely private pursuits that they are to learn for themselves the need for a constitutional state to make up for what individuals cannot achieve by themselves in the market. This modern state will be freer than ancient republics because in it individuals have rights as individuals, but also because citizens are not simply habituated into love for a state they cannot rationally defend, but are given space in which to work out freely for themselves how their liberty depends on a rightly constituted state, as they try out other ways of pursuing freedom in the family and civil society and come to see how these end by undermining themselves—unless the state steps in to compensate for their limitations and to maintain them in their proper spheres. This is a rather ingenious sort of Socratic pedagogy that puts Smith's argument concerning the "invisible hand" to quite a different use than Smith's.

Hegel's notion of *Sittlichkeit* thus describes the relation between a popular spirit of freedom and those institutions that support it in two different ways: the institutions prevent domination by dividing political power so that every part of society is included and mutually dependent, and they teach citizens, indirectly, that this is the sort of constitution on which their liberty depends. So why is this not a fruitful idea for contemporary theory? I have already said that it may be admitted if reworked as a mode of exercising popular sovereignty rather than as an alternative to it—although that invites ongoing conflicts between the authority of the constitution and the present popular will one will need a historical and Socratic theory to resolve. If one instead holds to a strictly antidemocratic view like Hegel's, however, one must answer the challenge from Hobbes, Rousseau, and Kant. If the "parts" of society are not natural, but depend on claims to corporate authority requiring a political justification, then how can one possibly defend those claims except on authority borrowed from the will of all the citizens against whom they will be enforced? And more generally, who is to judge when the constitution does or does not respect the conditions of citizens' freedom demanded by right reason, other than the citizenry as a whole or its representatives?

But the greater problem with *Sittlichkeit* is its second part, its displacement of politics by pedagogy. Despite Hegel's innovations, this remains in essence an idea based on a classical and religious conception of politics as grounded in a substantive ethical consensus (as is clear from his earliest writings). Its attraction is that it proffers the dream of a society without power, where everyone is naturally at home and free because all agree on regulating their lives on the tenets of a shared culture. But in fact, at least some decisions will be made and enforced by someone—even maintaining a space of free association requires at a minimum a rule of law and defense against external aggression. So one of the things that tends to happen is that arguments for consensus politics are used to defend certain sorts of political authority as natural or consensual by definition—for instance, in the family, a church, or a "nation"—in contrast to other forms, like a democratic state, where claims to authority are at least explicitly political and open to challenge.

But antipolitics is not an escape from politics; it is politics badly done. So the other thing that tends to happen is that—even in the best-case scenario, when cultural conformity is not made a police matter—defenders of pedagogical politics turn to schemes for engineering consensus. We saw Rousseau take this route, and on this Montesquieu and Hegel agreed. The particular problem with this for a theory like Hegel's is that Hegel wanted to engineer an ethical consensus around the notion of a radically groundless and critical post-Kantian freedom. But for that freedom to play the role it needs to play in justification, it cannot possibly also be the sort of thing on which empirical agreement could be manufactured by third parties, the way one might perhaps have hoped to teach everyone to behave in a conventionally virtuous way by habituating them to emulate figures of exemplary virtue.[18] Rather, an order justified on a radical, internal freedom of this sort must be one in which people are free to use their own reason and hence to disagree. Since decisions will need to be made anyway, one needs a way of showing why coercion can sometimes be justified, and this requires a theory of who will have the right to decide. None of this means that broadly democratic *mœurs* must play no role at all in democratic politics. But it does mean they cannot play the role defenders of this sort of politics usually want them to play—to stand in for a defensible account of political authority as a criterion and guarantee of justice. This is certainly what Hegel thought the right constitutional order might achieve, securing citizens' subjective freedom by leading them to recognize that order's rational necessity and thus to accept it

---

[18] Hegel, of course, offered arguments denying this, which ultimately depended on his rejection of Kant's solution to the antinomies, particularly the third antinomy of necessity and freedom (WL 21:30–2, 179–89, 228–33, 12:157–8, 229–30). The core of this objection was taken over from Reinhold and Fichte, and the underlying philosophical issue is that Hegel's arguments assume, with Plato, that the whole point of philosophical thinking is to determine which concept is most "true" because logically self-sufficient. What Kant was really suggesting, however, was that explaining logically contingent empirical phenomena can be shown to require different presuppositions than explaining timeless logical truths (or noumena), and against this the monist objection begs the question because the point is that experimental methods have a logic of their own that allows one to answer a different sort of question than that of conceptual self-sufficiency. The philosophical issues at stake are particularly clear in Kant's 1799 open letter "Clarification Concerning Fichte's *Wissenschaftslehre*" (12:370–1), and in Schelling's late criticisms of Hegel in his 1842 Berlin lectures, available in English as *The Grounding of Positive Philosophy* (Albany: State University of New York Press, 2007). But if the philosophical arguments against Kant's position were weak, the debate was also closely bound up with period political worries over admitting the possibility of a reason divided against itself. This was widely criticized as supporting the independence of a "mechanical" or "positive" state from an ethical life modeled on a religious community united by shared belief, and Hegel's pursuit of "reconciliation" was a reaction to this he shared with the early Romantics, long before he seriously engaged the detailed arguments of Kant's first *Critique*.

as their own, even though in it their general will does not actually make the laws. This is how *Sittlichkeit* was supposed to be an alternative to Rousseau's dangerous voluntarism yet still grounded wholly in the freedom of the citizens.[19] In recent decades, this element in Hegel has seemed attractive to both conservative and ethical-socialist critics of a liberal individualism grounded in pre-political moral rights. But it is essential to see how profoundly undemocratic it is—just so much as the moralizing liberalism it criticizes. I have argued that this sort of liberalism was not Kant's, but one he also contested, following Hobbes and Rousseau, in a more political and hence more radical way that pointed toward democracy. And for these reasons I think we ought to conclude that for contemporary theory, what Hegel has to offer over Kant is not his theory of ethical life.

Freedom in History

What Hegel does have to offer is a revolutionary way of thinking about the relation of freedom to historical change. To make sense of it, the first thing to see is that when he claimed that "reason rules the world, and that world history has therefore been rational in its course" (*VPG* 20), he meant this in the standard idealist sense that anything that can be said to be "true" about history must be expressed through concepts whose use can be rationally justified. He mentioned Anaxagoras and Socrates; the point is what I have described as the method-dependence of knowledge first theorized by Plato and later developed by Kant. This is why Hegel described reason as a "presupposition" justified by philosophy that makes the interpretation of history possible (ibid., cf. 40). Reason, freedom, and spirit, then—which are all more or less fully elaborated names for the same concept—are not metaphysical entities that stand behind, above, or before history: they are all simply, in this use, regulative assumptions for interpreting history itself. As Hegel puts it:

> Even the common and average historian, who thinks and says that he comports himself only receptively, surrendering himself to the data, is not passive in his thinking; he brings his categories with him, and sees the given through them. . . . To him who looks at the world rationally, the world looks rational, too; the relation is reciprocal. (23)

Compare the famous passage at the end of the preface to the *PhR*: "What is rational is actual and what is actual is rational" means that reality can be interpreted

---

[19] See *PhR*, §258. One must not be misled by Hegel's crediting Rousseau with establishing the will as the basis of the state, since his point is that Rousseau was wrong to do this in a way that reduced the general will to the arbitrary choice of individuals. Cf. §29.

only in terms of rational concepts, but those concepts have no independent existence beyond their use in interpreting that reality (14:14). This is not to deny that Hegel thought freedom also "causal" in a final sense, but to stress that the reason we are warranted in presupposing it is as an *interpretive principle* required to distinguish what is "true" in the flux of events from what is merely irrational appearance—the signal from the noise.[20]

The second point is that in the philosophy of history (as distinguished from the philosophy of nature), the version of "reason" Hegel thinks we must presuppose is reason as "spirit"—that is, history must be conceived not *merely* as a system governed by mechanical or organic laws but also as the work of a social subject comprised of free individuals in relations of mutual recognition, becoming conscious of their own freedom and working out its content over time. Hegel's full argument is found in the *Phenomenology* and the *Encyclopedia*, where he offers an immanent critique of the sufficiency of naturalistic reason: human or *geistige* phenomena cannot be fully explained this way since their explanation requires the reflexive application of human reason to itself and its own practical conditions of possibility (which must therefore logically precede its application to natural phenomena as well).[21] But the central point is easily grasped: questions of justice, ethics, or political legitimacy require a justification in terms of human freedom (as Kant had also insisted in different terms), and Hegel's interest in history is essentially with this sort of question:

> The insight to which ... philosophy ought to lead ... is that the actual world is how it *ought* to be, that the truly *good*, the universal divine reason is also the power of actualizing itself [in history]. ... In the pure light of this divine idea ... the appearance that the world is an insane or foolish happening disappears. Philosophy wants to know the content, the actuality of the divine idea, and to *justify* the despised actuality [of the world]. ... (*VPG* 53, emphasis added, cf. 28)

In other words, Hegel's concern in the philosophy of history is in the first place practical in the Kantian sense: he wants to show the modern state can be *justified*,

---

[20] Cf. *Enz* (§549): "A history without a [presupposed] aim and without a... judgment [of events in relation to that aim] would be an imbecilic product of the imagination, not even a fairy tale for children, since even children demand in their stories an interest, that is, at least a hint of an aim and the connection of events and actions to it. In the historical existence of a *people* the substantial aim is to be a state and to maintain itself as such" (emphasis in original). Or again at *VPG* 68, Hegel compares the use of rational ideas in history to the way Kepler had to understand ellipses and other mathematical forms before he could invent laws "out of the empirical data," since one who did not understand the mathematics "could not so much as understand those laws, much less invent them—although he stared at the heavens and the movement of the heavenly bodies ever so long." Cf. also the similarly Socratic argument of the *PhG*'s first chapter, "Sense-Certainty."

[21] *Enz* §375, cf. *VPG* 23–4.

not to give an account of its causal antecedents for its own sake. His goal is to show that the final purpose of the world "has become actual [in history] and that evil has not imposed itself in the end" (28). In the *PhR*, he makes the same point regarding the aim of the systematic study of the state: "To recognize reason as the rose in the cross of the present and to take joy in this, this rational insight is the reconciliation with the actual which philosophy affords . . ." (14:15–6). If Hegel could show only that the state necessarily arose by a mechanical process but not that the same process could also be understood as free and therefore legitimate, this would not accomplish the task he thinks philosophy sets for us. What we need to ask is: "If we assume that history is to be understood as the work of freedom (as we must when considering spirit or practical questions), do we find in the historical record evidence that it has actually gone the way it should?" Or does the evidence, sorted on this assumption, instead suggest that the modern state, where we have arrived, is less justified than some other choice?

The third point is that the assumption that spirit's self-actualization is the "final purpose of the world" is only a principle that makes possible the actual work of interpreting history in its details—it is not a general cause behind history that explains and justifies the entire phenomenal world at a stroke. As Hegel took pains to emphasize:

> It must come to light through the examination of world history itself that it has happened rationally, that it has been the rational, necessary course of the world spirit, which is the substance of history—a spirit whose nature is always one and the same, and which manifests this its one nature in the existence of the world [*Weltdasein*]. . . . This must, as I said, be the result of history itself. But we must take history as it is; we must proceed historically, empirically. (*VPG* 22)[22]

He also stresses that not everything in history is rational, that many periods and places show no signs of freedom's progress (76–7, 86). So we cannot simply presume that history will turn out to be rational in the sense Hegel wants to show it to be. Reason is "presupposed" only as a principle we must assume in making this sort of judgment, the way we might suppose in constructing a reading of a text that the author means to advance some coherent line of thought. We need to go on to provide an interpretation of actual particular events in accordance with this principle, evaluating it implicitly against competing interpretations on

---

[22] Contrast Fichte, "The philosopher, who as a philosopher concerns himself with history, pursues every a priori developing thread of the world-plan, which is clear to him without any history; and his use of history is in no way to prove anything through it, since his propositions are proven already and independent of all history" (*Characteristics*, IX, 8:304).

the same assumption. What presupposing a final purpose of history allows us to do is to pick out those historical events that matter in trying to justify the present. But whether or not the modern state turns out to be justified will depend entirely on whether the details of the interpretation we put forward hold up better than other possible interpretations of these actual events. The point of the presupposition is not to save us this work, but only to limit the field of the *kind* of competing interpretations we must consider: we need to show whether the modern state is justified if we compare different possible ways of interpreting history as a history of freedom, but we do not need to show that the same events cannot also be read, from an altogether different point of view, as a mere welter of particulars or a chronicle of violence, even as a slaughter-bench.

The way Hegel put this was to insist that we cannot simply impute "external" purposes behind history with no demonstrable connection to actual events; those could only be arbitrary "imaginings," not philosophy (*VPG* 26–7). The freedom we must presuppose in history is not an abstract ideal floating mysteriously above or behind events; it must present itself *as actual*, which is to say we must be able to find evidence of it in the course of events themselves. And this is why the Smithian mechanism is of such interest to Hegel here: it allows one to see how actual events can be taken as empirical evidence of history moving in the right direction, *without* having to show that actors themselves had consciously pursued history's ethical purpose. (Again, contrast Fichte's *Characteristics*.) So it is useful in interpreting history because it shows that actors' bad motives do not rule out the possibility of viewing events also ex post as a development of freedom, from a different point of view.

The fact that one must first justify an interpretive principle and then go on to use that principle in interpreting actual events explains the otherwise rather inscrutable relation between the two halves of the *Phenomenology*, and in the later works between the *Encyclopedia* philosophy of spirit and the *Lectures on the Philosophy of History*.[23] The first half of the *Phenomenology* and the *Philosophy of Spirit* develop the concept of "spirit" by drawing out the concept of freedom

---

[23] This has long been a subject of controversy and confusion over the *PhG*, which is not sufficiently explained by the chronology of composition. See, for instance, Otto Pöggeler, "Die Komposition der Phänomenologie des Geistes" in *Materialien zu Hegels "Phaenomenologie des Geistes,"* 4th ed., eds. Hans Friedrich Fulda and Dieter Henrich (Frankfurt: Suhrkamp, 1998), 329–90; Jean Hyppolite, *Genesis and Structure of Hegel's Phenomenology of Spirit* (Evanston, IL: Northwestern University Press, 1974), 321–33; Michael N. Forster, *Hegel's Idea of A Phenomenology of Spirit* (Chicago: University of Chicago Press, 1998), 501–43. Cf. the lack of attention in Pinkard, *Hegel's Phenomenology*, 135 ff. Hegel himself explained that the shapes through which spirit must pass in the second half of the *PhG* "distinguish themselves from the preceding in that they are the real spirits [of peoples], actual realities [*eigentlich Wirklichkeiten*], and instead of shapes only of consciousness, are shapes of a world" (§441). Note that the *PhR* has a similar structure in which the two sections on abstract right and morality first justify the concept of ethical life, and then the third section applies that concept in interpreting and evaluating institutions.

implicitly presupposed (according to Hegel) in asking any question about ultimate truth or justification. This argument proceeds by systematically running through competing epistemologies and refuting each of them on its own terms, much the way Plato's dialogues arrived at the doctrine of ideas by systematically leading traditional authorities into *aporia*. The *Phenomenology*'s second half then applies this concept of spirit in interpreting actual history. Accordingly, history appears in the *Phenomenology*'s first half only as a repository of stylized, competing philosophical positions to refute, whereas the second half offers an evaluative interpretation of the actual prehistory of the modern European state and culture stretching back to the rise of the Greek *polis*. This second part is only needed because Hegel thinks the philosophical argument cannot provide a determinate conception of spirit or freedom that the philosopher can simply apply to history on his own authority. To the contrary, because philosophy shows that the only coherent understanding of freedom in history is a reflexive one—that history ought to be understood as one in which free spirit freely interprets and actualizes *itself*—all the philosopher can do is to reconstruct the course of actual historical events post facto to argue over which conception of freedom's social conditions the people should be taken to have accepted for themselves. Minerva's owl only flies at dusk.

This is confusing in the text because Hegel writes of spirit producing itself, developing itself further, or functioning as its own cause. It is natural to suppose that this means at some point (in ancient Athens, for instance) spirit was only implicit potential, which then causally propelled its own development the way an acorn grows into an oak.[24] But Hegel cannot think this: spirit in ancient Greece was already *spirit, already* a relation of an idea to the actual life of a people. What Hegel means by the principle of freedom's "development" in history is that looking back (from the standpoint of the oak), we can understand the relation of past to present as a *relation of development rather than some other kind* (degeneration, for instance, or contingency), not that we could have known from some point in the past, looking ahead, that freedom is organically or logically compelled to develop itself in any particular direction. The acorn only has meaning *in its relation* to the oak, once we know the course of the intervening process. Hegel is exceedingly clear that one cannot on this basis predict the future, that if one had only ever seen an acorn, it would provide no knowledge whatsoever of oaks. (Moreover, one can only generalize from the development of one oak to another because nature exists in the form of regular organic processes, whereas history must be understood to the contrary as the self-development of conscious freedom that creates what is entirely new, singular, and unpredictable, *VPG*

---

[24] Hegel invites this by writing, for instance, that "as the seed carries in itself the whole nature of the tree, the taste and the form of its fruit, so do the first traces of spirit contain, virtually, the whole of history" (*VPG* 31).

74.) For Hegel, the notion of development is the notion of a relation between potential and actualized result; it allows us to understand a phenomenon like accomplished history *as the relation of a present to its past*. This is not to project one of that relation's isolated terms into the past as the true, independent, and substantial cause of the other, but to insist to the contrary that what history is at every point is always a way of relating past and present.[25] So it is clearest to say not that freedom develops itself in history, but that looking back, history should be read as one in which freedom can be said to have developed. As I have stressed, this is only an interpretive presupposition, which means that one will then need to see if historical events actually line up as plausibly interpreted in this way. But the point is that this is always the question to ask, because to claim that the present is justified over the past is just to claim they do.

Hegel's point is that if we are concerned with justifying the present historically, we cannot take its history to be the "product" of anything *other than* freedom freely producing itself, since no mechanistic or organic natural cause could possibly provide the sort of justification we are looking for. What we need to ask, then, is whether or not the particular events that have led to the present order can be reconstructed as the work of a freedom freely choosing to reject previous modes of expressing itself in the world in favor of ones that count ex post as more consistently and therefore truly and perfectly free. Consider by analogy how if one looks back over the course of one's own life, one might conclude that one has freely chosen the person one has become if, on considering all the other paths on which one started out or might have started out, one finds some reason why one would not now choose to have pursued those paths instead. One's choices would then count ex post neither as mistakes nor external compulsions but as the free development of one's own freedom, even if one's actual choices at the time had been motivated by drives, passions, or circumstances rather than a conscious intention to act on the reasons that appear later to be good ones. This is the sort of evaluative story Hegel is concerned to tell about the history of the modern state.[26]

Finally, we can see here why the shape of this particular sort of development—the development of freedom as explicitly *contrasted* to a natural or organic development—must take an indirect and tortuous path, why

---

[25] Hegel introduces the notion in the *Lectures* in just this way: "The principle of *development* contains the further [principle] that an inner definition, an implicitly present presupposition that lies as its ground, brings itself into existence" (75). In other words, to call something a "development" is to relate the present to some anterior state defined as a ground considered to have led to it in the transition from potential to accomplished act. The thought that every idea is implicitly relational is a central thesis of Hegel's *Logic*.

[26] For how this fits with Hegel's general theory of agency, see Tanner McFadden, "Actuality, Integrity, and Freedom in Hegel's Philosophy of Right," Western Political Science Association 2011 Annual Meeting Paper.

"development, which in nature is a calm process, is in spirit a hard and endless struggle against itself" (76, cf. 98–9). The reason is that unlike in organic nature, "in spirit the transition of its definition in its actualization is mediated by consciousness and will" (76). We cannot, therefore, know the end of the story ahead of time because what it means for spirit to "actualize itself in history" is just that the people must be able to determine freely for themselves what their freedom is to mean, and which constitutional forms it will require. So in asking whether or not the course of historical events fits a pattern consistent with the presupposition that it can be seen as a history of freedom actualizing itself, we cannot presume already to know what such a course would look like and then simply to check whether or not the historical record corresponds. Rather, we must examine that course on its own terms, to see whether its twists and turns add up to justifying its result by showing how historical alternatives have undermined themselves as interpretations of free regimes. The key principle, which will *appear* post facto as a sort of motor or organizing principle lending coherence to the progression, is that every concrete form of freedom requires a justification. No form is naturally free (just because freedom is not natural); what makes it count as free is that it can be justified as freely chosen over alternatives whose own competing claims have turned out to be arbitrary and unfounded. Demonstrating this will require sifting through the different sorts of claims to freedom implicit in defenses of diverse historical regimes, and to show that the present—the modern state—ends up with a less arbitrary claim than any of its predecessors, just because it manages to incorporate whatever claims they had advanced that cannot be ruled out as self-contradictory. The point is that a dialectical history proceeding this way through immanent refutations is the only sort that could possibly *count* as a history of peoples freely working out for themselves the meaning of their own freedom.

The Cunning of Reason, Montesquieu, and the Scots

The obvious objection is that Hegel did not draw the neat distinction I have suggested between an interpretive principle and a causal power, and clearly meant his account of freedom history not *only* as a practical assumption (which sounds too much like Kant), but also as showing why history necessarily turned out the way it did.[27] It is certainly true that Hegel thought justice and necessity went hand in hand in history (if not in every detail, at least in the big picture). But

---

[27] Another objection might be that it leaves out Hegel's explicit identification of history with divine providence, but Hegel is always quite clear, at least after 1800, that in identifying the two, he is not adding anything extra-rational to philosophy, but showing to the contrary that philosophy is the truth of religion. For example, at *Enz* §573: "[P]hilosophy can indeed recognize its own forms in the categories of the religious mode of representation, and thus also its own content in religious content, and do justice to religious content; but the converse does not hold, since the religious mode

the question is why. Now when Hegel wrote that "the *final purpose* [*Endzweck*] *of the world* ... is spirit's consciousness of its freedom and therewith the actuality of that freedom," the most natural way to read this is as asserting that spirit is a metaphysical force driving history toward a natural teleology that is also God's providential plan (*VPG* 32, emphasis in original). Herder, for instance, defended just such a view.[28] But Hegel departed from this in two key ways. First, he followed in the vein of Kant's criticisms of Herder's *Ideen* by insisting on the priority of rational justification. Although he continued to use organic metaphors, he recognized in a way Herder did not that competing interpretations of freedom will conflict and these conflicts could only be resolved with (Socratic) arguments over criteria. (This is also why he insisted on the importance of a rational state, whereas the implications of Herder's views were broadly anarchistic and religious.) The second point is that Hegel integrated into his philosophy of history a sophisticated analysis of empirical causation drawn from Montesquieu and the Scots.[29] For Herder, as for Romantics and members of the historical school of law, this sort of "mechanistic" explanation was not merely unnecessary but anathema—because they rightly saw it to compete with their own directly causal interpretation of organic development as the motor of history.[30] Now the most characteristic concept in Hegel's philosophy of history—the "cunning of reason" [*List der Vernunft*]—turned precisely on the relationship between the two distinct perspectives of rational justification and mechanical explanation, *neither of which had any place* in Herder's framework, where metaphysical-theological principles of organic development were meant to stand in at once for both. So although Hegel continued to use some of the same language, it is essential to see that he was using it in a very different way.

The point is that Hegel thought he actually needed to show why, on a strictly mechanical account, it still turns out that self-interested individual actions end

of representation does not apply the critique of thought to itself and does not comprehend itself, and is therefore exclusive in its immediacy." Philosophy, after all, is in the *Enz* a higher stage than revealed religion.

[28] Herder, *This Too a Philosophy of History for the Formation of Humanity* (1774), *Ideas for the Philosophy of the History of Humanity*, 4 vols. (1784–1791), *Letters for the Advancement of Humanity* (1793–1797).

[29] Hegel's early unpublished notes on history include a brief discussion of Hume's *History of England* (2:604–5). His personal library included English editions of Robertson's *History of Scotland*, *An Historical Disquisition Concerning the Knowledge which the Ancients had of India*, and *The History of the Reign of Emperor Charles V*; Gibbon's *Decline and Fall*; and Smith's *Wealth of Nations* (Waszek, *The Scottish Enlightenment*). He also owned German editions of Kames's *Elements of Criticism* and Steuart's *Inquiry into the Principles of Political Economy*, on which Karl Rosenkranz reports Hegel wrote a running commentary in 1799, now lost (as well as English editions of Bolingbroke and Clarendon). *Georg Wilhelm Friedrich Hegels Leben* (Berlin: Duncker & Humblot, 1844), 86.

[30] Herder, for instance, asked: "Hume! Voltaire! Robertsons! Classical specters of the twilight! What are you in the light of the truth?" (*This Too a Philosophy*, in *Herders Sämmtliche Werke*, 33 vols., ed. Bernhard Suphan [Berlin: Weidmann, 1877–1913], 5:508).

up producing an outcome that can then be seen, from another point of view, as also serving the "purpose" of freedom.[31] Even in the purposive view, it is still strictly *through the mechanism* of conflicting individual wills that the larger end of reason is served: "The cunning [of reason] consists precisely in the mediating activity which, in letting objects act upon one another according to their own nature, and wear each other out, without itself mixing directly in the process completes only *its* purpose" (*Enz* §209, emphasis in original). If this story is to work, it requires a mechanical account sufficient to show what produced the outcome (in the sense of an efficient cause), although this will not also be sufficient to explain its *meaning* (or purpose, Aristotle's final cause).[32] The latter requires one to view history from the standpoint of reason and freedom, but the former is just the sort of empirical account Hegel found in the historical thought of Montesquieu, the Scots, and Gibbon. He followed Montesquieu and Gibbon in taking the "spirit" of a people in a certain age as the principal causal factor that determines whether or not their political order is able to subsist. And he also took the point that spirit itself may be advanced or undermined by the unintended consequences of particular actions and events—paradigmatically in the decline and fall of Rome. As we saw, he also took, however, from the examples of the Reformation and Enlightenment philosophy the thought that spirit is a matter not only of virtues and dispositions, but also of publicly shared beliefs open to rational criticism. On this he particularly followed Fichte's post-Kantian view

---

[31] Here, contrast Schelling. Hegel began his career as Schelling's protégé, but broke with him after 1803 in part in reaction to Schelling's Spinozism. Schelling's 1800 *System of Transcendental Idealism* set out some of the core problems Hegel's philosophy of history would address, particularly the notion of how lawless subjective freedom could be reconciled with the objective necessity of natural laws. Schelling's solution, however, was to suggest that one must posit over and above both elements an absolute identity that cannot be known but only believed as a presupposition of action, and which he identifies with God's continual self-revelation (9:291–303). It is because Hegel was unwilling to make a similar move to "intuition" [*Anschauung*] that he instead saw the need for the sort of empirical mechanism provided by Montesquieu and the Scots. The contrast between Hegel's history of "reason" and Schelling's of "revelation" [*Offenbarung*] would become only more pronounced in Schelling's later *Philosophical Investigations into the Essence of Human Freedom* (1809), his unpublished manuscripts on *The Ages of the World*, and the 1842 Berlin lectures previously cited.

[32] Hegel emphasized the sense of purpose or final cause as an explanation in terms of meaning: "[The] purpose [of history]... is spirit in accord with its essence, the concept of freedom. This is the fundamental object and therefore also the guiding principle of the development, that through which it receives its sense and meaning (the way in Roman history Rome is the object and therefore what guides the consideration of events), as conversely the events have proceeded only from this object and only in relation to it have a sense and content" (*VPG* 76). Although Hegel described the teleological perspective as more "true" than the merely mechanical, it did not replace the mechanical but added to it and completed it by showing also why relationships among particular events ought to be included among the stuff of "world history" in the first place. See James Kreines, "Hegel's Critique of Pure Mechanism," *European Journal of Philosophy* 12, no. 1 (2004): 38–74; Christopher Yeomans, *Freedom and Reflection: Hegel on the Logic of Agency* (Oxford: Oxford University Press, 2012), 183–91.

of ethics as requiring reflexively justified principles in an order in which agents mutually recognize one another as free.

If one puts together Montesquieu with Fichte in this way, one arrives at the conclusion that spirit plays a necessary role in the causal explanation of history because social orders premised on indefensible accounts of their own legitimacy are bound to fail. When conventional definitions of justice prove no longer able to resolve conflicts and orient citizens' actions to a single common good, the power of the laws, which depend on citizens' support, will collapse, and the social order will succumb to internal or external violence.[33] It also explains how a new order appropriate to the needs of the age may come about, and why that order will subsequently hold up in a newly established balance of forces, without any assumption that people pursue the good for the sake of the good, that God makes sure the good will win out in the end, or that society naturally organizes itself always toward ever greater perfection. This strictly mechanical interaction of competing wills will also count, from another point of view, as simultaneously serving the end of spirit's self-actualization in history, just because if the new order is to stick, this must be because it resolves some inconsistency that had become acute in the previous order's claim to legitimacy. Otherwise, that order would not have collapsed and a new one would not have managed to establish itself by aligning individual wills to support the power of new laws.

Hegel developed this distinctive position over time. Early works of the 1790s called for revitalizing the "spirit" of Christian religion. The 1802 "German Constitution" essay turned to the actual history of the Holy Roman Empire to chart the growing danger of fragmentation as laws on paper lost the backing of effective power. The "Natural Law" essay of 1802–1803 criticized both empiricist and moralistic approaches to law (the latter associated with Kant and Fichte), citing Gibbon and particularly Montesquieu on the need to develop a consistent constitutional system in accordance with the ethical customs of

---

[33] Hegel presents his view in the *PhR* as a response to Montesquieu: "When Montesquieu [writes] that England in the seventeenth century gave a fine show of endeavors to found a democracy showing themselves impotent, since the leaders lacked virtue—and when he adds furthermore that when virtue disappears in the republic, ambition seizes those whose character is capable of it, and avarice seizes everyone, and the state, as an object of general plunder, has its strength only in the power of a few individuals and the intemperance of all—one should note that in a more cultivated state of society, and with the development and freeing of the powers of *particularity* [i.e., of individual citizens *qua* individuals], the virtue of the heads of state becomes insufficient, and another form of rational law besides mere sentiment or disposition [*Gesinnung*] is required, if the whole is to possess the force to hold itself together and to allow itself to grant the forces of developed particularity [i.e., individuals] both their positive and negative right" (§273). Here, one sees disposition replaced by rational law as appropriate to a modern world in which individuals have come to demand personal liberty and rational justifications, but also how this law is meant to play the same role in history as was Montesquieu's spirit, by uniting individual wills to make possible a rule of law with sufficient force to be effective and hold together society.

a specific historical people. Although history had replaced theology, it served in these essays to identify a problem, rather than to explain progress toward a solution. Hegel first mentioned "political economy" in the "Natural Law" essay, before taking up the subject in greater detail in the 1803–1804 and 1805–1806 *Jenaer Realphilosophie* lectures. The first of these contained Hegel's first explicit reference to Smith, whose *Wealth of Nations* was cited by page number in Garve's German translation in a marginal note to a characterization of the division of labor as leading to a "monstrous system of sociability and mutual dependency, a self-animating life of the dead [in money], that in its movement moves blindly and elementally this way and that" (6:323–4). The notion of "cunning" [*List*] first appeared in both the 1803–1804 and 1805–1806 lectures, but "the cunning of reason" did not appear until the sections on mechanism and teleology in the 1816 second volume of the *Science of Logic* and the 1817 *Encyclopedia*.

In the meantime, Hegel had introduced his own distinctive theory of history in the second half of the 1807 *Phenomenology*. Between 1803 and 1807 history had become for him a story of progress, as for Kant, Fichte, and Schelling. Schelling had argued in his 1800 *System of Transcendental Idealism* that the necessary perspectives of freedom and necessity in history could be reconciled only if freely willed lawless actions nevertheless turned out unconsciously to serve a divine plan (9:300). But Schelling had no mechanism to explain this; he argued that one must simply accept it as a transcendental assumption. What Hegel added was an account of how this might work empirically, strictly through the interaction of contending human wills. In the *Phenomenology*, his account of the collapse of classical civilization paralleled the breakdown story familiar from Montesquieu and Gibbon. But Montesquieu had also emphasized that the binding role of virtue in republics had been replaced in modern monarchy by the ambition for preferment that left nobles dependent on the central government,[34] and Hegel's discussion of the early modern state closely followed the logic of that account (§509–§510), whereas his criticism of the Terror drew on the arguments for an organic constitution he had attributed to Montesquieu in the essay on "Natural Law." The *Phenomenology* did not refer to the "cunning of reason," which did not appear until the *Logic* nine years later. In Hegel's later discussions the competition of individual interests and passions replaced entirely the language of virtue and honor in Montesquieu, thus making the purely mechanical quality of the causal explanation even more emphatic. There is no dispositive evidence of a source for this further move, but Hegel had first associated the term "cunning" with political economy in the *Jenaer Realphilosophie*

---

[34] "[I]t is like the System of the Universe, where there is a force that incessantly draws all Bodies away from the center, and a force of gravity that brings them back. Honor makes all parts of the Body politic move; it binds them by their own action, and one finds that each moves to the common Good, believing that he goes to his particular interests" (*De l'esprit des Loix*, III.7, 1:51).

lectures and he devoted renewed attention to the logic of Adam Smith's arguments in the *PhR*, just as he began to develop his more detailed account of world history. Smith's *Wealth of Nations*, of course, had also applied to history the logic of private interest unconsciously serving public ends: "A revolution of the greatest importance to the publick happiness," Smith wrote, "was ... brought about by two different orders of people, who had not the least intention to serve the publick," although "[n]either of them had either knowledge or foresight of that great revolution which the folly of the one, and the industry of the other, was gradually bringing about."[35] In Europe this progress had even reversed the very course of nature (377–8). But Hegel might have drawn a similar point, for instance, from Schiller's *History of the Thirty Years War*, which had argued that "through a strange course of events, it had to be the *split in the Church* that led the states to a closer *union* among themselves. ... Europe emerged non-oppressed and free from this terrible war, in which she first recognized herself as a society of interdependent states, and this participation of states with each other, which was first learned through this war, would by itself already be sufficient gain to reconcile the citizen of the world to its horrors."[36] Hegel defended just the opposite view of that war in "The German Constitution," and Rosenkranz reported that Hegel had begun a critical work on Schiller's *Thirty Years War* in the early 1790s.[37] Or Hegel might simply have built on Kant's "unsocial sociability."

What matters is not attribution of direct influence, but the fact that Hegel's philosophy of history clearly incorporated a version of these strictly mechanical arguments that set him off sharply from contemporaries such as Herder, Goethe, Fichte, and Schelling, with whom in other ways he shared a great deal. And what this shows is that Hegel's account of history as freedom's self-realization cannot depend on assuming that account also materially effective in determining the course of history—just because Hegel went to great lengths to provide an entirely independent explanation of history's course instead in strictly empirical terms, of the sort he found in Montesquieu and the Scots. Hegel's characteristic notion of "the cunning of reason" depends on holding these two perspectives distinct and yet together, and this sharply distinguished his view from those such as Herder's that did, in fact, depend on a developmentalist metaphysics and the causal efficacy of providence. Today, one ought not to accept Hegel's empirical story as a general law of history—although it *might be* that sometimes arbitrary wills cancel each other out and a rule of law can be sustained by uniting

---

[35] Adam Smith, *Wealth of Nations* (Indianapolis: Liberty Fund, 1981), 422.

[36] *Schillers Werke, Nationalausgabe* (Weimar: Böhlau, 1943), 18.10, emphasis in original. See also Schiller's inaugural address as professor of history at Jena in 1789, translated as "The Nature and Value of Universal History: An Inaugural Lecture," *History and Theory* 11, no. 2 (1972), 327, 333; *Nationalausgabe* 17:359–76.

[37] *Hegels Leben*, 60.

enough people around rationally justified ideas, it might well be that people can be united by nonsense, or that power can survive merely by prior monopoly on arms or incomparable brutality, or through the self-perpetuating tendencies of bureaucracies in which no one any longer really believes. These are the sorts of possibilities that would concern later thinkers including Marx and Weber, and they are possibilities that can hardly be ignored today. Which scenario unfolds is an empirical question on which Hegel's methods offer no purchase whatsoever. But none of this touches the other side of the story, the point of view of evaluation in terms of progress in freedom, considered strictly as a principle of interpretation and judgment. Hegel was wrong, on the one hand, to think an undemocratic constitution justifiable in terms of freedom. And he was also wrong, on the other, to think a justified constitution is a historical necessity. Both of these theses would cause problems for Hegelianism, already splintering and weakened, by the 1840s, and particularly after the failed revolution of 1848, when the actual Prussian monarch flatly refused to abide any sort of constitution compatible with freedom. Hegel's reason no longer seemed on the side of power—which was after all always part of the promise with which Hegel had tantalized by marrying so closely freedom and necessity—and other ways of thinking about what it meant to put oneself on the side of power would soon come to take its place.

The Ways of Historical Refutation

In this final section, I consider a few of the details of Hegel's historical story of the progress of freedom. I am not concerned here with his general argument for the modern state, but rather with the way he tells the story that is supposed to make that case. My concern is to look behind the content of specific claims in order to draw out the distinctive *sort* of interpretive argument Hegel thinks his conceptual framework allowed him to make about history. It is in showing how this sort of argument might be made, an argument that shows how the present might be justified as freely chosen through the immanent refutation of the past, that I suggest is perhaps the most enduring of Hegel's contributions to the history of political thought. My discussion will draw from several of Hegel's works, including particularly the *Phenomenology*, where the elenctic shape of the argument is clearer than in the *Lectures on the Philosophy of History*. This final section of the chapter considers not only what Hegel's views were, but also what we might make of some of them today, from the standpoint of democratic theory.

Consider first how Hegel's treatment of Socrates in his *Lectures on the History of Philosophy* illustrates the general point that a consistent interpretation of freedom must be one that can be defended as already accepted by an entire people. The example supports Hegel's argument elsewhere that abstract moral reason is insufficient to ground determinate social obligations (*PhG* §599–671, *PhR* §105–41). Hegel claims that while Socrates is right in principle to suggest that the "natural" traditions of democratic Athens ought to be subject to the free criticism of individuals, he is nevertheless ethically in the wrong because there does not exist in Athens the possibility of erecting a new form of consensual ethical life on the basis of Socratic critique. Socrates is wrong not because of what he says but because in saying it he stands alone, and freedom requires a community acting under laws it freely recognizes as its own.[38] In the modern period, the lessons of the Reformation, the Enlightenment, and Kantian morality have made possible a real social world consensually governed by what is, in effect, a freethinking Socratic ethos. But in Socrates's time, his argumentative practice could only contradict its avowed aim of promoting justice, since it undermined religious respect for established laws that made possible collective life under laws of freedom, as opposed to internecine war and violence.

The more general point, which a historical and Socratic theory will take, is that in assessing a criticism of the state, one must consider not only the content of that criticism, but also whether or not it can be understood to express the view of the citizenry as a whole. This requires attending not only to argument but also to historical evidence of actual persons' views—but because we cannot know ex ante who really speaks for the citizenry, the argument can only proceed through immanent refutations of competing claims to represent them. In Socrates's case, his own claim to speak for Athenians' better nature is tested and confuted by their verdict, not because the principle of individuality he avows is disproven *qua* principle, but because the state fairly resists his claim to interpret and apply that principle for himself (154–5). (In Plato's *Crito*, moreover, Socrates explicitly accepts the authority of that decision by refusing to go against the laws even when he thinks they have ruled unjustly.) For Hegel this is a genuine tragedy that expresses the conflict of two valid ethical principles, and the Athenians also do violence to themselves by refusing to incorporate a recognition of individuality into the state. Philosophers turn from politics and the ethical basis of the polis soon collapses into self-interest in a world in which the unifying power of old certainties can no longer be relied on—and a weakened Athens finally succumbs to Sparta and Macedon. The significance of this sort of tragic symmetry is considered below, in the parallel case of Antigone. But what Socrates's fate particularly illustrates is how the direct assertion of rational principles of freedom and justice contradicts itself if those principles are not recognized by the actual citizenry.[39] A historical

---

[38] *Lectures on the History of Philosophy*, 148–53. Cf. *VPG* 328–30.

[39] Cf. *Enz* §552. The general problem then recurs in inverted form in the Roman Empire, when abstract individual legal right is the prevailing positive order, but it ceases to express the active ethical allegiance of the people. The same is later true also of the Holy Roman Empire.

and Socratic theory of democracy incorporates this thought in Principle (II)*'s practical condition.

A second strategy of refutation is illustrated by Hegel's discussion of the French Revolution, what he called in the *PhG* "absolute freedom and the Terror" (§582–95). Here, the point is that not every historical outcome can be attributed to the people's will, even if it is widely supported, if it fails also to respect the objective conditions of a state that secures the freedom of each and all. Hegel's criticism of the Jacobins was not that they, like Socrates, failed to rally the people to their cause; here, the problem was the cause to which they were rallied. Hegel took Jacobinism to be animated by a view of freedom as arbitrary self-will, which failed to acknowledge that individual freedom can exist only on the condition of the mutual recognition of the freedom of others, since only in that case can the freedom of individuals be confirmed, secured, and given objective content. The ensuing refutation follows the general logic previously worked out in the struggle for recognition between master and slave. Because the "absolute freedom" Hegel associates with the revolutionary Jacobins admits no objective constraints whatsoever on the power of choice of the people's general will, it can put into practice its vision of freedom only by abolishing every element of the existing social order, which it can see only as fetters because they have not been consciously legislated by the people (*PhG* §588–9). When nothing of the ancient régime remains, "absolute freedom" will continue to prove itself by casting up new enemies from its own ranks, only for the spectacle of destroying them and showing they are nothing before the irresistible force of the *voluntée générale* (§590).

According to Hegel, a regime of this sort can only end up undermining the real conditions of the freedom it purports to serve. Although it does teach the important positive lesson that a social order must be consciously chosen by the people, it fails to recognize that such a choice must constrain itself in accordance with the constitutive conditions without which the consistent realization of freedom is impossible. As we saw, Hegel followed Montesquieu in taking these conditions to require a complex constitutional order of mutually dependent powers within a sovereign whole. I have suggested that this is not quite right—whereas Hegel was correct to insist on the rule of law and certain rights of individuals, and although a constitutional division of powers is admissible and may well often be a good idea, Hegel left out the no less important requirement of final democratic control over legislative and executive decisions. What a historical and Socratic theory will take from his discussion of the Terror is not his specific institutional response, but the general point that any coherent conception of political freedom must be able to furnish some criterion to distinguish free institutions from organized tyranny. Which institutions these are will be the subject of struggle, but one can rule out any view that, in effect, defends certain institutions not on their own merits but as the self-evident expression of a "popular will" defined entirely by whom it chooses for its enemies. This is the thought behind the conceptual condition of Principle (II)*.

Consider finally Hegel's discussion of the ancient Greek polis, and particularly fifth-century Athens, as the paradigm of an order of mutual recognition understood as natural (§443–475). In this order, Hegel supposes, the laws in fact secured a consensual basis for a shared life respecting the equal freedom of all citizens (although not, of course, of women, slaves, or metics). Individuals also understood these laws as the natural expression of their own essential character; they thus freely reproduced them through their own actions rather than feeling their weight as an alien yoke. Yet there was a fundamental problem with this order: because individuals understood it as immediate and natural, they could not consistently acknowledge their own role in interpreting its demands and putting them into effect through their actions. This role is necessary if abstract notions of law, justice, duty, or virtue are to be instantiated in the phenomenal world by particular persons, as they must if they are to perform their role in securing the consensual grounds of social coexistence required for the exercise of freedom. But it also necessarily gives rise to conflicts of interpretation, and the failure of the "natural" view is that it can provide no principled grounds for resolving them. Who acts rightly, for instance, on the principle of duty to family—Clytemnestra or Orestes? The *Orestia* suggests that the state's public law may claim priority to competing familial obligations due to its claim to impartiality and reason. But *Antigone* points out that the state has no principled basis on which to substantiate this claim: since its authority is understood as immediate and direct precisely on the model of natural familial loyalty, it can only confront the family itself as an interested party, and each is just as fairly accused as the other of merely masking the pursuit of individual ambition and willful self-assertion in the trappings of piety and reason.

Hegel's point is that this problem is insoluble in any ethical order taken to be natural. In both the *Orestia* and *Antigone* (although in different ways), the state's prerogative is shown to depend ultimately on the borrowed authority of divine law; and as Hegel emphasizes, this implies that the state's power dissipates whenever it departs from that higher law (§447–8). The divine law, however, is supposed to have its power just because it is natural and immediately accessible to every individual, and this means the state is never safe from individuals' accusations that it has departed from the order rightful in itself (§454). Hegel's ultimate conclusion is that the only political order that could escape this contradiction would be one, like the modern state, which justifies itself not as natural, but as freely willed by all citizens in accordance with the conceptual conditions of understanding it as so willed.

Here, we encounter once again the problem of judgment, and one should note that Hegel's concern applies to any legitimating ground presented as self-evident, whether that claim is expressed in the language of religion, reason, or tradition. One way of taking the point is as showing why it is not enough to justify an order even to derive it from certain first principles. The logical possibility too frequently overlooked is that some competing view may also follow, either from the same principles or from others with an equal claim to certainty. So one must do more than to show one's own view is defensible; before imposing that view by force, one must also make sure that no one else's is. The problem with Creon's and Antigone's views is not that either is wrong in itself, but that neither acknowledges the other's equally valid claim, and each thus mistakes its own subjective certainty for certainty *tout court*. And this, of course, is only too common a problem in both philosophy and politics.

What one needs, then, is a reason for preferring one interpretation to all others even when several are internally consistent, without appealing to any self-evident final ground. Hegel illustrates two very clever ways of managing this. The first is to show that one option—like the "natural" order of the polis—could exclude rival interpretations only by appealing to some arbitrary positive foundation whose authority cannot be demonstrated in a way consistent with the freedom of a community that governs itself. The modern state is then justified over that alternative because it avoids any similarly self-defeating appeal to natural foundations by instead working out the content of a legitimate constitution from the very notion of such a free community. Even if we do not know ex ante that this interpretation is "right," it is uniquely admissible (if the alternative is a natural order) and this is sufficient to justify its claim by elimination.

The second way Hegel offers to justify the modern state over the polis turns on the claim that the modern state makes possible a reconciliation of the subjective individual certainty of religious conviction, purified and rationalized by Enlightenment philosophy, and the rightful claim of the legal state, similarly rationalized in line with the equal freedom of every individual citizen. The result may therefore be defended simultaneously from the point of view of the individual or the people as a whole, from that of subjective morality and that of objective public right. In the polis these principles could only be contradictory, as the *Antigone* so dramatically illustrates.[40] And so the modern state is justified not because we know it to follow from the one correct interpretation of justice or natural law, but just because it is *possible* to defend it consistently on *either* of the major competing interpretations, whereas the alternative cannot exclude competitors unless we already know that only one of those interpretations is ultimately "right," and this we cannot know.

---

[40] Patchen Markell rightly emphasizes that this conflict is not between stable archetypes, but rather that because each side asserts a self-certifying claim to justice and identity while ignoring the interpretive ambiguity inherent in acting among a plurality of persons, each in acting enters into conflict with him- or herself so that each is ultimately destroyed not merely by the other but in a deeper sense by his or her own hand (*Bound by Recognition* [Princeton, NJ: Princeton University Press, 2003], 62–89).

The details of Hegel's dialectical interpretations of key historical reversals, then, offer insight into some of the ways one might go about working through competing interpretations of freedom in order to see which hold up on their own terms and which do not. And this is helpful, because this is a difficult and in many ways much more demanding way of thinking about how to evaluate historical change than simply appealing to some ready-made external standard. Its advantage, however, is that it is the only way that allows one to argue about what the people have already decided for themselves, rather than what is "right" in the abstract and ought therefore to be imposed on the people. That is why this way of thinking will be so helpful for democratic theory, which shares Hegel's concern for justifying political decisions in terms of freedom, even if it breaks with much of his own view of what followed from this in early-nineteenth-century Germany.

Conclusion

This chapter has suggested that Hegel's philosophy of history is best understood as, in one of its major parts, a theory of how to work out what would count as a political order freely chosen by the citizenry as a way of organizing their own freedom. Although Hegel's solution did not build directly on Kant's, it agreed in placing the act of political judgment front and center, and in working out an answer from the conceptual conditions of any judgment that might be understood to be endorsed by the citizenry as a whole. Both Kant and Hegel insisted that a free constitution cannot be reduced to a formal ideal; although reason sets certain objective constraints with which defensible outcomes must accord, judging actual constitutions requires attending not only to the ideal but also to the acts through which that ideal might be brought to bear in the course of political disagreements among actual citizens in specific polities. It is these acts, and not only the abstract ideal, that must be free, and it is the need always to consider this subjective side of judgment that led both Kant and Hegel, in different ways, to break from traditional natural law theories and to build a theory of historical change into the very content of justice. Whereas Kant projected this change forward as a practical postulate, Hegel projected it backward as a principle for interpreting the present in relation to its past. But in both cases, historical change was a field opened up for ongoing political judgment that is radically free just because it depends on no external foundation. It was not, as for so many of Kant's and Hegel's contemporaries, a natural or metaphysical process of development on which we might rely to make our political judgments for us.

This is why familiar narratives in the history of political thought are wrong to pose a clean break between the two that assimilates Kant to eighteenth-century natural law and Hegel to nineteenth-century organicist historicism. Hegel did not simply point the way to Marx, to the historicist German nationalism of the Wilhelmine period, or even, via Mead, to an intersubjectivist sociology of action. But neither was he simply one of the last great metaphysical holdouts against the forward march of positive social science, much less a leading figure of an irrationalist Counter-Enlightenment. Kant, for his part, had already denied that morality or right reason could rule alone, without mediation by the sort of sovereign political decision emphasized by Hobbes, and he had introduced historical change into the definition of right itself in a way that set him quite apart from his contemporaries. So Kant cannot readily be assimilated to a mainstream liberal tradition of the sort associated with J. S. Mill (and sometimes anachronistically with Locke), or his political thought reduced to a moralistic alternative to the dominance of consequentialist and instrumental reason in postwar analytic philosophy and social science. But neither is Hegel simply a good liberal who also recognizes the value of community.[41] The distinctive character of Kant's and Hegel's political thought has been obscured by reading them through the lenses of twentieth-century debates—first over Enlightenment, democracy, and the so-called German *Sonderweg* in light of the Second World War, and then in struggles for dominance among Marxism, positivist social science, and a broadly Millian Anglophone liberal tradition in the Cold War era. Although Kant and Hegel shared a central concern for freedom with Millian liberals—and with Marx—they were much more interested than either of those traditions in the problem of political judgment, and much less willing to accept question-begging answers to conflicts over who speaks for the people or what it means for the citizens truly to be free.

Within their shared turn to historical judgment, however, Kant and Hegel differed over the conditions a free judgment must meet. Whereas Kant held that any consistent judgment of the laws must presume the authority of the existing sovereign, Hegel showed to the contrary how one might interrogate a sitting sovereign's claim in Socratic fashion, by working through the competing claims of historical alternatives it had replaced to see which held up better on its own terms as a consistent interpretation of freedom. This was Hegel's great insight into the solution of what I have called the paradox of authorization, and it is the point on which the theory of democracy defended in this book builds, which makes it not only historical but also Socratic.

But Hegel also made two key mistakes, where Kant's arguments had been stronger. First, in his political theory, Hegel thought his notion of ethical life

---

[41] Cf. Rawls: "I interpret Hegel as a moderately progressive reform-minded liberal, and I see his liberalism as an important exemplar in the history of moral and political philosophy of the *liberalism of freedom*. Other such exemplars are Kant and, less obviously, J. S. Mill. (*A Theory of Justice* is also a liberalism of freedom and learns much from them.)" John Rawls, *Lectures on the History of Moral Philosophy* (Cambridge, MA: Harvard University Press, 2000), 330.

could stand in for democratic control of the state, by showing how the citizens might learn to recognize the laws objectively required as conditions of their freedom also as their own even though they had no power actively to author or to change them. He presented this as an explicit rejection of Rousseau and Jacobinism, and it was part of a very widespread trend during the Napoleonic and Restoration periods to provide freedom-based alternatives to democratic republicanism, in order to save the larger project of grounding a state on freedom and the rule of law from the perceived failures of the Revolution.

Hegel's second great mistake was that his philosophy of history was not content only to show whether or not the present was defensible; he thought he also needed to prove that what was most defensible had also been historically necessary, and this was what the empirical side of that theory was to show. The deep philosophical reason for this was that Hegel rejected Kant's radical distinction between theoretical and practical reason, and so was unwilling to contemplate that history might play out in a way that could be explained causally but would not match up also with a different sort of argument built on principled justifications. The political reason, which in this case may well have been deeper than the philosophical since it predated the latter and remained consistent throughout Hegel's life, was that Hegel, like so many before and since, was unwilling to accept the idea of a wholly political state that did not depend in the final instance on a pre-political ethical consensus of the sort Montesquieu had called the spirit of a people's laws. Hegel insisted on the unity of reason and on social reconciliation, so that meaning and justice on the one hand, and power on the other, should never come wholly apart. And, of course, this was in a way the ultimate point of the theory, and the source of much of its appeal. But Kant was right that the logics of causality and justification need not match up, and Montesquieu and the long tradition on which he drew wrong that social order could be sustained only on the basis of a substantive ethical consensus across the entire citizenry. What Hegel missed—or too quickly ruled out on the basis of its apparent failure in 1790s France—was the possibility of a thoroughly political order of the sort for which Kant had argued, following Hobbes and even more radically, on this point, than Rousseau. In Kant's version, this sort of order preserved space for principled criticism *within* an ongoing process of political judgment, but rejected appeals to any putatively pre-political moral consensus that might be thought to put a floor under politics by removing the need for coercive decisions and thus the importance of a principled theory of who has the right to make them.[42] But this was the direction of democracy, and the historical irony here was that it was in seeking to exclude democracy through

---

[42] Note the vanishing place of political decision in Hegel's discussion of the monarch in the *PhR*, *Zusatz* to §279.

constitutionalism that Hegel opted for one view of political freedom over another in a way that would come to seem more and more arbitrary and indefensible in light of popular struggles for universal suffrage over the course of the later nineteenth century and into the twentieth. It is for these reasons that the historical and Socratic theory defended in the second half of the book insists on reworking Hegel's critical framework in a resolutely democratic direction, and in stressing that it is strictly a theory of judgment, a theory for use in debating what ought to happen but not also one that could ever promise that it has or that it will.

PART TWO

Part One of the book had several aims. In arguing for a certain way of understanding Plato, Kant, and Hegel, it first of all sought to recover a distinctive sort of argument called elenchus, which allows one (at least sometimes) to defend principled conclusions even in the absence of any foundational certainties. This required close attention to the logic of this sort of argument and to its limits, in order clearly to separate it from more familiar invocations of "dialectic" (or worse, "the dialectic" or "dialectics") that end up meaning very little and working more as evocative imagery than as arguments. Chapters 3–5 then went on to consider how Kant and Hegel later put this sort of argument to work in their moral and political theories. I argued that familiar interpretations of all three thinkers as dogmatic rationalists are thus profoundly misleading; rather, what unites their "idealisms" is attention to the active side of reasoning in defending one's claims to know, and a critical attention to the conditions one's arguments must meet if they are not to end up undermining themselves when confronted by arguments from others. This changes the way one understands the sort of moral and political claims Kant and Hegel made, and helps one to see how these fit with their larger philosophical views. In particular, it allows us to see that Kant was a radical critic of just the sort of moralizing rationalism of which he is often presented as an avatar (by both supporters and critics), and that neither his nor Hegel's views depended directly on any sort of tendentious positive metaphysics. It also allows us to appreciate the unique contribution of these leading German idealists to political thought, in placing the question of political judgment before the traditional question of the best regime, and in working out the conditions of defensible judgments in a way that brought historical change into the very content of right itself. Others in the period were also concerned with history, and after the French Revolution, theories of historical change would come to dominate the field. But Kant's and Hegel's approaches to history—which despite their differences agreed in viewing it as a space of contestable political judgment according to principles—would be eclipsed by other less reflective theories of progress in the century that followed.

These notions of elenchus and of history as a space of judgment are two that a historical and Socratic theory of democracy takes up and develops. But the discussions of Kant and Hegel in Part One also put on the table a number of powerful substantive arguments for what follows from thinking about politics and history this way. First of all, I have suggested, the reason democratic government is the only legitimate sort is just that any other basis for a claim to political legitimacy can only be self-defeating. Since any obligation to obey a particular government must presuppose the autonomy of those citizens it is to bind, Rousseau and Kant were right to argue that only a broadly republican government in which laws count as legislated by the people themselves can ever be fully legitimate.[1] Democracy is thus justified not because it is built on a true theoretical foundation, but just because it is the only form of government that requires no foundations whatsoever. It is the least legitimate form of government except for all those other forms that have been tried from time to time.

Three important points follow. First, the notion of a "people" in this conception of democracy is only a principle of judgment: what we can say is that any political judgment contradicting the idea of a self-determining people composed of free and equal citizens cannot be a good one, but this does not mean there actually exists such a people "out there" somewhere in the world that we might find and simply allow to rule. The point is that we can never get away from making and defending our own political judgments, but it is better to do this in democratic terms than in any other sort. Reifying "the people" and losing sight of our responsibility for the judgments we make is one of the greatest mistakes a democrat can make.

---

[1] Of course, this theory emerged as an immanent critique of natural law theories with religious roots that presupposed the category of obligation, and so in principle one might defend a political claim on some competing principle. But one would still need to show why that principle deserves to win out, and that becomes a real challenge once some citizens begin to raise objections in terms that question their obligation to obey. Historically, objections of this sort have spread farther around the globe than the religions and natural law theories in relation to which they first emerged. On my view, this is all perfectly fine, because one is not presupposing that any of this is necessary or universal, but only responding to particular conflicts as they arise, and whether or not any particular people want to make use of concepts like freedom or democracy in their domestic politics is entirely up to them to work out.

Second, it also follows that the interpretation of any democratic ideal must remain perpetually open to Socratic critique and contestation. Not only can one not derive any particular institutional system directly from the a priori idea of a self-governing people, but even the underlying notions of freedom and universality are radically indeterminate and always open to ongoing reinterpretation. So the fact that one understanding of citizens' equal freedoms seems to make sense in a certain country or in a certain historical period is no reason to suppose it also applies universally to other peoples or that it sets a timeless standard of human progress. But neither can one presume that certain "peoples" have no concern for freedom or equality, or that they are united around any timeless interpretation of those terms insulated from political struggle and contestation. Instead, one must always work out which view holds up best in a particular context, depending on the range of options citizens themselves bring to the table and the shape of specific historical conflicts as they arise. Hegel's phenomenological account of freedom in history offers, I suggested, some thoughtful examples of how to think through conflicts in this way, although Hegel certainly also held some indefensible views about what followed (particularly concerning non-Western societies and international relations, but also in his rejection of democracy).

Third, we saw that Kant and Hegel agreed, in different ways, that abstract concepts like a constitution respecting the freedom of all citizens matter for politics only when citizens act to interpret and apply them. Concepts of right do not exist as such in the social world; what exists are actions that either accord with or contradict those concepts, and so it is essential always to consider not only what is a good ideal but also whether the particular acts of actual persons are consistent with the ideals that they invoke. For Kant that meant individual revolutionaries could not simply overturn any order they disagreed with and impose their own views of a free constitution on the rest of the citizens. And this meant that citizens must ultimately trust the existing constitution to reform itself in a republican direction—although they might argue as much as they liked, they must nevertheless obey.

Hegel suggested another possibility. (In fact, we saw he offered two, but the appeal to pedagogical politics in the *Philosophy of Right* is both antidemocratic and indefensible.) Hegel's philosophical history of the rise of the modern state shows how one might defend a certain institutional interpretation of citizens' freedom by showing that the interpretations it replaced undermine themselves on their own terms. This Socratic approach does not, like Kant's, begin by presuming the legitimacy of the present system. To the contrary, the whole point for Hegel was to demonstrate that legitimacy by providing immanent refutations of the historical alternatives. There are certainly some problems with the way Hegel went about this and some of the conclusions he drew. But if one considers his philosophy of history not as a substantive doctrine but as a series of illustrations of how one might think about history and legitimacy in this Socratic way, then it makes points worth considering. The power of Hegel's core insight is that it finally shows a way out of the paradox of authorization. Or if one prefers, it shows why it was wrong to mistake the problem of political disagreement for a logical paradox in the first place, and how it is instead a challenge intrinsic to politics that can only be addressed by a theoretical framework allowing one to defend contextual judgments as conflicts unfold.

A historical and Socratic theory of democracy works out the logic of such a framework in a thoroughly democratic way that breaks with other of Hegel's views. Although it draws inspiration from the understanding of Socrates, Kant, and Hegel presented in Part One of this book, its substantive claims do not depend on the authority of any of those thinkers or any particular interpretation of them. Part Two accordingly defends a freestanding theory of democracy and democratic change that stakes out unique space in contemporary democratic theory. Its core principles were introduced in Chapter 1, and its first distinguishing feature is that it is a theory of political judgment rather than a theory of institutions or timeless ideals. Second, it asks us to begin by considering the course of actual democratic struggles already in progress, to ask which among the competing positions defended by different parties and factions has the best claim to represent a judgment of the democratic people as a whole. And finally, it recognizes that we will be able to answer this in a consistent way only if we can show that some of those judgments are indefensible on their own terms—not on ours. That is, unless we are to impose our own judgments undemocratically in the place of actual citizens', all we can argue is that certain judgments defended as "the people's" do not actually hold up that way when we go on to ask why those claims ought to be believed. This is what it means to call the theory Socratic.

Chapter 6 considers in greater detail the four conditions of Principle (II)* introduced in Chapter 1. Chapter 7 then goes on to consider a range of cases that show how they can be put to work. Although these cases help to illustrate the theory, one may perfectly well disagree with my treatment of specific cases while accepting the theory itself. The book's conclusion addresses some potential confusions and objections.

Throughout, less space is devoted to rebutting criticisms than some philosophically trained readers might expect. This is because I have found it more important here to present clearly the overall position I am arguing for, and to try to convey something of what it might be good for and what issues are really at stake in opting for a position of this sort over more familiar alternatives. A theory like this will have to be judged as a whole in comparison to other theories, and so the first order of business is to show what it entails and where the real differences lie. This is the major aim of Part Two.

6

The Four Conditions of Principle (II)*

This chapter considers in detail the four conditions of Principle (II)* first introduced in Chapter 1. A historical and Socratic theory of democracy begins from the competing interpretations of democratic legitimacy defended by actual political actors in struggles over change. It asks which of those interpretations deserves to win out because it has the best claim to be endorsed by the democratic people as a whole. To work this out, we cannot assume we already know how to check what "the democratic people" have decided, since this is just what the fighting is about. Instead, we need to consider each party's or faction's claim that its interpretation is the one the larger citizenry has endorsed, to see which holds up best on its own terms. The four conditions of Principle (II)* are constraints that any consistent claim of this sort will have to meet. For instance, I have already suggested that even if most citizens vote to install a despotism, that does not make despotism democratic, or that even if one brilliant citizen's view of democracy is supported by the best philosophical arguments, it cannot be the view the people have chosen if everyone else actively rejects it. These are the sorts of conditions Principle (II)* is meant to capture. They should be taken in a Socratic fashion, not as algorithms of the sort once fashionable in interpretations of Kant. The point is that these are ways of contradicting oneself that, if real, ought to be demonstrable in dialogue with any interlocutor—and there is no other way of proving them than by trying this out repeatedly in particular cases (as in Plato's exemplary dialogues). So interpreting and applying them are a matter for ongoing debate in context; they are not a way of ending debate but a way of thinking about how best to engage in it.

Throughout the chapter, it will be helpful to hold in mind a typical scenario of democratic struggle in which an opposition movement proposes some sort of social or political reform. The sitting government rejects the reform, and each side claims to speak on behalf of the people. Imagine further that we cannot confidently write off the opposition simply as sore losers, because their program challenges the democratic authority of the elected government on some prima facie plausible grounds. For instance, in the U.S. civil rights movement, a minority challenged the legitimacy of local majorities for violating the equal rights of citizens they claimed ought not to be subject to majority decision. Although the four conditions are clearest if one imagines this sort of classic scenario, however, they may also be applied to conflicts among more than two factions, or among factions in the absence of an established state. And they can also be applied with some modifications at other levels, both inside social and political movements themselves and in international affairs. But because these further applications raise additional complications, I will focus on the important state-versus-challenger-movement scenario in this book.

The Conceptual Condition

The first of the four conditions, *the conceptual condition*, holds that any admissible democratic system must be consistently defensible on some principled account of what distinguishes a system that respects the equal freedoms of all citizens as both authors and addressees of law from one that does not. It does not require any further reason for thinking this account the "true" one. All it demands is some such account and an argument from it that consistently supports the proposed system over others. It is thus strictly a requirement of internal consistency on any claim that a given system ought to count as democratic. (It corresponds to the so-called What-is-F? question in the Socratic elenchus.)

In conflicts over social and political change, competing sides often defend their positions explicitly in democratic terms. And if they do not, we may charitably attribute such arguments to each to consider the best possible case for its position. One side's case may, of course, fail the consistency test if its own interpretation of citizens' equal freedoms does not, in fact, support its program uniquely over its rivals. But the more interesting case is when the account does support the program, but still fails to show why that program should count as "democratic" because it fails to provide any determinate criterion for distinguishing democratic from undemocratic regimes. This is the problem, for instance, with a strictly Hobbesian or decisionist interpretation of democracy at the constitutional level, of the kind found in Carl Schmitt: if all that matters is that a decision is made and attributed to the people, but no formal conditions are allowed that might limit the range of such a choice or who is empowered actually to make it, then "democracy" becomes indistinguishable from despotism, the term is emptied of all content, and it can no longer mean anything to defend a political system as "democratic" as opposed to anything else.[1] As we saw, this was already Hegel's criticism of the "absolute freedom" he associated with the Jacobin Terror.

---

[1] See particularly Schmitt's *Constitutional Theory* (Durham, NC: Duke University Press, 2008), 75–88.

This is important for politics because it serves as a check on an entire range of otherwise potentially tantalizing populisms. Many such movements, including classic fascisms in Italy, Germany, and Spain, Mao's cultural revolution, contemporary European *Volksparteien*, and antipolitical populisms of left and right, have mobilized broad popular support in the people's name. What distinguishes all such movements, however, is that in explaining what it is that makes them count as expressing "the people's" voice, they answer by naming the people's enemies. The problem with this way of defining democracy is not that we know independently that some other definition is true, but that if one goes about it like this, then every autocrat is also a democrat. If calling governments or movements "democratic" is instead to have any meaning, one must provide a criterion for distinguishing democratic political forms from despotic ones. I have argued that this criterion is best expressed as the demand to respect the equal freedoms of all citizens as both authors and addressees of law. (This makes it possible to show why fascism, for instance, is not democratic—although an argument is still required.) If a political movement were to reject this formulation, it would need to provide some other criterion with institutional purchase capable of distinguishing democracy from nondemocracy, in a way that continued to show why we ought to think "democracy" supports a claim to rule. And that would take refuting the sort of arguments from Rousseau and Kant considered in previous chapters.

Some may accept that a criterion is needed but argue that my formulation in Principle (I) is either too thick or else too thin. Consider first the possibility that insisting on the equal freedoms of citizens as authors and addressees of law is too thick, that it builds in arbitrary demands that democrats might consistently reject. Now one cannot simply define democracy any way one likes, because the point of "democracy" in the sort of use we are considering is that it is meant to support a claim to legitimate rule. And on the argument from Rousseau and Kant, such a claim is defensible only if it respects the equal freedoms of those it purports to bind. So other ways of defining democracy, for instance as majority rule, cannot be primary in this use but must depend on a further argument that in a particular context majority rule is a good way of instantiating a more general principle requiring collective decisions to respect citizens' equal freedoms. It is important to see that Principle (I) does not require arbitrarily supposing any positive value of freedom or equality—which might be thought to impose liberal individualist assumptions on others who might prefer justice or the common good, for instance. The argument is elenctic—freedom and equality as they are used here are only limit-concepts on consistent claims of obligation, not positive foundational commitments that others might reject. And so you do not have to believe freedom is more important than other values to accept that other people should respect your equal freedom to pursue whatever values you believe in, insofar as that pursuit is consistent with the reciprocal claims of other citizens.

But is it really necessary not only that the laws respect citizens' equal freedoms but also that citizens make the laws? Liberals have often argued the contrary. François Guizot, for instance, argued against extending the suffrage under the French July Monarchy on the grounds that a truly "representative government" should express by "the sovereignty of reason" rather than the sovereignty of the people.[2] But since reason always requires interpretation by some empirical power, the real question is who has that power and how should it be structured.[3] And so a further argument would always be required to show why certain citizens are incapable of participating in that decision—the sort of argument Guizot advanced from *capacité*, J. S. Mill from civilization, and even Kant from freedom from private dependence. Now it is important to stress that on my view, such arguments are prima facie admissible, and indeed every contemporary democracy continues to deny the vote to children for just these reasons. What made the case for universal suffrage—and subsequently for women's suffrage—was that excluded persons organized political movements to rebut these claims of incapacity and dependence. But this is part of the historical baseline, not something built in a priori to the notion of any consistent interpretation of legitimate government. This is what it means to say the criterion is as minimal as it can possibly be, and strictly a requirement of internal consistency.

This may be an uncomfortable conclusion, but I think one needs to bite the bullet here and admit that even limitations on suffrage could be defensible on broadly republican grounds, of the sort advanced by Kant, in a particular context where no otherwise defensible popular movement supports extending it. The only alternative is to assert that some particular interpretation of "universal" suffrage follows a priori from Principle (I)—but then the question is whether that universal logical certainty is, for instance, that eighteen-year-olds should vote but seventeen-year-olds should not. Or why not twenty-one or sixteen? The point is that these are political judgments that may rightly be the subject of controversy—as they were, for instance, in the United States during the Vietnam War before the passage of the Twenty-sixth Amendment in 1971. It is not "safe" even to suppose that reason requires extending suffrage, for example, to all adult citizens, since it is not obvious that nonadults should be excluded,

---

[2] Indeed, he already wrote in 1821 that "the sovereignty of justice, of reason, and of right, that is the principle that one must oppose to the sovereignty of the people." François Guizot, *Des moyens de gouvernement et d'opposition dans l'état actuel de la France* (Paris: Ladvocat, 1821), 118.

[3] This is the ground on which republicans like publicist Armand Marrast challenged Guizot's defense of the regime: "You claim that your opinion is the only good one—but from my side, I have the same pretense in supporting the opposite opinion.—Where is the judge? It is reason, one will say.—Very good. But this reason, where is its organ?... We need a judge to decide, and this judge, it is the majority" (*Dictionnaire Politique*, ed. Pagnerre [Paris, 1842], 900).

or that noncitizen residents should be barred, for instance, from voting in local and supra-national elections where they live (as a number of European states presently allow). Some line will always be drawn and line-drawing is an act of judgment that always excludes some other persons. What can be ruled out on the conceptual condition alone is the notion that some people ought to be ruled by others *even though* they are capable of ruling themselves and reject others' claim to rule them. But these latter conditions are empirical and need to be demonstrated either positively by showing one's ability to organize politically, or at least negatively through evidence of repression aimed at preventing one from doing so. Otherwise, once one starts insisting in this way on more and more a priori content that no consistent interpretation of democracy could possibly contravene, it is hard to see where one will stop, and how to show that one is really building one's arguments out from the internal logic of actual political struggles rather than imposing one's own conventional truisms on others who may not share them.

So the conceptual condition will rule out very little a priori—slavery, active disenfranchisement, stripping citizens of citizenship, or the permanent alienation of popular sovereignty (as distinguished from conditional acceptance of a particular mode of exercising it). All the rest will depend on whose interpretation of the condition holds up best in context, and how it interacts with the other three. This does not mean everything else is permitted, but that the point of the condition is not primarily to rule out specific outcomes a priori but to set the terms in which particular judgments ought to be challenged and defended. Of course, in point of fact, at least some interpretation of universal suffrage is very widely demanded by some faction in almost every contemporary struggle. And once it has been anywhere established, it is hard to see how it could ever legitimately be rolled back, since that would appear to require showing certain citizens capable of making the political decision to declare themselves incapable of making political decisions, which is absurd.[4] But requirements on the other side, for instance, protecting certain liberal rights and civil liberties, may not be as widely demanded in every case. On my view, such rights and liberties will often deserve to win out when citizens demand them, but this does not mean that one can look in from the outside and rule that any constitution lacking them is entirely without legitimacy and may therefore be overturned at will (perhaps by an outside power), or placed under supervisory tutelage. Moreover, civil liberties and universal suffrage regularly conflict or are held to conflict, and in that case it depends whether or not an argument holds up that some particular

---

[4] Perhaps one could argue even this in a very particular case—say, hypothetically if the voting age were dropped to five but no five-year-olds actually came to vote and a proposal to raise it back was not met by any significant public criticism from five-year-olds. But this only supports my larger point that the conceptual condition should be taken as a test of internal consistency in context.

interpretation of rights and liberties deserves protection against majorities—I argue in the next chapter that some recent struggles over same-sex marriage are cases where they did, but that *Lochner*-era substantive due process in the United States was a case where they did not. And sometimes both sides may have equal claims; then only a negotiated settlement can be legitimate, if possible, and otherwise the situation will be tragic. On my view, then, one must always resist the temptation to confuse one's own particular judgments with a priori demands of universal reason. That is the point of distinguishing between the conceptual condition as a minimal formal demand of consistency, and the historical baseline, through which content may be added to the notion of citizens' equal freedoms through the course of actual political struggles among the citizens involved. In judging ongoing struggles, it does not help to project back certain outcomes as historically inevitable or logically preordained, and presuming that a particular interpretation of the past must continue also into the future is just to deprive actual citizens in the present of the chance to decide the issue for themselves.

In order to test the consistency of competing positions during the course of an actual struggle, it is important that we first canvass major arguments actually advanced on all sides of a controversial issue, both by political actors and by scholars. We should not be too quick to presume that we can identify "inconsistencies" a priori. Rather, determining what counts as consistent or inconsistent will often be the subject of debate. Understanding competing arguments and challenging our own unexamined presuppositions about what does or does not follow from what require, I think, what Arendt has called "visiting"—the exchanging of standpoints with others as a means of enlarging one's intellectual horizons, as a prerequisite for informed judgment.[5] The point of the conceptual condition is not, then, that "consistency" is obvious or an easy standard to apply. It is that despite the difficulty, there is nevertheless an important difference between debating which of several competing arguments holds up best *as an argument*, or searching instead for some self-certifying Archimedean point *beyond all argument*, from which the final truth might then be derived. In democratic debate the second strategy can only lead to paradox, and so we do better to focus on the first.

The Practical Condition

The second, *practical condition*, holds that any admissible democratic program must show a balance of positive empirical evidence in favor of its claim to enjoy the people's support, consistent with its own interpretation of how the people's

---

[5] Hannah Arendt, *Lectures on Kant's Political Philosophy*, ed. Ronald Beiner (Chicago: University of Chicago Press, 1992), 42.

will is expressed. Here again, we do not need to know which institutions or acts really do express the one true will of the democratic people. As we have seen, every democratic program must put forward some account of which organizational forms are to count as expressing "the people's" authoritative decisions. If, then, that program itself is to count as self-imposed by the people, it must provide some evidence of support *on its own account* of the forms that should be taken to express the people's will. If it does not, then it cannot consistently be defended as democratic even on its own interpretation of "democracy," and so it may fairly be ruled out as self-defeating. Actually imposing any program will require the ongoing coercion of citizens who reject it, and unless that program meets its own standards, it cannot consistently explain why that coercion is justified. In other words, if one imposes one's own view of democracy without showing consistent evidence that the people should be taken also to have endorsed it for themselves, then the pursuit of democracy—even if well-intentioned—flips over into its opposite and becomes indistinguishable from the despotic use of unaccountable force against the citizens.

To see why this matters for politics, consider two parallel cases. Imagine that in each a party endorses the same program of nationalizing major industries as a means of alleviating poverty and social inequality held to conflict with the equal freedoms of democratic citizens. (For the sake of argument, assume this program otherwise admissible.) Now imagine in the first case that a small, vanguardist minority imposes this program on an unwilling population, resorting to political violence and a "dictatorship of the proletariat" in order to overcome widespread and foreseeable resistance. In a second case, by contrast, large-scale nationalization is voted in through a system of free and fair elections grounded in a stable rule of law, the legitimacy of which is accepted by all major political parties, even though they continue to disagree over the results. The democratic legitimacy of these two outcomes is hardly identical. Or consider a second contrast: in one country liberal-democratic institutions result from a settlement hammered out over time by local political factions, whereas in another the very same institutions are instead imposed by conquest and propped up only by means of perpetual military occupation at the hands of a foreign power. The practical condition captures the difference between these two cases; focusing narrowly on formal conditions obscures it. That condition thus shows what is wrong with the supposition that either theorists or political actors unaccountable to any popular constituency should presume to legislate their preferred interpretation of democracy, without subjecting that interpretation to the practical test of actually demonstrating a following among the people for whom it purports to speak.

This does not mean that every valid program must demonstrate majority support, either in elections or public opinion. This would be so only if one could presume ex ante that a particular organized form of majoritarianism always represents the people's one true will. But this is just what cannot fairly be presumed, since conflicts over democratic change will involve arguments—first, over how to balance minority and majority rights in ways consistent with the equal freedoms of all citizens, and second, even when majority rule is appropriate, over the particular institutional forms in which it is to be administered. (That is, should a majority include only adult citizens and not minors or permanent residents, should it be determined by referendum or by electing representatives, nationwide or geographically based, with what qualifications for candidates or initiatives, on first-past-the-post or proportional representation, etc.?) In the most interesting cases, rival programs are bound up with competing accounts of the sort of empirical evidence that counts as manifesting the people's democratic will. And so all we can require is that whatever account each competing side advances, it must at least be able to show that its program is consistently defensible on its own account.

Consider, for instance, the U.S. civil rights movement in the 1950s and 1960s. In this dispute, segregationists backed the right of local white majorities to govern themselves without interference from outside powers like the federal government. Civil rights leaders invoked the competing democratic right of African American minorities to the equal protection of the laws. This argument had, of course, long been available, but what changed in this decade was first, the Supreme Court's 1954 decision in *Brown v. Board*, and second, most dramatically after the Montgomery Bus Boycott of 1955–1956, the fact that civil rights leaders built mass organizations that powerfully demonstrated support for their position among African Americans in the South.[6] Both developments dramatically bolstered the democratic credibility of segregation's critics. And yet the civil rights movement hardly raised any doubt that the majority of white southerners, and thus overall majorities in the South, remained overwhelmingly hostile to integration. Indeed, segregationists quickly organized their own popular mobilization through White Citizens' Council chapters to drive home the point. So does this not prove that segregation was democratic, if "wrong," and that if we wish to object to it, we have no choice but to appeal directly to individual judgments of justice?

The answer is that since the civil rights movement was defending a minority's democratic rights against a majority, it did not need to show support among that larger white majority in order to advance a consistent democratic claim. It was enough to show strong support among African Americans in the South (what in Chapter 7 I call "convincing supermajority support" among the relevant minority). Segregationists also demonstrated consistent support on their own majoritarian principles, but such majorities could not rule out the civil rights

---

[6] For precursors, see Aldon D. Morris, *The Origins of the Civil Rights Movement: Black Communities Organizing for Change* (New York: Free Press, 1984).

activists' competing claims. In this case, each side showed popular support on its own terms, and this is a major reason the struggle was so important, so hotly fought, and would have such far-reaching consequences. Because both sides met the practical condition, deciding will involve further questions considered later on. But what is clear is that it would be unfair to have demanded of African Americans in the South that they first win over an absolute majority of the entire population, including a major segment of southern whites, before their objections to the democratic legitimacy of local segregationist majorities could even be considered. This would have begged the question in favor of a majority whose right to speak for the people as a whole had plausibly been called into question.

Although my point here is only to show why the practical condition does not necessarily require majorities, one can see that the particular case raises a number of further issues that point to other conditions. One might well think the civil rights movement case is best resolved another way. One cannot appeal directly to justice without inviting democratic problems already considered. But perhaps segregation can be ruled out directly on the conceptual condition, as I suggested slavery could be? Whereas slavery denied legal personhood explicitly and in principle, however, the Jim Crow regime in the South claimed to respect that principle while instantiating judgments about its application. It might seem obvious that this was in bad faith, but only the democratic people have the right to issue and enforce a binding judgment. "Separate but equal" may be wrong but it is not a priori absurd, and so a judgment is required to show why it is wrong and it matters who is judging.

One could also argue that segregation was at least already ruled out by the principle of equal protection established as part of the historical baseline in the United States with the passage of the Civil War amendments. Here, one must distinguish two issues. Equal voting rights had indeed been established by the Fifteenth Amendment and actually put into practice during Reconstruction. They were subsequently rolled back through a policy of active disenfranchisement supported by extensive political violence.[7] This has all the hallmarks of an undemocratic power grab, and should be considered illegitimate. So on the question of voting rights, the movement culminating in the 1965 Voting Rights Act is best understood as reestablishing in effective law a principle already firmly established in the democratic baseline.

---

[7] See William Gillette, *Retreat from Reconstruction, 1869-1879* (Baton Rouge: Louisiana State University Press, 1979); Xi Wang, *The Trial of Democracy and Northern Republicans, 1860-1910* (Athens: University of Georgia Press, 1997); Richard M. Vallely, *The Two Reconstructions: The Struggle for Black Enfranchisement* (Chicago: University of Chicago Press, 2004); Alexander Keyssar, *The Right to Vote: The Contested History of Democracy in the United States*, rev. ed. (New York: Basic Books, 2009).

But dismantling "separate but equal" in public and private accommodations is somewhat more complex. On this issue, the official interpretation of equal protection had been set by the *Civil Rights Cases* of 1883 and *Plessy v. Ferguson* in 1896. Because the elected branches had effectively accepted the overruling of the Civil Rights Act of 1875 and did not pass another piece of federal civil rights legislation until 1957, after *Brown v. Board of Education*, it is hard to deny the importance of the latter decision and the new phase of grassroots and electoral contestation it helped to open up. The question is whether the *Civil Rights Cases* and *Plessy* were themselves undemocratic reversals that were always illegitimate. The final version of the 1875 Act had allowed segregation in schools, so it is difficult to argue that *Plessy* violated a clear standing decision of the democratic people. The *Civil Rights Cases* might well have done so, but the Court's claim was that Congress had overstepped its legislative authority in a way that violated states' rights to self-governance as per the Tenth Amendment.[8] This was unlike voting rights because those had been passed by an amendment ratified also by the states, but on this issue the farther-reaching claims of the 1875 Act had not been included in the Thirteenth or Fourteenth Amendments, although they might have been, and so did not enjoy a similar presumption to express the will of the people as represented by the complex balance of state and federal powers in the larger constitutional system. Now this is not obviously true, but it is a prima facie admissible objection because there was a real issue about how this balance would be redrawn after the war, which was still being hammered out in the 1870s and 1880s. Had the Court decided the other way, the choice of the people would have been clear, but it did not, and this meant the test would come from the response of the other branches and organized citizens. But national Republicans had been retreating, under electoral pressure, from their more radical positions since the 1875 Act was passed, and a few weeks after the *Civil Rights Cases* were decided in 1883, Grover Cleveland became the first Democrat to win the White House since the Civil War (1876 having been already controversial). This does not prove the Court right or refute the contrary position, particularly because these electoral results depended in significant part on the direct results of the illegitimate disenfranchisement of African Americans in the South. But neither had the pro-civil-rights position ever been decisively confirmed as a judgment of the American people, and by the 1880s it became clear that no mass actor with a claim to speak for that people continued actively to defend it. On the other hand, the Court's position had not been confirmed either, because that would have required allowing African Americans in the South to vote freely and without intimidation, which is just what southern states would not allow. So in this case, neither side had a defensible claim already to represent

---

[8] *Civil Rights Cases*, 109 U.S. 3 (1883).

the clear judgment of the American people as a whole; although disenfranchisement and the violence that supported it were always undemocratic, it was not clear that the larger people had decided to do anything about it. And so this was not only a power grab, it was an acquiescence in it by that larger people. In this period, then, although there was good reason to suspect the existing settlement undemocratic—since its democratic credentials depended on disenfranchising African American voters—there was no democratic alternative in a position to establish any other judgment as instead the American people's.

On this view, then, the historical actions of civil rights activists who built a mass-based, democratically organized protest movement across the South mattered materially to the legitimacy of their cause. These organizers and activists were not only the instruments of a timeless democratic ideal. Instead, like French republicans who fought for universal manhood suffrage in the 1840s and women's suffrage activists across much of Europe and the United States in the century that followed, they helped to prove the justice of their cause by building a democratic vehicle for their demands, lending them demonstrable empirical evidence of popular support and contesting the pretense of segregationist majorities to rule in the name of the people in the southern states. If there had been no movement, if *Brown v. Board* had fallen on deaf ears, then efforts by the federal government to enforce *Brown* by repressing demonstrable popular opposition from white southerners—for instance, at Little Rock in 1957 and the University of Mississippi in 1962—would have been much more plausibly challenged as undemocratic outside interference in local affairs. Action at least on voting rights would have been legitimate in any case, because it could not consistently be opposed on the established baseline, but action on desegregation would have raised further issues about the balance of federal and states' rights that the federal government was not obviously in a position unilaterally to renegotiate. It would have called a question that might have gone either way, although even if the federal government had eventually capitulated, this would not have proved the recalcitrant states right but only left the question still undecided (so long as local voting rights were not respected).

But the fact that a mass movement among African Americans in the South instead rose up to challenge the existing settlement, even in the face of violent repression, offered spectacular evidence against that settlement's claim to speak even for the people in the southern states. The civil rights movement challenged the monopoly on democratic legitimacy claimed by official, segregated institutions, and offered an alternative democratic partner for negotiation with federal reformers. In both ways, it radically altered the democratic equation from what it would have been had it been left up to the federal government to interpret, without input from democratic organizations representing African Americans in the South, the institutional steps necessary for securing their equal freedoms, and how far to push those steps in the face of consistent popular opposition from the other side. One result of this struggle's success is that it radically reinterpreted the principle of equal protection in the historical baseline, so that today it seems nearly impossible to imagine there was ever a consistent defense of the claim that the federal government lacked the right to overrule segregation. But we do a disservice to the work of civil rights activists, I think, to suppose that this was always so—to overlook what a profound historical achievement it was to establish this particular interpretation of principle in the United States, and how it durably reshaped American democracy in ways the effects of which are still being felt. It matters that civil rights activists did more than make good arguments; they also built the democratic organization that corroborated their claim in making those arguments to speak, as well as anyone, for the larger democratic people with the right to put them into force. If some of this work had been done already by the Civil War and Reconstruction, much of it had been left radically undecided—not only, as in the case of voting rights, incomplete. There was no guarantee that the American people would ever come to accept a judgment that required desegregation, and this was not already decided by the Civil War, much less by any self-correcting core principles already inscribed in the U.S. constitution in 1789 or 1791. In this case, it was not history that secured the justice of the civil rights activists' cause; it was their own democratic organizing and argument, in its interplay with the acts of other citizens. Segregation is a case in which for a certain period no available option already had a good democratic claim and it took political action rather than better arguments to change that.

In assessing the practical condition, then, we do not presume to know what kind of evidence expresses the people's one true will. Instead, we look for the evidence we *should expect to see* on either of the views defended by competing parties. In most cases, the key sources will be election results on the one hand and evidence of mass support for challenger movements outside official institutions on the other. The latter includes records of public demonstrations, petitions, and membership in advocacy organizations. Public opinion polls should be used with caution; they may sometimes yield useful indirect evidence for second-guessing the representative claims of elected officials or movements spokespersons, but on their own it is unclear what they show. On my view, there is good reason no existing state governs directly by opinion poll: first because a process is required to sort through competing evidence of opinion and to determine which opinions deserve to be made into law, and second because there is a difference between a process in which all citizens are invited actively to participate in the making of an actual collective decision, and another in which some are randomly selected and asked to record responses to questions about their beliefs posed to them by others. The former, I contend, has a much stronger claim to justify law as actually self-imposed, and it is at any rate the interpretation inscribed in the historical baseline in every existing democracy. If elections are more authoritative than opinion polls, however, then so is evidence of actual popular mobilization by opposition movements. How a law polls, in other words, does not immediately tell us anything about its legitimacy, if it was passed through a fair and representative electoral process. If the legitimacy of that process is to be called into question, then opponents must at least actually turn out to protest, the way supporters (presumably) actually turned out to vote. The practical condition thus turns our attention to the important fact that much of social movement practice is devoted to producing just such public "demonstrations" of popular support, often with the explicit aim of corroborating the movement's claim to representative status in order to speak on behalf of the larger people (or of an otherwise underrepresented segment thereof). The logic of this condition, then, taps into a logic already at work in the actual organizing practice of movements for social and political change.

Of course, in many cases empirical evidence may be skewed, either because dominant factions repress or frighten others into apparent acquiescence, because they mobilize unequal resources to distort outcomes, or else because the dominated themselves buy into the ideological mystification of their own oppression. A historical and Socratic theory takes these concerns seriously, but points out that if these assertions are to be meaningful, they must be taken as empirical claims susceptible in principle to assessment based on evidence. One should consider them always as possibilities, but in order to demonstrate their positive relevance in a particular case, one must find (1) some actual empirical evidence of actions tending to skew observed results, *and also* (2) evidence that in the absence of such actions the persons affected would indeed endorse the particular program one puts forward in their name. Otherwise, one can only impute "distortions" wherever one finds actual citizens not to share the view one has reasoned out for oneself a priori that the people "ought" to hold. And this contravenes the basic democratic demand that citizens play an actual—and not merely hypothetical—role in the making of the laws. Consistently pursued, it renders democracy indistinguishable from tutelage.

As I have explained it, then, the practical condition is a requirement of consistency that allows us to rule out certain democratic programs strictly on their own terms. It does not require any independently valid constitutional ideal against which competing programs might be measured. It simply points out that if a program is to count as democratic, it must enjoy the people's support on some account consistent with its own claim of how democratic consultation should proceed. Debates will and should continue to turn on what the available empirical evidence either does or does not show. Sometimes evidence will be insufficient to determine whether or not a side has met this condition, and sometimes this is not a problem of the quantity or quality of the evidence but a problem in the world, because the answer will depend on future actions that one side or another may or may not take, and how the other may or may not manage to respond. This is why applying the conditions justifies only provisional judgments and requires continued attention to shifting historical realities.

The Historical Baseline

The notion of the historical baseline asserts that a legitimate democratic program in the present must respect principles established by past democratic struggles, in the absence of evidence that the people have since reversed those decisions. This is not a claim that the past binds the present, but one about how to interpret the people's present will. The difficulty is that in conflicts over democratic change, there is no way of ever directly knowing that any particular present manifestation of that will is authoritative. All we can do is to eliminate some options that cannot consistently be defended. Now imagine for the sake of argument that we had managed to do this in a past case, to show that some particular struggle—for instance, establishing universal manhood suffrage or the equal protection of the laws—ought to count as a democratic decision of the people. This does not mean that that decision can never be reversed, or that it binds future generations for all time. But it does raise a certain bar that later movements must clear if they are rightly to convince us they have managed to reverse it.

The reason is this. Any institutional interpretation of the abstract notion of democratic citizens' equal freedoms must, if it is to be coherently defensible, be consistent across cases. For example, if we defend a concrete interpretation of democracy as requiring equality under the law, we cannot consistently argue that this applies only to white citizens but not to others *in principle*. Or if all males of a certain age deserve the right to vote because, since the 1840s, it has been accepted by the people that alleged intellectual or material incapacities for self-governance cannot actually justify withholding the suffrage, then no other group of citizens *who meets similar standards* can be denied it either. But it is essential to see that this is not to say that general principles interpret and apply themselves: it does not immediately follow a priori from granting unpropertied of-age men the right to vote that either women or minors deserve it, too. An intervening judgment needs to be made: Is there good reason to think women similarly capable of self-governance to unpropertied men? What about minors? Consider how even if a good argument supports lowering the voting age, for instance, from twenty-one to eighteen—especially if you are going to send people to war at eighteen—it does not follow that there is also a good reason to lower it to five or two. A real judgment is required in every instance, and so one cannot deduce particular instances directly from general principles. What can fairly be insisted on is that one consistently apply the principle.

This is a familiar notion in jurisprudence. To fairly apply a certain law, one ought to consider both the general law (or principle), and other relevant cases of how that law has been applied. To judge a particular case, one should reason by analogy to similar cases; one will apply the law fairly if one concludes likewise in like cases, and if, when one decides differently, one is able to show a principled ground for distinguishing the present case from those that appear similar but are, in fact, different in some dispositive way. If we did not do this, there would be no consistency in our application of general laws or rules, and therefore no grounds for accepting the legitimacy of any particular decision. The legitimacy of the law, then, depends on its integrity (and its democratic provenance), and maintaining that integrity requires working through particular cases and reasoning by analogy, in order to argue that one should be seen as treating like cases alike and unlike cases differently.[9]

Now in the judicial case, this injunction to treat like alike also holds over time, until the law is changed by legislatures, since judges are supposed to interpret rather than make the laws. But this is different for democratic principles, because the democratic people are always free to change their minds and make new laws. So why should past cases matter here? The reason is that the principles underlying a controversial present case will often bear on other cases that are not presently controversial. And so, if those principles clearly continue to be accepted in other instances, this will provide prima facie evidence against any interpretation of the people's present will that rejects them only in the controversial one. These principles constrain our decisions, then, because they continue to be principles we accept as structuring the institutional expression of our own democratic will. The reason it is useful to look at history is that these general principles were established by past struggles—principles like universal suffrage or equality under the law. And it commonly occurs that over time the people ratify further diverse instances of such principles. So in order to interpret which principles structure the democratic system today, we ought to look at the major struggles that shaped that system, and the range of particular consequences the people have drawn from them. If struggles in the past led to legitimate democratic outcomes that reformed the democratic system, then we ought to recognize that overturning those principles in the present would require rolling back all the other particular judgments that continue to depend on them. It may be that we should do this, that the democratic people have really changed their minds. But to tell, we need at least to know which other, historical decisions are at stake, in order to consider whether or not there is consistent present evidence

---

[9] On all this, see Ronald Dworkin, *Law's Empire* (Cambridge, MA: Harvard University Press, 1986). Dworkin's "integrity" further stresses that one must ascribe principles below the surface of individual terms, statutes, and decisions; on my view, this is also how we uncover historical baseline principles.

that the people have now reversed themselves across the range of instances. If we ignore the history and look only at the present moment, we will miss the principled interconnectedness of elements in the existing democratic system, and the ways that our particular present decisions might put us at odds with general principles we continue to affirm in other cases. This is what the notion of the historical baseline is meant to rule out.

Consider again the case of universal suffrage, for instance, in France. The principle itself was extremely controversial in the 1840s, even among defenders of modern liberty and "representative government." Blood was spilled in the streets and a revolution eventually fought in 1848, which managed (as it turned out) definitively to establish it. This revolution, I would argue, was democratically justified and showed ultimately that the democratic people had opted to ratify the principle of universal suffrage. (This is not because that principle is self-evident, but rather because the actual political organizing of unpropertied men confuted Guizot's claims that they were incapable of independent political action, and defenders of the Orleanist monarchy failed to accept compromise once their position was shown up as arbitrary and indefensible in context.) The course of subsequent French history would show that this achievement would prove durable, at least over the *longue durée*. The conquest of universal suffrage in 1848 thus succeeded in shifting the historical baseline against which future democratic struggles could be measured. When women's suffrage was debated in the early twentieth century, then, the validity of the argument for universal manhood suffrage could henceforth be presumed as a point of departure. If women's suffrage could be denied only on a premise that also contradicted universal manhood suffrage, then, and unless a case could be made to show that the French people had now decided to reverse course and give up on universal male suffrage as well, then women's suffrage could no longer consistently be denied. In the twentieth century, its advocates could ask: On what grounds can women consistently be denied the suffrage based on assertions of inferior intellectual capacity or a lack of requisite material independence when the very same considerations had already been rejected as applied to unpropertied men? (Of course, this is not to say that argument was bound to work—in fact, women received the vote in France only at the end of the war, from General de Gaulle rather than a democratically elected body—but the point is that the French Senate was undemocratic in blocking it for the duration of the Third Republic.) The point is that this is an argument that could be made after 1848 but not before, because the historical event served to establish a particular principle as willed by the democratic people, and later interpretations of that people's will ought, on democratic grounds, to take that principle into account.

Now this does not mean that even a principle today as uncontroversial as universal suffrage could never be reversed. Any of the principles of the historical baseline can be overturned at any time, and even short of this, they may well be radically reinterpreted. For instance, U.S. constitutional law in the period from the Supreme Court's decision in *Lochner v. New York* in 1905 to the New Deal in the 1930s used the notion of substantive due process, based on the Fourteenth Amendment, to defend a very strong reading of individual contract rights as inviolable property, and a very narrow interpretation of the commerce clause to limit strictly the federal government's authority to regulate economic activity. This view ruled out not only the kind of programs the New Deal would eventually usher in—such as the National Labor Relations Act and Social Security—but even the most basic federal child labor legislation. The same underlying principles were used regularly to quash strikes through court injunctions backed up by the force of federal troops or the National Guard.[10] New Deal legislation would eventually overturn this constitutional framework, but only after early New Deal programs had been struck down by the Court, Roosevelt responded with his court-packing threat, and the Court eventually shifted position in a series of watershed decisions beginning in 1937.[11]

I contend that in the struggle over the New Deal, as in that over universal suffrage in 1840s France, the result should count as democratically legitimate, but not because the alternative *Lochner* doctrine was conceptually incoherent or even an indefensible interpretation of prior standing constitutional law in the United States. On my view, a real decision was made in the 1930s, a democratic decision that might have gone another way. The reason the New Deal counts as legitimate is because between its own interpretation of the equal freedoms of democratic citizens and the *Lochner* Court's, it did a better job of consistently making its case as events unfolded in the 1930s. Roosevelt's electoral victories gave majoritarian backing, and the self-organization of working people into labor organizations and a mass labor movement put the lie to the Supreme Court's claim to speak on its own, unaccountable authority for workers who showed they, in fact, preferred a different interpretation of economic freedom, one allowing not only individual contract rights but also collective bargaining. Since this aligned majoritarian institutions and representative organizations of the very minority the antimajoritarian institution of the Court claimed to protect, and because it was not countered by comparable mass organizing in favor of the Court's interpretation among working people, it undercut the practical consistency of the *Lochner* interpretation of fundamental liberties and thus

---

[10] Felix Frankfurter and Nathan Greene, *The Labor Injunction* (New York: MacMillan, 1930); Irving Bernstein, *The Lean Years: A History of the American Worker, 1920–1933* (Boston: Houghton-Mifflin, 1960), 190–243; William E. Forbath, *Law and the Shaping of the American Labor Movement* (Cambridge, MA: Harvard University Press, 1991).

[11] On this "Roosevelt Revolution," see William E. Leuchtenberg, *The Supreme Court Reborn: The Constitutional Revolution in the Age of Roosevelt* (New York: Oxford University Press, 1995); and Bruce Ackerman, *We the People*, Vol. 2 (Cambridge, MA: Harvard University Press, 1998).

its democratic legitimacy. Here is a case, then, in which an established baseline principle was overturned (or at least very radically reinterpreted). But it took an awful lot to pull this off, and to show why doing so ought to count as democratic. It would take something even more dramatic to reverse a principle like universal suffrage today.

In interpreting the historical baseline, constitutional law and major legislation play a central role. They are not necessarily sufficient—there can be other extra-legal institutions, practices, or customs that might be considered a part of the baseline in certain cases or for certain questions—but it is a good place to start; and even where laws are silent, this is itself often positive evidence of what the prevailing baseline allows. At least three kinds of arguments can be made about the baseline. Sometimes the relevant baseline simply needs to be reconstructed. Other times it will be controversial whether the outcome of a certain historical struggle should be considered a democratic advance shifting the baseline, or instead a step backward, an illegitimate de facto abrogation of democracy. In this case, one applies all four conditions of Principle (II)* to the historical case; in theory one can always push the chain of analysis further back, but in practice a given question will require one only to go back so far, since those on opposite sides in a given democratic struggle usually do not disagree about everything (or if they do, it will not be the historical baseline that will decide). All this is open to debate, but these are the debates to be had. Finally, the third sort of argument is one in which some general baseline principles are accepted as established, but one is concerned to show either whether a contemporary struggle should be taken to overturn them, or else which side in such a struggle should be understood to interpret them correctly. This sort of case is considered in the next chapter.

The historical baseline, then, should be understood strictly as an immanent constraint of consistency on competing democratic programs, one that requires those programs to defend their proposed institutional principles consistently across cases, given the standing decisions of a particular democratic people. In practice, this will require drawing principles out of the history of democratic struggles and distinguishing frontal assaults on those principles themselves from battles over their interpretation. In the first sort of case, a high bar will be required to overturn the principles because it must be shown that other historical decisions that continue into the present also deserve to be overturned because the people have since changed their minds across the board. In the second sort of case, one will need to see whether or not the particular decision in controversy can be distinguished from otherwise analogous cases. Not every program that meets the first two conditions of Principle (II)* will also meet this historical condition, or at least they will not all do so equally well. And so sometimes considering the history of a particular people's experience of working out for itself the meaning of its own democratic freedom also helps us better to interpret its democratic decisions in the present.

The Condition of Exclusivity

Each of the first three steps served to rule out certain democratic programs because they cannot consistently be defended, in context, as chosen by a particular democratic people. Some of the most interesting and momentous democratic struggles, however, are just those in which these conditions prove insufficient to rule out every program but one. In such cases, we are left with more than one internally consistent interpretation of democratic institutions. The problem is that we need to choose only one of these competing programs actually to enforce. And this may seem to suggest that at the end of the day, we have no choice but to appeal to some sort of external positive foundation in order to decide among them. It may seem to show that arguing by elimination cannot be enough to justify the sort of positive claim of obligation that democratic legitimacy requires.

The problem, however, can be turned into its own solution: if our problem is that we need to choose one program uniquely to enforce, the solution is that the only program that could legitimately be enforced would be one that was not only internally coherent and thus admissible, but which also provided some nonarbitrary reason for *excluding all the live alternatives*. (This was the thought behind Plato's *archē anhupothetos*, as I argued in Chapter 2.) A theory that claims to be true, or a democratic system that claims to be legitimate, implicitly commits itself to the claim that incompatible views must be false or illegitimate. So if among two coherent theories, one can also provide a consistent reason for excluding the other, while the second cannot provide a similar reason for excluding the first, then we have good reason to accept the first and rule out the second. This is not because we know that the reason for excluding the second is independently true. It is just because the second cannot provide *any* such reason that would not contradict the substance of its own interpretation of democracy, and this means that view cannot consistently be defended as legitimate, since "legitimate" is always implicitly shorthand for *uniquely* legitimate, "true" for *uniquely* true. In this case enforcing the second view would be arbitrary and indefensible, whereas enforcing the first—even though we do not know it "true" in any positive or independent sense—at least does not involve us in contradictions when we are pressed to account for our right to put down by force, when necessary, defenders of a competing, equally admissible view.

But what sort of consideration might this be that would rule out an otherwise coherent interpretation of the people's will without appealing directly to any positive foundation? There are at least two sorts. The first turns on the fact that some theories can exclude others only by invoking some democratically arbitrary and inadmissible premise, such as God's authority or a particular scientific view of natural human ends. For instance, it might be that two different regimes of marriage law are equally admissible on competing interpretations of democracy: the first is a wholly contractual system based on the priority of individual rights (democratically legislated and affirmed), whereas the second is a system in which the state imposes conditions that make it more difficult to divorce, grounded in the people's democratically avowed commitment to promoting stable families. Imagine for the sake of argument a society in which both positions can plausibly claim popular support on their own terms. Now consider the first, contractual regime. Although it is defensible on some coherent interpretation of democracy, the question is how it can explain why it alone is defensible and the priority-of-the-family view must be excluded. It might be defended as uniquely legitimate because it rests on the true Lockean doctrine of the natural priority of individual rights to collective democratic decisions, but *that* explanation could not consistently be defended as a democratic one. A better explanation, then, would be one that began from the notion of the equal freedom of democratic citizens, and tried to show, for instance, that imposing the opposite view would privilege some citizens over others. Even if it could not be shown that this interpretation was the only interpretation conceptually possible, it would at least count as a democratically admissible ground for excluding the competing view.

Now consider the priority-of-the-family position. In order to show why this and only this view must be enforced, one might invoke substantive moral truths, tradition, or the will of God. These explanations, however, are inadmissible because they place an external authority above the people's own democratic freedom; they cannot be reasons to choose one shape of democracy over another, only for choosing something other than democracy. Here too, then, a better approach would be to defend an interpretation of the citizens' democratic rights that would somehow be violated if the contractual regime were imposed instead. Perhaps such an argument could appeal to the rights of a married couple's children or potential children, or else to second-order rights of individuals who want the opportunity freely to bind themselves in certain institutional ways other than individual contracts. Again, the question is not whether or not this is the "true" interpretation of democratic rights. At issue is only whether or not it is at least admissible.

The reason this provides leverage for excluding certain views is that, *once one works out their democratically admissible grounds for excluding competing programs*, this adds to the content of the views on each side that must also meet the other conditions. In this case, it means, for instance, that it will not be enough to demonstrate the consistency of the contractual regime to show that a Lockean natural rights view has wide support among the people. Rather, what we need to consider is whether the *admissible* ground for excluding alternatives—the specific interpretation of citizens' equal freedoms—also manages to demonstrate practical support consistent with the historical baseline. Similarly on the other side, it might be that a priority-of-the-family regime has wide popular support from those who think it the word of God. This alone does not rule it out—it may well be that the same program is defensible on both religious *and* democratic grounds. But what has to be shown is that the democratic argument, the explanation of why the priority-of-the-family regime uniquely follows from democratic citizens' equal freedoms, *also* has popular support consistent with the historical baseline. If the *only* view we could plausibly attribute to the people in favor of that program were the view that God demanded it, then because basing the legitimacy of state coercion on that sort of claim would be incompatible with democracy, the program could fairly be excluded.

The second way of applying the exclusivity condition is to show that when we are left with two or more competing views of what democracy requires, neither of which can be ruled out as inconsistent, one institutional program can be defended on *both* sets of starting assumptions, whereas any competing view requires presuming one of those sets uniquely true in the absence of any democratic ground for such a presumption. Consider the familiar device of institutional compromise: the U.S. Constitution, for instance, includes a compromise between the representation of states and the representation of individual citizens. The solution was to juxtapose the two principles by requiring law to be passed by both a House representing population and a Senate representing states. It is possible to defend this solution from either point of view: even if one thinks states have natural sovereignty, their agreement to cede *absolute* sovereignty to a system in which they retain a permanent veto power can be defended as compatible with states' rights. A similar argument can be made on the other side, that the national people has freely recognized certain internal conditions on the exercise of its will by distributing powers among federal and state authorities. Now there is no a priori necessary reason for either side to accept this deal, but if they do, then it is possible to justify that deal ex post on both competing sets of assumptions. Finally, the same outcome is also justified on a third set, which each party accepts in signing the deal, according to which final authority henceforth rests in a more encompassing constitutional system comprising both state and national institutions. Unlike any other outcome, then, this one cannot be ruled out no matter the set of assumptions from which one begins. (In Chapter 6, we saw that Hegel illustrated a similar point with *Antigone*.)

By contrast, if in a particular historical context, there was no other way of ruling out either the sovereign claims of states or the competing sovereign claims of a national people, then imposing either of those solutions uniquely, and putting down the other by force, would be arbitrary and democratically indefensible. For this reason, a certain compromise program may sometimes be uniquely more defensible than any of the more one-sided alternatives it reconciles. Notice, however, that this is not always so. It is not obvious, even if the House–Senate compromise was legitimate in 1787, that the conditions that made it so then continue to hold today. Indeed, many of them clearly do not, given intervening events such as the Civil War and New Deal, although it is unclear exactly how far the change should be taken to go, and this accordingly remains a central issue in ongoing struggles over change. On the other hand, the "grand compromise" of 1787 also ratified slavery. Whether or not there is some democratic way of defending this compromise in context while admitting that slavery itself cannot be justified, one can at any rate imagine a case in which one specific compromise between two historical factions would be justified, but another between the same factions would not. What is justified is not compromise for the sake of compromise, but only specific compromises that manage to resolve conflicts among otherwise defensible democratic programs.

This general sort of thinking reaches back at least to Aristotle's *Politics*, and underlay the classical defense of the mixed constitution. According to Aristotle, the sign of the best regime likely to be attainable is that it be "possible for the same regime to be spoken of as both a democracy and an oligarchy," since democracy and oligarchy were the two major contending parties in the classical polis.[12] "[A] finely mixed regime," Aristotle explains, "should be held to be both and neither."[13] (Of course, Aristotle is using the term "democracy" in a different way than I do; he holds to the classical view that defines democracy as the rule of the poor, hence not of the entire "people" in the modern sense, but of one social group called "the people" as opposed to another.) For Aristotle, the competition between oligarchic and democratic regimes arises because each embraces a different, and equally partial, view of equality.[14] And this leads to factional conflict, since each side mistakenly takes its own view as true absolutely, or without qualification, and thus feels justified in trying to impose it on the other. In a finely mixed regime, by contrast, "none of the parts of the *polis* would wish for a different regime," because unlike democracy or oligarchy, that regime can be embraced from either point of view.[15] Although Aristotle also appreciates this constitution for its inherent moderation,[16] the sort of constitutional mean he calls for is not a mere half-measure—it is one in which "each of the extremes can be seen," and equally so.[17]

To see how applying the exclusivity condition might work, consider two historical cases. First look again at the U.S. civil rights movement, which is what

---

[12] 1294b14–16. I have benefited from Lord's translation in Aristotle, *The Politics*, ed. Carnes Lord (Chicago: University of Chicago Press, 1984).
[13] 1294b33–35.
[14] 1301a27–1302a15.
[15] 1294b38–40.
[16] In *Politics*, see particularly book IV, Chapter 11; in *Nichomachean Ethics*, books II and V.
[17] 1294b17.

we might call an easy case because in it one of the competing sides ends up meeting the condition, while the other does not. The second case, the founding of the Third French Republic in the early 1870s, is a hard case in which a compromise different from what either side initially demanded ended up being the only defensible solution. In the civil rights movement, as we have already seen, although segregation might be defended directly on racist grounds, in fact, its apologists commonly styled their case as a defense of states' rights against encroaching federal tyranny. For instance, in his 1963 inaugural address as governor of Alabama, George Wallace vowed to defend "segregation forever" against the interference of federal courts, calling upon his fellow southerners to "rise to the call of the freedom-loving blood that is in us and send our answer to the tyranny that clanks its chains upon the South."[18] Now this argument is perfectly admissible from a democratic point of view. While there is no obvious reason that states' rights should win out over the will of national majorities, neither is there an obvious reason they should not. Recognition of states' rights, moreover, is an integral part of the American constitutional tradition and the historical baseline, and had previously been upheld by the United States Supreme Court specifically on the segregation issue in the 1883 *Civil Rights Cases*. There was a fair question, then, as to whether or under what conditions the federal government had the right unilaterally to redraw those lines.

The best tack for segregationists was thus to stake their case on states' rights, and to cast the federal government as an imperialist interloper. Of course, it is no more obvious why it should be states rather than the federal government to interpret the limits of states' rights in the established post–Civil War settlement. And the New Deal had changed the legal calculus in the interim by radically expanding federal power under the commerce clause, which states at that time had accepted. But there still remained a question about a new extension of that principle from the federal side, since it was at least possible for states to point out that this was not what they had meant to agree to in ratifying the Civil War amendments. And so they could, and did, force a constitutional crisis over the right to interpret the existing settlement. As long as the only popular mobilization in the South was of white segregationists, they might portray federal intervention as incursion, since they could cast the NAACP (who brought *Brown* to court) as outside agitators with no genuine right to speak for southerners. Before *Brown*, the U.S. federal government, through the Supreme Court, had sided explicitly with the segregationists. But the shift in *Brown* did not immediately decide the issue the other way; what it did was to force the further question of which, if any, side would be able to defend its position as less arbitrary than the other.

---

[18] "North Denounced by Gov. Wallace: Alabama Inaugural Pledges Fight on Integration," *New York Times*, January 15, 1963.

There could be no more powerful refutation of the claim that overturning segregation was a plot foisted on the South by outside interlopers, however, than the civil rights movement itself. Once African Americans in the South began organizing massive popular protests for their own rights, the conflict could no longer plausibly be portrayed as simply one of southern self-determination versus northern *imperium*. The movement's actions shattered the pretense of segregated state and local governments to speak univocally for the South. Of course, that claim had always rung hollow because it was supported through the active and violent disenfranchisement of local African American voters. But it mattered that there was now an actual democratic challenger to deal with, accountable to actual southerners unrepresented by official institutions. Enforcing desegregation could now be justified as actually self-legislated by some southerners with as good a claim to speak for the whole of the democratic South as anyone else, rather than as imposing some outsider's interpretation of what southerners *would hypothetically* legislate for themselves under the right conditions, in the absence of any actual consultation with representative organizations of those citizens and in the face of powerful observable evidence of popular mobilization to the contrary. It reframed the choice, in other words, from one of principle versus reality into one of choosing between the representative claims of two real and democratic organizations of the same people. Only in this latter case could one not only criticize the contradictions of the Jim Crow system but also show in a decisive way why a particular action to change it was democratically justified.

Now the federal government could play the role of arbitrator in a conflict between two competing southern factions, reestablishing a local rule of law in the South's own interest, rather than imposing its own views of southern social institutions from outside. As President Johnson put it in a televised interview during the debate on the 1964 Civil Rights Act, passing the bill would go "a long way to taking the battle from the streets into the legislative halls and into the courthouses," thus working to reunite a divided country under law.[19] With this historical shift, the only consistent objection favoring segregationists was canceled out, whereas civil rights advocates still had on their side arguments from freedom and minority rights, which segregationists themselves had used for their own ends to contest the authority of federal majorities. Nor, of course, could it possibly any longer be pretended that African Americans were incapable of self-government. Although this argument had been more explicit in the struggle over slavery a century before, the fact that African Americans in the South fighting for their rights also helped prove to others they deserved those rights remained, I think, an important performative aspect of the civil rights

---

[19] Anthony Lewis, "Johnson Details Domestic Plans in TV Interview," *New York Times*, March 16, 1964.

struggle. Consider, for instance, famous images of African American sanitation workers marching in Memphis in 1968 holding out placards reading in simple block letters "I am a man." Against this background there was no longer any consistent democratic case for the proposition that southern state governments had a right to resist federal enforcement of desegregation under *Brown* and the new Civil Rights Acts of 1964 and 1968.

So the civil rights movement is an "easy case" because as events unfolded, only one side was able to sustain a consistently democratic argument for excluding the other's position. In that case, desegregation deserved to win outright; there was no principled reason for requiring a compromise with segregationist holdouts. But in other cases, no one side manages to refute the claims of all the others. In these cases, it may be that only a compromise is legitimate, or else compromise may be impossible and then there is nothing left but either resignation or continued struggle. This is the sort of case one saw repeatedly in French revolutions from 1789 until the 1870s. The point can be illustrated by comparing the founding of the Second and Third Republics.

On April 23, 1848, the fledgling French Second Republic held its first elections, widely recognized as enshrining the principle of universal manhood suffrage.[20] The day before, Alexandre-Auguste Ledru-Rollin, minister of the interior and a leading figure in the provisional government that had ruled the country since a popular uprising in February, issued a public circular. He assured the newly enfranchised masses that, with the proclamation of universal (male) suffrage:

> The science of politics has now been found. It has been revealed not only to one; it was revealed to all the day the Republic proclaimed the principle of the sovereignty of all. The application of this science of politics will henceforth ... involve merely convoking the people in great masses, the whole and complete sovereign, and invoking its universal consent, by acclamation, on those questions where popular consciousness speaks so eloquently and in unison.[21]

The following day, however, the French people overwhelmingly elected the conservative, recent converts to republicanism called *républicains du lendemain*, or "republicans of the day after" the revolution, as opposed to the *républicains de la veille*, or "republicans of the evening before," like Ledru-Rollin. Key early

---

[20] Votes in 1792 and 1793 had also been conducted on universal manhood suffrage, as had Napoleon's plebiscites, but the epochal quality of the 1848 elections was universally acknowledged by contemporaries. See Raymond Huard, *Le suffrage universel en France: 1848–1946* (Paris: Aubier, 1991).

[21] *Bulletins de la République*, April 22, 1848.

proclamations of the provisional government had proclaimed the *droit au travail*, or the "right to labor," and established National Workshops to provide (some) work for the masses of Parisian unemployed, and the Commission du Luxembourg, where the socialist Louis Blanc presided over a chamber of workers' representatives in the palace that had until February housed the Chamber of Peers.[22] From March to May, a series of demonstrations and counterdemonstrations pushed tensions between radical and conservative republicans to the brink, culminating in a failed coup attempt on May 15 by inveterate *putschistes* Barbès and Blanqui.[23] In response, the Assembly abolished the National Workshops and tens of thousands of workers took to the barricades two days later.

The government replied by handing dictatorial powers to republican stalwart General Eugène de Cavaignac, who crushed the rebellion with great loss of life.[24] These "June Days" proved a trauma from which the Second Republic would never fully recover—they fatefully divided the ranks of the Republic's genuine supporters, and strengthened the hand of conservatives more concerned with maintaining order than with republican ideals. Adolphe Thiers, who had led the center-left parliamentary opposition under the July Monarchy, became a driving force behind the Réunion de la Rue de Poitiers, a committee that pulled together a broad coalition of the party of order behind the presidential candidacy of Louis-Napoleon Bonaparte, who was elected the first president of the Republic by a crushing margin in the freely contested election of December 1848.[25] The left regrouped from this humiliating defeat by the elections of 1849, when they organized as *démocrates-socialistes* and made significant inroads in the Assembly.[26] But as the center collapsed in an environment of mutual suspicion, the prospects of a durable agreement that all parties could live with rapidly

---

[22] See Louis Blanc, *La Révolution de février au Luxembourg* (Paris: Michel Lévy Frères, 1849); Rémi Gossez, *Les Ouvriers de Paris: Bibliothèque de la Révolution de 1848, v.23* (La Roche-Sur-Yon, 1967), 225–66; William Sewell, *Work and Revolution in France: The Language of Labor from the Old Regime to 1848* (Cambridge, UK: Cambridge University Press, 1980), 251–5.

[23] See Peter Amann, "A 'Journée' in the Making: May 14, 1848," *The Journal of Modern History* 42, no. 1 (1970): 42–69.

[24] See the *Rapport de la commission d'enquête, sur l'insurrection qui a éclaté dans la journée de 23 juin et sur les événements du 15 mai*, 3 vols. (Paris: Imprimerie Nationale, 1848); Charles Tilly and Lynn Lees Tilly, "Le peuple de juin 1848," *Annales: Économies, Sociétés, Civilisations* 29, no. 5 (1974): 1061–91; Peter H. Amann, *Revolution and Mass Democracy: The Paris Club Movement in 1848* (Princeton, NJ: Princeton University Press, 1975).

[25] Ledru-Rollin, at that time still a leading political figure, had come in third, with roughly 370,000 votes to Bonaparte's 5,400,000, from a total of 7,300,000. See Michel Winock, "La poussée démocratique: 1840–1870," in *L'invention de la démocratie*, eds. Serge Bernstein and Michel Winock (Paris: Éditions du Seuil, 2003), 135.

[26] See Raymond Huard, "Un parti en mutation: Le parti républicain (1848–1851)," in *Des Républiques françaises*, eds. Paul Isoart and Christiane Bidegaray (Paris: Economica, 1988), 94–121.

dimmed. As Tocqueville put it in a letter of September 24, 1848, to Gustave de Beaumont:

> The decent and moderate republican party has nearly disappeared from the assembly. We are placed between a small minority that wants a social or red republic and an immense majority that doesn't want to hear talk of a republic of any kind whatsoever.[27]

When Tocqueville, at Foreign Affairs, sent French troops to Rome to help put down Mazzini's Republic, Ledru-Rollin demanded the government be impeached and threatened to defend the constitution "by all means possible, even by arms!"[28] But two days later he fled to exile in London, where he would remain for twenty years. The exhaustion of the *quarante-huitard* dream that the establishment of the right sort of republican constitution would end conflict over the constitution itself was patent. But neither Ledru-Rollin nor anyone else—right, left, or center—managed to come up with an alternative that did any better. In the end, Bonaparte would provide one based on force, finally delivering the Republic a coup de grâce with his coup d'état in December 1851. The French people overwhelmingly ratified Napoleon III's Second Empire in a plebiscite the following year—conducted on universal suffrage.

When Bonaparte's own regime collapsed in 1870 after Sedan, the founders of the Third Republic faced many of the same problems as had the founders of the Second. But this time the outcome would be different. Once again, a provisional government, this time called the Government of National Defense, was set up and controlled by men of the left, ranging from the moderate republican Jules Favre to the radical Léon Gambetta. Once again, the first elections under universal suffrage returned an overwhelming conservative majority: 1871 saw some 400 monarchists elected to only 150 republicans. Again, the new government was confronted almost immediately by a radical uprising of Parisian workers, this time the storied Commune of 1871. And again, the government put down the insurrection with overwhelming force—some 20,000 were killed, another 10,000 imprisoned or shipped to New Caledonia.[29]

But then the stories diverged: unlike in 1848, in 1870 the government did not hurry to entrench a republican constitution. Indeed, it was content to

---

[27] *Œuvres Complètes*, eds. Jean-Paul Mayer and André Jardin (Paris: Gallimard, 1951), 8:53.

[28] Ledru-Rollin, *Discours politiques et écrits divers*, 2 vols. (Paris: Librairie Germer Baillière, 1879), 2:349.

[29] According to Furet's best estimates; see *Revolutionary France, 1770–1880* (Malden, MA: Blackwell, 1992), 504. On the Commune, see Robert Tombs, *The War Against Paris, 1871* (Cambridge, UK: Cambridge University Press, 1981), and *The Paris Commune, 1871* (Harlow, UK: Pearson, 1999); and Jacques Rougerie, *Paris Libre 1871* (Paris: Seuill, 2004).

operate without any settled constitution for five long years, and in 1875 what it finally passed was not a detailed charter and proclamation of natural rights, but three brief statutes defining, in the most minimal terms, the working of its central institutions. Much was left deliberately unresolved. But it was this makeshift "constitution," the least characteristically "French" of any since 1789, that finally managed to establish a working republic in France, and which remains to this day that which has governed that country longer than any other.

The 1870s were different from the late 1840s because even though familiar conflicts on the right and left soon reemerged, this time enough of the key players ultimately chose to hold in suspense their own views about ultimate ends and to search for a settlement that might be justifiable to others who did not share them. Thiers was elected the first president of the Republic by the monarchist Assembly; he was the man of the Rue de Poitiers, and he met expectations early by crushing the Paris Commune. But then he shocked the nation on November 13, 1872, by declaring publicly for the Republic on the grounds that:

> Events have given us the Republic, and to return to its causes to debate and to judge them today would be an enterprise as dangerous as it would be useless. ... The Republic exists; it is the legal government of the country: to want something else would be a new revolution and the most terrible of all.[30]

At the same time, he insisted that the Republic must also be "conservative, or it will not be at all," by which he meant that it must be a republic of compromise, one made acceptable also to those disinclined to support it for its own sake (28). "For the Republic is nothing but an absurdity [*un contresens*]," he explained, "if, instead of being the government of all, it is the government of one party, whichever it may be" (29). In 1870s France, Thiers's *République conservatrice* was just the sort of regime that could be seen as "both—and neither" by the major parties on the ground.

On the republican side, Gambetta, the radical and the man of National Defense, reciprocated with a concession of his own: if monarchists would accept the Republic, republicans would accept a republic with a Senate designed to overrepresent rural areas as a guarantee of conservative interests. And it was this compromise that finally made possible the passing of the 1875 laws on institutions that laid the foundations of the regime. Gambetta later defended his policy, known as "opportunism," in a speech to his Belleville constituents:

---

[30] *Discours parlementaires de M. Thiers, publiés par M. Calmon*, Vol. 15 (Paris: Calmann Lévy, 1883), 27.

I only know two ways of doing politics: one must negotiate or one must fight. And me, I am for negotiations.... We've had enough of the painful crises through which France developed her attempts at reform for one hundred years.... And what's the result [of this violence]? Much wasted time, much spilled blood, and setting back the idea that one wants to serve.[31]

Thiers paid for his disloyalty when he was forced by the duc de Broglie to resign in 1873, and replaced with the more reliable General MacMahon. But the monarchists were as ever divided among themselves, and the uncompromising nature of the comte de Chambord, the Bourbon heir, made a restoration in the short term impossible. So the monarchists played for time, refusing to constitutionalize the status of the de facto republic. Gambetta nevertheless managed to wrangle 353 votes from center-right, center-left, and the left—against 352 from the monarchists—for the crucial vote on the Wallon amendment that institutionalized the office of the Président de la République on January 30, 1875, in exchange for establishing the Senate. The monarchists were confident they would win the upcoming elections to fill the two new houses, and thus reestablish a monarchy sooner or later, perhaps after the passing of the comte de Chambord. But the elections of 1876 returned only the narrowest conservative majority in the Senate—151 to 149—and an overwhelming republican majority of 340 to 155 in the Assembly. Now it was the monarchists' turn to find that they had backed themselves into a corner by placing their faith in universal suffrage to resolve always according to their own lights.[32]

And so the Third Republic put down roots in France not because the French had been converted en masse to republican principles, but strictly *faute de mieux*. Some, like Thiers and Gambetta, accepted this result explicitly as a compromise that promised to end the nearly century-long cycle of revolution and reaction stretching back to 1789. Others, like the legitimists, accepted it at first only tactically but later found it impossible to extricate themselves, since they were unable to offer any alternative even comparably viable. And yet in the end, it was this least republican of French republics, every party's second choice, that was the one that took.

---

[31] October 27, 1876, in *Plaidoyers Politiques de M. Gambetta*, Vol. 6, ed. Joseph Reinach (Paris: G. Charpentier, 1882), 160–1.

[32] On the transition to the republic, see Odile Rudelle, *La République Absolue, 1870–1889* (Paris: Publications de la Sorbonne, 1986); Léo Haman, ed., *Les Opportunistes: Les Débuts de la République aux Républicains* (Paris: Fondation de la Maison des Sciences de l'Homme, 1991); and Philip Nord, *The Republican Moment: Struggles for Democracy in Nineteenth-Century France* (Cambridge, MA: Harvard University Press, 1998).

Now the claim is not that this solved everything or that there were no democratic costs to an institution like the Senate, which would turn out to block every attempt to extend the suffrage to women until German Panzers overturned the republic and General de Gaulle's provisional government took the initiative in 1944. But it is still the case that the Third Republic was a great democratic advance over the cycle of revolution and authoritarianism that had continued since 1789. The fact that this was a settlement monarchists had become willing to accept was more important on democratic grounds than the fact that it looked less like an Athenian assembly. And that it took putting down the Commune is a hard fact, but one for which responsibility must be assumed, because democracy is not, as the *quarant-huitards* had supposed, a magic spell that dissolves all differences and allows one to escape ever having to defend the use of coercion. When citizens use force against each other, choices must be made, and the maximalism of the *Communards* was incompatible with the sort of compromise other factions had become willing to accept and which was required if any generally defensible solution was to be possible. This does not mean the *Communards'* social and direct-democratic ends were necessarily wrong in principle, but that to be admissible, they would need to be fought out another day in a different register, within a republican framework that had become acceptable to the country as a whole.

In France in the 1870s, we see the use of two devices—institutional compromise and deferring certain controversial issues to the outcomes of future contested elections—that helped to make possible a solution palatable to the major contending parties. In other cases, constitutionalizing toleration has played a similar role, for instance, in England in 1689. But it must be stressed that compromise is only warranted where neither party's claim to represent the larger people can be ruled out as inconsistent, and even then compromise is not always possible. In some cases divisions may be so fundamental that compromise is unworkable or even inconceivable, and then we may have to accept a tragic outcome in which we are forced simply to choose sides, even though we recognize that our choice is no more defensible than that of those we oppose. But this is still a positive finding, and I think an important one. We cannot expect democratic theory to solve for us every problem of democratic practice, and the fact that we need a legitimate solution cannot guarantee that one can always be found. And so even in these cases there is value in an awareness of the democratic failings of our choices, although we are still forced to make them. It is one thing to act aware of the ultimate illegitimacy of one's actions, because one sees that no more legitimate course is available, another to suppose self-righteously that the justice of one's acts is unimpeachable. At the same time, the conclusion that no legitimate solution is possible can never be final, since it always depends, in part, on our imagination in inventing new and better arguments and, in part, on the political choices of historical actors, which may change. And so sometimes one will be able to work out both why no presently available solution is democratically legitimate and also what might have to change before such a solution could become possible in the future.

We have seen, then, three types of cases: easy cases in which one side deserves to win outright, hard cases in which only a compromise is defensible, and tragic cases in which no legitimate solution is presently available. The condition of exclusivity allows us to distinguish in context among these different types, rather than presuming that every case must have the same sort of solution (or even a solution at all). The reason this fourth condition is so important is that it always provides a determinate answer that either one single constitutional program or discrete range of programs is legitimate, or else that no program is.[33] Because it requires a legitimate program to exclude every competing possibility, it solves the problem of how to choose among multiple programs coherently defensible on their own terms, and responds to our practical need to enforce one program to the exclusion of others. And it continues to do so, like the other three conditions, strictly by elimination. It draws out tacit requirements of any consistent claim to democratic legitimacy, without appealing to any external foundation whatsoever that might compete with the people's right to decide how they will govern themselves.

Conclusion

Taken together, Principle (II)*'s four conditions define the conditions of possibility of any consistent claim to democratic legitimacy. This makes possible a very different way of discriminating among competing democratic systems than by measuring them against any timeless ideal of "the" good democratic constitution. Instead, a historical and Socratic theory forces us to engage with actual history, and with evidence of what real political actors actually do on the ground to try to bolster their democratic claims and undercut those of their rivals. It also continues, however, to require attention to conditions that afford critical leverage on the claims of competing democratic factions, so it does not make the mistake of confusing what merely is (or is to come) with what ought to be. It does not suppose that the application of the four conditions is uncontroversial, but that ongoing debate over how they may be applied is the sort of debate that can help advance arguments over democratic legitimacy in the face of continued political struggle over what it means to put "democracy" into practice. The next chapter discusses some exemplary cases that show how this can work.

---

[33] A range is possible when several options are acceptable to all relevant parties, in which case any one may be chosen; exclusivity applies only to those programs that compete because they depend on conflicting justifications, among which one must at least tacitly choose.

7

Cases

The last chapter explained the ideas behind the four conditions of Principle (II)*. This chapter considers several cases that show how this framework can be put to use. One need not agree with the conclusions in these particular cases to accept the general claims of a historical and Socratic theory. But even if one disagrees, the theory argues that one ought to make one's contrary case in this sort of way rather than another. Shifting the language in which struggles over change are debated is one of the theory's major aims.

What is most characteristic of democratic elenchus is that it looks to defend judgments of particular struggles entirely by drawing out contradictions internal to the positions defended by actual political actors. It does not appeal to any external, putatively universal yardstick of democratic progress. Nor does it take for granted that any particular way of organizing a collective decision always best represents the voice of the democratic people—in particular, it does not presume that either majorities or whichever institutions happen to be in place always speak reliably for the people as a whole. Instead, it focuses on drawing out latent contradictions entailed when particular interpretations of democracy are defended in particular contexts. That is what the conditions of Principle (II)* are for.

This chapter considers a range of cases that illustrate some of the different ways the theory allows one to resolve conflicts over democratic rights, representation, and change. The case of same-sex marriage in the United States shows how majority decisions may sometimes be undemocratic, and how in a constitutional system like the American, court action may sometimes be justified when supported in the right way by extra-parliamentary organizing. A brief comparison to contemporaneous reforms in France and the United Kingdom shows how the arguments work also in systems without American-style judicial review. The historical case of the New Deal, on the other hand, shows how elected powers may also be justified in resisting courts, and a brief discussion of the more recent struggle over the Affordable Care Act of 2010, against that background, illustrates how principles may become inscribed in the historical baseline in ways that bear on later struggles. Finally, recent debates over gun control in the United States show a case in which conservatives have so far made a stronger democratic case than liberal reformers. If this range of cases focuses largely on the United States, this is partly because that is the political culture with which I am most familiar, but it should be clear from discussions here and in other chapters that the general arguments apply equally well in other countries against the background of their own distinctive political traditions.

Democracy and Minority Rule

On June 26, 2013, the U.S. Supreme Court handed down two historic rulings. In *U.S. v. Windsor*, the Court overturned section 3 of the 1996 federal Defense of Marriage Act (DOMA), which had defined "marriage" for the purposes of federal law as "a legal union between one man and one woman as husband and wife."[1] In *Hollingsworth v. Perry*, the Court denied plaintiffs' standing to sue on behalf of the state of California, thereby allowing to stand a District Court ruling invalidating California's Proposition 8, which had inserted in the state's constitution a new section reading, "Only marriage between a man and a woman is valid or recognized in California."[2] Together, these decisions established as a matter of federal law that Fifth Amendment protections of "the equal liberty of persons" include a right of same-sex couples to marry, which cannot be overridden by legislative majorities, while declining to rule directly on the further question of whether or not the U.S. Constitution also requires enforcing the same principle against the states.[3] At the time, twelve states plus the District of Columbia had legalized same-sex marriage, thirty states banned it by constitutional amendments passed by referendums, and seven more expressly prohibited it by law.[4] Within one year of the decisions, by July 2014, six additional states legalized same-sex marriage, and federal courts overturned marriage bans in eleven more where decisions were stayed pending appeal.[5] The situation has continued to evolve as this book has been in press. What I have tried to do in what follows is to approach the issue strictly from within the time-horizon of July 2014—to

---

[1] 1 U.S.C. §7.

[2] Cal. Const. art I §7.5.

[3] *United States v. Windsor*, 133 S. Ct. 2675 (2013).

[4] In New Mexico, a case was pending over the interpretation of existing law that did not explicitly address the issue. The state supreme court ruled in 2014 that the state constitution's equal protection clause protected same-sex marriage.

[5] The six states to legalize were NJ, HI, IL, NM, OR, and PA (the last two by declining to appeal a federal court decision). The eleven states with stayed federal court decisions were UT, OH, OK, VA, TX, TN, MI, IN, ID, WI, and KY. Of those, UT and OK had been upheld by the 10th Circuit Court and VA by the 4th. In several other states, state courts had ruled for same-sex marriage but decisions were appealed to state supreme courts.

call attention to, rather than to paper over, the fact that every conclusion here is time-limited and must be continually revisited in light of still-unfolding events. You, the reader, will necessarily have information I did not have in writing. But if the theory has done its job, it will have made a case as to whether the Supreme Court rulings in *Windsor* and *Hollingsworth* were democratic when they were handed down, on the basis of what was (or should have been) known to actors at the time. And no less important, it will point to possible events that had not yet occurred, but which would, if they should occur later, either strengthen or undermine confidence in that case. The point is to avoid a vicious circle in which one reads historical decisions in light of present values, in order then to justify the present as the natural outcome of the past. Rather, the fact that these *scripta* I have written *manent*, while their meaning may not, makes them an analogue of the political decisions they describe, and requires from the reader an act of contextual appraisal similar to the one that they perform. But this does not make the cases considered here of only local or historical interest; because they are instances of the perennial democratic problem of how to sort out conflicts between majority rule and minority rights, the general lines of argument will speak to a large range of other cases, *mutatis mutandis*.

Now it is often supposed that judicial interventions like *Windsor* are not democratic, and so if they are to be justified, this could only be on the basis of arguments from morality or justice held to trump the sovereignty of the people. Influential arguments to the contrary include John Hart Ely's, according to which courts should play a role in "policing the process of representation" to make sure that process is open and competitive and that minorities are fairly represented within it.[6] And we have seen that Corey Brettschneider has argued that democracy requires protecting the equal rights of citizens both in the political process and in its results.[7] But these sorts of claims are rightly controversial, because the underlying question remains why the Court and not the elected branches has the right to decide which rights of this sort need to be protected. Consider, for instance, how Brettscheinder defends a more robust conception of relevant rights than Ely—so who is to choose? Democratic elenchus tackles this question directly. On my view, one cannot presume the sovereign legitimacy of either side in a contest over "democratic rights"—or what I call the interpretation of the equal freedoms required by Principle (I). Rather, it depends on the particular struggle whether or not there is a good case to make against the legitimacy of decisions by elected officials or referendum. In the absence of a specific objection, those decisions deserve a presumption in their favor, since they at

---

[6] John Hart Ely, *Democracy and Distrust: A Theory of Judicial Review* (Cambridge, MA: Harvard University Press, 1980), Chapters 4–6.

[7] Corey Brettschneider, *Democratic Rights: The Substance of Self-Government* (Princeton, NJ: Princeton University Press, 2007).

least enjoy a prima facie claim to represent the entire citizenry wherever elections are free and conducted on universal suffrage.

There are two major reasons a political decision supported by elections may fail to count as democratic. (I am concerned here only with cases in which there is nothing in principle amiss with the way a referendum, say, was conducted, and yet there remains a question as to whether its outcome is defensible on democratic grounds.) A decision may violate rights or principles established by other standing decisions of the citizens, without providing reason to suppose the citizens have chosen to abandon those rights. Or that decision may violate the equal freedoms of either a minority—if the process is majoritarian—or a majority, if an antimajoritarian process allows a minority to decide. On the issue of same-sex marriage in the United States, although both issues come into play, the latter is most centrally at issue: Is or is not denying same-sex couples a right to marry a violation of the equal rights of citizens belonging to an electoral minority? One will also need to consider whether the opposite outcome would violate the equal freedoms of some other group—for instance, certain religious believers.

On my theory, a majority decision like a referendum should count as an undemocratic violation of minority rights only if four conditions are met. First, a coherent argument has been made that that decision violates the equal freedoms of citizens in the minority. Second, that argument is not countered by an equally good argument that the alternative would violate the equal freedoms of any other group. Third, a convincing supermajority of the relevant minority supports the claim that its equal freedoms have been violated. And fourth, no convincing supermajority of the entire population rejects the minority's claim.

On an issue like same-sex marriage, in which it is clear that the equal rights of a minority are at least potentially at stake, one cannot simply presume a majoritarian process competent to rule in the name of all the citizens. One must consider whether the majority's claim or the minority's is more consistently defensible as an interpretation of all citizens' equal freedoms. Now in most elections (say, an election for president), the losing side is just an electoral minority whose equal freedoms are not violated simply because they lost. (The contrary position cannot consistently be maintained since the alternative outcome would violate an equal claim on the other side.) To raise a serious challenge, one first needs a consistent argument from principle that a majority decision violates the equal freedoms of a specific minority of citizens, which may or may not coincide with the minority who voted on the losing side. If a majority votes to enslave some ethnic or religious minority, this condition would be met. Crucially, one need not prove that the minority's equal freedoms *actually are violated*, in some dispositive way—since who is to determine this is precisely the question at issue. One need only judge that a consistent argument to this effect has been made. Then one must consider whether or not an equally consistent principled argument exists on the other side. Would banning slavery violate the equal freedoms of slaveholders? Certainly, this was claimed. But because no such right is natural or self-evident (there cannot be any natural property right or natural right of states against federal intervention), any such claim can be defended only as an interpretation of the principle of equal freedoms for all. And since a right to enslave another cannot consistently be grounded on that principle, it cannot be a democratic right. So here there is no principled argument on the other side to counter the admissible objection of the minority.

Now things become difficult, because we need a way of choosing between a majoritarian interpretation of the popular will and one that constrains majority decisions to respect certain rights of minority citizens. The majority's right to rule depends on its claim best to represent the citizenry as a whole. But the minority, in effect, charges the majority with representing not the whole but only a despotic faction. So the real question that must be resolved is whether the citizenry should be understood as united, so that disagreements are only innocent differences of opinion concerning a general will they in fact share, or whether that people is instead already divided, so that the same disagreements appear as the efforts of one faction to impose its will on another.[8] Now the challenge is to answer in a way that counts as interpreting evidence of citizens' own judgments, rather than simply imposing *our* a priori judgment of the substantive merits of the minority's claim. In this case, that means we ought not to answer by deciding for ourselves whether or not a "right to marriage" really "is" a "fundamental right" of all persons that deserves to be protected against the will of the majority—or by handing that decision over to a court.[9] But how can we allow the citizens to decide?

First of all, if the minority view is correct, then we would expect most of that minority itself to agree. If half or nearly half of the minority instead vote with the overall majority, then it will be very hard to see why we should believe the claim of the rest to speak for the minority as a whole. Indeed, we must require not merely a bare majority within the minority but a *convincing supermajority*—since the claim at issue is that a bare majority of the whole is not sufficient to decide, defenders of that claim must at least meet a comparable standard relative to their own self-described constituency. Of course, it is possible to argue that even a small enlightened minority within the minority represents its "true" view, but there can be no way of corroborating such a claim without relying directly on our judgment of that view's substantive truth, and this is what democratic principles disallow.

---

[8] This is really an argument with and against Rousseau; cf. *CS* IV.II, 3:441.

[9] Contrast Martha Craven Nussbaum, *From Disgust to Humanity: Sexual Orientation and Constitutional Law* (New York: Oxford University Press, 2010), 233–4.

The situation is different, of course, if a minority within the minority raises its own claim that its equal freedoms would be threatened by a *departure* from majority rule. Consider, for instance, the claim of southern U.S. states against laws passed by majorities based in the North. Now on some issues—say, tariff policy—this may have been an admissible complaint. But on the issues of slavery or segregation, it was not because on that issue the result was open to a direct challenge on the part of local minorities within the geographic minority. Rights of geographic, ethnic, or religious minorities may sometimes conflict, for instance, with rights claims from women, LGBT persons, or other ethnic or religious minorities within their ranks. Where the claims of the minority-within-a-minority meet all the other conditions, this second-order question must be answered first. Obviously, the problem is iterative—in principle, there can always be another minority within any minority, but not every imaginable claim will meet all the other conditions, and one needs to go back only as far as admissible challenges have actually been raised in a given case.

These examples raise two further points. First, in a case like slavery, it may be nearly impossible for the minority publicly to demonstrate support for its claims because of repression; but we have seen that the only reasonable response is to include evidence of repression among the evidence supporting a presumption about the views certain persons would express if left free to do so. Second, in some cases a group such as women may comprise a relevant group whose equal freedoms are threatened by a majoritarian or putatively majoritarian process, even if they are not a numerical minority in the population. This may be so if positive evidence can be provided that barriers exist to women (or others) freely expressing themselves through normal political channels. This raises difficult issues one must approach with care, but the key will be to distinguish between a judgment that the substance of a particular decision "could not" be supported by most women because it violates their "true" interests—which is not allowed, short of a limiting case like slavery—and a judgment that women lack or are prevented from forming sufficient vehicles for the public expression of their own views. The latter objection is admissible, and although it suggests that when possible actions by a larger majority ought to focus on mitigating barriers to women's self-organizing rather than jumping directly to acting on its own unilateral interpretation of women's best interests, there may be cases where separating the two is virtually impossible and hard calls simply have to be made. Here, too, slavery is a limit case.

Now consider the other side of the question—how the majority in the larger polity might defend its brief for majoritarianism even against a minority objection from equal freedoms that has cleared all these hurdles. The issue, recall, is whether or not the majority has a right to decide for the whole because the people count as united rather than already divided into factions. Now in a referendum, for instance, one may consider voters to express their views on two questions at once—first, what is my interpretation of the general will, and second, are the people united such that one may take the majority view of that general will fairly to represent it? The first concerns the substance of the issue and the second the procedure to decide it. In fact, this is not implausible even in a literal sense, because if one thinks through an actual case, one sees that on a question of potential violation of minority rights, one's views on both issues are likely to be determined by the same considerations, and at any rate when people go to vote, they know that a decision on the second question will decide the outcome.[10] But the issue is not really about the empirical mental processes of individuals, which cannot be determined objectively apart from the observable evidence of how people actually vote. (Here, I assume a scenario capped by a free vote, in which that vote is recognized as authoritative in a way an exit poll, for instance, is not.) So the question is: What outcome in the vote is sufficient to justify the claim that a majority decision may indeed be taken in this case for a decision of the whole?

Obviously, majoritarianism must at least win a majority, but that is not very interesting because if it does not, then the claim against minority rights loses on both substance and procedure. Can it be enough then to require a bare majority in favor of majoritarianism? The answer must be no, because that position could only beg the question. If we insist that a minority must win over a majority to the view that its rights have been violated by majority decisions *before* that minority's rights could ever deserve protection, this amounts to denying that majorities can ever wrong minorities. And if we presume a majority competent to decide the justice of majoritarianism, then we have, in fact, already opted for majoritarianism a priori before any actual citizens have had a chance to weigh in on the matter. That is, we have substituted an a priori judgment of our own for any judgment that might possibly be defended as an interpretation of what citizens themselves have decided. Not only is this objectionable on general democratic grounds, but it also directly contravenes the only plausible rationale for majoritarianism. For surely the intuitive appeal of majoritarianism as a decision mechanism is that it allows the views of actual citizens to decide by taking into account how many among them line up on one side or the other. But if one lets a majority decide on majoritarianism, the decision has been made before voting begins, and it depends in no way at all on how actual citizens vote (except in the uninteresting case in which the majority already supports the minority). On the other hand, if we require a convincing supermajority to ratify the majority's claim to represent the entire people, then the number of people who vote one

---

[10] Compare the way a procedural vote like a cloture vote on the floor of the U.S. Senate commonly determines substantive outcomes. Of course, one might similarly separate procedure from substance even in referendums, which is sometimes done.

way or the other *does* play the decisive role in determining the outcome. We actually have to count the votes.

Ironically, then, it is only by insisting on a *supermajority for majoritarianism* that one can preserve the merits of majoritarianism in a decision on majority rule itself. Of course, such a result is only evidence for an interpretation lacking the certainty of a logical proof, but if one were to challenge that result by claiming, for instance, that a supermajority was only an even larger faction, one would need to provide a way of testing such a claim in accordance with the same sort of logic just laid out. In the absence of such further arguments, if the majoritarian position fails to carry a supermajority, then we should acknowledge that the minority has done everything we can ask it to do to make its case without requiring it first to become the majority. The majority, however, has not managed to rebut the minority's argument, to persuade a significant number among the minority of its view, or even to shore up convincing supermajority support among its own putative constituency—the united larger people. These are all things the majority can try to do, and they are just those things we have required of the minority—to provide and answer arguments, to shore up supermajority support among its avowed constituency, and to work to convince others to reconsider their views in order to pare down the supermajority on the other side. The burdens of proof are symmetrically distributed, and this is therefore the fairest basis for decision there can be.

Obviously, there are no precise quantitative thresholds for what makes a supermajority "convincing." As a rough rule of thumb, one might think that less than three-fifths is unlikely to suffice, and either two-thirds or three-fourths probably to do so. But one might also require a higher supermajority where the minority with a rights claim is likely to be large, and a smaller one where it is likely to be small. It would be unreasonable in any case to insist on consensus or near consensus, because at issue is not whether every single individual agrees, but whether the citizenry is broadly divided into antagonistic factions. Four further points must be stressed. First, these conditions are nothing like a standing supermajority requirement—on my view, those requirements will favor the wrong side maybe half the time, since minorities are neither always well-intentioned nor always right. Everything depends on working out which side's position is most consistent on a case-by-case basis. Second, the first two conditions require attending to arguments of principle—this interaction between principle and organizing is characteristic of democratic elenchus, and means it rejects the possibility of any general institutional solution to a problem such as how to reconcile minority rights and majority will. Third, this does, of course, mean we must make some judgments of our own, but we are asked to judge only whether arguments advanced by citizens are consistent with their own claims to represent the people as a whole, not also if those arguments are true. The reason this is allowable is that it is part of interpreting citizens' own decisions in light of their actual expressed views, and I have argued that there is really no way of avoiding this—only ways of being more or less up-front and reflective about the judgments one is making. Finally, some may worry (like Kant) that judging this way on a case-by-case basis undermines the rule of law. But some judgments are required even for the rule of law to function (hence judges), and so there are ways of using these principles to guide judgments within existing law or existing political institutions. Judgments that would call into question elements in the existing constitution will require clearing a higher bar of justification.

Working through these four conditions allows one to understand the course of democratic struggles in the following way. By default, majority rule is justified unless a minority puts forward a consistent argument that this would violate its equal freedoms. (In practice, most electoral systems have already built in some claims of this sort on historical grounds, so one must start from the electoral system one actually has.) An argument of this sort poses a question, but to substantiate that argument, its defenders must go on to organize support for their position among the minority whose rights they claim to defend. If they cannot manage plausible evidence of convincing supermajority support among their own declared constituency, a democratic struggle cannot get off the ground. But if they do, then a democratic struggle begins in which other citizens have a chance to push back. On the one hand, members of the majority may produce a counterclaim that their rights would be violated if the minority got its way, and organize to show support for that claim among the majority. On the other, actors claiming to speak for minorities-within-the-minority may raise their own objections. This initiates a phase of organizing and counterorganizing in which each side takes actions to bolster its own claim and challenge those of its opponents. Only if the minority manages to undercut the counterclaims of every other group can it sustain its challenge to majority rule, since otherwise admissible claims on opposite sides cancel each other out. (On the other hand, negotiated settlements acceptable to all parties may always be admissible and sometimes required if competing claims among different groups do not neatly line up.)

If the minority's rights claim uniquely holds up, the struggle may move from the phase of *organizing and counterorganizing* to the phase of *decision*. Then the question is called by appealing to the polity as a whole, for instance, through a general election or referendum. If in such a contest a convincing supermajority fails to reject the minority's claim, then in this special case *it is the minority who turns out to have the best claim to represent the citizenry as a whole*. This is not rights trumping democracy, but one interpretation of the popular will, backed by a substantial number of citizens but less than half, beating out another. If, on the other hand, a convincing supermajority does reject the minority's claim, this does not immediately refute it in a final way. If the minority concedes, this ratifies the majority's decision (until and unless actors within the minority subsequently launch the struggle anew, from square one). If the minority instead reacts by reaffirming its rejection of the result, one of three things may ensue. If all sides agree to some negotiated settlement, that settlement will be legitimate. Or all may return to the previous stage of organizing and counterorganizing, in which the minority works to improve its position in anticipation of another round of decision at some point in the future. Finally, in exceptional cases the minority may *escalate* the struggle by refusing to obey the majority decision and provoking a constitutional crisis. In this case, another round of organizing and counterorganizing follows in which what is at stake is no longer only the particular decision but also the legitimacy of the institutional powers involved in making it. This additional element in the struggle may shift citizens' judgments—that is, some may well hold that institutions ought to judge a certain way, but that if they do not, they ought still to be obeyed because of the democratic value of maintaining the existing system as a whole. But this does not go without saying in every case, as it did for Kant. Sometimes even revolutions can be justified on democratic grounds, and even within broadly democratic systems, there may sometimes be space for reform outside established constitutional channels. These sorts of actions must clear very high bars of justification, but the four conditions explain both how this may sometimes be managed and why it usually is not. A later section will consider a case of constitutional crisis in the New Deal. But first let us consider how this framework helps one to makes sense of recent contests over same-sex marriage.

Same-Sex Marriage

It is important to recognize that what would come to be called "marriage equality" was not at the center of the organized gay and lesbian movements that emerged in the United States after the 1969 Stonewall riots.[11] Antidiscrimination and later also AIDS activism played a much greater role in the 1970s and 1980s. It was a series of legal battles involving a small number of persons that pressed the marriage issue until Hawaii's landmark 1993 decision in *Baehr v. Lewin* forced it suddenly onto the national political stage. The ensuing turmoil led to DOMA in 1996, passed with bipartisan support and signed into law by President Clinton.

---

[11] Nor was it a central concern of the earlier "homophile" movement. See Craig A. Rimmerman, *From Identity to Politics: The Lesbian and Gay Movements in the United States* (Philadelphia: Temple University Press, 2002); George Chauncey, *Why Marriage? The History Shaping Today's Debate Over Gay Equality* (New York: Basic Books, 2004); and Marc Stein, *Rethinking the Gay and Lesbian Movement* (New York: Routledge, 2012). I will use "gay and lesbian" and "LGBT" interchangeably in what follows, while recognizing that all these terms may themselves be the subject of controversy.

But this backlash also had the effect of politicizing the issue and putting pressure on participants in gay and lesbian movements to work out a position. The issue was highly controversial. Many rejected the idea of pursuing marriage as a movement goal, and major membership organizations were deeply divided.[12] But the 2003 Massachusetts Supreme Court decision in *Goodridge v. Massachusetts Department of Public Health* proved to be a turning point. Unlike in Hawaii, in Massachusetts the legislature (narrowly) failed to act to change the state constitution, and in 2004 Massachusetts became the first state in the nation to allow same-sex couples to marry. This had two important effects on the movement. First, it called the question of who really spoke for the larger constituency of gays and lesbians on the issue. When in 2004 San Francisco Mayor Gavin Newsome ordered the city to issue marriage licenses, over 4,000 couples flooded City Hall over a period of twenty-eight days before the state supreme court intervened; similar scenes played out in Oregon and in Massachusetts, where the marriages remained legal.[13] Massachusetts registered over 6,000 same-sex marriages in 2004 alone, and it is estimated that some 18,000 couples married between 2004 and 2012.[14] On the other hand, the Republican Party moved to capitalize on the electoral advantage offered by opposing same-sex marriage, placing constitutional amendments to ban it on the ballot in eleven states during the 2004 presidential election cycle. Voters approved all eleven by significant margins.[15] It was the direct threat of further legislative action by opponents of the LGBT movement and the public demonstrations of grassroots support for marriage among its own constituents that conspired to lead major segments of the movement to unite in active support of marriage equality. In 2005 some twenty-two leading LGBT organizations including the nation's two largest—the Human Rights Campaign and the National Gay and Lesbian Task Force, previously so often at

---

[12] See Ronald G. Shaiko, "Same-sex Marriage, GLBT Organizations, and the Lack of Spirited Political Engagement," in *The Politics of Same-Sex Marriage*, eds. Craig A. Rimmerman and Clyde Wilcox (Chicago: University of Chicago Press, 2007); and Stephen M. Engel, "Organizational Identity as a Constraint on Strategic Action: A Comparative Analysis of Gay and Lesbian Interest Groups," *Studies in American Political Development* 21, no. 1 (2007): 66–91. For influential criticisms of marriage from inside the movement, see inter alia Paula L. Ettelbrick, "Since When Is Marriage a Path to Liberation?," *OUT/LOOK* 6 (1989): 14–7; and Michael E. Warner, *The Trouble with Normal: Sex, Politics, and the Ethics of Queer Life* (Cambridge, MA: Harvard University Press, 2000).

[13] Dean E. Murphy, "San Francisco Sees Tide Shift In Battle Over Marriage," *New York Times*, March 13, 2004; Pam Belluck, "Same-Sex Marriage: The Overview; Hundreds of Same-Sex Couples Wed in Massachusetts," *New York Times*, May 18, 2004. On developments from *Goodridge* to Proposition 8, see Chauncey, *Why Marriage?*, and Daniel R. Pinello, *America's Struggle for Same-Sex Marriage* (Cambridge, UK: Cambridge University Press, 2006).

[14] "Health of Massachusetts," Massachusetts Department of Public Health, 2007, 19. http://www.masslive.com/politics/index.ssf/2012/05/massachusetts_marks_eighth_ann.html.

[15] The closest result was 57 percent in favor in Oregon. Two other states had passed amendment referendums earlier the same year, and three in previous years. President George W. Bush also called for a federal constitutional amendment in his successful reelection campaign.

loggerheads—issued a joint statement of purpose that included marriage equality as one of eight core priorities.[16] In the following years, state-based coalitions actively organized several high-profile campaigns, including most famously California's unsuccessful "No on 8."

Consider first the role of same-sex marriage supporters in this phase of the struggle. It is hard to deny that they managed early on to advance a consistent argument in terms of equal freedoms. This was the argument on which *Baehr v. Lewin* had been won already in 1993, although the result was subsequently reversed. But the consistency of an argument does not depend on the courts; what the record of legal decisions shows is that the argument was, in fact, publicly made. During this period, however, it was made by a small number of lawyers and not by a mass movement among gays and lesbians. Many movement organizations focused on other issues through the 1990s, and even the Human Rights Campaign, which did campaign vigorously against DOMA and later state-level referendums, did so in response to external events. It was only after 2004 that one finds convincing evidence of broad agreement in the movement on an actively pro-marriage-equality agenda. Real disagreements remained, but after 2005 it was hard to deny the existence of an organized mass movement for same-sex marriage including the major LGBT membership organizations, and supported by the individual acts of tens of thousands of couples who took advantage of opportunities to marry.[17] Continued disagreements over principle may well have great theoretical interest and perhaps even point toward future political possibilities, but after 2005 they no longer called into question the existence of convincing supermajority support among gays and lesbians for the claim that legally denying them an opportunity to marry violates their equal freedoms.

There was nothing inevitable about this development. Political divisions before 2004 were real, and they might have been resolved another way or not at all. The sort of judgment democratic elenchus asks us to make does not require supposing that marriage is, in fact, a good idea, or even that it really

---

[16] Evelyn Nieves, "Gay Rights Groups Map Common Agenda," *Washington Post*, January 17, 2005. A subplank referring to marriage equality had been included in the official platform of the 1993 March on Washington for Lesbian, Gay, and Bi Equal Rights and Liberation, but it was only one small point among dozens (reprinted in Rimmerman, *From Identity to Politics*).

[17] The Human Rights Campaign alone claims over 1 million members and supporters (*Annual Report 2011*, http://www.hrc.org/files/assets/resources/AnnualReport_2011.pdf). Although the National Gay and Lesbian Task Force does not advertise its membership figures, it has in the past reported several tens of thousands; on the history of these two organizations, see Engel, "Organizational Identity." One may acknowledge the significance of large organizations of this type, especially when they agree with each other, even while admitting that the HRC's numbers and supporters, for instance, include many people who have only made small donations or purchases and that its leadership is not directly accountable to its base through strong democratic institutions. See Steve Koval, "HRC 'Members' Include All Who Ever Donated $1," *Washington Blade*, May 6, 2005.

is a "fundamental right." What matters is only that the best evidence of gays' and lesbians' own organized political will—in this case supported by dramatic examples of spontaneous individual acts—supports the claim that they came to decide unequal legal barriers to marriage were an injustice incompatible with their democratic rights. This is what it means to say a historical and Socratic theory is democratic all the way down. It does not require one to posit any essential interests or identity of LGBT persons, or even to decide who is and is not objectively a part of that community. Democratic elenchus considers relevant minority groups as self-defined political constituencies rather than sociological entities (although people may, of course, choose to make certain social categories politically relevant by organizing around them). In this, it treats LGBT persons like any other group, including the democratic people as a whole. It is a strength of this radically antifoundationalist approach that it allows one to acknowledge deep historical contingencies and avoid unwarranted essentialisms, without thereby surrendering possibilities for political judgment and action. It is democratic politics itself, on this theory, that provides the content of justice.

One must next consider the relation of this movement to the larger democratic people. The first question to ask is whether a consistent claim had been advanced that the marriage equality position violates the equal freedoms of some other group of citizens. It has been argued, for instance, that normalizing marriage does an injustice to gays and lesbians who value other ways of life, but I do not believe these arguments suffice to show why removing a legal barrier denying all gays and lesbians a choice of whether or not to marry is more unjust than allowing that barrier to remain.[18] Nor is it clear that most critics of marriage really mean to rule out legalization, or how many other actual persons would support such a position. One must conclude therefore that there is presently no good evidence that marriage equality would violate the equal freedoms of a minority-within-the-minority. On the other hand, a range of arguments has been advanced to show why the rights of other persons, usually children or

---

[18] In addition to Ettelbrick and Warner, various grounds for disestablishing marriage have been offered by Nancy D. Polikoff, *Beyond (Straight and Gay) Marriage: Valuing All Families Under the Law* (Boston: Beacon Press, 2008); Martha Albertson Fineman, *The Autonomy Myth: A Theory of Dependency* (New York: New Press, 2004); Katherine Franke, "The Politics of Same-Sex Marriage Politics," *Columbia Journal of Gender and Law* 15 (2006): 236–48; Lisa Duggan and Richard Kim, "Beyond Gay Marriage," in *Sex Wars: Sexual Dissent and Political Culture*, 10th anniv. ed., eds. Lisa Duggan and Nan D. Hunter (New York: Routledge, 2006), 231–8; Lawrence G. Torcello, "Is the State Endorsement of Any Marriage Justifiable? Same-Sex Marriage, Civil Unions, and the Marriage Privatization Model," *Public Affairs Quarterly* 22, no. 1 (2008): 43–61; Cass Sunstein and Richard Thaler, "Privatizing Marriage," *Monist* 91, no. 3/4 (2008): 377–87; Tamara Metz, *Untying the Knot: Marriage, the State and the Case for Their Divorce* (Princeton, NJ: Princeton University Press, 2010). Elizabeth Brake goes half-way with disestablishmentarians but defends "minimal marriage" in her *Minimizing Marriage: Marriage, Morality, and the Law* (New York: Oxford University Press, 2012).

those committed to certain religious beliefs, would be threatened by same-sex marriage. These arguments have been extensively rebutted by others, and I will not rehash them here except to remind readers that any admissible argument must be compatible with democracy—and so cannot depend directly on religion or natural law—and must also be consistently principled, which means that one's equal freedoms cannot include a right to demand that laws reflect one's own moral and religious views when doing so would violate the reciprocal demands of others with different views.[19] This is not to say religion and morality must be kept entirely out of politics; a majority decision inspired by religion is perfectly legitimate if it respects all citizens' equal freedoms (unless it violates a specific commitment to secularism in the baseline), but the point is that its legitimacy depends entirely on the presumption for majority rule. In fact, campaigns like "Yes on 8" in California routinely juxtaposed arguments from majority rule and substantive appeals to tradition or religion.[20] Those appeals were perfectly admissible ways of mobilizing electoral support, but they did not also amount to good principled arguments from equal freedoms that might offset arguments on the other side.

But if same-sex-marriage supporters had met their burdens of argument already before 2008, they could not also claim to have shown that their arguments were endorsed by the larger citizenry. *Baehr v. Lewin* was reversed by a referendum that cleared the way for legislative action subsequently affirmed by Hawaii's state supreme court.[21] DOMA in 1996 and the unbroken string of referendum victories for state-level same-sex marriage bans until 2006 continued to provide clear evidence of supermajorities opposed.[22] Indeed, *Goodridge* in 2003 stepped out ahead of any public mass movement among supporters, and so its bold decision to call the principled question anyway ran a real risk of overstepping any democratic mandate—but in that case the grassroots reaction and the ultimate choice of elected branches to acquiesce ended up confirming the Court's interpretation and providing a popular mandate *post factum*. As a national

---

[19] Nussbaum provides a systematic rebuttal in *From Disgust to Humanity*. For the argument from reciprocal freedom of religion, see Mark Strasser, "Same-Sex Marriage and Civil Unions: On Meaning, Free Exercise, and Constitutional Guarantees," *Loyola University of Chicago Law Journal* 33 (2002): 597–630.

[20] The opening lines from the website www.yeson8.info are typical: "Proposition 22, which was passed in 2000 by an overwhelming margin of 61%, is better known as the California Defense of Marriage Act prohibiting same-sex marriage. Unfortunately, our state judges have overturned the will of the people and reinterpreted God's definition of what a marriage, a family, and a society should look like."

[21] The 1998 referendum passed 69 percent to 31 percent. Office of the Hawaii Secretary of State.

[22] Arizona narrowly rejected a 2006 referendum that also banned civil unions. However, a second referendum limited to marriage passed in 2008. No other referendum had lost before 2012, when a ban was rejected in Minnesota and voters for the first time passed referendums *requiring* same-sex marriage in Maryland, Maine, and Washington.

movement began to coalesce around marriage equality, all eyes turned to the hard-fought 2008 campaign over California's Proposition 8. At the time, no jurisdiction besides Massachusetts recognized same-sex marriage. In 2005 California had become the first state to pass a legalization bill through its legislature without instigation from the courts, but the bill was vetoed by Governor Arnold Schwarzenegger, and the scenario was repeated by the new legislature in 2007. The state supreme court then ruled in May 2008 that banning same-sex marriage violated a fundamental right to marry and the equal protection clause of the state's constitution.[23] So here was a real test-case to see whether California's citizenry as a whole might have shifted its interpretation of democratic rights since 2000, when Proposition 22 banning same-sex marriage passed by a margin of 61 percent to 39 percent.[24] This was a move to the phase of decision.

On November 4, 2008, Proposition 8 passed by a margin of 52 percent to 48 percent. On the view I have defended, this is not convincing evidence of a united people rejecting a minority's claim of rights violation. In this case, the minority rather than the majority had the stronger democratic mandate. And it raised the possibility that the country as a whole might turn out to decide the same way if the question should be put to it again. As I have emphasized, this is not to deny that the result was legally binding—given the existence of a constitutional system with a presumption of legitimacy, those who rejected the result as undemocratic had three choices. They might give up and accept the narrow majority. Or they might radically escalate to provoke a constitutional crisis through direct action and civil disobedience. But the third option was to continue to work within the system to gain legal recognition of a claim already democratically sound, and this is the route the movement took. In the United States, one of the obvious channels for pursuing this is through the courts, but, in fact, the movement pressed its case on multiple fronts. Within a year state supreme courts had followed Massachusetts in legalizing same-sex marriage in Connecticut and Iowa, and by 2011 three states and the District of Columbia had for the first time legalized it entirely through legislation. Maine had also done so in 2009, but a referendum reversed the result later the same year. In 2012, however, Maine changed course again to join Maryland and Washington as the first three states to legalize same-sex marriage by popular vote. Three more states legalized it through legislation in 2013, bringing the balance on the eve of *Windsor* and *Hollingsworth* to thirteen jurisdictions (including Washington, DC) with same-sex marriage to thirty-eight without. By June 2014, North Carolina had been the only state to pass an anti-same-sex-marriage referendum since 2008.[25]

---

[23] *In re Marriage Cases*, 183 P.3d 384 (Cal. 2008).

[24] Figures from the Office of the California Secretary of State.

[25] A concerted effort to reverse the Iowa state supreme court decision by recalling justices in statewide ballots failed in 2012 by the narrowest of margins, after earlier successes.

In retrospect, it is clear that Proposition 8 was a turning point, and its supporters' victory decidedly pyrrhic. After 2008—and only after 2008—there was a real question as to whether a convincing supermajority of the nation as a whole continued to reject the claim that on this issue a minority's equal freedoms deserved protection from majority rule. This had emphatically not been the case in 1996 when DOMA was passed by a bipartisan vote of 342 to 67 in the House, 85 to 14 in the Senate, and signed into law by President Clinton, who publicly supported it. Although opponents of same-sex marriage continued to frame the issue as one of democratic majorities versus elite judges imposing their own views, this was much less plausible after 2008 then it had been in the 1990s. Now two organized grassroots movements squared off in their claims to speak for the considered views of the citizenry as a whole. The minority claim was bolstered by appealing to principles of equal protection firmly established in the historical baseline and which continued to enjoy strong majority support. This meant, in effect, that even majorities clearly accepted the principle that majorities should not be able to rule alone on everything, if a minority's equal freedoms were at stake.[26] So although there remained a real question as to whether same-sex couples' freedom to marry should number among those freedoms, the choice posed was not between democracy and rule by judges but between two ways of interpreting the popular will. Because of their acknowledged place in the established legal system in the United States, judges would be forced to opt for one view or the other. And after 2008, but not before, judges could entertain the possibility that an organized marriage equality movement had established the democratic credentials of its position, and that subsequent developments had undercut the presumption that overturning a majority decision such as DOMA would contravene the best interpretation of a popular will attributable to the American people as a whole.

Although public opinion polls were shifting, polls alone are not sufficient evidence.[27] In 2013 the balance of jurisdictions, as we saw, stood at thirteen to thirty-eight, or 25 percent to 75 percent. Although I have suggested that California perhaps should not count in principle, and although a case in New Mexico was under way to resolve ambiguity in the law (subsequently decided in 2014 to protect same-sex marriage), these would still count as jurisdictions with standing state-level interpretations against marriage equality. But

---

[26] In California, for instance, the state constitution's equal protection clause (art. 1 §7) was approved by referendum in 1974 with 72 percent support, and so its claim to overrule at least certain majorities had a clear majoritarian credential (and a stronger margin than Prop. 8). Bud Lembke, "Nov. 7 Election Analysis: Democrats, Minorities, Students Vote Low," *Los Angeles Times*, December 11, 1978.

[27] Trends across major national public polls are graphed in Nate Silver, "How Opinion on Same-Sex Marriage Is Changing, and What It Means," *New York Times*, March 26, 2013.

states are not obviously dispositive of the national will, and the direction of momentum appeared overwhelmingly if not entirely on the side of change. Against this background, the 2012 elections would be decisive. These were the first national elections in which a major-party presidential nominee supported same-sex marriage, and the first in which a major-party platform did so.[28] Obama was reelected to the presidency, and the party supporting marriage equality retained a 53-45-2 majority in the Senate.[29] The House, on the other hand, remained under GOP control, but its margin there was well short of a convincing supermajority (234 to 201, or approximately 54 percent to 46 percent). Of course, marriage quality was hardly the central issue in the campaign, so these results are far from proving a positive mandate in its favor. But they do make it very difficult to argue that there existed after 2012 a convincing supermajority *against* same-sex marriage anywhere in the U.S. federal government, and that is what would be needed to counter the argument from principle.[30]

On balance then, when the U.S. Supreme Court overturned DOMA in June 2013, it was acting in line with the best available interpretation of the country's democratic will, everything considered. In his dissent, Justice Antonin Scalia denied this, asserting that prior to the ruling, the issue was being decided through "plebiscites, legislation, persuasion, and loud voices—in other words, democracy" (24). The Court should have refrained from imposing its own views and overturning "democratically adopted legislation" (1); instead it "might have let the People decide" (26). But whatever one thinks of Justice Scalia's legal theory, his democratic theory here is bad—it simply ignores the possibility that electoral majorities may sometimes fail to represent a will attributable to "the People" if their decisions violate the equal freedoms of all, on which their own claim to rule ultimately depends. Notice that my view does not imply that one ought to leave minority rights to courts; to the contrary, it insists on the importance of a dynamic interaction among courts, elections, and grassroots citizen organizing in justifying an overall decision. But in a system like the American one where courts have a recognized role to play, they ought to play it when

---

[28] Obama became the first sitting U.S. president to endorse same-sex marriage in May 2012, and the 2012 Democratic Party Platform was the first major party platform to do so.

[29] The two independents in the Senate, Bernie Sanders of Vermont and Angus King of Maine, also both publicly support same-sex marriage. By June 2013 Republican Senators Rob Portman of Ohio, Mark Kirk of Illinois, and Lisa Murkowski of Alaska had also come out publicly for same-sex marriage. Democrat Joe Manchin of West Virginia was publicly opposed, Mary Landrieu of Louisiana personally in favor but unwilling to vote against her state, and Mark Pryor of Arkansas personally opposed but undecided as to federal law. Lindsay Boerma, "Then There Were 3: The Democratic Holdouts on Same-Sex Marriage," *CBS News*, April 8, 2013.

[30] A further contrast to the 1990s was offered by congressional repeal of "Don't Ask Don't Tell" in September 2011.

they can in a more democratic rather than a less democratic way—as should everyone else.

Hollingsworth raised further issues. On the one hand, the principle established in *Windsor* would have to hold as a matter of law also for states given widely accepted interpretations of the incorporation of federal amendments, as Scalia emphasized in his dissent and other courts since 2013 have, at the time of writing, overwhelmingly affirmed. On the other hand, if the Supreme Court directly overturned California's Proposition 8 in *Hollingsworth*, it would immediately void standing majority decisions in thirty-eight jurisdictions, many (although not all) of them backed by convincing local supermajorities. On my reasoning, it might have been possible to justify such a course of action if one argued that the direction of change was such that voters would be unlikely to reaffirm all existing bans had the Court boldly called the question. But this would have been extremely perilous, since the most plausible reading was, to the contrary, that on the federalism issue—unlike DOMA—a clear supermajority of the relevant constituencies continued to oppose same-sex marriage. It would have been a decision like *Goodridge*, avowedly ahead of public opinion on the wager that it might be supported by the people ex post—but there is little reason to doubt that at least in many jurisdictions, such an act by the Court would have provoked a deep backlash, leaving its democratic legitimacy at best cloudy for years to come.[31] At the same time, however, I have argued that in California itself the democratic credentials of Proposition 8 were extremely poor, and the Court would be failing to play its acknowledged role in the larger constitutional system if it were to reverse the 9th Circuit Court of Appeals decision voiding the referendum. In this context, the most defensible course of action would be to find a way to overturn Proposition 8 in California without immediately ruling either way

---

[31] Consider that when *Brown v. Board* was decided in 1954, seventeen states required segregated public schools and another four permitted them by law. James T. Patterson, *Brown v. Board of Education: A Civil Rights Milestone and Its Troubled Legacy* (Oxford: Oxford University Press, 2001), xiv. In 1967 *Loving v. Virginia* overturned laws in sixteen states prohibiting interracial marriage, *Loving v. Virginia*, 388 U.S. 1, 7 (1967). And when *Roe v. Wade* was handed down in 1973, thirty states banned abortion entirely, fifteen allowed it in cases of danger to the health of the woman, and one only in cases of rape (MS), while only four had legalized it generally before fetal viability (AK, HI, NY, and WA). *Roe v. Wade*, 410 U.S. 113, 119 (1973). Of these, *Roe* clearly ventured beyond popular opinion. The Court should have waited, and any eventual ruling should have relied on equal protection rather than a privacy right, because the former enjoys a stronger democratic warrant. The predictable backlash was, however, met by organized support and the balance has never yet quite tipped in favor of rolling back the decision, although it has come exceedingly close. The democratic credentials of the status quo, however, remain more ambiguous than following *Brown* or *Loving*, and the way the decision was handled has distorted subsequent debate by turning it away from the democratic question of who has a more defensible claim to speak—not merely for a majority—but for the democratic people as a whole, considered as free and equal citizens. My view broadly supports that of Justice Ruth Bader Ginsburg, "Some Thoughts on Autonomy and Equality in Relation to *Roe v. Wade*," *North Carolina Law Review* 63 (1985): 375–86.

on the bans in other states. This would allow *Windsor* to establish the principle that equal protection demands marriage equality, but it would allow both other courts and—most importantly—also political branches in various jurisdictions to have a chance to weigh in in response before the Supreme Court would make a final decision. This is just what the Court did by ruling in *Hollingsworth* to deny standing to appeal and allowing to stand the lower district court ruling against Proposition 8, without ruling directly on its merits.

Within a year of these decisions, as we saw, two further states had legalized same-sex marriage through legislation and two by state court decisions accepted by the elected branches, while in two more elected officials opted not to appeal federal court decisions. In California itself, marriage equality came to enjoy clear majority support, and Schwarzenegger, who had vetoed previous marriage bills, had been replaced in 2010 by supporter Jerry Brown. This brought the balance of jurisdictions to twenty versus thirty-one, or 39 percent to 61 percent. Was this still a convincing supermajority? One might well argue that it was, but it is at most a very narrow one trending down, and much less convincing than 25 percent to 75 percent a year earlier. Although the Court would still be taking some risk if it were to strike down the remaining bans in these conditions, I would argue that the best interpretation of the people's will, all considered, would already narrowly support this in 2014 in a way it had not yet in 2013; and if any more states were to legalize same-sex marriage in the interim, the case would only be clearer. If the Court were so to rule, however, the final test would be in the response from local officials and citizens—in how many of the remaining states would they continue actively to fight such an interpretation of constitutional principles to which they remain generally committed? The issue, of course, is that a Supreme Court ruling locks in a certain interpretation, making it much harder to revisit in a few years' time, even if without a ruling the balance of opinion in the country might dramatically have changed. This is obviously a risk either way, but given the overwhelming (if not perfect) recent trend in one direction, I would suggest that locking in the view that the U.S. Constitution does not protect same-sex marriage would stand a much greater chance of turning out ex post to have been out of step with citizens' own evolving views.

It might appear the safest route for the Supreme Court is thus to leave the issue permanently to the states, but that cannot be right because if the whole citizenry judges that a minority's rights are threatened by certain majority decisions, then state-level majorities have no democratic mandate against federal courts, especially if those courts should appear to be supported both by national majorities and the organized efforts of minorities within recalcitrant states. The obvious historical parallels are slavery and segregation, and the general point is well established in the existing constitutional baseline in the United States—originally by the Fourteenth Amendment. This is why Scalia anticipated that *Windsor* would invalidate state-level bans by establishing the general principle that equal protection applies also to same-sex marriage. Now it is possible to imagine states rejecting the extension of that principle to this case by such an overwhelming margin that one would face a constitutional crisis over courts' right to impose it against the will of local minorities—which is, of course, also what happened with slavery and segregation. But in that scenario one would need to consider how united was the judiciary (presently very much so), how united were the states (presently not so much and declining), in addition to the balance of national representation and grassroots organizing on the ground. If the Supreme Court were to force this issue, I find it very difficult to see how a nullifying escalation from recalcitrant states could be justified democratically in the state of play in 2014. By the time you read this, you will doubtless have more evidence to draw on. But one of the characteristics of a historical and Socratic theory is that it allows one to justify judgments at a given point in time, while also pointing toward possible future developments that might either confirm those judgments or cause us to revisit them. So one can judge for oneself how well these considerations *in medias res* hold up also in retrospect.

Finally, consider briefly how the same struggle played out in different ways at just the same time in the United Kingdom and in France. Both of these countries legalized same-sex marriage in 2013 through legislation. In the United Kingdom, the bill had broad crossparty support, passing 400 to 175 in the Commons (despite a majority of the sponsoring Conservative Party voting against), and although it was opposed by the Church of England, public protests were small and dwarfed by turnout at annual gay pride parades.[32] In France, by contrast, massive protests drew hundreds of thousands repeatedly to the capital in the run-up to final votes on the bill.[33] Although hundreds of thousands also rallied in support, they were outnumbered by opponents.[34] The measure passed in the National Assembly 331 to 225 and in the Senate 179 to 157. In France then, unlike in the United States or the United Kingdom, organized grassroots opposition was dramatic and would be sufficient to raise questions about the result if other conditions were also met. But they were not—protesters in France were not challenging a countermajoritarian judicial ruling but majority rule itself, and principled arguments for a positive violation of equal freedoms that might justify overriding the majority simply were not forthcoming.[35]

[32] The (French) organizers of the largest London protest claimed 2,000 participants, whereas Pride London 2013 drew hundreds of thousands. Charlotte Philby, "Large Anglo-French Rally Against Same-Sex Marriage Held in London," *The Independent*, March 24, 2013; Costas Pitas, "Hundreds of Thousands Out for London's Gay Parade," *Reuters*, June 29, 2013.

[33] "Mass Paris Rally Against Gay Marriage in France," *BBC News*, January 13, 2013; "Gay Marriage Opponents March in Paris Before Vote," *Reuters*, March 24, 2013.

[34] Stephen Erlanger, "Thousands Rally in Paris for Same-Sex Marriage," *New York Times*, January 27, 2013.

[35] See the argumentation offered by the major protest organizer, La Manif Pour Tous, at http://www.lamanifpourtous.fr/en/why/the-heart-of-the-matter.

So in all three countries, we see cases of reform justified on democratic principles even though citizens remained divided, and indeed in the United States, a case in which, at the time of writing, further change is still required. In the United States, courts played an important role, but so did grassroots activists and voters. This time the various actors and arguments lined up in such a way that courts had to act and were justified in doing so, but this is not a general argument for courts or against electoral majorities. It is an argument about how to give particularities of context their due, without giving up the possibility of defending principled judgments on democratic grounds. This way of thinking about the issue stands in marked contrast to dominant approaches in the theoretical literature. Despite their disagreements, conservatives, liberals, and queer theorists and other radical constructivists widely agree in approaching the issue as one of morality or ethics—in asking what justice or morality requires from marriage, or what sorts of harms state actions might engender to different ways of life.[36] But my claim is that although these sorts of arguments may have theoretical import, and may also play a legitimate role in rallying actual citizens to one side or another in the course of actual struggles, none of them suffices to justify coercive state policy or law. Only democracy can do that. And so when we argue over issues like same-sex marriage, we ought to argue in democratic terms.

The New Deal

I have argued that in the controversy over same-sex marriage in the United States, the Supreme Court was justified in overturning the elected branches. But this is not a general brief for judicial review. Indeed, there is a good principled case that the U.S. system would be more democratic without it, but what there is not is presently a good case that the American people have already endorsed that view. As I understand it, the baseline in the United States expects courts to play a role as arbiter but does not grant them sovereign interpretive authority; rather, other branches and organized citizens may challenge even Supreme Court decisions through political action in and outside formal channels whenever those decisions are not defensible on democratic grounds.[37] In extreme cases, such conflicts might provoke a constitutional crisis that ends by renegotiating the baseline settlement itself. One must be very careful to avoid either of three easy

---

[36] Conservatives and liberals sometimes also rely on positive law, but although this has a point for arguing before judges, it cannot on its own also determine larger questions about democratic legitimacy.

[37] See notably Larry Kramer, *The People Themselves: Popular Constitutionalism and Judicial Review* (Oxford: Oxford University Press, 2004), although as should be clear, I am rather more troubled than he by the problem of figuring out who speaks for those "people."

presumptions—that such actions are always wrong, that they are always right, or that they are right whenever one personally agrees with their substantive ends but not otherwise. The point of a historical and Socratic theory is that it allows one to judge particular conflicts of this sort in a principled way by working out which position has a consistent claim to be endorsed by the citizenry as a whole. The New Deal is a good example of a case in which courts deserved to come out on the losing side.

The events were briefly considered in the last chapter; the key issue is that during the *Lochner* era, courts relied on substantive due process to overturn protective social legislation and to block legislative action supporting workers' efforts to organize unions, while routinely granting injunctions enabling officials to crush unions by force. The Court's claim was that legislation cannot arbitrarily interfere with individual freedom of contract (although some regulation for public interests such as health was allowed), since this amounted to depriving citizens of liberty without due process of law in contravention of the Fifth and Fourteenth Amendments.[38] It was as though those citizens were being enslaved or thrown into jail without a trial. Although objections to federal action based on a narrow reading of the commerce clause were also used,[39] substantive due process was held to trump even the police power of the states. Now whatever one thinks of the argument, one must admit it is perfectly consistent and admissible as an interpretation of citizens' equal freedoms. At the same time, however, proponents of social legislation and union organizing rights also had perfectly good arguments on their side concerning the need for collective solutions to offset imbalances of power in market transactions between individuals with and without capital. For instance, whether so-called yellow-dog contracts prohibiting employees from joining unions were a fair exercise of employers' contractual freedom, as the Court found in *Adair v. U.S.* (1907) and *Coppage v. Kansas* (1915), or instead a way of robbing workers of theirs, as dissents in *Coppage* by Justices Holmes and Day insisted to the contrary, was a decision that required a judgment not merely from the Court but from the people.

Here, the Court could not rely on the existing baseline. The Fifth, Thirteenth, and Fourteenth Amendments applied to very different sorts of freedoms—as indeed the Court itself had ruled on the latter two in the 1873 *Slaughterhouse Cases*. Although some elected powers supported the *Lochner* Court's position, there was no good evidence for any higher-order democratic claim that might support the Court trumping legislatures that instead voted the other way (as there at least arguably had been for the *Civil Rights Cases*). So here everything depended on the Court's claim to protect an individual liberty from state control. Although the Court's language often sounded echoes of a doctrine of

---

[38] *Lochner v. New York*, 198 U.S. 45 (1905).
[39] *Hammer v. Dagenhart*, 247 U.S. 251 (1918).

pre-political natural rights, its position may be defended on strictly democratic grounds as a case for protecting individual citizens' freedoms from hostile legislative majorities—much as in the same-sex marriage case. So one needs to ask whether the minority supported by the Court had met the burdens required to justify a democratic claim against those majorities.

The Court insisted it was protecting an equivalent freedom of contract of both employers and employees, but the other side argued legislation was needed precisely to protect the contractual freedoms of employees from effective domination by employers. So employers on their own had no unique claim of rights violation and nothing that might justify trumping majorities who opted for workers' contrary interpretation. This meant that everything really came down to the Court's claim that social legislation interfered with the contractual freedoms of those workers themselves—that it prevented them from freely agreeing to take substandard jobs they really wanted, from entering into "those contracts in relation to labor which may seem to him appropriate or necessary for the support of himself and his family."[40] Now in certain contexts this might be true—there could exist a system of labor regulation ostensibly protecting all workers' interests but, in fact, functioning primarily to secure certain workers' monopoly position against competition from others. But although this can always be asserted, it is just as possible to hold that minimum standards, in fact, best serve the interest of employees generally by countering an unfair bargaining advantage otherwise held by employers. On my view, there can be no a priori and universal answer—so what is needed is a judgment attributable to the democratic people concerning specific measures in a specific context, taking into account the views of the actual citizens who will have to live with them.

And this means the Court was in no position to decide on its own. Since the Court claimed to protect the freedoms of workers, it matters what actual workers thought. When given the chance freely to organize themselves, did workers in the period line up behind the Court's interpretation of their rights? Did they take to the streets organizing dramatic demonstrations against unions and social legislation, and rally behind anti-union candidates? Although dissent existed, as it always will, the overwhelming balance of evidence was clear. The much more convincing interpretation was that the Court's view was supported by employers and elected officials where workers had less influence. There was no convincing evidence of a supermajority of workers behind the *Lochner* Court. And this put the lie to the Court's claim to speak for the equal freedoms of all citizens, which might be held to trump legislative majorities, rather than merely one interested faction in a fight that ought to be left instead to the political branches. If anything, the principled democratic argument might have supported judicial

---

[40] *Lochner*, 198 U.S. 57.

intervention on the other side; but that would have raised further democratic challenges that would have to have been sorted through, and in any case such action was not in the cards.

The case also raises an important point about individual rights. Because individuals as such are coextensive with the citizenry as a whole, there is no democratic way of adjudicating a conflict framed strictly as one of individual rights versus majority rule. A majority at one point in time may well seek to constitutionalize such rights, but there is really no democratic way of defending them against future majorities other than by the appeal to integrity in the historical baseline—that is, to point out that rolling back habeas corpus for citizens declared "enemy combatants," for instance, may not be able to be squared with the underlying principle of habeas corpus in general, and asking the larger political system to weigh in on whether the people accept that judgment and whether or not they would be willing to accept the consequences of rolling back the general principle everywhere it applies in the law. Sometimes, of course, individual rights deserve to lose, like individual rights to property in slaves. So in the absence of a historical claim—in a straight conflict between a minority opinion favoring some interpretation of individual rights and a majority opposed and unwilling to negotiate a compromise—the majority ought to win because the majority itself shows that most "individuals" disagree with the contrary view of their own rights and freedoms.

The better route for critics of untrammeled majoritarianism, then, is typically to reframe individual rights claims as claims of injustice to a particular minority. So free speech or religious toleration is an individual right, but the best democratic warrant for them where majorities disagree is that certain minorities of dissenters would otherwise be unfairly deprived of the equal freedoms of democratic citizens. Similarly, one cannot really judge a conflict between an abstract "freedom of contract" and legislative majorities (unless it is strictly a claim of integrity in the baseline), but if one breaks down that freedom into a claim of a minority of employers, on the one hand, and a relevant group of employees (even if these are a numerical majority in the population), on the other, then one can test representative democratic claims from either side that might counterbalance the analogous claims of legislative majorities. And keep in mind that since electoral systems are rarely strictly majoritarian by popular vote (even Westminster uses first-past-the-post constituencies), in a particular case one might in this way end up arguing against *legislative* majorities on either majoritarian or countermajoritarian grounds. Many individual rights built into constitutional traditions are actually best understood in this way as solutions to factional conflicts, and part of the point of the historical baseline is that it draws our attention to these historical conflicts in a way that allows us to consider which among them are or are not still relevant to politics in the present day. Equal protection, then, is generally a more democratic principle than appeals to fundamental rights, particularly in contests between courts and legislative majorities. If framing political choices in terms of "rights" leads majorities to back limits on their own majority powers, that is fine, but then the warrant is really majoritarian and always open to revision by future majorities. (Perhaps these should be the sustained majorities Ackerman emphasizes in the U.S. Constitutional system, but I agree with him that other systems may be defensible in other contexts.)

On my account of the New Deal, then, Roosevelt was right to challenge the Court and was on solid democratic ground in forcing a potential constitutional crisis with his Court-packing plan. On my view, it did matter that Roosevelt and the Democrats won a series of convincing electoral victories. But that is not the whole story, because although movement majorities might well win a series of victories in favor of stripping minorities of their equal freedoms as citizens—as in the period after Reconstruction—that would not necessarily mean they enjoyed a democratic mandate from the people as a whole. They might simply represent a large but tyrannical faction. On the other hand, the Court's actions were already wrong even before Roosevelt's transformative victories, because its argument to justify overruling normal legislation was indefensible on democratic grounds. Unlike in Ackerman's story, although elections and the interaction of constitutional branches played important roles, what was decisive in this case was the relationship of a principled argument against majoritarianism to extra-parliamentary grassroots organizing, which served to test the Court's pretense to stand for individual rights against majority tyranny. This is the key internal contradiction. Although Ackerman's history chooses to focus on positive steps in a narrative of constitutional progress, there is no reason to suppose that great, historic majorities in periods of higher lawmaking are, in general, better guarantors of citizens' equal freedoms than other majorities in the meantime—did not the American founders constitutionalize protections for slavery just to insulate it from challenge in normal politics? And why should not national capitulation to the retreat from Reconstruction and the building of Jim Crow count also as an episode of higher lawmaking, in which the victorious reformers were the segregationists? Again, this is not necessarily a problem for Ackerman's theory of constitutional interpretation, but it does show why a larger democratic theory is also needed to provide critical perspective on positive constitutional law, whatever that law may be.

This interpretation of the New Deal also departs from Habermas's. The reason the New Deal was justified on democratic grounds is not that in retrospect all parties came to agree that "with the inclusion of marginalized groups and the empowerment of deprived classes, the hitherto poorly satisfied presuppositions for the legitimacy of the existing democratic procedures are better realized."[41] It is true

---

[41] Jürgen Habermas, "Constitutional Democracy: A Paradoxical Union of Contradictory Principles?," trans. William Rehg, *Political Theory* 29, no. 6 (2001): 775.

that many parties would come to adopt that view ex post (although "all parties" is perhaps too strong in the United States since the 1980s), but that is just to say that this is the view that won out (to the extent it did and so long as it continues to hold). When it mattered, however, at the time of the struggle, the competing *Lochner* view was just as coherent as an interpretation both of general a priori principles of equal freedoms and of "progress" in the U.S. constitutional tradition. A real decision was required to choose between these two competing but equally admissible views, just as a real decision had been required in the Civil War and Reconstruction to choose between two admissible interpretations of the status of the U.S. Constitution and the place of slavery within it. And there was no guarantee in a moral arc of history or the unforced force of the better argument that the interpretation that won out would also be the one that deserved to—or that this interpretation, say, of the New Deal, will not one day appear to future generations the way the era of Jim Crow and *Lochner* appear to (many of) us. So if the New Deal was a political decision, it needs to be defended as such, on democratic grounds. And this requires asking who at the time had a better claim to speak for the entire democratic people, even though actual citizens were divided and deliberation in the public sphere had failed to resolve interpretive disagreements and unite all around a common sense of justice. This is not to contest the point Habermas's story is meant to make—that since it is at least *possible* to view democratic change ex post as progress, there is no reason to suppose democracy and constitutional rights intrinsically incompatible. But we also need grounds for distinguishing, for instance, between the period after Reconstruction and the New Deal that followed, if we are to provide any defensible framework for judging history in democratic terms, and to avoid projecting back into the past the rational seeds of the inevitable triumph of those outcomes we personally happen to support. This is what a historical and Socratic theory adds that is otherwise left out of the story. And in this case what matters greatly is that workers in the period before the New Deal did more than deliberate in the public sphere over democratic ideals—they also built vast, representative organizations that challenged the claims of their opponents in the courts and elsewhere to interpret democratic citizens' equal freedoms in their name.

    The New Deal, then, was a constitutional revolution that chose to expand and radically reinterpret certain elements in an earlier legal tradition while dramatically repudiating others. In addition to renegotiating the balance of powers between states and the federal government and among the federal branches, it served decisively to entrench most of the principles of social democracy mentioned in Chapter 1, in the general form in which they remain in effect today—notwithstanding important later modifications and ongoing controversies of the sort symbolized by the battle over the 2010 Affordable Care Act. The exception is the principle of *social emancipation*, which was established by the Thirteenth Amendment, fixed in a certain interpretation by the *Civil Rights Cases* and *Plessy v. Ferguson*, and later radically reinterpreted by *Brown* and the 1964 and 1968 Civil Rights Acts. The principle of *protective legislation* was dramatically extended by the Fair Labor Standards Act of 1938, which first succeeded in extending federal protections against unfair market practices to relations among employers and employees, of the sort that had been pioneered in relations among owners of businesses and capital by the 1887 Interstate Commerce Act and the 1890 Sherman Antitrust Act. The principle of guaranteed *social minimums* was radically extended by the 1935 Social Security Act; although earlier laws had provided limited support for veterans, public education, and maternity and infant care, the Social Security Act for the first time established a permanent and universal right of citizens to a floor of federal support, at least upon reaching sixty-five years of age. The principle of government protection for the *right to organize unions* was established generally and effectively only with the National Labor Relations Act of 1935, which built on the earlier efforts of the 1914 Clayton Act, the 1926 Railway Labor Act, and the 1932 Norris-LaGuardia Act.

The principle of *public planning compatible with private property* was the most complex in the New Deal. The 1933 National Industrial Recovery Act (NIRA) was overturned by the Supreme Court in 1935. The Roosevelt administration and the New Deal Congress responded not by fighting for a new NIRA, but with the Social Security and National Labor Relations Acts (along with a new Agricultural Adjustment Act in 1938), and it was these latter that were eventually affirmed by the Court, faced with Roosevelt's Court-packing threat, in the famous "switch in time." These and subsequent decisions greatly expanded federal powers under the commerce clause, allowing even federal price controls, but the elected branches never again attempted a corporatist reorganization of the economy as a whole, and when the Court blocked Truman's attempted nationalization of the steel industry in 1952, the elected branches did not contest the decision as they had in 1935–1937.

Subsequent decades saw many controversies and reinterpretations, but none of these general principles has been overturned or, I think, any new ones of comparable generality been added. (The creation of the Environmental Protection Agency in 1970, for instance, falls under the planning power for public ends, antidiscrimination law under protective legislation.) For instance, the 2010 Affordable Care Act combines elements of protective legislation (regulated exchanges), social minimums (subsidies), and the planning power (mandates on individuals and businesses). Mass protests over that Act from citizens and some elected officials raised questions about its democratic mandate, but were countered by grassroots and elected support on the other side.[42] No good argument was provided that core provisions of the Act violated minority freedoms consistent with standing interpretations of baseline principles entailed by other

---

[42] See, for instance, two *New York Times* articles from September 12, 2009: Jeff Zelny, "Thousands Rally in Capital to Protest Big Government"; and Sheryl Gay Stolberg, "Thousands Rally in Minnesota Behind Obama's Call for Health Care Overhaul."

programs like Social Security, which continued to enjoy wide popular support. The Act's legitimacy was sealed in 2012 when it was upheld by the Supreme Court and President Obama was reelected over GOP nominee Mitt Romney, who campaigned on repeal—but the key factor in this case was the lack of any good argument for why the elected branches that had passed the law should not be taken to speak for the people in choosing between conflicting interpretations of citizens' freedoms, on the one side to be free from government interference, on the other to be secured the possibility of acquiring affordable health insurance. Nor, in my assessment, is there any clear ground in either the baseline or minority rights claims for preventing the federal government from making the continuance of existing Medicaid funding to states contingent on Medicaid expansion, and so that part of the decision in *National Federation of Independent Business v. Sibelius* is best seen as undercutting the democratic people's expressed will to make sure affordable health insurance is actually available to all.

The Court's 2013 decision in *Burwell v. Hobby Lobby* is more defensible on democratic grounds, even if it does open up an interpretation of protected religious liberty that may lead to new problems in attempts to apply it consistently across cases. *Burwell* allowed closely held private companies to avoid paying for insurance covering contraception if this went against their owners' religious beliefs; in doing so, it extended an exemption already written into the law for religious employers such as churches, and drew on the Religious Freedom Restoration Act of 1993 (passed by voice vote in the House and 97 to 3 in the Senate). If another workable solution is found that does not undercut the popular will by, in effect, making women's access to contraception insurance contingent on the arbitrary wills of their employers, then that solution will be defensible. (Otherwise, women's claims would still demand redress.) At the time of writing, a challenge suggesting the Act permits federal subsidies only for insurance purchased on state exchanges but not the federal one had been upheld by the U.S. Court of Appeals for the D.C. Circuit in *Halbig v. Burwell*, but this interpretation contravenes the express aim of the law to secure access to affordable coverage for citizens in all states (hence the federal exchange in the first place), and so is clearly an attempt to use the courts to undercut the people's expressed democratic will and should be thrown out.

It is important to stress that the Affordable Care Act is not the natural completion of New Deal social principles. Although those principles matter in showing why not every battle needs to be refought and opening constitutional space in which the Affordable Care Act is defensible on one possible interpretation of standing principles among others, a choice among competing interpretations is still a real political choice that demands a democratic justification. In this case, the struggles of the 1930s—and the vicissitudes of the intervening decades—provide background against which more recent struggles must be considered, but it is the struggle from 2009 to 2012 through which the American people chose to include a right to affordable health insurance among those social minimums a democratic government has a duty to secure for all its citizens. That decision might have gone the other way, as it had for three-quarters of a century since the Roosevelt administration and the New Deal Congress decided to leave medical insurance out of the Social Security bill. One must also bear in mind that any of the social principles established by the New Deal might be overturned at any time, the way *Lochner* doctrine was overturned in the 1930s. It might be that unions, for instance, will turn out to be no longer relevant to modern-day workers, as conservatives have long argued, or else that some new principle will be established entailing at least certain limits on inequalities of wealth, of the sort implied by Occupy Wall Street protests. But neither of these possibilities has yet received a convincing endorsement from the democratic people as a whole. And that is why the five social principles, along with the seven political principles, continue to set the baseline from which analyses of contemporary conflicts ought to begin.[43]

Gun Control or Gun Rights?

Same-sex marriage and the New Deal are two cases in which democracy demanded change, and in which that change supported broadly left-of-center outcomes. But this will not always be the case. Because democratic elenchus is a resolutely democratic theory, it will sometimes support conservative conclusions, other times reformist ones, still other times radical change. It all depends on how democratic citizens in a particular context understand their equal freedoms, and what is required to resolve conflicts among them in a principled and democratic way that respects those freedoms in deciding. The gun control debate in the United States offers a good example of a recent case in which liberal reformers have so far deserved to lose out to conservatives, for the most part, on democratic grounds.

Consider first the principled arguments on each side. Gun rights advocates have long argued that these rights protect a system of free and democratic government against the threat of tyranny, and they draw support from the Second Amendment claim that "[a] well regulated Militia, being necessary to the security of a free State, the right of the people to keep and bear Arms, shall not be infringed." This view was explicitly upheld in 2008 by the 5 to 4 Supreme Court majority in *District of Columbia v. Heller* and extended in *McDonald v. Chicago* (2010), in effect overturning the standing view since 1939 established in *United States v. Miller*. Now the weak point in this argument has always been the leap

---

[43] Here, this holds for the United States, but similar investigations of constitutional traditions in other contemporary democracies turn out to uncover similar broad principles, interpreted in a variety of ways. See the Appendix.

from protection of a military-political use of firearms in citizen militias to protecting their general use for purposes, such as private self-defense and recreation, with no direct relation to "the security of a free State." But whatever one thinks of the logic of the argument or the historical debate over the Framers' intent in 1791, it is certainly an admissible interpretation that a general right of individuals to own firearms is a necessary condition toward the democratic end of preserving a free constitution. On this view, it is a civil right like freedom of speech and assembly that majorities should not abridge. And some interpretation is required, on democratic grounds, because the Second Amendment is indeed a part of the standing constitutional structure with a defeasible presumption to represent a decision of the people, in the absence of a visible mass movement to overturn it.

On the other hand, gun control proponents can argue that the basic democratic principle of protection of the laws (political principle one) requires a publicly accountable police power to stand in, as a general rule, for private acts of violence even for the protection of legitimate individual rights. *In extremis* the contrary view leads not to a free state but to no state at all, and there is nothing democratic about the sort of armed vigilantism historically practiced by groups like the Ku Klux Klan. But the weak point in this argument is that if unlawful uses of guns are prohibited, it is not clear a priori why possession of them for otherwise lawful uses must be criminalized as well. And although the argument in principle might be used to reserve all firearms for police and a standing army, that conclusion at least is clearly ruled out by the Second Amendment. So one of two things is required—either gun control advocates would need to press a democratic case that the people no longer endorse the Second Amendment, although repeal through the formal Article V process has been too onerous, or else one will need to choose between competing interpretations of what that Amendment requires by determining which commands more consistent and convincing support from the American people today.

Consider first whether defenders of gun rights can justify their countermajoritarian claim. Although the Court might allow local jurisdictions to set their own rules, there is certainly good precedent for incorporating constitutional amendments against states and localities, and so for the same reason it is not clear that every state should be able to make up its own mind concerning same-sex marriage according to local majorities, it is not clear that local majorities should be able to abridge federally recognized gun rights if those rights are indeed democratically defensible. So the issue is whether a relevant minority of gun owners (or those who would be gun owners if allowed) can substantiate a claim of equal rights violation against gun control supporting majorities. We do not need to show that gun owners "really are" an independently disadvantaged minority; as with the LGBT community or workers, we allow the relevant group to define itself politically. We have already seen gun rights advocates have an admissible argument from principle, and it is unique because the counterargument lies in favor of majoritarian police powers, but not a competing rights claim from another minority. So the question is whether advocates demonstrate convincing supermajority support among gun owners for their interpretation of the people's prevailing view of the Second Amendment. Now the National Rifle Association claims 4.5 million members; according to Cook and Goss, "A more reliable estimate is about 3.4 million" but "either way, it is one of the largest pressure groups in the country" (190). Although the NRA also doubles as an industry lobby, there is little gainsaying the fact that it represents the views of millions of American gun owners. The gun rights movement is larger than this, with other groups such as Gun Owners of America self-reporting some 300,000 members,[44] but the NRA figures serve as a useful benchmark for comparison (since membership in many organizations doubtless overlaps). On the standard we used in considering movements for marriage equality and labor during the New Deal—looking to the balance of citizens' organized political action—this is good evidence of convincing support among the relevant constituency and little sign of organized dissent.

Next consider mobilization on the other side: Have gun control proponents demonstrated a clear supermajority of the people as a whole united against the claims of gun rights advocates? Although the 1990s saw some popular organizing for gun control, it declined precipitously after. In 1993, urged by the Brady Campaign to Prevent Gun Violence, the nation's largest gun control organization, Bill Clinton signed the Brady Handgun Violence Prevention Act, which requires background checks by federally licensed gun dealers, and a national assault weapons ban. The largest public demonstration for gun control in U.S. history was the 2000 Million Mom March in Washington, DC (a year after the Columbine school shootings), which drew crowds of several hundred thousand (750,000 according to organizers' reports).[45] According to Goss, the Brady Campaign (which absorbed the Million Mom March in 2001) reportedly had fewer than 200,000 members by 2005, and total membership in all gun control organizations was "at most 268,000 people and almost certainly fewer," or 7 percent of membership in the NRA.[46] The assault weapons ban expired in 2004 and has not been renewed. In 2006 then Mayors Michael Bloomberg of New York City and Thomas Menino of Boston founded Mayors Against Illegal Guns; in December 2013 it claimed 1.5 million "supporters" and joined in an umbrella group with Moms Demand Action for Gun Sense in America, a group founded after the Newtown shootings and at the time reporting 130,000 members.[47] Also in 2013, former

---

[44] According to its website at http://gunowners.org/larry-pratt.htm.

[45] Robin Toner, "Mothers Rally to Assail Gun Violence," *New York Times*, May 15, 2000.

[46] Kristin A. Goss, *Disarmed: The Missing Movement for Gun Control in America* (Princeton, NJ: Princeton University Press, 2006), 18. See also Philip J. Cook and Kristin A. Goss, *The Gun Debate: What Everyone Needs to Know* (Oxford: Oxford University Press, 2014).

[47] Greg Toppo, "High-Profile Gun Control Groups Join Forces," *USA Today*, December 18, 2013.

U.S. Rep. Gabrielle Giffords and her husband Mark Kelly founded Americans for Responsible Solutions PAC, which self-reported 500,000 members and 72,000 donors six months later.[48]

Even if these developments in response to high-profile shootings (still recent as this book goes to press) turn out to represent a lasting mobilization, they have yet to match the NRA, much less to demonstrate a convincing supermajority among the citizenry as a whole. In the twelve months following the Newtown shooting, the balance of legislative activity was thirty-nine acts strengthening gun regulations to seventy loosening them, and a federal bill for universal background checks died in the Senate.[49] It is true that opinion polls often demonstrate large supermajorities for specific tighter gun regulations such as background checks,[50] but as I have argued throughout, polls alone are a poor indicator (partly because they generate inconsistent results depending on the questions asked), and so dispositive evidence of support should come from elections, legislation, and citizen organizing. At any rate, national opinion polls do not show clear evidence of supermajorities for tighter gun control in general: Pew polls show a decline from 57 percent to 34 percent in favor in 1993 to a low of 45 percent to 49 percent against in 2012, and a temporary reversal after Sandy Hook dissipating by early 2014, to leave a 49 percent to 48 percent plurality against.[51] Gallup shows similar trends over the same period, with an uptick in the minority position in favor of loosening laws in late 2013 from 5 percent to 16 percent.[52] (Support for loosening restrictions nevertheless remains low across polls that offer an option of keeping laws as they are now.) As Cook and Goss note, "Unlike a lot of other issues, civil rights for example, gun control has not relied on a mass movement from below to secure many key laws" (203). Although it is always possible that recent developments will eventually change this dynamic, there is little evidence that this has already happened.

What this means is that in the absence of a clear grassroots challenge or an argument from minority rights, gun control advocates must bank their democratic claims on representation through the elected branches. But the gun rights movement, by contrast, does at least have an admissible argument from equal freedoms backed by consistent popular support, and because that argument can be defended as an interpretation of a standing baseline decision represented by the Second Amendment, the Court may justifiably invoke it to overrule certain

---

[48] Fredreka Schouten, "Giffords' Super PAC Raises $6.5 Million," *USA Today*, July 26, 2013.

[49] "State Gun Laws Enacted in the Year Since Newtown," *New York Times*, December 10, 2013.

[50] http://www.people-press.org/2013/01/14/in-gun-control-debate-several-options-draw-majority-support/.

[51] http://www.gallup.com/poll/1645/guns.aspx, http://www.people-press.org/question-search/?qid=1851413&pid=51&ccid=51#top, http://www.pewresearch.org/fact-tank/2013/12/12/a-year-after-newtown-little-change-in-public-opinion-on-guns/.

[52] http://www.gallup.com/poll/167135/americans-dissatisfaction-gun-laws-highest-2001.aspx.

majority decisions. As in the New Deal and the same-sex marriage controversy, showing that the Court was wrong to do so would require a concerted response from the elected branches, mass protest from citizens at the grassroots, or both, in order to escalate the struggle. But this has not happened; Congress failed even to pass universal background checks in the wake of Sandy Hook, much less to take on the Court directly. That does not mean the courts ought to strike down all gun regulations (because judgments are required as to which regulations actually vitiate the protected right), but it does mean that they cannot fairly be faulted on democratic grounds for what they have done so far—even if one should remain unconvinced by the legal or historical bases of their decisions.[53]

So here is a case in which the better democratic argument (in 2014) supports a right-of-center rather than a left-of-center position, and one in which the status quo, rather than reform, is presently most consistent with democracy. This does not mean that gun control is necessarily a bad idea in principle, but it means that if its supporters want to show that it is also an idea the democratic people support, then they need to become much more successful at organizing in elections and at the grassroots level. If they cannot, then this will suggest that the American people, all considered, do in fact support gun rights and think these ought to rule certain policy solutions out of bounds—even if national majorities sometimes support them in polls. In that case this democratic view will need to be respected, even by those who think it wrong. On the other hand, gun rights activists remain free to press their claims even further, although doing so might risk overreach and finally provoke the sort of broad backlash that has so far, I have suggested, failed to materialize. It remains an open question which of these scenarios will play out in the future. The answer will be decided not by theory but by the dynamic of political action among committed citizens on all sides of the debate.

Conclusion

The cases in this chapter have shown several ways that the demands of certain parties in struggles over democratic change may fail to hold up consistently, when one goes on to ask why one ought to believe they are also backed by the people as a whole. These arguments often turned on Principle (II)*'s *practical condition*, on showing different ways that majoritarian or countermajoritarian arguments may fail to demonstrate the sort of popular support required to justify their claims. But it should be clear from working through these cases that one must draw freely on all four conditions in order to interpret exactly which

---

[53] Cf. the interesting and broadly confluent discussion in Reva B. Siegal, "Dead or Alive: Originalism as Popular Constitutionalism in *Heller*," *Harvard Law Review* 122 (2008): 191–245.

claim one is testing for support, what sorts of answers may be ruled out by the historical baseline so long as it holds, and when support on one side is sufficient to overrule backing for competing claims on the other. I focused particularly on the issue of majority rule and minority rights, because this is an important and perennial problem in democratic struggles. I also discussed more briefly some of the considerations involved when claims turn instead principally on the presumptive legitimacy of an existing baseline settlement, suggesting that overturning that settlement in the face of organized opposition requires reformers to sustain consistent democratic support through a series of escalating contests that ultimately force a constitutional crisis—and in the most extreme cases, a democratic revolution. I hope also to have conveyed something of the dynamic sense in which democratic history ought, I think, to be approached—although I have given a certain account of how events played out much of the point is that they might instead have played out another way, and might still do so in the future. Struggles for democracy are not the natural unfolding of self-correcting ideals or the march of truth in the world. They are a series of political acts in which different actors make spontaneous decisions in the face of uncertainty, against the background of certain contexts of possibilities, constraints, and interpretive schemes, and turn out for a time to succeed more or less well in rallying others and making things difficult for their opponents. None of this is written in the stars. But that does not mean there is no point in arguing over what would make a democracy better or worse. What it means is that these are always political decisions that require a democratic defense. This chapter has offered a few illustrations of how such a defense might go.

Conclusion

This book had two major aims—to draw renewed attention to a distinctive sort of antifoundational argument called elenchus, and to defend a democratic theory that adapts this broadly Socratic sort of argument to the problem of judging democratic change. I also argued that appreciating the uses Kant and Hegel made of similar strategies challenges familiar understandings of their ethical and political theories and their place in the history of political thought.

Part One argued that commonplace portrayals of Plato, Kant, and Hegel as paragons of foundationalist metaphysics get their arguments here almost exactly wrong. Elenchus is a counterintuitive way of arguing that allows one to arrive at conclusions only indirectly, and justifies those conclusions strictly by elimination without ever seeking a certain positive ground. It takes up Socrates's radically skeptical assault on every comfortable dogma, and goes on to build the possibility of defending one's judgments entirely from inside this method of skeptical critique. But just for this reason, it is a kind of argument easy to miss if one is not looking for it, and it will be easy to mistake claims about the assumptions entailed in posing certain sorts of questions for bald assertions about human nature or ontology. Kant and Hegel, however, took the difference to matter a great deal, which was why Kant wrote "Critiques" and Hegel called his way of philosophizing "dialectic," which he described as advancing further down paths opened by Plato and Kant. This thoroughgoing commitment to thinking without foundations distinguished Kant and Hegel not only from the eighteenth-century natural lawyers they criticized, but also from many of their own interpreters since.

Although I have made some claims about Plato, the historical part of my argument has been most concerned with showing how Kant and Hegel both drew on Plato's idealism and broke with it, in a period seen by many as the threshold of the modern world in which we still live. How Kant and Hegel are positioned in the stories people tell about that period often says a great deal about where it is they want to think we have ended up. I have been particularly concerned to challenge two familiar ways of telling this story. The first holds Kant up as the epitome of a rationalist Enlightenment that was then beaten back on the Continent by the forces of historicist reaction, leading ineluctably down the *Sonderweg* to the horrors of the Second World War. Luckily, in the Anglophone world, it was instead the Liberals destined to succeed the Whigs. And so now we are free to make our way back to Kant, ironing out whatever too much unsettles the sort of liberal common sense we have in the meantime inherited from the likes of J. S. Mill, and projected back onto Locke. (If we are magnanimous, we may even, like Rawls, bring in Hegel as a less individualist sort of liberal.) The first problem with this is that it ignores Kant's radical critique of both conventionalism and the tradition of rational natural law, his avowed embrace of skeptical method, and the profound debt of his moral and political philosophy to the eminently political line of thought running from Hobbes to Rousseau. The second problem is that it posits a clean break between a rational Kantian Enlightenment and a historicism that assimilates Hegel to Marxism or to the German nationalism that would come to loom so large a century later. But this ignores how Kant already took the problem of constitutional authorization in the social contract tradition to point to the need for a theory of historical judgment, and how Hegel's continued commitment to principled justification sharply distinguished him from the less self-critical historicisms that came to predominate after 1848.

Politically speaking, this approach aims to vindicate one version or another of a revived liberal or democratic story of the progress of human reason, by cordoning off all the complications and failures of that story over the past two centuries as the work of obscurantism and reaction. But it is rather more plausible, I suggest, to see the nineteenth and twentieth centuries, broadly speaking, as ones in which self-described modern views won out, with varying degrees of thoroughness and in much of the world—and yet rather than this ushering in a rational consensus and putting an end to politics, people promptly began to fight new and even more terrible wars pitting different interpretations of emancipation and popular self-government against each other. (The United States, of course, was no exception—its nineteenth-century revolution just happened to be called the Civil War.) This is not to say the ideas caused the conflicts, but that this became increasingly the language in which conflicts would be fought. The point is that it would thus be strange if, say, after the Second World War or after the Cold War, it turned out that politics had finally been solved because we are all liberals or all democrats now—just because that is exactly the sort of view temporarily victorious revolutionary factions had taken over and over again since 1789, only to find themselves soon confronted with deep-seated political disagreements their triumphalist ideologies were unable to accommodate or to resolve (much as had religious reformers in the centuries immediately preceding). This is not, of course, to disparage Enlightenment thought, but to suggest that the less consensual and progressive aspects of what happened after 1789 are every bit as much a part of its history as those pieces one might like to pick out ex post as evidence of progress in reason and political culture.

The second story I mean to contest is one that ranks Kant and Hegel among the last great political metaphysicians. In positivist and certain Marxist versions, the social sciences have since learned to do better by purging themselves rigorously of "ideas." Post-structuralist versions do them one better by painting positivism and Marxism themselves as further iterations of the sort of metaphysical illusion they claimed to dispel. Now there are certainly problems in Kant and Hegel, on which some of the positivist and post-structuralist critiques are entirely right, but what this sort of story again leaves out is Kant's and Hegel's debt to skeptical method, their attention to political disagreement and the problem of interpretation in justifying coercion, and how in response they shifted the focus of theories of justice from human nature and the best regime to the activity of political judgment and the conditions on which defensible judgments might be said to depend. There was a democratic moment in this turn to political action and judgment that was lost again in positivism and which post-structuralism has not revived. Though many of the post-structural critiques of the traditions from which it emerged may be valid, there are other ways in which it may remain too faithful to assumptions of those traditions. What has gone is the point of view of action and of politics as a space of judgment, and it is not obvious that the best alternative to positivism is postpositivism. The theory defended in this book supports renewed calls to attend to the properly political in politics, but it also resists the temptation to collapse politics too quickly into brute decision and war, because it considers politics from the standpoint of actors who always retain at least the option of trying to organize themselves in concert with their fellow citizens—not only as an alternative to power but also in its pursuit—and in so doing to defend the judgments and the actions that they take. The historical point is that these were among the questions Kant and Hegel were wrestling with against the background of the French Revolution and the Napoleonic Wars, and that their turn to theories of historical judgment offered a sophisticated approach to issues of popular revolution and democratic change that have remained at the center of politics for the past two centuries, but of which our understanding today is hardly any better than when they wrote.

Part Two then took up this challenge by defending a freestanding theory of democracy and democratic change. On this theory, when faced with a struggle over the legitimacy of an existing constitution or a movement for reform, we ought to judge not by appealing to any external standard, but instead to begin from the positions defended by competing parties on the ground, to ask which has the most consistently defensible claim to represent the decision of the citizenry as a whole. A democratic decision must respect all citizens' equal freedoms as both authors and addressees, but what this means is itself open to political controversy. To show a decision is democratic, therefore, one needs to show that it respects all citizens' equal freedoms on the interpretation of those freedoms chosen by the citizens themselves. This is the idea expressed by Principle (I). To avoid an infinite regress, however, one cannot sort this out by deciding for oneself whose interpretation of equal freedoms is "right," or simply looking to see which "the people themselves" have picked. All one can do is to sort through competing claims in Socratic fashion to see which holds up as most consistent. This is Principle (II). Together, these principles show what it means to call this theory both historical and Socratic.

To show how this sort of critique can be given some teeth, Principle (II)* then works out four conditions any consistent democratic claim will have to meet. I call these the *conceptual condition*, the *practical condition*, the *historical baseline*, and the *condition of exclusivity*. In discussing some examples of how they might be put to use, I tried to emphasize the importance of context and also the dynamic and open-ended nature of the judgments this sort of theory allows one to make. One must always engage with shifting political realities and think through controversies across the points of view of all contending parties on the ground. One can thus defend judgments *in medias res*, but one must also remain attentive to which future developments might either reinforce these judgments or call them into question. One way of taking the theory, then, is as a critique of democratic judgment that seeks to make it aware of its own limits.

I have argued that this theory has a number of strengths. It provides a solution, drawn from Hegel but reworked in a thoroughly democratic way, to the centuries-old problem in democratic theory I called the paradox of authorization. That does not mean it hopes to end disagreements over democratic change. To the contrary, by providing a Socratic and consistently democratic way of arguing through those struggles, it gives up on the hopeless search for any ultimate foundation that might take the politics out of politics, and simply suggests that as struggles continue to unfold, we do better to argue about them in these terms than in others. Democratic elenchus also provides a distinctive account of what makes a "people" a "people." A people simply means all those citizens subject to a common political power, considered under conditions of equal freedom. But a "people" is only a practical principle that democratic judgments must not contradict; it is not a freestanding sociological entity "out there" that we might locate and simply allow to rule (for instance, by clearing away its enemies). This does not yet solve the further "boundary problem," but it does at least guard against populisms that trade on deflecting attention from the power relations among those who claim to speak for "the people" and everyone else. Finally, because the theory provides a *general framework* for defending *particular judgments* in context, it avoids familiar pitfalls on either side of longstanding debates over "universal values," and supports principled objections to any effort to impose a particular vision of democracy or progress on persons who are not best understood as having chosen it for themselves.

In closing I would like to address two foreseeable objections. The first worries that the theory is too conservative, too accepting of the way things have turned out even when this is better seen as a result of unaccountable power than as expressing popular consent. I may, of course, have erred this way in judging certain cases, but if so, then I have suggested that the way to correct this is still to argue it out within the general framework laid out by the theory. But there is a deeper issue because it is true that one of the theory's major claims is that one cannot responsibly argue in democracy's name without giving at least some weight to evidence of what actual citizens decide. I have insisted this does not mean that what is widely accepted is necessarily right, but it does mean that some criticisms of the status quo will not be defensible, even if supported by very good reasons, so long as they are not also accepted by those citizens who would have to live with their results. One must see that there is a bullet to bite here either way. I mean to stress that my view does not rule out the value of more radical utopian critiques, in raising questions and possibly opening up new avenues for subsequent political action. But it does mean that showing such critiques deserve to win out requires more than making arguments; it also requires political organizing to demonstrate a claim that one's fellow citizens endorse them. And this means engaging with others in a political way, not only to criticize or proselytize but also to work out common decisions in awareness of the political relations one is building and refashioning in the process. This means sometimes one will need to revise one's own ex ante views, but it might also mean that one discovers new avenues for change, more closely tied to the actual concerns of other citizens and therefore both more possible and arguably more important. It might even be that political theory could attend more seriously to the perspective of political agents in their interactions and less exclusively to the ideals and ends they claim to pursue. On these points I rather take democratic elenchus to side with Marx.

Finally, an opposite objection may see in this theory only another in a long line of attempts to revive the tired fetish of progress, with all its self-serving biases and political perils. But I take a historical and Socratic theory to support and require rigorous criticism of every such attempt, just because they always divert attention from the problem of defending political judgments in a thoroughly democratic way, which this theory places front and center. And yet it is also true that democratic elenchus does not limit itself to showing up illusions. If having the right religious or rational beliefs is no guarantee of making good decisions, then neither is not having the wrong ones, just because politics is about more than beliefs. What politics also requires is action of a sort capable of reaching collective decisions and putting them into effect, and this always creates new relations of power both among those persons involved in deciding and between them and all the others their decisions will affect. The point of critical principles of judgment of the sort I have defended is that they can play a role in reflecting on how democratic citizens might go about this in better rather than worse ways, as they work out answers for themselves (or fail to), and while remaining attentive to the very real risks contained in every political act. These are among the sort of questions that preoccupied theorists such as Kant, whatever one thinks of their answers. But they are questions that have too often been overshadowed in more recent theory further removed from the perspective of citizens who might actually participate in politics. Popular revolutions and struggles over democratic change have not ceased in recent times. Nor have they ceased to pose fundamental questions about the legitimacy of competing acts and orders defended in democracy's name. They deserve political theory that takes seriously both them and the questions that they pose.

Appendix

The following table lists forty-seven countries widely considered democratic without interruption since at least 1999. Country selection was based on rankings from Monty G. Marshall and Keith Jaggers, *Polity IV Project: Political Regime Characteristics and Transitions, 1800–2013* (Severn, MD: Center for Systemic Peace, 2010), http://www.systemicpeace.org/inscr/inscr.htm; and José Antonio Cheibub, Jennifer Gandhi, and James Raymond Vreeland, *Democracy and Dictatorship Revisited Dataset*, https://netfiles.uiuc.edu/cheibub/www/DD_page.html; with discrepancies resolved on my own appraisal of relevant histories. These are all such countries with populations of at least 4 million—besides the United Kingdom, where the lack of a discrete set of constitutional texts precludes one-to-one comparison with other countries' constitutions. For Israel, I followed the selection of "Basic Laws" at http://www.knesset.gov.il/description/eng/eng_mimshal_yesod.htm. Several borderline cases were excluded because of disagreement over whether they were democratic or had become so by 1999. Use of these datasets does not imply a substantive endorsement of their methodology, since my aim is only to provide a relatively uncontroversial selection. Because of broad agreement across cases, including somewhat smaller states or more recent democracies does not greatly alter the results.

An "X" indicates that the relevant principle appears in at least one *explicit provision* in the country's *formal constitutional text*. This means the numbers are extremely conservative, since many countries have established the same principles through normal legislation. Because my point is to identify areas of broad agreement, however, the case is most uncontroversially made by limiting myself to the narrowest possible text base, namely formal constitutional texts. I have not counted general statements of principle in constitutional preambles, but I did count the specific enumerated provisions in the Preamble to the French Constitution of 1946 and the 1789 Declaration of the Rights of Man and Citizen it incorporates, as well as the Preamble to the 1975 Constitution of Papua New Guinea. Here, I have listed principles of "public planning" and "private property" separately, which reflects their typical presentation in the constitutional texts. In this book, I have combined these on conceptual grounds into a single principle of a "public planning power compatible with rights to private property,"

Table A.1 **Principles of Democracy's Social Dimension**

Country	Social Emancipation	Protective Legislation	Guaranteed Minimums	Right to Organize	Public Planning	Private Property
First Wave						
1 Switzerland	X	X	X	X	X	X
2 New Zealand		X				
3 USA	X					
4 France	X	X	X	X	X	X
5 Canada			X		X	
6 Belgium	X	X	X	X		X
7 Norway	X			X		X
8 Australia			X			
9 Denmark	X		X			X
10 Netherlands	X		X	X	X	X
11 Sweden	X	X	X	X		X
12 Finland	X	X	X			X
13 Ireland			X	X	X	X
Second Wave						
14 Austria	X	X	X	X		X
15 Italy	X	X	X	X	X	X
16 Israel	X					
17 Germany	X	X	X	X	X	X
18 Costa Rica	X	X	X	X	X	X
19 India	X	X	X	X	X	X
20 Japan	X	X	X	X		X
21 Colombia	X	X	X	X	X	X
Third Wave						
22 Papua New Guinea	X	X			X	X
23 Greece	X	X	X	X	X	X
24 Portugal	X	X	X	X	X	X
25 Spain	X	X	X	X	X	X
26 Dominican Republic	X	X	X	X	X	X
27 Bolivia	X	X	X	X	X	X
28 Turkey		X	X	X	X	X

Country	Social Emancipation	Protective Legislation	Guaranteed Minimums	Right to Organize	Public Planning	Private Property
29 Argentina	X	X	X	X	X	X
30 El Salvador	X	X	X	X	X	X
31 Brazil	X	X	X	X	X	X
32 Philippines	X	X	X	X	X	X
33 South Korea	X	X	X	X		X
34 Poland	X	X	X	X	X	X
35 Chile	X	X	X	X	X	X
36 Nicaragua	X	X	X	X	X	X
37 Romania	X	X	X	X	X	X
38 Hungary	X	X	X	X	X	X
39 Bulgaria	X	X	X	X	X	X
40 Benin	X	X	X	X	X	X
41 Czech Rep.	X	X	X	X	X	X
42 Slovakia	X	X	X	X	X	X
43 South Africa	X	X	X	X	X	X
44 Ghana	X	X	X	X	X	X
45 Guatemala	X	X	X	X	X	X
46 Taiwan		X	X		X	X
47 Indonesia	X	X	X	X	X	X
Totals	**41**	**39**	**42**	**38**	**35**	**42**
% all democracies	87.23%	82.98%	89.36%	80.85%	74.47%	89.36%
% since 1945	94.12%	97.06%	94.12%	91.18%	88.24%	97.06%
% since 1975	92.31%	100.00%	96.15%	92.31%	96.15%	100.00%

because unlike the other principles, these two potentially conflict and should thus be considered as two sides of a single judgment that limits each by recognizing also the other. Although I have also consulted constitutions of states widely considered nondemocracies, I have not included these here because my aim is to show not a correlation but which principles are widely supported across democracies (whether or not nondemocracies also support them).

BIBLIOGRAPHY

Achenwall, Gottfried. 1763. *Ius naturae in usum auditorum*, 5th rev. ed., 2 vols. Göttingen: Victorinus Bossiegelius. Volume two, *Iuris naturalis pars posterior*, was reprinted in the Akademie edition of Kant's *Gesammelte Schiften*, Vol. XIX.

Ackerman, Bruce. 1991–2014. *We the People*, 3 vols. Cambridge, MA: Harvard University Press.

Allison, Henry E. 1987. "Transcendental Idealism: The 'Two Aspect' View." In *New Essays on Kant*, eds. Bernard den Ouden and Marcia Moen. New York: Peter Lang.

———. 1990. *Kant's Theory of Freedom*. Cambridge, UK: Cambridge University Press.

———. 2004. *Kant's Transcendental Idealism*, 2nd ed. New Haven, CT: Yale University Press.

———. 2009. "Teleology and History in Kant: The Critical Foundations of Kant's Philosophy of History." In *Kant's Idea for a Universal History with a Cosmopolitan Aim: A Critical Guide*, eds. Amélie Oskenberg Rorty and James Schmidt. Cambridge, UK: Cambridge University Press.

———. 2011. *Kant's Groundwork for the Metaphysics of Morals: A Commentary*. Oxford: Oxford University Press.

Amann, Peter. 1970. "A 'Journée' in the Making: May 14, 1848." *Journal of Modern History* 42, no. 1: 42–69.

———. 1975. *Revolution and Mass Democracy: The Paris Club Movement in 1848*. Princeton, NJ: Princeton University Press.

Ameriks, Karl. 2000. *Kant's Theory of Mind: An Analysis of the Paralogisms of Pure Reason*. Oxford: Oxford University Press.

Annas, Julia. 1992. "Plato the Skeptic." In *Oxford Studies in Ancient Philosophy*, supp. vol., *Methods of Interpreting Plato and His Dialogues*, eds. James C. Klagge and Nicholas D. Smith, 43–72. Oxford: Oxford University Press.

Arendt, Hannah. 1992. *Lectures on Kant's Political Philosophy*, ed. Ronald Beiner. Chicago: University of Chicago Press.

Aristotle. 1984. *The Politics*, ed. and trans. Carnes Lord. Chicago: University of Chicago Press.

———. 1995. *The Complete Works of Aristotle: The Revised Oxford Translation*, ed. Jonathan Barnes, 2 vols. Princeton, NJ: Princeton University Press.

Avineri, Shlomo. 1972. *Hegel's Theory of the Modern State*. Cambridge, UK: Cambridge University Press.

Baumgarten, Alexander Gottlieb. 1760. *Initia philosophiae practicae primae acroamatice*. Halle: Carl Hermann Hemmerde.

———. 1763. *Ius naturae*. Halle: Carl Hermann Hemmerde.

Beck, Gunnar. 1999. "Autonomy, History, and Freedom in Kant's Political Philosophy." *History of European Ideas* 25: 217–41.

Beck, Lewis White. 1960. *A Commentary on Kant's Critique of Practical Reason*. Chicago: University of Chicago Press.

———. 1965. "The Fact of Reason: An Essay on Justification in Ethics." In *Studies in the Philosophy of Kant*, 200–14. Westport, CT: Greenwood Press.

Beck, Lewis White. 1971. "Kant and the Right of Revolution." *Journal of the History of Ideas* 32, no. 3: 411–22.

Beerbohm, Eric. 2012. *In Our Name: The Ethics of Democracy*. Princeton, NJ: Princeton University Press.

Beiser, Frederick C. 1987. *The Fate of Reason: German Philosophy from Kant to Fichte*. Cambridge, MA: Harvard University Press.

———. 1992. *Enlightenment, Revolution, and Romanticism: The Genesis of Modern German Political Thought, 1790–1800*. Cambridge, MA: Harvard University Press.

———. 2005. *Hegel*. New York: Routledge.

———. 2011. *The German Historicist Tradition*. Oxford: Oxford University Press.

Benhabib, Seyla. 2006. *Another Cosmopolitanism*, ed. Robert Post. Oxford: Oxford University Press.

———. 2011. *Dignity in Adversity: Human Rights in Troubled Times*. Cambridge, UK: Polity Press.

Benson, Hugh H. 2000. *Socratic Wisdom: The Model of Knowledge in Plato's Early Dialogues*. Oxford: Oxford University Press.

———. 2003. "The Method of Hypothesis in the *Meno*." In *Proceedings of the Boston Area Colloquium in Ancient Philosophy 18, 2002*, eds. John J. Cleary and Gary M. Gurtler. Boston, MA: Brill.

Berlin, Isaiah. 2002. *Freedom and Its Betrayal: Six Enemies of Human Liberty*. Princeton, NJ: Princeton University Press.

———. 2002. "Two Concepts of Liberty." In *Liberty: Incorporating Four Essays on Liberty*. Oxford: Oxford University Press.

———. 2013. *Against the Current: Essays in the History of Ideas*. Princeton, NJ: Princeton University Press.

———. 2013. *The Roots of Romanticism*. Princeton, NJ: Princeton University Press.

Bernal, Angélica Maria. 2014. "The Meaning and Perils of Presidential Refounding in Latin America." *Constellations* 21, no. 4: 440–56.

Bernstein, Irving. 1960. *The Lean Years: A History of the American Worker, 1920–1933*. Boston, MA: Houghton-Mifflin.

Beversluis, John. 1987. "Does Socrates Commit the Socratic Fallacy?" *American Philosophical Quarterly* 24, no. 3: 211–23.

Blanc, Louis. 1849. *La révolution de février au Luxembourg*. Paris: Michel-Lévy Frères.

Bloch, Ernst. 1951. *Subjekt-Objekt: Erlaüterungen zu Hegel*. Berlin: Aufbau Verlag.

Borowiak, Craig T. 2011. *Accountability and Democracy: The Pitfalls and Promise of Popular Control*. New York: Oxford University Press.

Brake, Elizabeth. 2012. *Minimizing Marriage: Marriage, Morality, and the Law*. New York: Oxford University Press.

Brett, Annabel, and James Tully, eds. 2006. *Rethinking the Foundations of Modern Political Thought*. Cambridge, UK: Cambridge University Press.

Brettschneider, Corey. 2007. *Democratic Rights: The Substance of Self-Government*. Princeton, NJ: Princeton University Press.

Brickhouse, Thomas C., and Nicholas D. Smith. 1994. *Plato's Socrates*. Oxford: Oxford University Press.

Brownlee, Kimberley. 2012. *Conscience and Conviction: The Case for Civil Disobedience*. Oxford: Oxford University Press.

Brucker, Iacob. 1766–1767. *Historia critica philosophiae*, 2nd ed. Leipzig: Heirs of Wiedemann & Reich.

Busch, Werner. 1979. *Die Entstehung der kriticshen Rechtsphilosophie Kants, 1762–1780*. Berlin: de Gruyter.

Byrd, Sharon, and Joachim Hruschka. 2010. *Kant's Doctrine of Right: A Commentary*. Cambridge, UK: Cambridge University Press.

Chamley, Paul. 1963. *Economie politique et philosophie chez Steuart et Hegel*. Paris: Dalloz.

Chauncey, George. 2004. *Why Marriage? The History Shaping Today's Debate Over Gay Equality*. New York: Basic Books.

Christiano, Thomas. 2008. *The Constitution of Equality: Democratic Authority and Its Limits*. Oxford: Oxford University Press.

Cohen, Joshua. 2009. *Philosophy, Politics, Democracy: Selected Essays*. Cambridge, MA: Harvard University Press.

Connolly, William E. 1995. *The Ethos of Pluralization*. Minneapolis: University of Minnesota Press.
———. 1999. *Why I Am Not a Secularist*. Minneapolis: University of Minnesota Press.
———. 2002. *Identity/Difference: Democratic Negotiations of Political Paradox*, expanded ed. Minneapolis: University of Minnesota Press.
———. 2005. *Pluralism*. Durham, NC: Duke University Press.
Cook, Philip J., and Kristin A. Goss. 2014. *The Gun Debate: What Everyone Needs to Know*. Oxford: Oxford University Press.
Dahl, Robert A. 1989. *Democracy and Its Critics*. New Haven, CT: Yale University Press.
Descartes, René. 1998. *Regulae ad directionem ingenii* [Rules for the Direction of the Natural Intelligence: A Bilingual Edition of the Cartesian Treatise on Method]. Ed. and trans. George Heffernan. Atlanta, GA: Rodopi.
Dickey, Laurence. 1987. *Religion, Economics, and the Politics of Spirit, 1770–1807*. Cambridge, UK: Cambridge University Press.
Duggan, Lisa, and Richard Kim. 2006. "Beyond Gay Marriage." In *Sex Wars: Sexual Dissent and Political Culture*, 10th anniversary ed., eds. Lisa Duggan and Nan D. Hunter, 231–8. New York: Routledge.
Dworkin, Ronald. 1986. *Law's Empire*. Cambridge, MA: Harvard University Press.
Ellis, Elisabeth. 2005. *Kant's Politics: Provisional Theory for an Uncertain World*. New Haven, CT: Yale University Press.
———. 2008. *Provisional Politics: Kantian Arguments in Policy Context*. New Haven, CT: Yale University Press.
———, ed. 2012. *Kant's Political Theory: Interpretations and Applications*. University Park: Pennsylvania State University Press.
Elshtain, Jean Bethke. 1981. "Kant, Politics, & Persons: The Implications of His Moral Philosophy." *Polity* 14, no. 2: 205–21.
Ely, John Hart. 1980. *Democracy and Distrust: A Theory of Judicial Review*. Cambridge, MA: Harvard University Press.
Engel, Stephen M. 2007. "Organizational Identity as a Constraint on Strategic Action: A Comparative Analysis of Gay and Lesbian Interest Groups." *Studies in American Political Development* 21, no. 1: 66–91.
Erhard, Johann Benjamin. 1795. *Ueber das Recht des Volks zu einer Revolution*. Jena and Leipzig: Christian Ernst Gabler.
Estlund, David M. 2008. *Democratic Authority: A Philosophical Framework*. Princeton, NJ: Princeton University Press.
Ettelbrick, Paula L. 1989. "Since When Is Marriage a Path to Liberation?" *OUT/LOOK* 6: 14–7.
Euben, J. Peter. 1997. *Corrupting Youth: Political Education, Democratic Culture, and Political Theory*. Princeton, NJ: Princeton University Press.
Feuerbach, P. J. A. 1798. *Anti-Hobbes: Oder über die Grenzen der höchsten Gewalt und das Zwangsrecht der Bürger gegen den Oberherrn*. Erfurt: Hennings.
Fichte, J. G. 1964– . *Gesamtausgabe der Bayerischen Akademie der Wissenschaften*, eds. Erich Fuchs, Reinhard Lauth, Hans Jacobs, and Hans Gliwitzsky. Stuttgart-Bad Cannstatt: Frommann.
———. 2013. *Addresses to the German Nation*, trans. and eds. Isaac Nakhimovsky, Béla Kapossy, and Keith Tribe. Indianapolis, IN: Hackett.
Fine, Gail. 2003. *Plato on Knowledge and Forms*. Oxford: Oxford University Press.
Fineman, Martha Albertson. 2004. *The Autonomy Myth: A Theory of Dependency*. New York: New Press.
Flikschuh, Katrin. 2008. "Sidestepping Morality: Korsgaard on Kant's No-Right to Revolution." *Jahrbuch für Recht und Ethik* 16: 127–45.
———. 2012. "Elusive Unity: The General Will in Hobbes and Kant." *Hobbes Studies* 25: 21–42.
Forbath, William E. 1991. *Law and the Shaping of the American Labor Movement*. Cambridge, MA: Harvard University Press.
Forst, Rainer. 2007. *The Right to Justification: Elements of a Constructivist Theory of Justice*, trans. Jeffrey Flynn. New York: Columbia University Press.
Forster, Michael N. 1998. *Hegel's Idea of a Phenomenology of Spirit*. Chicago: University of Chicago Press.

Forster, Michael N. 2008. *Kant and Skepticism*. Princeton, NJ: Princeton University Press.
Forsyth, Murray. 1978. *Reason and Revolution: The Political Thought of the Abbé Sieyès*. Leicester, UK: Leicester University Press.
Fossen, Thomas. 2014. "The Grammar of Political Obligation." *Politics, Philosophy & Economics* 13, no. 3: 215–36.
Franco, Paul. 1999. *Hegel's Philosophy of Freedom*. New Haven, CT: Yale University Press.
Frank, Jason. 2010. *Constituent Moments: Enacting the People in Postrevolutionary America*. Durham, NC: Duke University Press.
Franke, Katherine. 2006. "The Politics of Same-Sex Marriage Politics." *Columbia Journal of Gender and Law* 15: 236–48.
Frankfurter, Felix, and Nathan Greene. 1930. *The Labor Injunction*. New York: MacMillan.
Frederick II of Prussia. 1740. *Anti-Machiavel, ou Essai de Critique sur le Prince de Machiavel, publié par M. de Voltaire*. The Hague.
Furet, François. 1992. *Revolutionary France, 1770–1880*. Malden, MA: Blackwell.
Furet, François, and Ran Halevi. 1989. "Introduction." In *Orateurs de la Révolution française, I, Les Constituants*. Paris: Gallimard.
Gadamer, Hans-Georg. 1980. *Dialogue and Dialectic: Eight Hermeneutical Studies on Plato*, trans. P. Christopher Smith. New Haven, CT: Yale University Press.
———. 1991. *Plato's Dialectical Ethics: Phenomenological Interpretations Relating to the Philebus*, trans. Robert M. Wallace. New Haven, CT: Yale University Press.
Gambetta, Léon. 1880–1885. *Discours et plaidoyers politiques de M. Gambetta*, 11 vols., ed. Joseph Reinach. Paris: G. Charpentier.
Geach, Peter. 1966. "Plato's Euthyphro: An Analysis and Commentary." *Monist* 50, no. 3: 369–82.
Gentzler, Jyl. 1991. "'συμφωνεῖν' in Plato's *Phaedo*." *Phronesis* 36, no. 3: 265–76.
———. 2005. "How to Know the Good: The Moral Epistemology of Plato's *Republic*." *Philosophical Review* 114, no. 4: 469–96.
Geuss, Raymond. 2008. *Philosophy and Real Politics*. Princeton, NJ: Princeton University Press.
Gillette, William. 1979. *Retreat from Reconstruction, 1869–1879*. Baton Rouge: Louisiana State University Press.
Ginsburg, Ruth Bader. 1985. "Some Thoughts on Autonomy and Equality in Relation to *Roe v. Wade*." *North Carolina Law Review* 63: 375–86.
Goldman, Loren. 2012. "In Defense of Blinders: On Kant, Political Hope, and the Need for Practical Belief." *Political Theory* 40, no. 4: 497–523.
Gonzalez, Francisco J. 1998. *Dialectic and Dialogue: Plato's Practice of Philosophical Inquiry*. Evanston, IL: Northwestern University Press.
Goss, Kristin A. 2006. *Disarmed: The Missing Movement for Gun Control in America*. Princeton, NJ: Princeton University Press.
Gossez, Rémi. 1968. *Les ouvriers de Paris*, Vol. 1: *L'Organisation, 1848–1851*. Bibliothèque de la Révolution de 1848, Vol. 23. Paris: Société d'histoire de la Révolution de 1848.
Green, Jeffrey E. 2009. *The Eyes of the People: Democracy in an Age of Spectatorship*. Oxford: Oxford University Press.
Griswold, Charles L. Jr. 1988. "Plato's Metaphilosophy: Why Plato Wrote Dialogues." In *Platonic Writings/Platonic Readings*, ed. Charles L. Griswold Jr., 143–67. Boston, MA: Routledge & Kegan Paul.
Grote, George. 1888. *Plato and the Other Companions of Socrates*, 2nd ed. London: John Murray.
Guizot, François. 1821. *Des moyens de gouvernement et d'opposition dans l'état actuel de la France*. Paris: Ladvocat.
Gutmann, Amy, and Dennis Thompson. 1996. *Democracy and Disagreement*. Cambridge, MA: Harvard University Press.
Guyer, Paul. 2000. *Kant on Freedom, Law, and Happiness*. Cambridge, UK: Cambridge University Press.
———. 2007. *Kant's Groundwork for the Metaphysics of Morals*. New York: Continuum.
Habermas, Jürgen. 1960. "Verrufener Fortschritt—Verkanntes Jahrhundert: Zur Kritik an der Geschichtsphilosophie." *Merkur* 14: 468–77.
———. 1984–1987. *The Theory of Communicative Action*, 2 vols., trans. Thomas McCarthy. Boston, MA: Beacon Press.

———. 1985. "Civil Disobedience: Litmus Test for the Democratic Constitutional State." *Berkeley Journal of Sociology* 30: 95–116.

———. 1989. *The Structural Transformation of The Public Sphere: An Inquiry into a Category of Bourgeois Society*. Cambridge, MA: MIT Press.

———. 1990. *Moral Consciousness and Communicative Action*, trans. Christian Lenhardt and Shierry Weber Nicholson. Cambridge, MA: MIT Press.

———. 1996. *Between Facts and Norms: Contributions to a Discourse Theory of Law and Democracy*, trans. William Rehg. Cambridge, MA: MIT Press.

———. 2001. "Constitutional Democracy: A Paradoxical Union of Contradictory Principles?," trans. William Rehg. *Political Theory* 29, no. 6: 766–81.

Hamann, J. G. 1949–1957. *Sämmtliche Werke, historisch-kitische Ausgabe*, 6 vols., ed. Josef Nadler. Vienna: Herder & Co.

———. 1956–1979. *Briefwechsel*, 7 vols., ed. Authur Henkel et. al. Frankfurt am Main: Insel.

Hamon, Léo, ed. 1991. *Les opportunistes: Les débuts de la République aux républicains*. Paris: Maison des sciences de l'homme.

Hänsel, Werner. 1926. "Kants Lehre vom Widerstandsrecht." *Kant-Studien Egränzungsheft* 60.

Harris, H. S. 1972–1983. *Hegel's Development*, 2 vols. Oxford: Clarendon Press.

Hartmann, Klaus. 1972. "Hegel: A Non-Metaphysical View." In *Hegel: A Collection of Critical Essays*, ed. Alasdair MacIntyre. Notre Dame, IN: Notre Dame University Press.

Hegel, G. W. F. 1968– . *Gesammelte Werke*, ed. Rheinisch-Westfälischen Akademie der Wissenschaften. Hamburg: Felix Meiner.

———. 1971. *Werke in zwanzig Bänden*, eds. Eva Moldenhauer and Karl Markus Michel. Frankfurt am Main: Suhrkamp.

———. 1983–2007. *Vorlesungen*, 17 vols., eds. C. Becker et al. Hamburg: Meiner.

———. 1999. *Political Writings*, eds. Laurence Dickey and H. B. Nisbet, trans. H. B. Nisbet. Cambridge, UK: Cambridge University Press.

———. 2006–2009. *Lectures on the History of Philosophy 1825–6*, 3 vols., ed. and trans. Robert F. Brown. Oxford: Oxford University Press.

Heimsoeth, Heinz. 1967. "Plato in Kants Werdegang." In *Studien zu Kants philosophischer Entwicklung*, eds. Heinz Heimsoeth, Dieter Henrich, and Giorgio Tonelli, 124–43. Hildesheim: Georg Olms.

Henrich, Dieter. 1975. "Die Deduktion des Sittengesetzes. Über die Gründe der Dunkelheit des letzten Abschnittes von Kants *Grundlegung der Metaphysik der Sitten*." In *Denken im Schatten des Nihilismus: Festschrift für Wilhelm Weischedel*, ed. Alexander Schwann, 55–110. Darmstadt: Wissenschaftliche Buchgesellschaft.

———. 1989. "Kant's Notion of a Deduction and the Methodological Background of the First Critique." In *Kant's Transcendental Deductions: The Three Critiques and the Opus Postumum*, ed. Eckart Förster, 29–46. Stanford, CA: Stanford University Press.

———. 1993. "On the Meaning of Rational Action in the State." In *Kant and Political Philosophy: The Contemporary Legacy*, eds. Ronald Beiner and William James Booth. New Haven, CT: Yale University Press.

Herder, Johann Gottfried von. 1877–1913. *Sämmtliche Werke*, 33 vols., ed. Bernhard Suphan. Berlin: Weidmann.

Herman, Barbara. 1996. *The Practice of Moral Judgment*. Cambridge, MA: Harvard University Press.

Hill, Thomas E. Jr. 2002. "Questions about Kant's Opposition to Revolution." *The Journal of Value Inquiry* 36: 283–98.

Hochstrasser, T. J. 2004. *Natural Law Theories in the Early Enlightenment*. Cambridge, UK: Cambridge University Press.

Holtman, Sarah Williams. 2002. "Revolution, Contradiction, and Kantian Citizenship." In *Kant's Metaphysics of Morals: Interpretive Essays*, ed. Mark Timmons, 209–31. Oxford: Oxford University Press.

Honig, Bonnie. 1993. *Political Theory and the Displacement of Politics*. Ithaca, NY: Cornell University Press.

———. 2001. "Dead Rights, Live Futures: A Reply To Habermas's 'Constitutional Democracy.'" *Political Theory* 29, no. 6: 792–805.

Honig, Bonnie. 2006. "Another Cosmopolitanism? Law and Politics in the New Europe." In *Another Cosmopolitanism*, ed. Seyla Benhabib, 102–27. New York: Oxford University Press.

———. 2009. *Emergency Politics: Paradox, Law, Democracy*. Princeton, NJ: Princeton University Press.

Honneth, Axel. 1995. *The Struggle for Recognition: The Moral Grammar of Social Conflicts*, trans. Joel Anderson. Cambridge, UK: Polity Press.

———. 2012. *The Pathologies of Individual Freedom*. Princeton, NJ: Princeton University Press.

———. 2014. *Freedom's Right: The Social Foundations of Democratic Life*. Cambridge, UK: Polity Press.

Hont, Istvan. 2005. *Jealousy of Trade: International Competition and the Nation-State in Historical Perspective*. Cambridge, MA: Harvard University Press.

Horkheimer, Max, and Theodor Adorno. 2002. *Dialectic of Enlightenment: Philosophical Fragments*, trans. Edmund Jephcott. Palo Alto, CA: Stanford University Press.

Horstmann, Rolf-Peter. 2008. "The *Phenomenology of Spirit* as a 'Transcendentalistic' Argument for a Monistic Ontology." In *Hegel's Phenomenology of Spirit: A Critical Guide*, eds. Dean Moyar and Michael Quante. Cambridge, UK: Cambridge University Press.

Huard, Raymond. 1988. "Un parti en mutation: Le parti républicain (1848–1851)." In *Des Républiques françaises*, eds. Paul Isoart and Christiane Bidegaray. Paris: Economica.

———. 1991. *Le suffrage universel en France: 1848–1946*. Paris: Aubier.

Humboldt, Wilhelm von. 1969. *The Limits of State Action*. Cambridge, UK: Cambridge University Press.

Hume, David. 2000. *An Enquiry Concerning Human Understanding*, ed. Tom L. Beauchamp. Oxford: Clarendon Press.

———. 2007. *A Treatise of Human Nature*, eds. David Fate Norton and Mary J. Norton. Oxford: Clarendon Press.

Hunter, Ian. 2001. *Rival Enlightenments: Civil and Metaphysical Philosophy in Early Modern Germany*. Cambridge, UK: Cambridge University Press.

———. 2012. "Kant's Political Thought in the Prussian Enlightenment." In *Kant's Political Theory: Interpretations and Applications*, ed. Elisabeth Ellis, 170–207. University Park: Pennsylvania State University Press.

Hyppolite, Jean. 1974. *Genesis and Structure of Hegel's Phenomenology of Spirit*. Evanston, IL: Northwestern University Press.

———. 1996. *Introduction to Hegel's Philosophy of History*, eds. Bond Harris and Jacqueline B. Spurlock. Gainesville: University Press of Florida.

Irwin, Terrence. 1995. *Plato's Ethics*. Oxford: Oxford University Press.

Jakob, Ludwig Heinrich. 1794. *Antimachivel, oder über die Grenzen des bürgerlichen Gehorsams*. Halle: Renger.

Kahn, Charles. 1996. *Plato and the Socratic Dialogue: The Philosophical Use of a Literary Form*. Cambridge, UK: Cambridge University Press.

Kant, Immanuel. 1902– . *Kants Gesammelte Schriften, herausgegeben von der Preussichen Akademie der Wissenschaften zu Berlin*. Berlin: de Gruyter.

Keenan, Alan. 2003. *Democracy in Question: Democratic Openness in a Time of Political Closure*. Stanford, CA: Stanford University Press.

Kelly, George Armstrong. 1969. *Idealism, Politics, and History: Sources of Hegelian Thought*. Cambridge, UK: Cambridge University Press.

Keyssar, Alexander. 2009. *The Right to Vote: The Contested History of Democracy in the United States*, rev. ed. New York: Basic Books.

Kleingeld, Pauline. 1995. *Fortschritt und Vernunft: Zur Geschichtsphilosophie Kants*. Leiden: Königshausen & Neumann.

———. 2012. *Kant and Cosmopolitanism: The Philosophical Ideal of World Citizenship*. Cambridge, UK: Cambridge University Press.

Kneale, William, and Martha Kneale. 1962. *The Development of Logic*. Oxford: Oxford University Press.

Knight, Jack, and James Johnson. 2011. *The Priority of Democracy: Political Consequences of Pragmatism*. Princeton, NJ: Princeton University Press.

Korsgaard, Christine M. 1996. *Creating the Kingdom of Ends*. Cambridge, UK: Cambridge University Press.
———. 1996. *The Sources of Normativity*. Cambridge, UK: Cambridge University Press.
———. 2008. *The Constitution of Agency: Essays on Practical Reason and Moral Psychology*. Oxford: Oxford University Press.
———. 2009. *Self-Constitution: Agency, Identity, and Integrity*. Oxford: Oxford University Press.
Koselleck, Reinhart. 1988. *Critique and Crisis: Enlightenment and the Pathogenesis of Modern Society*. Cambridge, MA: MIT Press.
Kramer, Larry D. 2004. *The People Themselves: Popular Constitutionalism and Judicial Review*. New York: Oxford University Press.
Kraut, Richard. 1983. "Comments on Gregory Vlastos, 'The Socratic Elenchus.'" *Oxford Studies in Ancient Philosophy* 1: 59–70.
———. 1984. *Socrates and the State*. Princeton, NJ: Princeton University Press.
Krienes, James. 2004. "Hegel's Critique of Pure Mechanism." *European Journal of Philosophy* 12, no. 1: 38–74.
———. 2006. "Hegel's Metaphysics: Changing the Debate." *Philosophy Compass* 1, no. 5: 466–80.
Kuehn, Manfred. 2005. "The Reception of Hume in Germany." In *The Reception of David Hume in Europe*, ed. Peter Jones, 115–30. New York: Thoemmes Continuum.
Landemore, Hélène. 2013. *Democratic Reason: Politics, Collective Intelligence, and the Rule of the Many*. Princeton, NJ: Princeton University Press.
Lane, Melissa. 1998. *Method and Politics in Plato's Statesman*. Cambridge, UK: Cambridge University Press.
Larmore, Charles. 2008. *The Autonomy of Morality*. Cambridge, UK: Cambridge University Press.
Laursen, John Christian. 1992. *The Politics of Skepticism in the Ancients, Montaigne, Hume, and Kant*. New York: E.J. Brill.
Lear, Jonathan. 2006. "Myth and Allegory in Plato's Republic." In *The Blackwell Guide to Plato's Republic*, ed. Gerasimos Santas, 25–43. Malden, MA: Blackwell.
Ledru-Rollin, Alexandre-Auguste. 1879. *Discours politiques et écrits divers*, 2 vols. Paris: Librairie Germer Baillière.
Lefort, Claude. 1988. *Democracy and Political Theory*, trans. David Macey. Minneapolis: University of Minnesota Press.
Lesher, J. H. 1987. "Socrates' Disavowal of Knowledge." *Journal of the History of Philosophy* 25: 275–88.
Leuchtenberg, William E. 1995. *The Supreme Court Reborn: The Constitutional Revolution in the Age of Roosevelt*. New York: Oxford University Press.
Liddell, Henry George, and Robert Scott. 1996. *A Greek-English Lexicon*. Oxford: Clarendon Press.
Longuenesse, Béatrice. 2007. *Hegel's Critique of Metaphysics*. Cambridge, UK: Cambridge University Press.
Losurdo, Domenico. 1983. *Autocensura e compromesso nel pensiero politico di Kant*. Naples: Bibliopolis.
Lukács, Georg. 1977. *The Young Hegel*. Cambridge, MA: MIT Press.
Luther, Martin. 1883– . *D. Martin Luthers Werke: Kritische Gesamtausgabe*. Weimar: Hermann Böhlaus Nachfolger.
MacIntyre, Alasdair. 1981. *After Virtue: A Study in Moral Theory*. Notre Dame, IN: University of Notre Dame Press.
Maliks, Reidar. 2013. "The State of Freedom: Kant and His Conservative Critics." In *Freedom and the Construction of Europe*, Vol. 2, eds. Quentin Skinner and Martin van Gelderen, 188–207. Cambridge, UK: Cambridge University Press.
———. 2014. *Kant's Politics in Context*. Oxford: Oxford University Press.
Manin, Bernard. 1987. "On Legitimacy and Political Deliberation." *Political Theory* 15, no. 3: 338–68.
———. 1997. *The Principles of Representative Government*. Cambridge, UK: Cambridge University Press.
Markell, Patchen. 2003. *Bound by Recognition*. Princeton, NJ: Princeton University Press.
Marrast, Armand. 1842. "Suffrage Universel." *Dictionnaire politique, encyclopédie du langage et de la science politiques*, eds. Eugène Declerc and Louis-Antione Pagnerre. Paris: Pagnerre.

Marx, Karl. 1982– . *Marx-Engels Gesamtausgabe*. Berlin: Dietz.
McCormick, John P. 2007. "Rousseau's Rome and the Repudiation of Populist Republicanism." *Critical Review of International Social and Political Philosophy* 10, no. 1: 3–27.
McDowell, John. 2009. *Having the World in View: Essays on Kant, Hegel, and Sellars*. Cambridge, MA: Harvard University Press.
McFadden, Tanner. 2011. "Actuality, Integrity, and Freedom in Hegel's Philosophy of Right." Paper presented at Western Political Science Association Annual Meeting. http://ssrn.com/abstract=1766821.
Meckstroth, Christopher. 2009. "The Struggle for Democracy: Paradox and History in Democratic Progress." *Constellations* 16, no. 3: 410–28.
———. 2012. "Socratic Method and Political Science." *American Political Science Review* 106, no. 3: 644–60.
Meinecke, Friedrich. 1950. "Mass Machiavellism." In *The German Catastrophe: Reflections and Recollections*, 51–5. Cambridge, MA: Harvard University Press.
———. 1984. *Machiavellism: The Doctrine of Raison d'Etat and Its Place in Modern History*. New York: Routledge and Keegan Paul.
Mendelssohn, Moses. 1843–1845. *Gesammelte Schriften*, 7 vols., ed. Georg Benjamin Mendelssohn. Leipzig: F.A. Brockhaus.
Metz, Tamara. 2010. *Untying the Knot: Marriage, the State and the Case for Their Divorce*. Princeton, NJ: Princeton University Press.
Michelman, Frank I. 1998. "Constitutional Authorship." In *Constitutionalism: Philosophical Foundations*, ed. Larry Alexander. Cambridge, UK: Cambridge University Press.
Montesquieu, Charles-Louis de Secondat de. 1749. *De l'esprit dex Loix*, rev. 2nd ed. Amsterdam: Chatelain.
Morris, Aldon D. 1984. *The Origins of the Civil Rights Movement: Black Communities Organizing for Change*. New York: Free Press.
Möser, Justus. 1798. *Vermischte Schriften*. Zweiter Theil. Berlin: Friedrich Nicolai.
Mosher, Michael A. 1984. "The Particulars of a Universal Politics: Hegel's Adaptation of Montesquieu's Typology." *American Political Science Review* 78, no. 1: 179–88.
Mouffe, Chantal. 2000. *The Democratic Paradox*. New York: Verso.
Muthu, Sankar. 2003. *Enlightenment Against Empire*. Princeton, NJ: Princeton University Press.
Nakhimovsky, Isaac. 2011. *The Closed Commercial State: Perpetual Peace and Commercial Society from Rousseau to Fichte*. Princeton, NJ: Princeton University Press.
Näsström, Sofia. 2007. "The Legitimacy of the People." *Political Theory* 35, no. 5: 624–58.
Natorp, Paul. 2004. *Plato's Theory of Ideas: An Introduction to Idealism*, trans. Vasilis Politis and John Connolly. Sankt Augustin, Germany: Akademia Verlag.
Neuhouser, Frederick. 2000. *Foundations of Hegel's Social Theory: Actualizing Freedom*. Cambridge, MA: Harvard University Press.
Nord, Philip. 1998. *The Republican Moment: Struggles for Democracy in Nineteenth-Century France*. Cambridge, MA: Harvard University Press.
Nussbaum, Martha. 2010. *From Disgust to Humanity: Sexual Orientation and Constitutional Law*. New York: Oxford University Press.
O'Neil, Onora. 1989. *Constructions of Reason: Explorations of Kant's Practical Philosophy*. Cambridge, UK: Cambridge University Press.
———. 2012. "Kant and the Social Contract Tradition." In *Kant's Political Philosophy: Interpretations and Applications*, ed. Elisabeth Ellis, 25–41. University Park: Pennsylvania State University Press.
Ochoa Espejo, Paulina. 2011. *The Time of Popular Sovereignty: Process and the Democratic State*. University Park: Pennsylvania State University Press.
Olson, Kevin. 2006. *Reflexive Democracy: Political Equality and the Welfare State*. Cambridge, MA: MIT Press.
———. 2007. "Paradoxes of Constitutional Democracy." *American Journal of Political Science* 51, no. 2: 330–43.
Otsuka, Michael. 2005. *Libertarianism without Inequality*. Oxford: Oxford University Press.
Pasquino, Pasquale. 1998. *Sieyes et l'invention de la constitution en France*. Paris: Jacob.

Patten, Allen. 1999. *Hegel's Idea of Freedom*. Oxford: Oxford University Press.
Patterson, James T. 2001. *Brown v. Board of Education: A Civil Rights Milestone and Its Troubled Legacy*. Oxford: Oxford University Press.
Pettit, Philip. 2012. *On the People's Terms: A Republican Theory and Model of Democracy*. Cambridge, UK: Cambridge University Press.
Pinello, Daniel R. 2006. *America's Struggle for Same-Sex Marriage*. Cambridge, UK: Cambridge University Press.
Pinkard, Terry. 1994. *Hegel's Phenomenology: The Sociality of Reason*. Cambridge, UK: Cambridge University Press.
———. 2000. *Hegel: A Biography*. Cambridge, UK: Cambridge University Press.
Pippin, Robert B. 1989. *Hegel's Idealism: The Satisfactions of Self-Consciousness*. Cambridge, UK: Cambridge University Press.
———. 2008. *Hegel's Practical Philosophy: Rational Agency as Ethical Life*. Cambridge, UK: Cambridge University Press.
Plant, Raymond. 1983. *Hegel: An Introduction*, 2nd ed. Oxford: Basil Blackwell, 1983.
Pöggeler, Otto. 1998. "Die Komposition der Phänomenologie des Geistes." In *Materialien zu Hegels "Phaenomenologie des Geistes*," 4th ed., eds. Hans Friedrich Fulda and Dieter Henrich, 329–90. Frankfurt am Main: Suhrkamp.
———. 1999. *Kegels Kritik der Romantik*. Munich: Fink, 1999.
Polansky, Ronald. 1985. "Professor Vlastos' Analysis of Socratic Elenchus." *Oxford Studies in Ancient Philosophy* 3: 247–60.
Polikoff, Nancy D. 2008. *Beyond Straight and Gay Marriage: Valuing All Families Under the Law*. Boston, MA: Beacon Press.
Polledri, Elena. 2000. "Friedrich Höderlin e la Fortuna di Platone Nel Settecento Tedesco." *Avevum* 74, no. 3: 789–812.
Popkin, Richard H. 1951. "David Hume: His Pyrrhonism and His Critique of Pyrrhonism." *Philosophical Quarterly* 1, no. 5: 385–407.
———. 1992. *The Third Force in Seventeenth-Century Thought*. Leiden: E.J. Brill.
———. 1993. *The High Road to Pyrrhonism*, eds. Richard A. Watson and James E. Force. Indianapolis, IN: Hackett.
Popper, Karl. 2002. *The Poverty of Historicism*. London: Routledge.
———. 2013. *The Open Society and Its Enemies*. Princeton, NJ: Princeton University Press.
Potter, Nelson. 1998. "The Argument of Kant's *Groundwork*, Chapter 1." In *Kant's Groundwork of the Metaphysics of Morals: Critical Essays*, ed. Paul Guyer, 29–50. Lanham, MD: Rowman & Littlefield.
Prior, William J. 2004. "Socrates Metaphysician." *Oxford Studies in Ancient Philosophy* 27: 11–12.
Pufendorf, Samuel. 1927. *De officio hominis et civis juxta legem naturalem libri duo*, 2 vols. Oxford: Oxford University Press.
———. 1934. *De jure naturae et gentium libri octo*, 2 vols. Oxford: Oxford University Press.
Quine, W. V. O. 1980. *From a Logical Point of View*, 2nd ed. Cambridge, MA: Harvard University Press.
Ranke, Leopold von. 1867–1890. *Sämmtliche Werke*, 54 vols. Leipzig: Dunker & Humblot.
Rapport de la commission d'enquête, sur l'insurrection qui a éclaté dans la journée de 23 juin et sur les événements du 15 mai. 1848. 3 vols. Paris: Imprimerie Nationale.
Rawls, John. 1971. *A Theory of Justice*. Cambridge, MA: Harvard University Press.
———. 1980. "Kantian Constructivism in Moral Theory." *The Journal of Philosophy* 77, no. 9: 515–72.
———. 1989. "Themes in Kant's Moral Philosophy." In *Kant's Transcendental Deductions*, ed. Eckart Förster. Stanford, CA: Stanford University Press.
———. 1999. *The Law of Peoples*. Cambridge, MA: Harvard University Press.
———. 1999. *A Theory of Justice*, rev. ed. Cambridge, MA: Harvard University Press.
———. 2000. *Lectures on the History of Moral Philosophy*. Cambridge, MA: Harvard University Press.
———. 2001. *Justice as Fairness: A Restatement*. Cambridge, MA: Harvard University Press.
———. 2005. *Political Liberalism*, expanded ed. New York: Columbia University Press.
Redding, Paul. 1996. *Hegel's Hermeneutics*. Ithaca, NY: Cornell University Press.
Riedel, Manfred. 1984. *Between Tradition and Revolution: The Hegelian Transformation of Political Philosophy*. Cambridge, UK: Cambridge University Press.

Riker, William H. 1982. *Liberalism against Populism: A Confrontation between the Theory of Democracy and the Theory of Social Choice*. Prospect Heights, IL: Waveland Press.
Riley, Patrick. 2007. "Kant Against Hobbes in *Theory and Practice*." *Journal of Moral Philosophy* 4, no. 2: 194–206.
Rimmerman, Craig A. 2002. *From Identity to Politics: The Lesbian and Gay Movements in the United States*. Philadelphia, PA: Temple University Press.
Ripstein, Arthur. 2009. *Force and Freedom: Kant's Legal and Political Philosophy*. Cambridge, MA: Harvard University Press.
Robinson, Richard. 1953. *Plato's Earlier Dialectic*, 2nd ed. Oxford: Oxford University Press.
Rosanvallon, Pierre. 1998. *Le peuple introuvable*. Paris: Gallimard.
Rosen, Allen. 1993. *Kant's Theory of Justice*. Ithaca, NY: Cornell University Press.
Rosen, Michael. 1982. *Hegel's Dialectic and Its Criticism*. Cambridge, UK: Cambridge University Press.
Rosenkranz, Karl. 1844. *Georg Whilhelm Friedrich Hegel's Leben*. Berlin: Dunker & Humblot.
Rougerie, Jacques. 2004. *Paris libre 1871*. Paris: Seuil.
Rousseau, Jean-Jacques. 1959–1995. *Œuvres complètes*, 5 vols., eds. Bernard Gagnebin and Marcel Raymond. Paris: Gallimard.
Rubenfeld, Jed. 2001. *Freedom and Time: A Theory of Constitutional Self-Government*. New Haven, CT: Yale University Press.
Rudelle, Odile. 1986. *La République absolue, 1870–1889*. Paris: Publications de la Sorbonne.
Rüdiger Bubner. 1975. "Kant, Transcendental Argument and the Problem of Deduction." *Review of Metaphysics* 28, no. 3: 453–67.
Ruiz, Alain. 1977. "Neues über Kant und Sieyès: Ein unbekannter Brief des Philosophen an Anton Ludwig Théremin (März 1796)." *Kant-Studien* 68, no. 4: 446–53.
Runciman, David. 2009. "Hobbes' Theory of Representation: Anti-Democratic or Proto-Democratic?" In *Political Representation*, eds. Ian Shapiro, Susan C. Stokes, Elisabeth Jean Wood, and Alexander S. Kirshner, 15–34. Cambridge, UK: Cambridge University Press.
Ryle, Gilbert. "Philosophical Arguments." In Ryle, *Collected Papers*, Vol. 2. London: Routledge, 2009, 203–21.
Samsom, Antonie. 1927. *Kants Kennis der Grieksche Philosophie*. Alphen aan den Rijn, Netherlands: N. Samsom.
Sandel, Michael J. 1982. *Liberalism and the Limits of Justice*. Cambridge, UK: Cambridge University Press.
Satkunanandan, Shalini. 2011. "The Extraordinary Categorical Imperative." *Political Theory* 39, no. 2: 234–60.
Savigny, Friedrich Carl von. 1814. *Vom Beruf unserer Zeit für Gesetzgebung und Rechtswissenschaft*. Heidelberg: Mohr & Zimmer.
Sayre, Kenneth M. 1969. *Plato's Analytic Method*. Chicago: University of Chicago Press.
Schelling, Friedrich Wilhelm Joseph. 1976–2010. *Historisch-kritische Ausgabe*. Stuttgart: Frommann-Holzboog.
———. 2007. *The Grounding of Positive Philosophy*, trans. Bruce Matthews. Albany: State University of New York Press.
Schiller, Friedrich. 1943– . *Schillers Werke, Nationalausgabe, herausgegeben im Auftrag der Stiftung Weimarer Klassik und des Schiller-Nationalmuseums Marbach von Norbert Oellers*. Weimar: Hermann Böhlaus Nachfolger.
———. 1972. "The Nature and Value of Universal History: An Inaugural Lecture." *History and Theory* 11, no. 2: 327, 333.
Schmitt, Carl. 2008. *Constitutional Theory*, trans. Jeffrey Sietzer. Durham, NC: Duke University Press.
Schneewind, J. B. 1998. *The Invention of Autonomy: A History of Modern Moral Philosophy*. Cambridge, UK: Cambridge University Press.
Schubert, Friedrich Wilhelm. 1842. *Immanuel Kants Biographie: Zum grossen Theil nach handschiftlichen Nachrichten*. Leipzig: Leopold Voss.
Schumpeter, Joseph A. 1976. *Capitalism, Socialism and Democracy*. New York: Allen & Unwin.
Schwartzberg, Melissa. 2007. *Democracy and Legal Change*. New York: Cambridge University Press.

Bibliography

Sewell, William H. Jr. 1980. *Work and Revolution in France: The Language of Labor from the Old Regime to 1848*. Cambridge, UK: Cambridge University Press.
Sextus Empiricus. 1976. *Outlines of Pyrrhonism*, trans. R. G. Bury. Cambridge, MA: Harvard University Press.
Shaiko, Ronald G. 2007. "Same-sex Marriage, GLBT Organizations, and the Lack of Spirited Political Engagement." In *The Politics of Same-Sex Marriage*, eds. Craig A. Rimmerman and Clyde Wilcox. Chicago: University of Chicago Press.
Siegal, Reva B. 2008. "Dead or Alive: Originalism as Popular Constitutionalism in *Heller*." *Harvard Law Review* 122: 191–245.
Sieyès, Emmanuel-Joseph. 1970. *Qu'est-ce que le Tiers état?*, ed. Roberto Zapperi. Geneva: Droz.
Skocpol, Theda. 2003. *Diminished Democracy: From Membership to Management in American Civic Life*. Norman: University of Oklahoma Press.
Sonenscher, Michael. 2003. "Introduction." In Sieyès, *Political Writings*, ed. Michael Sonenscher, vii–lxiv. Indianapolis, IN: Hackett.
Stein, Heinrich von. 1862. *Sieben Bücher zur Geschichte des Platonismus*. Göttingen: Vandenhoeck und Ruprecht.
Stein, Marc. 2012. *Rethinking the Gay and Lesbian Movement*. New York: Routledge.
Stilz, Anna. 2009. *Liberal Loyalty: Freedom, Obligation, and the State*. Princeton, NJ: Princeton University Press.
Strasser, Mark. 2002. "Same-Sex Marriage and Civil Unions: On Meaning, Free Exercise, and Constitutional Guarantees." *Loyola University of Chicago Law Journal* 33: 597–630.
Strauss, Leo. 1964. *The City and Man*. Chicago: University of Chicago Press.
Strong, Tracy B. 2012. *Politics Without Vision: Thinking Without a Banister in the Twentieth Century*. Chicago: University of Chicago Press.
Sunstein, Cass, and Richard Thaler. 2008. "Privatizing Marriage." *Monist* 91, no. 3/4: 377–87.
Tarnopolsky, Christina H. 2010. *Prudes, Perverts, and Tyrants: Plato's Gorgias and the Politics of Shame*. Princeton, NJ: Princeton University Press.
Taylor, Charles. 1975. *Hegel*. Cambridge, UK: Cambridge University Press.
———. 1979. *Hegel and Modern Society*. Cambridge, UK: Cambridge University Press.
Thibaut, A. F. J. 1814. *Ueber die Nothwendigkeit eines allgemeinen bürgerlichen Rechts für Deutschland*. Heidelberg: Mohr & Zimmer.
Thiers, Adolphe. 1879–1889. *Discours parlementaires de M. Thiers, publiés par M. Calmon*, 16 vols. Paris: Calmann Lévy.
Tilly, Charles, and Lynn Lees Tilly. 1974. "Le peuple de juin 1848." *Annales: Économies, Sociétés, Civilisations* 29, no. 5: 1061–91.
Tocqueville, Alexis de. 1951. *Œuvres complètes*, eds. Jean-Paul Mayer and André Jardin, 18 vols. Paris: Gallimard.
Toews, John Edward. 1980. *Hegelianism: The Path Toward Dialectical Humanism, 1805–1841*. Cambridge, UK: Cambridge University Press.
Tombs, Robert. 1981. *The War Against Paris, 1871*. Cambridge, UK: Cambridge University Press.
———. 1999. *The Paris Commune, 1871*. Harlow, UK: Pearson.
Tonelli, Giorgio. 1997. "Kant and the Ancient Skeptics," trans. John Christian Laursen. In *Skepticism and Enlightenment*, eds. Richard H. Popkin, Ezequiel de Olaso, and Giorgio Tonelli, 69–98. Boston, MA: Kluwer Academic.
Torcello, Lawrence G. 2008. "Is the State Endorsement of Any Marriage Justifiable? Same-Sex Marriage, Civil Unions, and the Marriage Privatization Model." *Public Affairs Quarterly* 22, no. 1: 43–61.
Tuck, Richard. 1999. *The Rights of War and Peace: Political Thought and the International Order from Grotius to Kant*. Oxford: Oxford University Press.
Urbinati, Nadia. *Representative Democracy: Principles and Geneaolgy*. Chicago: University of Chicago Press, 2006.
Vallely, Richard M. 2004. *The Two Reconstructions: The Struggle for Black Enfranchisement*. Chicago: University of Chicago Press.
Villa, Dana R. 2001. *Socratic Citizenship*. Princeton, NJ: Princeton University Press.
Vlastos, Gregory. 1991. *Socrates, Ironist and Moral Philosopher*. Ithaca, NY: Cornell University Press.

Vlastos, Gregory. 1994. *Socratic Studies*, ed. Miles Burnyeat. Cambridge, UK: Cambridge University Press.

———, ed. 1971. *The Philosophy of Socrates: A Collection of Critical Essays*. New York: Anchor Books.

Waldron, Jeremy. 1996. "Kant's Legal Positivism." *Harvard Law Review* 109:1535–66.

———. 2006. "Kant's Theory of the State." In Immanuel Kant, *Perpetual Peace and Other Writings on Politics, Peace, and History*, ed. Pauline Kleingeld, 179–200. New Haven, CT: Yale University Press.

Wang, Xi. 1997. *The Trial of Democracy and Northern Republicans, 1860–1910*. Athens: University of Georgia Press.

Warner, Michael. 2000 *The Trouble With Normal: Sex, Politics, and the Ethics of Queer Life*. Cambridge, MA: Harvard University Press.

Waszek, Norbert. 1985. "Hume, Hegel, and History." *Clio* 14, no. 4: 379–92.

———. 1988. *The Scottish Enlightenment and Hegel's Account of "Civil Society."* Boston, MA: Kluwer.

Westphal, Kenneth R. 1992. "Kant on the State, Law, and Obedience to Authority in the Alleged 'Anti-Revolutionary' Writings." *Journal of Philosophical Research* 17: 383–426.

Williams, Bernard. 1985. *Ethics and the Limits of Philosophy*. Cambridge, MA: Harvard University Press.

Williams, Howard. 2003. *Kant's Critique of Hobbes: Sovereignty and Cosmopolitanism*. Cardiff, UK: University of Wales Press.

———. 2012. "Natural Right in Hobbes and Kant." *Hobbes Studies* 25: 66–90.

Williams, Robert R. 1992. *Recognition: Fichte and Hegel on the Other*. Albany: State University of New York Press.

Winock, Michel. 2003. "La poussée démocratique: 1840–1870." In *L'invention de la démocratie*, eds. Serge Bernstein and Michel Winock. Paris: Éditions du Seuil.

Wolff, Christian. 1740–1748. *Jus naturae methodo scientifica pertractatum*, 8 vols. Frankfurt, Leipzig, and Halle: Renger.

———. 1750. *Institutiones juris naturae et gentium, in quibus ex ipsa hominis natura continuo nexu omnes obligationes et jura omnia deducuntur*. Halle: Renger.

Wood, Allen W. 1990. *Hegel's Ethical Thought*. Cambridge, UK: Cambridge University Press.

———. 1999. *Kant's Ethical Thought*. Cambridge, UK: Cambridge University Press.

———. 2008. *Kantian Ethics*. Cambridge, UK: Cambridge University Press.

Woodruff, Paul. 1986. "The Skeptical Side of Plato's Method." *Revue Internationale de Philosophie* 40: 22–37.

———. 1987. "Expert Knowledge in the *Apology* and *Laches*: What a General Needs to Know." In *Proceedings of the Boston Area Colloquium in Ancient Philosophy*, Vol. 3., ed. J. J. Cleary, 79–115. Lanham, MD: University Press of America.

———. 1990. "Plato's Early Theory of Knowledge." In *Ancient Greek Epistemology*, ed. S. Everson, 60–84. Cambridge, UK: Cambridge University Press.

Wundt, Max. 1941–1942. "Die Wiederentdeckung Platos im 18. Jahrhundert." *Blätter für Deutsche Philosophie* 15: 149–58.

Yeomans, Christopher. 2012. *Freedom and Reflection: Hegel on the Logic of Agency*. Oxford: Oxford University Press.

Zuckert, Catherine H. 2009. *Plato's Philosophers: The Coherence of the Dialogues*. Chicago: University of Chicago Press.

INDEX

Note: Footnotes are designated with the letter *n*. Headings which appear periodically throughout the page range are designated with *passim*.

Achenwall, Gottfried, 21, 114, 119
Ackerman, B., 19, 49
  We the People, 34, 37–39
activism, 1, 5–6, 38–39, 184–189, 200, 217, 228. *see also* organizing, political
Adair v. United States, 229
Aeschylus, *Orestia,* 58, 164
Affordable Care Act, 1–2, 233–235
Allison, H. E., 102
Anaxagoras, 149
antifoundationalism, 47–52, 50n4, 61–64, 82
Antigone (Sophocles), 58, 164–165
Apology (Plato), 71, 73
aporia, 62, 69–73, 75, 88
Arab Spring, 1
archē anhupothetos, 76–78
Arendt, Hannah, 85n11–12, 87, 112, 182
Aristotle, 82
  Metaphysics, 66
  Organon, 66
  Politics, 198
authority, Kant on, 82, 94–98
authorization, paradox of. *see* paradox of authorization
autonomy. *see also* freedom
  formula of, 97–100
  Kant on, 54, 84–87, 97–115 *passim,* 172

Baehr v. Lewin, 217, 219, 221
Barbés, Armand, 202
Benhabib, S., 19
Blanc, Louis, 202
Blanqui, Louis Auguste, 202
Bloomberg, Michael, 238
Bonaparte, Louis-Napoleon, 202

borders, 11n4
boundary problem, 34, 245. *see also* borders
Bouterwek, Friedrich, 137
Brady Handgun Violence Prevention Act, 238
Brettschneider, C., 14–15, 210
British idealism, 50n5
Broglie, duc de, 205
Brown, Jerry, 224
Brown v. Board of Education, 186–187, 199, 201, 233
Brucker, Johann Jacob, 88, 92
Burwell v. Hobby Lobby, 235

categorical imperative, 53, 80–87, 94–107
Cavaignac, Eugène, 202
Chambord, comte de, 205
change. *see* democratic change; politics of change
Churchill, Winston, 55
citizens
  active *vs.* passive, Kant on, 128–129
  defined, 11
  equal freedoms of, 11–23 *passim,* 32, 178–182
  Hegel on, 146–147, 162–163
  Kant on, 128–129
De Cive (Hobbes), 121, 122n15
civil liberties, 31–32
Civil Rights Act of 1875, 186, 200–201
Civil Rights Act of 1964, 200–201, 233
Civil Rights Act of 1968, 234
Civil Rights Cases of 1883, 186, 199, 229, 233
civil rights movement, 39, 177, 184–201
Civil War, American, 2–4, 185, 188, 198–199
Clayton Act of 1914, 234
Cleveland, Grover, 186
Clinton, William J., 217, 223, 238

coercion, justifiability of, 12, 14, 35–37, 42, 99, 111n50, 112, 148.183, 197, 206, 244
   Hobbes, Pufendorf, and Rousseau on, 120–123
   Kant on, 115n4, 120, 122, 129, 131n28, 135n35, 168
coherentism, 76
Columbia v. Heller, 236
Communards, 206. *see also* Paris Commune of 1871
conceptual condition, 25–26, 178–182
consent, Kant on, 131–134
constitution. *see also* institutions of democracy
   common principles among democracies and, 31–33, 249–251
   Hegel on monarchical, 143–149
   Kant on republican, 129–130
   people's right to choose their own, 10–18
   United States, 2–3, 188, 197–198, 236–237
constitutional order. *see* institutions of democracy
constitutional rights. *see* democratic rights
Contest of the Faculties (Kant), 83, 129, 133
Cook, P. J., 238
Coppage v. Kansas, 229
Creating the Kingdom of Ends (Korsgaard), 101
critique, 47, 62–63, 80–91, 89n19, 110, 242–245
Critique of Judgment (Kant), 85, 87, 126n20
Critique of Practical Reason (Kant), 51, 83, 96, 109–111
Critique of Pure Reason (Kant), 51, 82, 84–86, 88–89, 91–95, 104–106
Crito (Plato), 69, 74
cultural rights, 33
cunning of reason, 142, 155–161

Day, William R., 229
decisions, political
   defined, 11–14
   freedom and, 15–23
   institutions of democracy and, 16
   legitimacy of democracy and, 14–15
   majority rule and, 12–13, 13n9
deduction
   direct, 61, 64–66, 72
   in Kant, 104–110, 105n41
Defense of Marriage Act (DOMA), 209, 217–228 *passim*
deliberation, democracy and, 3n3, 40–45, 233
democracy
   activism/organized contestation as integral to, 5–6
   constitution of (*see* institutions of democracy)
   defined, 1–7, 12
   deliberation and, 3n3, 40–45, 233
   disagreement in (*see* disagreement in politics)
   epistemic, 3n3, 20, 180
   founding of, 19, 40, 43–45, 126, 201 (*see also* paradox of authorization)
   historical dimension of, 6–7
   institutional (*see* institutions of democracy)
   Kant on, 127–128
   legitimacy of (*see* legitimacy of democracy)
   majority rule and, 13, 183–185, 209–217
   minority rule and, 209–217
   principles of social dimension of, 31–33, 249–251
   procedure and, 3n3, 13, 17, 38
   reflexive, 3–4, 19–20, 40–41, 188
   Rousseau on, 128n24
   values and, 12, 12n7
democratic change, 43–44
   democratic elenchus and, 23–45
   theories of, 3–7, 3n3
democratic elenchus, 9–45 *passim. see also* historical and Socratic theory of democracy
   Ackerman's dualist democracy and, 34, 37–39
   advantages of, 34–45
   defined, 9, 9n1
   democratic change and, 23–45
   disagreement and, 30n28
   Habermas's discourse theory of law and the democratic state and, 34, 39–43
   institutions of democracy and, 10–11
   legitimacy of democracy and, 10–23
   paradox of authorization and, 20–21
   politics of change and, 23–45
   principles of, 10–45 *passim* (*see also* Principle)
   Rawl's political liberalism and, 34–37
democratic institutions. *see* institutions of democracy
democratic order. *see* institutions of democracy
democratic revolution, 1–3, 39, 241. *see also* founding of democracy
democratic rights, 17, 27, 184, 196, 208–210, 220, 222
democratic system. *see* institutions of democracy
demos. see "the people" in democratic theory
diairesis, 64
dialectic, 10n3, 23, 47, 61, 64
disagreement in politics, 2–5, 30n28, 35–36, 41n49, 50, 123, 140n1, 174, 212, 233, 243–245
Doctrine of Right (Kant). *see Metaphysics of Morals*
DOMA. *see* Defense of Marriage Act
duty, Kant on, 53, 82–110 *passim*

elenchus, 25, 52–53, 61–79. *see also* democratic elenchus
   aporia and, 62, 69–73, 75, 88
   archē anhupothetos and, 76–78
   defined, 9–10, 9n1, 10n3, 61
   hypothesis and, 73–79
   Platonic theory of ideas and, 74–79
   producing positive conclusions through, 61–64
   reductio ad absurdum and, 64–68
   refutation and, 64–68
Ely, John hart, 210
emancipation, social, 32, 233, 250–251

Encyclopedia of the Philosophical Sciences (Hegel), 150, 152, 159
the Enlightenment, 50–51, 83, 140–167 *passim*, 242–243
environmental rights, 32–33
epistemic democracy, 3n3, 20, 180
equal freedoms of citizens, 11–15, 32, 178–182
  interpreting, 15–18, 21–22
equality, 12, 179. *see also* equal freedoms of citizens; social principles
  legal, 15n12, 27–28, 32
  Rousseau and Kant and, 28n26
ethical life *(Sittlichkeit)*, 57, 140, 143–149
ethics
  Hegel on, 56–57, 140, 143–149
  Kant on, 57
Euthyphro (Plato), 78
exclusivity condition, 25, 29–30, 29n28, 195–207

fact of reason, 109–111
Fair Labor Standards Act of 1938, 234
Favre, Jules, 203
Fichte, Johann Gottlieb, 48–49, 48n2, 145–146, 157–160
Ficino, Marsilio, 91
Fine, G., 76
Forst, R., 111n50
Forster, M. N., 90
foundational metaphysics, 47–52, 50n4, 96
founding of democracy, 19, 40, 43–45, 126, 201.
  see also paradox of authorization
France. *see also* French Revolution
  same-sex marriage in, 227
  Second Republic of, 201–204
  Third Republic of, 187, 199–206
  universal suffrage in, 180–182, 192
Frank, J., 19
Frederick II (king of Prussia), 83, 114
freedom, 11–12, 178–182. *see also* autonomy
  citizen's, interpretation of, 15–23
  Hegel on, 149–155, 161–166, 178
  Kant on morality and, 82, 84, 101
  objective *vs.* subjective, 22–23
  political judgment and, 48–50, 115–118
French Revolution
  of 1789, 44, 51, 56, 123–124n18, 127, 163, 171, 201, 244
  of 1830, 145
  of 1848, 38–39, 116, 192, 201–206
  of 1870, 203–205

Gambetta, Léon, 203–205
Gaulle, Charles de, 206
general will, 15n12, 84, 86, 121–134 *passim*
Gentzler, J., 76
"German Constitution" essay (Hegel), 158, 160
German idealism, 47–48, 51

Gibbon, Edward, 142, 157–159
Giffords, Gabrielle, 239
Goethe, Johann Wolfgang, 142, 160
Goodridge v. Massachusetts Department of Public Health, 218, 221, 225
Gorgias (Plato), 67, 69, 74
Goss, K. A., 238
Greek polis, 153, 162–165, 198
Grotius, Hugo, 119–122
Groundwork of the Metaphysics of Morals (Kant), 83, 89, 93–109
guaranteed social minimums, 32–33, 233, 250–251
Guizot, François, 130, 180, 192
gun control/gun rights, 236–240

Habermas, J., 14, 19, 34, 39–43, 45, 232
Hamann, Johann Georg, 91
health insurance, 1–2, 233–235
Hegel, Georg Wilhelm Friedrich, 7–8, 29, 45, 47–59 *passim*, 79, 244–247
  antifoundationalism and, 47–52 *passim*, 50n4
  on *Antigone* (Sophocles), 58
  constitutional theory of, 143–149
  dialectic and, 23, 47, 58, 155, 166, 242
  elenchus and, 25
  Encyclopedia of the Philosophical Sciences, 150, 152, 159
  on ethical life *(Sittlichkeit)*, 56–57, 140, 143–149
  on freedom, 149–155, 161–166, 178
  "German Constitution" essay, 158, 160
  Greek polis and, 153, 162–165
  historicism and, 49–51, 50n4, 167, 243
  on the Jacobins, 58, 145, 159, 163, 178
  Jenaer Realphilosophie, 159
  Kant and, 48, 139–140, 167
  Lectures on the History of Philosophy, 161
  Lectures on the Philosophy of History, 152, 161
  metaphysics and, 140–141
  on monarchical constitution, 143–149
  Montesquieu and, 48, 56, 57n13, 140–163 *passim*
  on natural law, 158, 165–166
  "Natural Law" essay, 158–159
  on *Orestia* (Aeschylus), 58
  on paradox of authorization, 139–140, 166–167
  Phenomenology of Spirit, 143, 150–163 *passim*
  philosophy of history of, 57–59, 143–169 *passim*
  Philosophy of Right, 22, 49, 56, 140, 146, 160, 173
  Philosophy of Spirit (Encyclopedia), 152
  political judgment and, 48–50
  political theory of, 56–59, 140–150, 157–169
  Principle (II)* and, 58–59
  on progress, 49–51, 58, 139–142, 161–169
  on providence, 142, 155–156n27
  J. Rawls on, 35, 35n38

Hegel, Georg Wilhelm Friedrich (Cont.)
  on reason, 142, 155–161
  on revolution, 145, 163
  Rousseau and, 140, 144–149, 168
  Science of Logic, 159
  Scottish Enlightenment and, 140, 142–143, 155–160
  on Socrates, 58, 149, 161–163
  on spirit, 56–57, 142–158 *passim*, 168
  on *The Spirit of the Laws* (Montesquieu), 146
  on teleology and mechanism, 155–158, 157n32
  on the Terror (1793-4), 58, 145, 159, 163, 178
Herder, Johann Gottfried, 142, 156, 160
  historicism and, 49–50, 156
  Ideas for the Philosophy of the History of Humanity (Ideen), 50n4, 58, 156
Herz, Marcus, 91
historical and Socratic theory of democracy, 7. *see also* democratic elenchus
  constitutional choice and, 15
  defined, 9, 9n1, 24
  democratic change and, 43–44
  institutions of democracy and, 10–11
  legitimacy of democracy and, 10–23
  paradox of authorization and, 20–21
  principles of, 10–30 (*see also* Principle)
historical baseline, 25–29, 28n26, 190–195
historical dimension of democracy, 6–7
historicism, 49–51, 117, 166–167, 243
History of the Thirty Years War (Schiller), 160
Hitler, Adolf, 134
Hobbes, Thomas, 52, 54, 56, 119–120, 167–168
  De Cive, 121, 122n15
  on coercion, justifiability of, 120–123
  Kant and, 48, 84–86, 118–127
  Leviathan, 121, 122n15
  paradox of authorization and, 19–20, 21n19, 118
  Rousseau on, 121n12
Hollingsworth v. Perry, 209–210, 222, 225
Holmes, Oliver Wendell, 229
Honig, B., 19
humanity, formula of, 85–86, 100–103
Humboldt, Wilhelm von, 54
Hume, David, 48, 81, 90
hypothesis, 73–79, 97
  archē anhupothetos and, 76–78

idealism
  British, 50n5
  German, 47–48, 51
ideas, Platonic theory of, 74–79, 88, 91–94
  Kant on, 87–88, 91–94, 96, 107
Ideas for the Philosophy of the History of Humanity (Herder), 50n4, 58, 156
immigration, 11, 11n4
Inaugural Dissertation on the Form and Principles of the Sensible and Intelligible World (Kant), 91

individual rights, 15–17, 31–33, 181–182, 193, 196–197, 231–232
induction, 64–66
institutions of democracy
  common principles of, 30–33
  popular choice of, 10–18
  Principle (I) and, 12–13, 16
  reform of, 3–4, 45
international politics, 31n29, 33. *see also* borders
Interstate Commerce Act of 1887, 234

the Jacobins, 48, 51, 58, 115, 123–124n18, 140, 144–145, 159, 163, 168, 178
Jenaer Realphilosophie (Hegel), 159
Johnson, Lyndon B., 200
judgment. *see also Critique of Judgment* (Kant)
  moral, 83–86
  political, 48–50, 85–86, 115–138 *passim*
judicial review, 16, 228

Kant, Immanuel, 7–8, 45–59 *passim*, 79, 177–180, 217, 244–247
  on active *vs*. passive citizens, 128–129
  antifoundationalism and, 47–52 *passim*, 50n4, 82, 97–98
  on authority, 82, 94–98
  on autonomy, 54, 84–87, 97–115 *passim*, 172
  categorical imperative and, 53, 80–87, 94–107
  on coercion, justifiability of, 115n4, 120, 122, 129, 131n28, 135n35, 168
  on consent, 131–134
  Contest of the Faculties, 83, 129, 133
  Critique of Judgment, 85, 87, 126n20
  Critique of Practical Reason, 51, 83, 96, 109–111
  Critique of Pure Reason, 51, 82, 84–86, 88–89, 91–95, 104–106
  deduction and, 104–110, 105n41
  on democracy, 127–128
  Doctrine of Right (*see Metaphysics of Morals*)
  on duty, 53, 82–110 *passim*
  elenchus and, 80–87, 91n24, 94–95, 103
  on freedom, 15n12, 82, 84, 101
  Groundwork of the Metaphysics of Morals, 83, 89, 93–109
  Hegel and, 48, 139–140, 167
  historical baseline and, 28n26
  historicism and, 49–51, 50n4
  Hobbes and, 48, 84–86, 118–127, 131n28
  on *Ideas for the Philosophy of the History of Humanity* (Herder), 50n4, 57–58
  Inaugural Dissertation on the Form and Principles of the Sensible and Intelligible World, 91
  liberalism and, 55–56, 116
  Metaphysics of Morals, 85, 89, 122, 124, 127, 133, 137

on monarchical and aristocratical government, 129–130
on morality and freedom, 82, 84, 101
moral theory of, 53–55, 80–113 passim
on natural law, 80–87, 98, 100, 108, 110–111, 114–118
on paradox of authorization, 19–21, 21n19, 136–138
Pedagogy (Pädagogik), 89
Perpetual Peace, 127, 129, 138
philosophy of history of, 125–127
Plato and, 87–93
on Platonic theory of ideas, 87–88, 91–94, 96, 107
political judgment and, 48–50, 85–86, 115–138 passim
political theory of, 55–56, 114–138 passim
on progress, 49–51, 117, 125–126
Pyrrhonism and, 81, 88–90
J. Rawls and, 35
on reason, 88–93, 109–113
Rechtslehre (see Metaphysics of Morals)
on regulative assumptions, 53–55, 75–76, 88, 108–109
on religion, 83, 88–89
Religion within the Limits of Mere Reason, 83, 95
on republic, 40, 116–117, 127, 133
on republican constitution, 129–130
on revolution, 56, 116–117, 116n6, 127–138
Rousseau and, 48, 84–86, 114–115, 119–123
skepticism and, 89–91, 109–113
Socrates and, 83, 85, 87, 89–90, 95–96
"Theory and Practice" essay, 127–128
"What Is Enlightenment?," 83, 85, 132
Kelly, Mark, 239
knowledge
method and, 69–73, 75
priority of definitional, 74
Korsgaard, C., 101–102
Creating the Kingdom of Ends, 101

Latin America, popular movements in, 1
Lectures on the History of Philosophy (Hegel), 161
Lectures on the Philosophy of History (Hegel), 152, 161
Ledru-Rollin, Alexandre-Auguste, 201–203
Lefort, C., 19
legislation, protective, 32, 234, 250–251
legitimacy of democracy, 7, 10–23
constitutional choice and, 11
decisions and, 14–15
exclusivity and, 195–207
historical baseline and, 190
historicism and, 139–140
Kant on, 117
slavery and, 14
Leibniz, Gottfried Wilhelm, 81
Leviathan (Hobbes), 121, 122n15

liberalism, 149, 167, 180, 243
democratic elenchus and Rawls', 34–37
Kant on republicanism and, 55–56, 116–117
Lochner v. New York, 182, 193, 229–236 passim
Locke, John, 21, 167
Louis XVI (king of France), 132

MacMahon, Patrice de, 205
Madison, James, 145
majority rule, 12–13, 13n9, 209–217
Marx, Karl, 145n14, 161, 167, 246
Marxism, 51, 161, 167, 243–244
Mazzini, Giuseppe, 203
McDonald v. Chicago, 236
Mendelssohn, Moses
adaptation of Plato's *Phaedo* by, 91
Morgenstunden, 82
Menino, Thomas, 238
Meno (Plato), 61, 63, 74–75, 95
metaphysics
foundational, 47–52, 50n4
Hegel and, 140–141
Metaphysics (Aristotle), 66
Metaphysics of Morals (Kant), 85, 89, 122, 124, 127, 133, 137
meta-republicanism, 117, 127, 133
method, knowledge and, 69–73, 75
Mill, John Stuart, 167, 180
minimums, guaranteed social, 32–33, 233, 250–251
minority rights, 12–13, 200, 209–220, 224
minority rule, 209–217
mobilization. *see* activism; organizing, political
Montesquieu
on constitutionalism, 144
Hegel and, 48, 56, 57n13, 140–163 passim
The Spirit of the Laws, 144–146
morality
freedom and, 82, 84, 101
judgment and, 83–86
Kant on, 53–55, 80–113 passim
vs. right in politics, 115–116, 134–135n35, 228
Morgenstunden (Mendelssohn), 82
Mouffe, C., 19
Müller, Adam, 142

Napoleon III, 202
National Federation of Independent Business v. Sibelius, 235
National Industrial Recovery Act (NIRA) of 1933, 234
National Labor Relations Act of 1935, 234
National Rifle Association, 238–239
natural law, 114–119, 221
Hegel on, 158, 165–166
Kant on, 80–87, 98, 100, 108, 110–111, 114–118

"Natural Law" essay (Hegel), 158–159
Neoplatonism, 48, 69n18, 88, 92, 93
New Deal, 193, 198–199, 228–236
Newsome, Gavin, 218
NIRA (National Industrial Recovery Act) of 1933, 234
Norris-LaGuardia Act of 1932, 234

Obama, Barack, 1–2, 234
objective freedom, 22–23
Occupy movement, 1, 236
Ochoa Espejo, P., 19
O'Neill, O, 87, 130
Opera Omnia (Plato, Ficino ed.), 91
Orestia (Aeschylus), 58, 164
organize, right to, 32, 229–234, 250–251
organizing, political, 30, 38–39, 184, 187–188, 192–193, 208, 213–217, 220, 224, 227, 230–233, 246, 248–249. *see also* activism
Organon (Aristotle), 66

paradox of authorization, 18–23, 21n19, 29
 Habermas on, 39–43
 Hegel on, 139–140, 166–167
 Hobbes on, 19–20, 21n19, 118
 Kant on, 19–21, 21n19, 136–138
 Rousseau on, 20, 21n19, 118
 Sieyès on, 124n18
Paris Commune of 1871, 204–206
Parmenides (Plato), 92
party politics, 23–45 *passim*
pedagogy, 89, 146–148
Pedagogy (Pädagogik) (Kant), 89
"the people" in democratic theory, 18–19, 21, 34, 172, 198, 245
Perpetual Peace (Kant), 127, 129, 138
perplexity, 95, 95n29. *see also* aporia
Phaedo (Plato), 74–76, 91
Phenomenology of Spirit (Hegel), 143, 150–163 *passim*
philosophy of history
 Hegel's, 57–59, 143–169 *passim*
 Kant's, 125–127
Philosophy of Right (Hegel), 22, 49, 56, 140, 146, 160, 173
Philosophy of Spirit (Hegel), 152
planning, public, 32, 234, 249–251
Plato, 8, 9, 47–48, 59, 242
 Apology, 71, 73
 coherence and, 76
 Crito, 69, 74
 dialectic and, 10n3, 23
 elenchus and, 25, 52–53, 61–79 *passim*
 Euthyphro, 78
 Gorgias, 67, 69, 74
 ideas, theory of, 74–79, 88, 91–94

 Kant and, 87–93
 Meno, 61, 63, 74–75, 95
 Opera Omnia (Ficino ed.), 91
 Parmenides, 92
 Phaedo, 74–76, 91
 Protagoras, 67
 Republic, 47, 63, 67, 74–79
Plessy v. Ferguson, 186, 233
polis, 153, 162–165, 198
political judgment, 48–50, 85–86, 115–138 *passim*, 182–190
political legitimacy. *see* legitimacy of democracy
Political Liberalism (Rawls), 34–37
political principles, 30–32
political theory
 of Hegel, 56–59, 140–150, 157–169
 of Kant, 55–56, 114–138 *passim*
Politics (Aristotle), 198
politics of change, 1–7, 3n3, 23–45
positivism, 50–51, 167
practical condition, 25–26, 182–190
pragmatism, American, 50n5
Principle (I), 179, 180
 defined, 10–23
 institutions of democracy and, 10–11, 12–13, 16
 legitimacy of democracy and, 14–15
 paradox of authorization and, 18–23
 relation of, to Principle (II), 23
Principle (II), 245
 defined, 23–30
 relation of, to Principle (I), 23
 relation of, to Principle (II)*, 25
Principle (II)*, 24–30, 245
 conceptual condition of, 25–26, 178–182
 exclusivity condition of, 25, 29–30, 29n28, 195–207
 Hegel and, 58–59, 162–166
 historical baseline in, 25–29, 28n26, 190–195
 practical condition of, 25–26, 182–190
 relation of, to Principle (II), 25
principles of democracy's social dimension. *see* social principles
priority of definitional knowledge, 74
private property, 32, 234, 249–251
progress, 8, 28, 43–44, 232–233, 243–247
 Hegel on, 49–51, 58, 139–142, 161–169
 Kant on, 49–51, 117, 125–126
Proposition 8 (California), 209, 221–226 *passim*
Protagoras (Plato), 67
protective legislation, 32, 234, 250–251
protest. *see* activism
public opinion, 40–42, 41n49, 188–189
public planning, 32, 234, 249–251
public sphere, 40–41, 233
Pufendorf, Samuel, 21, 114, 119–122
Pyrrhonism, 81, 88–90

Railway Labor Act of 1926, 234
Rawls, J., 51, 116, 130
   on Hegel, 35, 35n38
   Kant and, 35
   Political Liberalism, 34–37
reason/reasoning. *see also Critique of Practical Reason* (Kant); *Critique of Pure Reason* (Kant)
   cunning of, 142, 155–161
   fact of, 109–111
   in history, Hegel on, 149–151
Rechtslehre (Kant). *see Metaphysics of Morals*
reductio ad absurdum, 64–68
reflexive democracy, 19–20, 40–41, 188
reform, institutional, 3–4, 45
the Reformation, 146, 157, 162
refutation, 64–68
regulative assumptions, Kant on, 53–55, 75–76, 88, 108–109
religion
   Kant on, 83, 88–89
   the Reformation and, 146, 157, 162
Religion within the Limits of Mere Reason (Kant), 83, 95
representation, 14, 23, 32, 38, 116–124, 127–134
republic, 40
   as defined by Kant, 40, 116–117, 127, 133
   as defined by Rousseau, 13–14, 14n10, 40
Republic (Plato), 47, 63, 67, 74–79
revolution, 1, 116–117, 116n6. *see also* French Revolution
   democratic, 1–3, 39, 241 (*see also* founding of democracy)
   Hegel on, 145, 163
   Kant on, 56, 127–138
rights. *see* civil liberties; cultural rights; democratic rights; environmental rights; gun control/gun rights; individual rights; minority rights; social principles
right to organize, 32, 229–234, 250–251
Romanticism, 50–51, 57, 142, 156
Romney, Willard Mitt, 235
Roosevelt, Franklin D., 232, 234, 236
Rosanvallon, P., 19
Rousseau, Jean-Jacques, 8, 47n1, 54–55, 56
   on coercion, justifiability of, 120–123
   on constitutional change, 49
   on decision-making, 12
   on democracy, 128n24
   equality and, 28n26
   on freedom, 15n12
   on general will, 15n12, 49, 84, 86, 121–134 *passim*
   Hegel and, 140, 144–149, 168
   Kant and, 48, 84–86, 114–115, 119–123
   on majority rule, 13, 13n9
   on paradox of authorization, 20, 21n19, 118
   on republic, 13–14, 14n10, 40
   The Social Contract, 121, 121n12

Rubenfeld, J., 19
rule of law, 31, 115

same-sex marriage, 27, 39, 43, 182, 217–228
   in France, 227
   in United Kingdom, 227
Scalia, Antonin, 224
Schelling, Friedrich Wilhelm Joseph, 48, 142, 160
   System of Transcendental Idealism, 141n4, 157n31, 159
Schiller, Friedrich, *History of the Thirty Years War*, 160
Schmitt, Carl, 178
Schulz, Johann Heinrich, *Attempt at an Introduction to a Doctrine of Morals*, 108
Schwarzenegger, Arnold, 222, 226
Science of Logic (Hegel), 159
Scottish Enlightenment, 140, 142–143, 155–160
Second Republic, French, 201–204
segregation, 184–188, 199–201
Sherman Antitrust Act of 1890, 234
Sieyès, Emmanuel Joseph, 124n18
Sittlichkeit (ethical life), 57, 140, 143–149
skepticism, 89–91, 109–113
Slaughterhouse Cases of 1873, 229
slavery, 3–4, 13–14, 36, 39, 103, 120–121, 163, 181, 185, 198, 200, 211–213, 227–233
Smith, Adam, 140, 147, 152, 159–160
   The Wealth of Nations, 159–160
social contract, 19–22, 48–49, 56, 114–132 *passim*
The Social Contract (Rousseau), 121, 121n12
social democracy, principles of. *see* social principles
social dimension, principles of democracy's. *see* social principles
social emancipation, 32, 233, 250–251
social minimums, 32–33, 233, 250–251
social principles, 30–33, 233–234, 249–251
Social Security Act, 234–235
Socrates, 7–9, 47–48, 53, 83–96 *passim*, 95. *see also* Plato
   elenchus and, 61–79 *passim* (*see also* democratic elenchus; elenchus)
   Hegel on, 58, 149, 161–163
   trial of, 58
Socratic elenchus. *see* elenchus
Socratic method, 52–54. *see also* elenchus
   defined, 9–10, 9n1, 10n3
Sophocles, *Antigone*, 58, 164–165
spirit *(Geist)*, 56–57, 142–158 *passim*, 168
The Spirit of the Laws (Montesquieu), 144–146
   Hegel on, 146
Strong, T. B., 87
subjective freedom, 22–23
suffrage, 145n14, 180–182, 185, 187, 192, 201–206
supermajorities, 211–215
System of Transcendental Idealism (Schelling), 141n4, 157n31, 159

Taylor, C., 51
Tea Party, 1
the Terror (1793–1794), 13n8, 58, 145, 159, 163, 178. *see also* the Jacobins
  Hegel on, 58, 145, 159, 163, 178
"Theory and Practice" essay (Kant), 127–128
Thiers, Adolphe, 204–205
Third Republic, French, 201–206
Thomasius, Christian, 119
Tocqueville, Alexis de, 144–146, 203
Toward Perpetual Peace (Kant), 127, 129, 138
Truman, Harry S., 234

unions, right to organize, 32, 229–234, 250–251
United Kingdom, same-sex marriage in, 227
United States of America, constitution of, 2–3, 188, 197–198, 236–237
United States v. Miller, 236

United States v. Windsor, 209–210, 222, 226
universal law, formula of, 100, 103–104

Vattel, Emer de, 21, 119–122
Vietnam War, 180
Vlastos, G., 65, 70
das Volk an sich selbst, 20–22, 26, 38, 41

Wallace, George, 199
The Wealth of Nations (Smith), 159–160
Weber, Max, 57, 161
We the People (Ackerman), 34, 37–39
"What Is Enlightenment?" (Kant), 83, 85, 132
Wolff, Christian, 80–81, 84–85, 99, 114–115, 119
Wood, A. W., 102

zetetic inquiry, 89–91, 109–113

Printed in Great Britain
by Amazon